Dorothea Horst

Meaning-Making and Political Campaign Advertising

Cinepoetics

——

Edited by
Hermann Kappelhoff and Michael Wedel

Volume 2

Dorothea Horst

Meaning-Making and Political Campaign Advertising

A Cognitive-Linguistic and Film-Analytical Perspective on Audiovisual Figurativity

DE GRUYTER

The proofreading of this book was financially supported by the European University Viadrina.

ISBN 978-3-11-070906-3
e-ISBN (PDF) 978-3-11-057878-2
e-ISBN (EPUB) 978-3-11-057793-8
ISSN 2569-4294

Library of Congress Control Number: 2018951333

Bibliographic information published by the Deutsche Nationalbibliothek
The Deutsche Nationalbibliothek lists this publication in the Deutsche Nationalbibliografie; detailed bibliographic data are available on the Internet at http://dnb.dnb.de.

© 2020 Walter de Gruyter GmbH, Berlin/Boston
This volume is text- and page-identical with the hardback published in 2018.
Cover image: People walk by a rain puddle reflecting a giant election billboard (c) Johannes Eisele / Staff / AFP / Getty Images
Typesetting: Integra Software Services Pvt. Ltd.
Printing and binding: CPI books GmbH, Leck

www.degruyter.com

Acknowledgements

Thanks to my supervisor, Cornelia Müller, for opening me up to figurative thinking many years ago and for giving me the opportunity to investigate it in its lived contexts of use. Ever since the beginning of our joint collaboration, she has inspired and excited my curiosity about "experiencing and understanding something in terms of something else". Her invaluable feedback, motivation, and support kept me following my PhD journey.

I would also like to thank Hermann Kappelhoff for influencing my view on audiovisual media and making me think about metaphor and metonymy in a transdisciplinary manner.

I am indebted to my colleagues at the European University Viadrina in Frankfurt/Oder, Franziska Boll, Janett Haid, Lena Hotze, and Silva H. Ladewig, for their constant encouragement and invaluable support.

Furthermore, I want to thank Amber Shields for proofreading and polishing the English throughout the book, and Eileen Rositzka, Thomas Scherer, and Christina Schmitt for being always helpful companions I could rely on.

Kaspar Aebi, Lars Dolkemeyer, and Janine Schleicher deserve acknowledgement for their assistance in preparing the manuscript for publication.

My deepest gratitude goes to my husband, my parents, and my friends for their loving guidance and understanding over the past years.

Berlin, June 2018   Dorothea Horst

https://doi.org/10.1515/9783110578782-201

Contents

1 Introduction

Over the last two decades, cognitive-linguistic research on figurativity has increasingly taken into account its modality independence and, from an initial exclusive consideration and investigation of verbal expressions, turned towards its wide range of materializations in various modalities (e.g., gestural or pictorial). By contrast, the study of figurativity in audiovisual media is hitherto rather rare and has not gone beyond individual studies of television advertising and films. The field of audiovisual political advertising, such as campaign commercials, has so far not been taken into consideration at all by cognitive-linguistic research on figurativity, which "has traditionally been overshadowed by the study of metaphor" (Catalano and Waugh 2013, 32). This oversight is remarkable as both metaphor and metonymy are conceived of as fundamental tools of communication and of rhetoric in politics (see, e.g., Androshchuk 2014, Charteris-Black 2004, 2005, Lakoff 1996, 2008, Lakoff and Johnson 1980).

This book intends to bridge this gap. By analyzing metaphorical and metonymical meaning-making processes in German and Polish campaign commercials, it pursues the objective of contributing to metaphor and metonymy theory by taking a dynamic perspective on figurative meaning-making and refraining from former mainly static and cognitivist approaches. In this pursuit, two dynamically-oriented theoretical models from film studies and cognitive linguistics are combined to form the theoretical basis for a new approach to audiovisual figurativity. This dynamic approach will focus on three aspects of dynamics: time, attention, and experience. In brief, the dynamic approach as presented in this book brings together the following core statements:

Multimodal figurativity and audiovisual compositions are temporally dynamic.

Multimodal figurativity and audiovisual compositions are attentionally dynamic.

Multimodal figurativity and audiovisual compositions are experientially dynamic.

Drawing on a transdisciplinary cognitive-linguistic and film-analytical method of analysis (Müller and Kappelhoff 2018, Müller and Schmitt 2015, Schmitt, Greifenstein, and Kappelhoff 2014, Kappelhoff and Greifenstein 2016), this book elaborates on these three aspects in German and Polish campaign commercials and describes them in regard to the process of audiovisual figurative meaning-making. The point that thereby shall be made is:

https://doi.org/10.1515/9783110578782-001

The interplay of the two main modalities of language and audiovisual staging, which is analytically accessible through the respective configuration of their three dynamics each, gives rise to different variant forms of audiovisual figurative meaning-making.

The dynamic approach advocated in this book seeks to contribute to a better understanding of metaphor and metonymy as fundamental principles of meaning-making and communicating ideas and conceptualizations. Using the example of campaigning candidates, it focuses on figurative meaning-making as a process instead of a fixed product. Moreover, it does not assume a presumed default persuasive power of figurativity but addresses it as situated process of embodied experience and meaning-making at all medial and modal levels (and, this being the case, as a potential precondition of persuasion; see Section 9.3). This dynamic and embodied approach has fundamental consequences for a theory of figurative thinking and is, as shall be suggested, an unfilled gap in contemporary reflections on audiovisual metaphor and metonymy.

1.1 Audiovisual Figurativity as Product and as Process

A commonly shared assumption among researchers dealing with metaphor and metonymy is that both are usually complementary combinations of spoken or written language, moving images, sound, or music in audiovisual media, such as TV ads or films. The following example of a commercial for body lotion discussed by Charles Forceville (2007b, 21) may serve as a representative illustration:

> In a fast montage of close ups we see white thread winding itself on a wooden spindle. After a few seconds a female voice-over comments, "Silk reflects each ray of light. Hardly surprising, then, that it is so beautiful on your skin." The next shot shows the "spindle" standing upright, while the silk quickly unwinds to reveal a bottle of *Dove Silkening Body Moisturizing*, suggesting the metaphor DOVE BODY LOTION IS SILK. [...] The target is rendered both pictorially and verbally, the latter in spoken as well as written form (on the Dove bottle). The source, silk, is presented visually [...] and orally [...].

The metaphor in this example is clearly divided into a source and a target domain with the two of them unambiguously assigned to particular modalities. Metaphorical meaning is prompted from the unilateral mapping of features from the source domain to the target domain. Furthermore, both domains are exclusively constituted (verbally, audiovisually, or pictorially) by represented content from the commercial that is conceived of as pre-existing in terms of well-defined entities, ideas, or concepts, i.e., the silk thread on a spindle and the body lotion. Such a clear-cut and fixed form of metaphor in audiovisual media seems to be due to a top-down perspective conditioned by conceptual metaphor theory (CMT). Its fundamental tenet is that the "ordinary conceptual system, in terms of which we both think and act, is fundamentally metaphorical in nature" (Lakoff and Johnson 1980, 3). In order to verify the existence of such a mental figurative deep structure and to make reliable statements about its nature, proponents of CMT are looking for verbal, pictorial, audiovisual, etc. surface appearances of this deep structure. Gunnar Eggertsson's and Charles Forceville's (2009, 429) introduction to their study of a structural metaphor in the horror film genre gets to the heart of such an approach:

> However, assessing the validity of the Conceptual Metaphor Theory (CMT) paradigm launched by Lakoff and Johnson requires not only that non-verbal and multimodal expressions of conceptual metaphors are studied as such, but also that the extent of their systematic occurrence is investigated. After all, a central tenet of CMT is that human beings conceive certain phenomena systematically in terms of certain other phenomena, allowing for numerous different surface manifestations of a single conceptual metaphor.

From such a perspective, the level of the human conceptual system has primacy over the level of actual and situated use. Accordingly, what is relevant is how conceptual metaphors and metonymies are manifested or expressed in a particular film, TV ad, or campaign commercial. In order to outline this tenet and its analytical focus, it is subsequently illustrated by one of the campaign commercials to be analyzed in this book.

In the Christian Democratic Union's (CDU) TV campaign ad for the German parliamentary elections in 2009 the top candidate Angela Merkel is shown standing at and gazing out the window of her chancellery (Figure 1 left). In a voice-over she comments on her political career, significant past events for Germany, such as the German reunification or the FIFA World Cup in 2006, and achievements of her first term as Chancellor. Showing Merkel turning away from the window and striding through her office (Figure 1 right), the topic of her statements changes to future issues and challenges.

Figure 1: Angela Merkel looking back into the past and striding towards the future

From a CMT point of view, these two sequences would probably be considered as audiovisual instantiations of the conceptual metaphor TIME AS SPACE, more precisely PAST AS BEHIND and FUTURE AS IN FRONT OF OBSERVING EGO. PAST AS BEHIND OF OBSERVING EGO would possibly be analyzed as being cued by Merkel's statements about past events (verbally represented target) and her posterior view and look 'back', evoked by the camera angle (visually represented source). The conceptual metaphor FUTURE AS IN FRONT OF OBSERVING EGO would be regarded as being cued by Merkel's statements about future tasks (verbally represented target) and her turning around and striding forward (visually represented source).

In addition to these particular audiovisual manifestations of the conceptual metaphor TIME AS SPACE, two instantiations of the conceptual metonymy PLACE FOR PERSON would probably be detected: the interior perspective of the bureau locates Merkel in her official residence, which stands for her political life, her political office as German Chancellor, and her political work. In contrast, the space outside, i.e., beyond this political sphere, stands for the life beyond politics, namely the social life of the people. Both the metaphorical and metonymical instantiations would be considered to intertwine with the result that Merkel is understood as being both outside – knowing the shared history and people's concerns and thus having a private, civil side – and inside – knowing the political challenges of the future and thus having a formal or political side.

It strikes that such an approach and its focus of analysis have a rather identifying or deciphering character instead of a reconstructing one, so to speak. Put another way, it addresses finished products instead of unfolding processes. Due to its clear top-down orientation it is from the first geared towards presumed collective and ubiquitous patterns of meaning and might therefore disregard novel, creative, and unusual forms of figurative meaning. Moreover, the clear-cut, static form of the audiovisual manifestations unpicks the dynamic and multimodal unfolding of audiovisual media. As a consequence, these kinds of extracted metaphors or metonymies suggest meaningful items or instances of meaning-making that run contrary to the moving nature of audiovisual images.

These observations are the starting point for the argument unfolded in this book. It argues that drawing conclusions with regard to the meaning of a film or a commercial on such a narrow basis ignores the fundamental dynamic aspect of audiovisual figurative meaning-making. By contrast, a process-oriented, dynamic approach is suggested to allow for findings closer to the data and to the specific media mode of experience of audiovisual images that modulates the spectator's process of viewing. Including and applying dynamics in terms of the three aspects mentioned above (time, attention, and experience) to the analysis of figurative meaning-making in the CDU campaign commercial provides a somewhat different picture than the one outlined above.[1]

A process-oriented, dynamic approach first entails taking account of the *temporal dynamics of audiovisual compositions*. Although this statement may appear self-evident, neither cognitive-linguistic research on audiovisual figurativity nor film and media studies have sufficiently taken it into account. No matter in which disciplinary context, the analysis of audiovisual images frequently is based on extracting single shots or scenes from their temporal flow and treating as well as analyzing them as if they were static images. Nevertheless, the medium of film differs significantly from static images due to its dynamic unfolding in time, and it is this difference that has a fundamental impact on the process of meaning-making.

The two stills from the CDU campaign commercial in Figure 1, for instance, are made snapshots showing Angela Merkel standing in front of the window and walking through her office. Watching the TV campaign ad, a spectator does not perceive any one of them in a separate and static manner. Instead, they are embedded into a composition or, in other words, they are part of a temporally unfolding movement. This dimension of movement goes beyond the mere representation of walking, it implies "more complex forms of transformation (e.g., lighting, rhythmic arrangements of shot lengths, acoustics), that are called 'movement' in film theory with regard to their role in modulating perceptual dynamics" (Bakels 2014, 2052). Only within and through this compositional context and temporal course are the images connected and unfold their meaning: Merkel's walk through the office takes up her position of standing at the window in a contrastive manner. Accordingly, audiovisual images – like audiovisual figurativity – are not meaningful on their own terms, but only within their media context, i.e., their temporal composition and unfolding.

The change of perspective from single, constructed static images to a temporal unfolding of audiovisual movement goes hand in hand with the *attentional dynamics of audiovisual compositions*. The interrelation of images or figurations reveals a particular orchestration of this temporal movement that shapes the viewer's flow of attention. The audiovisual staging plays an important role here as it unfolds patterns in the viewer's perception: "Different articulatory modalities (e.g., camera movement, montage, or sound) create figurations of movement that establish different gestalt-like forms." (Scherer, Greifenstein, and Kappelhoff 2014, 2085) The respective composition of these movement gestalts (or *cinematic*

---

1 That is not to say that the potential existence of conceptual metaphors and metonymies in the two sequences described above is completely ruled out. However, the question is raised if TIME IS SPACE, PLACE FOR PERSON, or 'Angela Merkel is both outside and inside' is indeed the only thing the CDU campaign commercial is all about.

expressive movements, Kappelhoff 2004) and their arrangement in the course of time make particular aspects more salient in the viewer's perception. For instance, in the first half of the CDU campaign commercial the interplay of the underlying court-style music and temperate camera movement evokes and foregrounds a calm and solemn atmosphere. In the second half, a clear arrangement of the frame in center and periphery, making Merkel the unambiguous focal point of each shot, highlights balance and stability. In this way, the articulatory modalities of audiovisual staging build a salience structure throughout the campaign commercial in the viewer's perception.

Audiovisual staging does not only orchestrate the spectator's flow of attention, but also his or her affective experience. By the continuous interplay of articulatory modalities that compose to movement patterns throughout an entire film or campaign commercial, a path of various qualities, moods, and atmospheres emerges that the spectator goes through in the process of viewing (Kappelhoff 2004, Kappelhoff and Bakels 2011, Kappelhoff and Müller 2011, Müller and Kappelhoff 2018, Scherer, Greifenstein, and Kappelhoff 2014). Such a philosophical argument understands 'to be moved' by audiovisual images literally: as a dynamic modulation of a viewer's affective experiences (Scherer and Greifenstein 2014, 2083) or, in other words, as the *experiential dynamics of audiovisual compositions*.

In this understanding, the viewer is bodily affected by, for instance, the calm and moderate movement qualities that are foregrounded in the first half of the CDU TV campaign ad. Audiovisual compositions are considered to consist of movement patterns that shape time in an aesthetic manner. The spectator realizes their qualities as felt experiences and, on such an embodied basis, creates meaning.[2] In the case of the CDU campaign commercial, the audiovisual staging and composition unfolds an experience of dignified power and dominance that viewers ascribe to Angela Merkel and through it see her as a queen-like sovereign in the center of power.

---

[2] Note that experience as it is used here indicates an aesthetic mode of perceiving and reflexive feeling on the part of the spectator that follows John Dewey's idea of a 'feeling for the unity of experience' (Dewey 1980, 36–59) instead of alluding to reactions to and mental simulations of cognitively stored experience: "What experience means here is a becoming aware of an object through a deliberate process of perception; it is the unfolding of an object field into a perceived object through a temporally unfolding feeling for the perception of a concrete thing. The term experience therefore denotes the reflexive becoming aware of this operation, which unfolds automatically in our perception process and is completed without an awareness of the developing feeling." (Müller and Kappelhoff 2018, 53)

The illustration of the product- and the process-oriented perspective on figurative meaning-making by the example of the CDU campaign commercial concludes with a theoretical remark. The separate elaboration of the three aspects of dynamics for multimodal figurativity as well as for audiovisual compositions demonstrates that meaning in both contexts is neither a static property of single components or entities nor a product that results by default from their addition. The process-oriented approach to audiovisual figurative meaning-making as put forward in this book brings together and thinks through both contexts in the aspect of dynamics. This perspective indicates the fundamental role of a perceiving and sensing viewer, who participates affectively and cognitively in the process of meaning-making. In this respect, the spectator has so far rather been disregarded by cognitive-linguistic and cognitive media studies research within the two contexts. Without him or her, however, the three aspects of dynamics are unthinkable. Figurative meaning as well as audiovisual compositions unfold temporally, attentionally, and experientially only and exclusively for 'some-body' who is experiencing and understanding something in terms of something else (cf. Gibbs 2018, Jensen 2017, Kappelhoff 2004, Müller 2008a, Müller and Kappelhoff 2018, Müller and Tag 2010). This observation is of great relevance for this book's argument while also representing far-reaching consequences for a theory of metaphor and metonymy.

1.2 Audiovisual Figurativity as Construction of Meaning

One consequence of the dynamics outlined in the previous section and their key prerequisite of an experiencing and understanding participant is that they direct attention to the process of figurative meaning-making in audiovisual contexts itself. So far, little attention has been paid to the question of how a spectator in watching a film, advertising spot, or campaign commercial is actually enabled to make meaning and how this process occurs. Instead the main focus has rather been on how figurative meaning in audiovisual media is objectified in word-image form by a producer (without clarifying, who 'the producer' of audiovisual media actually is) with the aim of intentionally evoking a particular idea in the viewer (e.g., Carroll 1996, [1994] 2001, Eggertsson and Forceville 2009, Fahlenbrach 2007, 2010, 2011, Urios-Aparisi 2009, 2014). The process he or she experiences is thereby broken down into recognition and deciphering of such word-image forms that are suggested to be interspersed throughout the film or spot by the producer. In order to argue that the viewer is indeed able to identify and comprehend them, they are considered manifestations of interpersonally shared, entrenched mappings between conceptual domains, allowing viewers to easily process them. It seems to be very much taken for granted that the spectator deciphers higher-level figurative meaning by default from its audiovisual instantiation and due to a producer intending so; all the more, considering the lack of reliable empirical evidence for such a claim. As Chapters 3 and 4 develop, this holds for both cognitive-linguistic as well as for film-theoretical accounts of figurativity.

Forceville devotes some attention to this concern indirectly when dealing with the question of whether or not "comprehension of a non-verbal or multimodal metaphor [implies] that recipients 'mentally' verbalize the metaphor" (Forceville 2009a, 31). Since, in his viewpoint, non-verbal modalities differ from words as they do not have the 'A IS B' form, one has to focus on the "stylistic means" by which similarity is "*triggered*" (emphasis mine). Noël Carroll (2001, 362–367) touches upon the process of audiovisual figurative meaning-making when discussing "visual metaphors" as intentionally created symbols in an artistic medium with regard to their recognition and interpretation by a spectator. In both cases, figurativity merely plays a role in advocating a concept of intentional meaning-making that is based on the emphasized perspective of a creator. For the most part, this concept is based on an objectivist understanding of language use and meaning-making in audiovisual media. It does so by objectifying figurative meaning in terms of image plus word(s) and thereby making a process a product, by linking this product and its recognition to the intention of a producer, and thereby making the spectator a passive recipient.

Although Forceville and Carroll have different opinions in regards to the question of whether or not source and target domain are reversible in the case of audiovisual metaphor, both nevertheless share the idea of a producer who deliberately implements figurative meaning audiovisually in this or that way and wants it to be understood accordingly. As Forceville states, "[m]akers' intentions are an important factor in discussions about metaphor" (Forceville 2007b, 16).

> [A]n *intention* to produce a metaphor usually results in the provision of salient cues to that effect by the metaphor's producer. In the first place, some sort of similarity between A and B must be signalled. [...] The similarity may be of many different kinds: A and B may look similar, sound similar, occur in a similar space or [...] be simultaneously signalled [...]. A second type of cue that an A-as-B interpretation may be called for is that there is something odd or anomalous in the identification of A and B, because in the given situation A and B are experienced as entities belonging to different categories and do not normally constitute a single entity. (Forceville 2007b, 19)

According to such a way of thinking, the spectator's derivation of figurative meaning is the result of a prior intentional 'just so' presentation of a thing, a person, or an issue by the producer. The prerequisite for this is an objectification of figurative meaning, specifically, a clear formal manifestation of a conceptual source and target domain. Each of these has to be exclusively or predominantly represented in different modalities (Forceville 1996, 2007b, 2009a). Carroll follows a similar line of thought, but adds furthermore the salience of features to be mapped as a criterion for correct interpretation:

> Up to this point, our conception of a visual metaphor has been that a visual metaphor is a visual image in which physically noncompossible elements belong to a homospatially unified figure which, in turn, encourages viewers to explore mappings between the relevant constituent elements and/or the categories or concepts to which they allude. [...] This signals that the figure as a whole is recognizable perceptually as well as that the elements that serve in the viewer's mappings be perceptually recognizable. [...] Of course, in order to negotiate a visual metaphor, the viewer must not only be able to recognize the relevant elements. Her attention also needs to be drawn to them. So the relevant elements must stand out; they must be visually salient or prominent. (Carroll 2001, 362)

For both Forceville and Carroll it is of utmost concern that, first of all, the producer of audiovisual figurative meaning himself recognizes the contradiction of two similar yet actually incompatible things. On that basis, it is reasonable for him to suppose that the viewer does as well (Carroll 2001, 363). By implication this means that, for instance, a metaphor is only then a metaphor when viewers have reason to believe that the producer wanted them to see two actually incompatible things as identical (and not due to fiction or genre) (Carroll 2001, 363). Thereby, viewers play a subordinate and, above all, passive role in the process of audiovisual figurative meaning-making: they become deciphering recipients and figurative meaning a pre-existing meaningful entity that a producer can dispose of intentionally.

Such an understanding is reminiscent of CMT and its verification on the basis of linguistic metaphors and a "lexical-semantic approach" (Müller 2008a, 76) that primarily proceeds from a paradigmatic and systemic point of view. Indeed, audiovisual and linguistic figurative meaning are explicitly related to each other in such a perspective: "[T]here are some visual images that function in the same way that verbal metaphors do and whose point is identified by a viewer in roughly the same way that the point of a verbal metaphor is identified by a reader or a listener" (Carroll 2001, 347). Saying this results in the adoption of the lexical-semantic and static focus of the paradigmatic level, i.e., the selection from the assumed superordinate system of conceptual metaphors and metonymies. This, in turn, leaves out the combinational interplay with other aspects and entities of the context of use, i.e., the syntagmatic level. As Müller has aptly and thoroughly explained, the tacit assumption of CMT that conceptual figurativity is "collective in nature" and "psychologically realistic" (Müller 2008a, 68) is rather implausible and, moreover, hard to empirically verify.

The idea of relating producer and recipient with regard to meaning-making is not wrong by itself. After all, film just as face-to-face interaction has no end in itself, but is addressed to someone being involved in it. What is, however, prob-lematic is the notion of 'a producer', for it is never a single person but always a number of people involved in making a film. As the film only unfolds meaning by being perceived and experienced through a spectator, the immediate interac-tive situation takes place between these two, not between 'a producer' and the spectator. On the other hand, the notion of intention alludes to the psychological reality of figurative meaning for the producer and the addressee and thus also to consciousness. These psychological states are hard to argue and to prove empiri-cally from the paradigmatic perspective of the system as they are matters of indi-vidual use (Müller 2008a, 2011). It seems that exactly this difficulty of inspection in the spectator's individual perspective of use is the reason to de-emphasize his process of figurative meaning-making in terms of a static recognition and deci-phering of the producer's intentions.

The issue of the viewer (or the addressee) and his or her process of figurative meaning-making – the problem of comprehension – is a central one for traditional as well as cognitive metaphor and metonymy theories (see, e.g., Black 1993, Gibbs 2011, Müller 2008a, 2011, Steen 2006, 2011). However, it has not yet received pro-found attention by scholars dealing with audiovisual figurative meaning-making. This is a gap that this book intends to bridge. Instead of proceeding from a fin-ished product of meaning that the viewer automatically perceives and deciphers one-to-one according to the producer's intention, it is argued that retracing the process of figurative meaning-making has empirical relevance. Furthermore, it is suggested that such a close consideration of the situated media context also directly bears upon a theory of figurative meaning-making as it locates and anal-yses it where it actually emerges: in a situated manner with an involved viewer who experiences and understands something in terms of something else.

The dynamic approach proposed in this book makes for a change in per-spective with regard to the analysis of audiovisual figurative meaning-making: from a product to a process and from the producer to the recipient. This empiri-cal shift of focus entails a clear distinction of system and use (cf. Müller 2008a). So far, figurative meaning-making in audiovisual media has first and foremost been ascribed to entrenched, collectively shared patterns of thought (e.g., Eggertsson and Forceville 2009, Fahlenbrach 2007, 2010, 2011, Forceville 2009b, 2017, Urios-Aparisi 2009, 2014). Yet, such an exclusive orientation to the system level ignores the media specificity and the situatedness of the meaning-making process in the spectator's perception and experience as properties of the level of use. The spectator, on the other hand, turns through a dynamic approach from a passive recipient into an active participant: the constructer of figurative meaning in establishing metaphoricity or metonymicity (cf. Kappelhoff and Müller 2011, Müller 2008a). As a result, figurative meaning in audiovisual media can no longer be conceived of as a product of deciphered, pre-existent meaningful entities. By contrast, the term figurative meaning-making alludes to an *activity* (a 'doing', see Gibbs 2018, Jensen 2017), a process of constructing meaning in the course and context of viewing a campaign commercial.

As a result, the audiovisual metaphors and metonymies presented in Section 1.1 from a dynamic perspective would not be considered pre-existent meaningful entities that a producer has intentionally packaged in audiovisual images, spoken or written language. Instead, they are conceived of as emerging from the temporal, attentional, and experiential dynamics that a spectator goes through while watching a campaign commercial. As Kappelhoff and Müller have put it in more active terms, in the process of viewing the spectator is "enabled to construct" (Kappelhoff and Müller 2011, 143) figurative meaning through these aspects of dynamics, i.e., over the course of time, through foregrounded segments and aspects, and through embodied experience. Again, the fact that Angela Merkel is experienced as standing for the people or that she is seen in terms of a queen or sovereign in the CDU campaign commercial is not contained holistically or objectively in an image or a word, a phrase, or a sentence. The spectator is considered to construct these meanings in the 'encounter' with the audiovisual 'material' through perception, experience, and cognition. The issue of the empirical reconstruction of this process of meaning-making will be presented and discussed in detail in Chapter 5. The complete analysis of the emergence of figurative meaning in the CDU campaign commercial will be provided in Chapter 6.

The last idea to be suggested in these regards for the moment is that the first and foremost concentration on a producer's intentions and purposes of previous cognitive-linguistic, as well as cognitive media studies' research with regard to audiovisual figurativity, is replaced by the viewer's perspective. There are several reasons for doing this: as outlined before, the viewer has hitherto been widely disregarded and reduced to a passive receiver when it comes to audiovisual figurative meaning-making. Moreover, using the producer's intention as a central criterion and argument for the meaning-making of an addressed spectator seems theoretically as well as empirically problematic. First of all, intention refers to a mental state that is closely linked to activities like planning and forethought (cf., e.g., Bratman 1987). As such, it raises the question of its degree of consciousness, i.e., how aware the producer was of his or her intentions or intended impact on the addressee. These questions have philosophical, neuropsychological as well as psychological relevance and, as Müller (2008a) has convincingly pointed out, there is still no single comprehensive theory of consciousness. In order to make a reliable point about the intention of the producer as the decisive factor for audiovisual figurative meaning-making on the part of the spectator, empirical evidence for this intention would be necessary. Additional research instruments, such as questionnaires, would be needed for intentions that are not empirically observable from the audiovisual material. However, such additional research has not been carried out in previous studies on audiovisual figurative meaning-making. Instead, the equivalence between the analyst's interpretation and the (psychologically real) producer's intention has been tacitly presupposed.

Instead of reapplying such a problematic presupposition, this study follows Müller's decision "to rely on a facet of cognitive processes that is *empirically accessible* through microanalyses of language use" (2008a, 12; emphasis mine). This is as much as to say that by the results of the analyses in this book there will be no claims of their psychological reality. The type of argument that is developed instead is a philosophical one and, as such, it is theoretically motivated. On the basis of accessible and observable aspects a specific approach will be suggested that is above all – and thereby it is in line with Johnson (2007) – inspired by aesthetic perception and bodily experience as the driving forces for meaning-making. As this argument is fundamentally contrary to previous research on audiovisual figurativity, the main objective of this book is first of all to introduce and illustrate an alternative approach to audiovisual figurativity by means of campaign commercials. For this purpose, the dynamic approach to audiovisual figurative meaning-making and its practical application to campaign commercials will be developed step by step (see Chapter 5).

1.3 Audiovisual Figurativity as Embodied Experience

Former one-sided concentration on the assumed collective conceptual system in the context of analyzing audiovisual metaphors and metonymies has been shown to oversimplify figurative meaning-making in audiovisual media. It makes figurativity a pre-existent product, the spectator a passive recipient, and the producer an intentional and most influential factor in meaning-making. Following this tenet, respective studies also try to account for the affective dimension and persuasive impact of metaphor and metonymy. In the same manner that conceptual figurative meaning is considered to manifest objectively in words and/or audiovisual images, affective content – as an inherent feature of such superordinate concepts – is implicitly assumed to be contained in these manifestations (see, e.g., Androshchuck 2014, Charteris-Black 2005, Fahlenbrach 2007, 2010, 2011, Grady 1997, Kövecses 2000, Ortiz 2015). Just as these manifestations are considered to be more easily comprehended due to their status as collectively shared patterns, their immanent affective substance is suggested to be, by default, recognized and internalized by recipients. The following quote of Forceville is a representative example of such a cognitivist-informed conception of emotional appeal through figurative meaning:

Drawing on conceptual schema's, they [i.e., verbal metaphors] will retrieve from memory typical elements that belong in such schemas. In multimodal metaphors, many details need not be imagined or supplied, since they are already given. Such details are bound to evoke specific connotations, and hence will steer and constrain interpretation of metaphors in manners that are different from those cued in exclusively verbal terms. [...]

Apart from their greater degree of comprehensibility, metaphors drawing on images, sounds, and music also, I submit, have a more intense, immediate emotional impact than verbal ones. (Forceville 2007b, 27; emphasis mine)

Apart from the fact that Forceville does not offer any more precise differentiation or a definition of "typical elements" and "connotations" at this point, what is remarkable is the lack of a systematic accountability of what he calls elsewhere "clear-cut connotations for a community of users" (Forceville 2009b, 383). At this point, there is no known satisfactorily and thoroughly elaborated theory of these suggested culturally or nationally shared associative patterns. This is one of the reasons that makes it problematic to draw on such a conception of emotional appealing through figurative meaning. The lack of differentiation between a collective system and its realization in use is another factor for the necessity of an alternative account of the emotionalizing potential of audiovisual figurativity.

The usage-based and notably dynamic approach as advocated in this book is not consistent with the static and system-based understanding of emotional appeal of former cognitive-linguistic as well as cognitive media studies' work on audiovisual metaphor and metonymy. Their lack of concern for the necessity of distinguishing the collective and the individual level, i.e., system and use, of emotional experience (not to speak of the lack of differentiating between emotion, affect, and feeling; for a detailed discussion of these terms, see Kappelhoff 2018) is another research gap addressed in this work. Due to the one-sided orientation towards the system level (and its thereby tacitly postulated higher value), the emotionalizing of addressees through metaphor and metonymy becomes a mere response to a stimulus. Its basis is the already mentioned cognitively stored connotations and emotions that are said to be linked to a particular concept or issue.

Consider in some detail how cognitive-linguistic research has described and explained the issue of emotionalizing so far by taking the example of Forceville's study (2009b) of metaphors in commercials and fiction films. In it, he focuses on how sound and music can cue a metaphor's source domain as well as mappable features from source to target domain. In the case of an advertisement for a Senseo coffee maker Forceville suggests the metaphor COFFEE MAKER IS MOTORCYCLE, which he derives inter alia from the underlying sound of a motorcycle and the song "Born to be wild" from the film EASY RIDER (Dennis Hopper, USA 1969) accompanying the presentation of the coffee maker. In the following quote, he explains how music and sound come to evoke particular qualities with the promoted product on the part of the spectator:

> One mappable feature is clearly the high-tech design, but more importantly *the music evokes connotations* such as living life in the fast lane, freedom, unconventionality, youth, sixties' counterculture – a whole range of *qualities nostalgically associated with Easy Rider motorbiking* that are potentially mapped to making your coffee with a Senseo machine. (Forceville 2009b, 389; emphasis mine)

Here, it becomes apparent that Forceville links the suggested co-accessed connotations to cultural knowledge that he tacitly assumes to exist and to be shared collectively.[3] Although there is no explicit mention of particular emotions or emotional evaluation, the synonymous use of "connotations" and "qualities" indicates that Forceville attributes emotional content as an inherent feature to objects, entities, and figures on the level of representation, such as the film EASY RIDER. This is prompted by the following statement: "In most metaphors in commercials, the product is the target and the source is something else, which means that *it is positive features that are mapped* from source to target" (Forceville 2009b, 389; emphasis mine).

In a similar manner, film-analytical studies following CMT derive and explain emotional appeal through audiovisual figurativity. Kathrin Fahlenbrach (2011), for example, proceeds in her study about metaphors in the sound design of films from cognitively stored image schemas that as sonic and visual manifestations affect the viewer's perception. Drawing on Lakoff and Johnson's (1980) as well as Kövecses' (2000) work on the systematic metaphorical conceptualization of emotions, she argues that the sound design of films draws on entrenched image schemas and mappings when it comes to the perception and evaluation of objects, characters, and spaces. Using the example of the film THE SHINING (Stanley Kubrick, GB/USA 1980), Fahlenbrach explains the emotional impact of the stair sequence when Wendy is attacked by Jack by means of the unconsciously activated conceptual metaphor FEAR IS AN OPPONENT IN A STRUGGLE:

---

3 Boris Androshchuk argues similarly in his study of metaphor as an ideological tool of persuasion in the political discourse of the German Bundestag about family policy. Although he does not analyze audiovisual figurativity but verbal metaphors, he too presupposes a collectively shared system that is determinative of a particular shaping of emotions. Androshchuk suggests a social value system that, for instance, rates children high as something valuable in the life of man and family (Androshchuk 2014, 281). On that basis, he holds, a metaphorical substitution of the concept family by the concept child (*sic!* Actually, this is a case of metonymy and not metaphor) leads to a lower degree of criticism towards a respective statement. This way, the recipient is suggested to be more easily influenceable at the producer's will and intention.

Together with the music and the voice timbre of the characters, further key stimuli are triggered on the reflexive level of bodily response that is linked to the opponent metaphor: The high frequency of Wendy's voice and the dissonant sounds of the music contrast with the slow movements of the two characters through the hall. (Fahlenbrach 2008, 94)

Overall, both cognitive linguistics as well as cognitive media studies treat a systemic approach to figurative meaning-making and its emotional appeal as unproblematic. In focusing solely on assumed, but not thoroughly elaborated and accounted conceptual patterns and networks that are suggested to be shared by entire groups of people, figurative meaning as well as its emotional impact are reduced to static and pre-existent entities and features that a producer can dispose of intentionally and that are recognized and understood one-to-one. Compared with this, a dynamic approach to audiovisual figurativity shall be proposed that implies two fundamental theoretical changes of perspective:

1. *From an objectivistic view on figurative meaning-making in audiovisual media to a constructivist one that proceeds from bottom up.* This opens up an alternative, usage-based way of thinking that goes against the so far dominant systemic one and puts to the fore the viewer's participation and activity in meaning-making.

2. *From a cognitivist view on figurative meaning-making in audiovisual media to an embodied one that proceeds from the felt experience of the viewer.* This opens up an alternative way of thinking about the claimed affective or persuasive potential of figurativity that so far has been conceived of as a default effect on the cognitive level, but has never been convincingly discussed or demonstrated.

This is not to say that these two changes of perspective from top down to bottom up (i.e., from system to use) deny the existence of superordinate image schemas or conceptual metaphors and metonymies. Nor should the possibility of the existence and impact of shared cultural value systems or associative networks be ruled out. However, the previous exclusive commitment to the systemic level has entirely neglected the level of use, i.e., the situated media context, as a noteworthy aspect of audiovisual figurative meaning-making. This is the subject to which this book intends to contribute. By proceeding from the very situation in which audiovisual figurative meaning is emerging and playing out, i.e., when a spectator is watching a campaign commercial or a film and addressed by it temporally, attentionally, and experientially, it takes account of the respective individual medial context of use.

In this respect, the dynamic approach to audiovisual figurative mean-ing-making as proposed here is considered to complement the existing systemic approaches by opening up an alternative perspective to the object of research. By means of systematic analyses of a larger body of data, e.g., of all parties that released campaign commercials in particular elections, it becomes possible to draw conclusions on a higher level. In so doing, recurrent motifs and their respec-tive audiovisual presentation could be identified and considered. With a larger body of data, be it national or international, one could look for genre-specific features in a limited period of time or in general.[4] With regard to the identifica-tion and verification of systematic or superordinate meaning structures, such a bottom-up approach provides a more material-informed basis than a top-down take that, in a biased manner, intends to confirm ex ante assumed superordinate structures in the data. In order to arrive at a complete picture of the issue, the so far dominating static top-down approach that has considered audiovisual figu-rative meaning-making in an objectivistic and cognitivist light needs to be com-plemented and revised by a dynamic bottom-up approach. This is a conclusion drawn by Lynne Cameron in regard to metaphor in face-to-face interaction:

> [...] [I]f we take a purely cognitive approach or a purely socio-cultural approach to language use and, by extension, to an aspect of language use such as metaphor, we do not get pictures that are differently but equally valid; rather, we get partial and inaccurate pictures, since it is precisely the interaction between the cognitive and social in language use that produces the language and behavior that we observe and research. What we need is a view of language in use which prevents a one-sided or compartmentalized approach, by allowing the social and the cognitive to be integral parts of theory and analysis of data. (Cameron 1999b, 4)

By contributing an alternative approach that proceeds from the viewer's process of figurative meaning-making, this book intends to bridge the research gap Cameron is mentioning. Its understanding of dynamically emerging and unfolding figura-tive meaning gains support from recent usage-based approaches to metaphor that predominantly but not only have been developed within the field of face-to-face interaction (e.g., Cameron 2007, 2010, Cameron et al. 2009, Jensen 2017, Jensen and Cuffari 2014, Müller 2008a, 2008b, Müller and Ladewig 2013, Müller and Tag 2010, Musolff and Zinken 2009, Semino 2008, Semino and Demjén 2017). It is only recently that an increasing number of studies with a similar way of thinking

---

4 Such a comprehensive analysis has been conducted within the Hollywood war film genre (see Kappelhoff 2018, Kappelhoff, Gaertner, and Pogodda 2013, Kappelhoff 2010–2014 and the inter-net portal *Empirische Medienästhetik* [http://www.empirische-medienaesthetik.fu-berlin.de/en/index.html]). In this case, there was, however, no explicit focus on audiovisual figurativity but on recurrent strategies of staging and of affect mobilization.

appear and come up for discussion with regard to audiovisual forms of figurative meaning-making (e.g., Müller and Kappelhoff 2018, Kappelhoff and Müller 2011, Kappelhoff and Greifenstein 2016, Müller and Schmitt 2015, Schmitt forthcoming/2019, Schmitt, Greifenstein, and Kappelhoff 2014). This book is inspired by and considered in line with this body of research.

With campaign commercials as its particular object of research the dynamic approach to audiovisual figurativity as proposed here goes beyond the scope of the cognitive-linguistic theory of and research on metaphor and metonymy alone and provides a link to the social sciences (e.g., political science, political sociology, communication studies). Located at such an interdisciplinary interface, it poses figurative meaning-making on the part of the recipient or addressee of the campaign commercials as a shared question of central relevance to each of these disciplines and opens up a new, embodied perspective on it: bodily experience as the ground for the emergence of figurative meaning and thus for making sense of candidates and political issues.

Experience, however, is not considered as an instinctive simulation of cognitively stored and by default one-to-one processed emotional content, but as felt qualities of meaning (Johnson 2007, 17) evoked by in the situation of watching a campaign commercial. Johnson has aptly described this bodily 'encounter' with meaning: "[T] he situation is meaningful to us in the most important, primordial, and basic way that it can be meaningful – it shapes the basic contours of our experience" (Johnson 2007, 66). Such an idea of "understanding through experience" (Müller and Schmitt 2015, 319) makes it possible to look at the often-claimed persuasive power of figurativity in political communication in a new light. As a result, affective experience is no longer seen from an angle that is biased from the first in that it is equated with the adoption of the perspective it is expressing. Conceiving of affective experience as the ground for figurative meaning-making does not jump to such conclusions. Instead, it leads the way to understanding. In doing so, it raises the question of whether comprehension – achieved through embodied experience, as argued here – could be considered the prerequisite for persuasion. If so, then audiovisual figurativity's experiential aspect would have been wrongly prejudged as mere negative manipulation (as, e.g., by Androshchuck 2014). An in-depth treatment of this question is beyond the scope of this book. It shall, however, be briefly addressed in Section 9.3.

1.4 Objective, Scope, and Structure of the Book

The main objective of this book is to put forward a dynamic approach to the emergence of figurative meaning in political campaign commercials by taking the perspective of the viewing and experiencing spectator. By starting from a situated process of meaning-making instead of a by-default product, the line of argument put forward contrasts with a hitherto dominant top-down directed and intentionally driven understanding of figurative meaning in audiovisual political communication and instead conceives of it as a practice of experiencing and understanding. Along those lines, the dynamic approach to audiovisual figurativity as proposed here is rather consistent with dynamic approaches to figurative meaning-making in face-to-face interaction (e.g., Cameron 2010, Jensen 2017, Müller 2008a, Müller and Tag 2010). Metaphor and metonymies in audiovisual media are considered as emergent phenomena of a multimodal encounter of two 'interactants': the campaign commercial and the viewer. In the act of watching, both enter into an interactive situation in which figurative meaning emerges and unfolds dynamically in the course of time, in the flow of attention, and in the flow of experience (see also Müller and Kappelhoff 2018). The focus of this book is on empirically retracing these dynamic aspects in their audiovisual context in order to avoid premature or overgeneralized conclusions concerning the intentional use of and manipulation by conceptual metaphors and metonymies. Therefore, the constructivist and embodied understanding of audiovisual figurative meaning-making introduced sticks to the situated media context. In doing so, the dynamic approach is in line with Terrell Carver and Jernej Pikalo who have suggested that research on figurativity in the field of politics has focused too much on its interpretation and too little on its "creative-productive function" (Carver and Pikalo 2008b, 3). In this context, they emphatically point out the dynamic nature of figurative meaning-making, which corresponds to the major tenet of this book: "The defining characteristic of metaphor in the Aristotelian tradition is that it is defined in terms of movement, change with respect to location mainly movement 'from ... to' [...]" (Carver and Pikalo 2008b, 2).

It is with this emphasis on the processuality and productivity of audiovisual figurative meaning that the book addresses not exclusively metaphor or metonymy researchers from cognitive linguistics, but also political and social scientists as well as media scholars. On the one hand, it operates formally at the interface of the mentioned disciplines by its specific type of data, i.e., political campaign commercials. On the other hand, it intends to bring ideas into the above-mentioned fields of study by its transdisciplinary theoretical model and methodology that are a result of the connection of cognitive linguistics and film studies. Metaphor and metonymy as general cognitive (and therefore modality-independent) phenomena and social practices of meaning-making and constructions of reality provide a common reference point for this purpose.

As a result of such a transdisciplinary scope, the book and its leading argument of the dynamics of audiovisual figurativity are subject to maximum comprehensibility and clarity in order to address researchers from cognitive linguistics, film and media studies, and the social sciences. The discussed approaches and theories are not entirely exhaustive but the result of a selection process in the light of their relevance for the central question of this book. As this particular trans-disciplinary question about audiovisual figurative meaning-making in campaign commercials has not yet been previously posed by neither metaphor or meton-ymy research nor by the social sciences, only those aspects of existing models and theories will be discussed – in a systematic manner – that are relevant for the book's argumentation instead of treating them extensively one after another. Despite such a content-related reduction, the book aims to account for and give an overview of the range of existing and adopted research related to audiovisual figurativity and campaign commercials.

The selection of theories and approaches that, although being relevant for the subject matter, have until now received only little attention plays another major role in this regard. Bringing together and discussing Anglophone, Germanophone, and Polonophone research contributes to their increased mutual and international scientific awareness and reception. A closer look at parallels in the theoretical argumentation and empirical analysis when compiling the current state of research reveals that the single disciplines often pose similar research questions and share certain assumptions. For instance, metaphor research as well as the social sciences and film and media studies similarly ask for the interplay of modalities and different levels of communication with regard to the presentation of particular contents and issues. Another relevant subject is the relation between emotional appealing by audiovisual content and its impact on the spectator (e.g., in terms of manipulation or persuasion). The specific focus on audiovisual figur-ativity in campaign commercials opens up an interface to address these questions and makes for new insights within the single disciplines as well as for putting established and taken for granted assumptions up for negotiation. In this respect, the structure of the book is (metaphorically) considered an interweaving of so far unconnected research strands running in parallel: it proceeds from the single disciplines and their core themes relevant for the topic of the book in order to finally bring them together and to open up a new perspective (i.e., a mutual see-ing-in-terms-of).

Chapter 2 provides an overview of the state of research about campaign commercials that so far have been examined almost exclusively in the field of the social sciences (e.g., in political science, political sociology, communication studies). As will be shown, the focus of this research has been either on the rep-resented and expressed content of the TV campaign ads or on their persuasive impact on the spectator. However, both aspects have never been investigated in their mutual interplay and context; just as little as the aspect of the situated context, i.e., the media perception. This holds for Germanophone, Anglophone, as well as Polonophone studies.[5] Compared with this, cognitive-linguistic research has hitherto not taken account of campaign commercials. Instead it has dealt with figurativity in various contexts of political communication, most of all in spoken or written form, but not in audiovisual formats like campaign commercials. As will be demonstrated, hitherto existing cognitive-linguistic studies focus first and foremost on metaphor and leave metonymy to the side. A link to the beforehand-discussed state of research in the social sciences provides the question for the persuasive impact of figurativity in political communication. Finally, both research topics, i.e., campaign commercials and figurativity, will be brought together with regard to their central research desiderata and in view of the dynamic approach to audiovisual figurativity as put forward in this book.

Chapter 3 develops the first part of the theoretical background by starting from the fundamental role of metaphor and metonymy for human thinking, understanding, and action from a cognitive-linguistic perspective. On that basis, usage-oriented research is introduced that conceives of figurativity as a modality-independent phenomenon and accounts for questions such as how figurative meaning emerges in situ and unfolds dynamically as well as if and how it is comprehended. Such multimodal usage-based research enables empirical access to the embodied ground of figurative meaning-making and to its suggested affective dimension. The chapter concludes that research on metaphor and metonymy hitherto, however, – save for some exceptions – has given priority to the cognitive function and has also subordinated the affective dimension to this cognitive primacy. Taking up Lakoff and Johnson's well-known metaphor definition, it will be demonstrated that it is rather understanding that is brought to the fore instead of experiencing something in terms of something else.

Chapter 4 introduces accounts of metaphor and metonymy from a film-theoretical perspective. As will be shown, film studies – like most cognitive-linguistic studies of audiovisual figurativity – have predominantly considered metaphor and metonymy as static, meaningful entities in a filmmaker's hands. Apart from semiotic and rhetorical accounts that conceive of figurativity as a general principle of figuration in film or as a rhetorical device serving a film's elocution, recent approaches will be discussed that are informed by relevant linguistic and cognitive theories of metaphor and metonymy. Proponents of such a perspective, however, tend to disregard the media specificity of film or limit it to

---

5 A comparative analysis of German and Polish campaign commercials has been carried out by Musiałowska (2008). On the basis of content analysis she comes among others to the conclusion that compared to German campaign commercials, Polish ones are produced less professionally. The comparative analyses in this book avoid such an intuitive evaluation and instead focus on potential similarities and differences in the form of audiovisual figurative meaning-making.

the level of audiovisual representation. Compared with this, classical film theory focuses especially on the temporal dynamics of the cinematic movement-image and relates it the spectator's experience. In line with such a way of thinking, phenomenologically informed approaches consider cinematic expression, perception, and affective experience in the process of viewing as being interrelated. Regarding therein the basis for meaning-making on the part of the viewer, such approaches provide a fruitful link to a dynamic and embodied understanding of figurative meaning-making.

Chapter 5 brings together the perspectives of both disciplines regarding understanding and experience in a theoretical and methodological manner. Combining a dynamic cognitive-linguistic perspective on multimodal figurativity and a neo-phenomenological perspective on film-viewing as embodied experience, highlights the benefits of a transdisciplinary approach to audiovisual figurativity. The dynamic approach elaborated will thus rest on three shared aspects of dynamics of both multimodal figurativity and audiovisual compositions: temporality, attention, and experience. These dynamics will next be developed as an analytical access to reveal the particular interplay of language and audiovisual staging in terms of three dominance phenomena. The subsequent analyses of campaign commercials serve to illustrate these variant forms.

Chapter 6 introduces a case of close interplay between metonymy and metaphor – the former emerging multimodally in language and audiovisual staging, the latter almost entirely through audiovisual staging – on the basis of the Christian Democratic Union's (CDU) campaign commercial for the German federal elections in 2009. As will be demonstrated, the foregrounding of contiguity combines with an unfolding experience of power, balance, and stability and evokes a vital image of the protagonist of the TV campaign ad, the incumbent Angela Merkel, as a powerful sovereign with civil roots. Thereby, audiovisual figurative meaning-making transpires as a form of an equal interplay of language and audiovisual staging.

In comparison, Chapter 7 offers an analysis of the Polish party Platforma Obywatelska's (PO) campaign commercial for the parliamentary elections in 2011. Despite a similar structure and content conception, this ad creates an entirely different image of its protagonist, the incumbent Donald Tusk, by staging him as a leading builder of a still unfinished building project of a future Poland who is asking his voters for a deadline extension. Here, figurative meaning is primarily induced through verbal metaphors of building that are affectively substantiated by audiovisual staging throughout the campaign commercial. As such, it conveys its message more explicitly as compared with the CDU campaign commercial whose figurative meaning is rather non-verbally grounded in the spectator's affective experience.

Chapter 8 complements these two analyses of incumbent campaign commercials by presenting those of two challengers: the German Social Democratic Party (SPD) and the Polish party Prawo i Sprawiedliwość (PiS). The latter's TV campaign ad displays a variant form of audiovisual figurativity that is similar to the CDU's campaign commercial; however, without metonymy playing such a dominant role. In it, the candidate Jarosław Kaczyński is experienced and understood as a door opener for the so far segregated and excluded, thereby making for participatory equality. Here, figurative meaning emerges primarily from the audiovisual staging that provides its experiential grounds and is made explicit verbally through two faded-in slogans. By contrast, the SPD's campaign commercial is noticeably language-driven, conveying its central message – Frank-Walter Steinmeier's Germany plan as the realistic answer to existential questions – explicitly through the voice-over while the audiovisual staging is restrained and plays a subordinate role.

Lastly, Chapter 9 brings the findings of the analyses from the Chapters 5, 6, and 7 together and relates them to the classification of the three variant forms (or dominance phenomena) of audiovisual figurativity introduced in Chapter 5. On this basis, conclusions will be drawn for cognitive-linguistic research and analysis of figurativity in political contexts of use and, in a second step, for social sciences research on campaign commercials. Among these conclusions, the doubt regarding the often claimed, but unsubstantiated, manipulation and persuasion of the spectator by the affective dimension of figurativity will be the subject of a final reflection. The question will be raised if the interweaving of experience and understanding as put forward in the dynamic approach to audiovisual figurative meaning-making might not serve illustrative and evidence-based purposes in the first place (in order to fully understand issues and messages) before taking persuasive effect.

2 The State of Research on Campaign Commercials and Figurativity

Though linguistics has a long research tradition in the field of political communication (for an overview, see Burkhardt 1988, Girnth 2015, Wengeler and Ziem 2015), election advertising has not been a focal point. As compared to the social sciences that have dealt with it in more detail and for a longer period of time, linguistics has dwelled upon the topic for only the last two to three decades. Cognitive linguistics, critical discourse analysis, and the research branch of politolinguistics in their dominance in the field of political communication, have taken the fore in examining the construction, legitimation, and distribution of political and social reality both descriptively and critically (Wengeler and Ziem 2015, 493).

In this regard, also figurative language use has become a subject of research, not least due to the broad reception of Lakoff and Johnson's conceptual metaphor theory (1980, 1999) that attributes figurativity a fundamental reality-structuring role. The objective of metaphor analysis in the context of political science issues is to detect latent concepts that influence "core value judgements" in a significant way (Charteris-Black 2005). This way, it is intended to raise awareness of unconsciously formed beliefs, attitudes, and values of political actors and to make them accessible to critical reflection (Charteris-Black 2004, 2005, 2013, Cameron et al. 2009, Cameron 2011, Musolff 2004, 2012, 2016, Wodak and Chilton 2005, Wodak and Meyer 2009). Remarkably, the field of election campaign communication has thereby gone unnoticed although it provides a prime example of the (strategic) construction of reality by means of figurative language in order to achieve understanding, approval, and persuasion on the part of the voters. As a result, the field is instead dominated by examinations and studies from a social sciences perspective that seek to describe and classify different forms of election campaign communication especially in regard to their content. In doing so, language use and, more precisely, meaning-making, are neither analyzed in their dynamics, processuality, and multimodal emergence nor in respect of their contextual situatedness.

This becomes particularly apparent when it comes to political campaign commercials. Although the state of research in general is not significantly extensive, examinations from within the social sciences – in particular media and communication studies, political science, and sociology – are prevailing. Moreover, the German research landscape is characterized by a clear orientation to basic assumptions, terminology, and findings from American exploratory work and follows it in the substantive prioritization of the content and effects

https://doi.org/10.1515/9783110578782-002

of TV campaign ads. Consequently, the aspects of meaning-making mentioned above as well as the media specificity of audiovisual images are not taken into consideration. From a cognitive-linguistic perspective, there is hitherto no research on figurativity in political campaign commercials – a research gap that this book intends to fill.

In order to reveal its relevance, applicability, and added value for the object of investigation, this chapter initially introduces and outlines the social sciences state of research on campaign commercials with its respective foci. Following this, a summary and overview of existing cognitive-linguistic work on figurativity in political communication will be given. Both research topics and their central research desiderata will finally be summarized and elaborated on in view of the dynamic approach to audiovisual figurativity as put forward in this book.

2.1 Campaign Commercials as Simplistic and Emotionalizing Canvassing

The discussion and examination of campaign commercials is – also from a scientific point of view – ex ante biased in two regards: because of the competitive context of elections and due to the fact that the candidates and parties present and promote themselves audiovisually. Already in the opening remarks of their edited volume, Christian Schicha and Andreas Dörner (2008) set forth that election campaigns tend to focus less on argumentative structures than on the principle of association, i.e., that they are not run rationally but primarily emotionally. In this light, the "paradigmatic change from written to visual culture" (Schicha and Dörner 2008, 8), and thus precisely campaign commercials, seem to be a suitable means for realizing this associative emotional principle in a success-oriented manner.

What immediately comes up at this point is the comparison with product advertising which for a long time has not been able to survive simply by informatively pointing out the existence of a new product and directly inviting the customer to purchase it. In times of increased competition and replaceability, commercial advertising as well as campaign commercials are considered to instead make use of an added benefit: a psychological added value of the product and the candidate or party. This in turn builds a bridge to the consumer (Holtz-Bacha 2000, 15), to catch his attention and, finally, to persuade him. Such bridge building through advertising has negative connotations: it creates an intermediate world in which attributions and meanings that a product does not have as such are transferred to it (Holtz-Bacha 2000, 15). Schicha and Dörner (2008, 8) likewise point out that advertising in election campaigns has a bad image as it is accused of trivializing and undermining politics. What shows up solely from these quotes is representative for a large part of research carried out on campaign commercials: an exclusive juxtaposition of reason and emotion, argument and persuasion, issue and image. The (audiovisual) symbolic space that TV campaign ads are opening up is thus from the outset conceived of as an untruthful one, a deception, trying to conceal by means of veneer at the surface (i.e., aesthetically and emotionally) that it has nothing to offer 'inside' (i.e., substantially) (cf. also Dörner and Vogt 2008). Despite considering campaign commercials as sensorily graspable materializations and negotiation spaces of political culture (Holtz-Bacha 2000, Dörner and Vogt 2008), aesthetic aspects have hitherto to a large extent not been taken into consideration for their analysis (Dörner and Vogt 2008, 40). The present book intends to close that research gap, too, by drawing on a phenomenologically informed notion of aesthetics, which refers to the qualitative dimension of experiencing the campaign commercials as audiovisual compositions.

As elections increasingly have been losing their ritual character, voter turnouts are falling, and traditional party ties are strongly weakened, the outcome of elections becomes more and more uncertain and difficult to predict, which is why election campaigns have significantly become more important for the parties (Holtz-Bacha 2000, 13). In addition, election advertising has been strongly professionalized with the aid of spin-doctors from the field of public relations to conduct a more active communication management plan with strategic placing of topics and candidates (Holtz-Bacha 2000, 14). The major parties therefore most often draw on established advertising agencies for the conception, aesthetic arrangement, and production of their campaign commercials. In this scenario, minor parties with limited financial means are repeatedly said to come up with unprofessional TV campaign ads (Dörner and Vogt 2008, 49f.).

Since 1957, campaign commercials have been a permanent and legal, though regulated, feature of election campaigns in Germany (Holtz-Bacha 2000, 63, 97). The legal framework regulating these ads at once imposes strict regulations while also allowing for a certain degree of liberties. To begin with, campaign airtime is fixed to a period of four weeks before the election day[1] (see state media authorities [*Landesmedienanstalten*] 2013, 11). The possibility to broadcast campaign commercials has its basis in the single broadcasting acts of the Länder (Holtz-Bacha 2000, 64), whereby all parties with at least one approved national list are entitled to benefit ('principle of equality'; see Interstate Broadcasting Agreement

---

1 The period between the 31st and the penultimate day before the election is usually considered to be appropriate (cf. state media authorities [*Landesmedienanstalten*] 2013, 11).

[*Rundfunkstaatsvertrag*] 2016, Section 42(2)). However, not all of them have the right to get the same amount of time: based on the outcomes of the last elections and further factors, the allocation of time is fine-tuned among the parties (see state media authorities [*Landesmedienanstalten*] 2013, 7–9). The general conditions vary depending on whether the TV campaign ads are broadcasted by public service or commercial television. In the case of public service television, the broadcast is for free, but the broadcasting corporations are able to individually decide where in their programs they embed the campaign commercials. In contrast, commercial television charges prime costs for the broadcast, but grants the parties a say in which program environment their TV campaign ads shall be presented (Holtz-Bacha 2000, 66, 70).

In sum, though being labeled and thus recognizable as advertising,[2] campaign commercials provide the parties with the opportunity to address spectators and potential voters in a direct, unfiltered, and unedited way. It is this aspect that has led most scholars to compare them to product advertising, which is said to make strategic use of images in order to induce emotional stimuli on the part of the consumers (Kroeber-Riel 1993, 14). The parties are assumed to operate in a similar manipulative manner when they present themselves to the voters by means of moving images that are considered to be particularly effective in manipulating human behavior. For that reason, they are of great interest for social science scholars, as, for example, seen in the recent trend towards 'politainment' in the field of political communication (see Dörner 2001). In this respect, it is suggested that campaign commercials draw on popular entertainment culture and aesthetic mainstream in order to evoke a feel-good sensation. It is therefore deemed that in this context the focus of attention (also in their reception) has more and more shifted towards their well-made style (Dörner and Vogt 2008, 46, 47). Professionalization, personalization, and emotionalizing have become the keywords for such a modern way of campaign advertising that is deduced from a supposed general trend of Americanization (see, e.g., Holtz-Bacha 1994, Pfetsch and Schmitt-Beck 1994, Brosda and Schwarz 2001, Römmele and Falter 2002). This term, which is usually negatively connoted, assumes a sweeping adoption of American political communicative regularities and behavior to German (and also European) political communication.[3] In this context, campaign commercials are mostly seen and described as an indicator for the general tendency to the

---

2 The campaign commercials are beyond the responsibility of the broadcasters. This is expressed by announcements before and afterwards, pointing out that it is the parties who are responsible for their content.
3 For a detailed discussion of the term 'Americanization', see Siebel (2007) and Wagner (2005).

modernization of election campaigns,[4] especially for the last fifteen to twenty years, with an increased occurrence and use of images and staging compared with a decrease of content and issues. Due to the fact that television was and still is considered an essential source of information for most people, campaign commercials are understood as an important means for the parties to mobilize apolitical voters by offering identification and triggering positive emotions in a directed manner (Holtz-Bacha 2000, 235).

While an abundance of literature has been published on issues such as content, function, methods, and effects of campaign advertising in general, the amount of studies especially on campaign commercials is rather small in Germany (Schicha and Dörner 2008, 19). Jakubowski (1998) has pointed out that German compared with American research in this field is rather underdeveloped, as it comprises of only a few studies dealing with the effectiveness, content, conception, or form of the TV campaign ads. In her comprehensive study of German campaign commercials between 1957 and 1998, Holtz-Bacha (2000) states the same deficit but holds out the prospect of a rising interest for this research in the near future. However, the number of studies in these parts hitherto remains limited. In comparison, American research has devoted itself earlier and more comprehensively to the study of TV campaign ads.[5] As German research in this field makes ample recourse to American studies, the most important issues and developments in this field will be briefly addressed here. This will lead to greater understanding of the overview of the German state of research on campaign commercials as it has borrowed several theoretical assumptions, methodologies, and outcomes from American exploratory work.

Starting out as just one element of election campaigns among others, campaign commercials have been examined more systematically on an individual basis from the 1970s onwards (Kaid and Johnston 2001, 15). According to Kaid and Johnston (2001), the current body of research can be divided into two major fields: studies dealing primarily with the content and studies focusing on the effects of campaign commercials. In the field of content-related research, two aspects are key concerns for study: the dichotomies of image and issue and of negative and positive contents (Kaid and Johnston 2001, 16), both of which are

---

4 The parliamentary elections in Germany in 1998 rate as a prime example of an increased modernization and personalization of election campaigns due to Gerhard Schröder's (referred to as the 'media chancellor') extensive self-promotion in the media (Sarcinelli 2009, 223–224).

5 Campaign commercials have been an essential part of American election campaigns since the early 1950s: "The first television commercials were aired during the 1950 election cycle in a state race", while Dwight D. Eisenhower used them as an important aspect of his campaigning style for the first time during the 1952 presidential campaign (Kaid and Johnson 2001, 3).

deduced from the verbal level. In the case of image and issue, statements are differentiated according to their relation to public concern and to personal qualities and characteristics of the candidate (Kaid and Johnston 2001, 18). In the case of positive and negative contents, statements are distinguished according to their positive reference to the candidate, his or her issues, and to their negative reference to the opponent's alleged undesirable traits and issues. What is problematic about these contrastive categories is the lack of reliable defining criteria[6] and the exclusive focus on verbal content that pays no attention to the media context in which it is situated. Findings in this field suggest a predominance of image rather than issue content (e.g., Joslyn 1980, Payne, Marlier, and Baukus 1989) in campaign commercials. Based on their results, respective studies furthermore focus on ethical questions concerning the content of the TV campaign ads (Sinclair 1995, Winsbro 1987) or aim to reveal the connection between issue/image via positive/negative strategies and the electoral position of the candidate (Kaid and Johnston 2001, 18f.).

In the second major field of research focusing on the effects of campaign commercials, three types of possible outcomes can be distinguished in terms of influence on: the level of knowledge, the perception of the candidate, and voting preferences (Kaid and Johnston 2001, 19). Respective studies suggest, for instance, that campaign commercials increase voter's memory of the candidates' names, their issues, and positions (see Atkin and Heald 1976, Kaid 1982, Martinelli and Chaffee 1995) or influence voter's decision in the case of late deciders and politically low-involved people (see Bowen 1994, Rothschild and Ray 1974). It seems difficult to conclude possible effects of campaign commercials on viewers' voting behavior, as a complete certainty of their influence cannot be verified and a full insight into people's motivations for their voting behavior as such is not possible. The fact that most of the results of these studies were obtained by survey research and experimental designs (Kaid and Johnston 2001, 19; Paul Christiansen's 2018 analysis of music in American TV campaign ads is one recent exception) amounts to an abstraction from the actual viewing process and makes the outcomes at best valid on a higher level of consciousness on which further unknown factors might have played a role, too. For this branch of research, the media specificity of audiovisual images is not relevant either although it actually plays a significant role with regards to the perception of the candidate.

---

6 The mutually exclusive categorization of positive vs. negative and image vs. issue amounts to an oversimplification of things on the level of content, which are, moreover, being taken for granted.

As will be shown, German research on campaign commercials has adopted central assumptions – among them especially the distinction of image and issue-oriented spots and of positive and negative campaigning – and confirmed most of the outlined findings of American studies. In so doing, it has likewise adopted the theoretical and methodological problems outlined above. While in its beginning, it focused primarily on questions and problems in the field of media law, such as the allocation of broadcasting time and its distribution among the several parties, the first analysis of campaign commercials as a format was carried out in 1969 (Holtz-Bacha and Kaid 1993, 48). Within the context of the parliamentary elections of 1969, Dröge, Lerg, and Weißenborn (1969) analyze them by means of formal and content-based criteria. On the one hand, they rely on articulatory modalities of audiovisual staging, such as sound, montage, and camera movement, in order to infer different degrees of variety and dynamics. While the frequency of different levels of representation indicates a complex or low level of diversity, movement, volume, and cutting rate indicate a calm or moving level of dynamics. In this respect, the campaign commercials of the Social Democratic Party of Germany (SPD), the Christian Democratic Union (CDU), and the Christian Social Union (CSU) are classified as complex and moving, those of Free Democratic Party (FDP) and minor parties are suggested to be simple and calm. As for the content of the campaign commercials, the authors make use of qualitative content analysis and classify it according to factual [*Faktenwissen*], value [*Wertewissen*], and normative knowledge [*Normenwissen*]. They come to the conclusion that the parties primarily convey normative knowledge in their campaign commercials and thus rather focus on securing the existing power relations instead of offering alternatives.

After this first study, it was nearly twenty years until campaign commercials again became the topic of analysis. In 1988, Wachtel conducted an argumentation analysis of TV campaign ads of the 1987 parliamentary elections from a linguistic and semiotic point of view in order to find out how the parties tried to convey trustworthiness and competence. He concluded that they communicated their intentions in a credible manner but did not reasonably explain their lacking political course of action. According to Wachtel, most of the analyzed campaign commercials were image-oriented and contained elements of negative campaigning (cf. Schicha and Dörner 2008, 19).

Another, similarly oriented case study of a SPD campaign commercial for the 1989 European election was carried out by Werner Holly. He considers political campaign commercials as a type of text that prompts spectators to vote for the promoted party by making increasing use of symbolic implications, simplifications, and polarizations instead of objective messages (Holly 1991, 261). This pejorative evaluation of his object of research permeates the entire study. As a result of his interpretative and intuitive approach to the audiovisual material under discussion,[7] Holly exclusively focuses on elements and figures on the level of representation as well as on single aspects of audiovisual staging that he separates from the situated media context in order to attribute a fixed meaning and affective impact to them. He concludes that the interplay of image, sound, and language – which he considers in an isolated and static manner – aims at bringing about a 'vague', i.e., not argumentatively well-founded, approval (Holly 1991, 272).

What becomes apparent from these three early German studies is a strong focus on written and verbal language in the campaign commercials that is obviously considered to play a leading role from an argumentative point of view. In this respect, the audiovisual staging seems to have solely a supporting function for conveying a particular image, e.g., of trustworthiness and competence. It is not examined in view of its media-specific dynamics as a perceptual experience but rather by means of extracted single elements.

This conception is maintained in subsequent studies although they examine in more detail the form of campaign commercials, that is to say the way of (self-) presentation and the use of film techniques (e.g., Klein 1992, Holtz-Bacha and Kaid 1996). Those works are first and foremost about the identification and long-term consideration of recurrent patterns, such as testimonials or statements of the candidates, and their distribution among the campaign commercials of the parties (cf. Holtz-Bacha 2000, 79). Generally, comparative and long-term studies gain increasing importance at the beginning of the 1990s. Holtz-Bacha and Kaid (1993, 1996), for instance, compare campaign commercials of the first parliamentary elections after the German reunification in 1990 with those of the 1994 elections. Proceeding from the American dichotomy of image and issue orientation, they conclude that the TV campaign ads tend towards image orientation in 1990, while in 1994 they rather focused on issues. Furthermore, they observe that the issue and image orientation varies also with regard to the broadcasting television, i.e., if it was public or commercial. Concerning the distribution of incumbent and challenger strategies – a distinction that the authors borrow from Trent and Friedenberg (1991) and that is drawn from the language in the campaign commercial – Holtz-Bacha and Kaid confirm previous findings from American exploratory work.

Another recurring outcome in other studies is that TV campaign ads of the minor parties are considered as unprofessional and even boring as they make use of conventional patterns and production technique as well as long text passages

---

7 Holly himself admits his lack of a methodological procedure for the analysis of the campaign commercial and declares his approach to be rather reminiscent of an 'interpretation of a poem' (Holly 1991, 259).

(Holtz-Bacha and Kaid 1993, 68). Such an evaluative judgement, however, is problematic as it is grounded in personal taste[8] rather than in the empirical material, wherefore the distinction between professional and unprofessional is hard to substantiate. This appears mainly due to the analysis of selected formal aspects and elements, isolated from their media context of the campaign commercial. In doing so, respective studies however disregard that it is only within the situated experience of the campaign commercial that these features unfold their particular form, sensation, and meaning for the viewers.

The foci of existing American and German research on campaign commercials from a social sciences perspective, i.e., content and effect, determine a level of analysis that takes the meaning and impact of the TV campaign ads for granted and deals with them in terms of a static object that can be taken in piece by piece. In doing so, the inherent dynamic nature of meaning-making in language and equally in audiovisual media is underestimated and disregarded. Jakubowski mentions in the context of his own study on campaign commercials that only few studies deal with audiovisual data by using content analysis due to the difficulty of properly analyzing and bringing together image, sound, and text (Jakubowski 1998, 168). He even discusses the possibility of using film analysis but comes to the conclusion that it does not suit for research methods that work with ex ante formulated hypotheses: while content analysis relies on assumptions and perspectives formulated in advance and therefore only focuses on relevant aspects in a selective way (top down), film analysis rather proceeds from the object of research itself (bottom up) (Jakubowski 1998, 171).

Overall, most of the studies proceed from similar assumptions (image vs. issue, positive vs. negative), use similar methodologies (first and foremost content analysis), and come to similar conclusions (among others the tendency towards images and increasing personalization) against the strategic and persuasive backdrop of the TV campaign ads. In comparison, the central study in this field has a wider agenda which makes it possible to subject the prevalent hypothesis of the Americanization of German election campaigns to a critical review. Christina Holtz-Bacha's (2000) comprehensive long-term study of campaign commercials in Germany describes and analyzes them in the historical and political context of the respective elections over a large period of time. On that basis, she illustrates correlations between topics within the TV campaign ads and political, social, and legal circumstances and developments, putting forward that campaign commercials are highly contextual and reflect both already legitimized political culture

---

8 It seems that the recourse to the distinction of image and issue as put forward by American research in this field restricts the analysis of the campaign commercial from the outset with regard to the evaluation of content and certain aspects of audiovisual staging.

[*Soziokultur*] and new interpretative offers [*Deutungskultur*] (Holtz-Bacha 2000, 20). Presenting a broad historical overview of all parliamentary elections from 1957 to 1998 with their candidates, topics, and contents as well as a synopsis of the legal developments concerning the broadcasting, Holtz-Bacha concludes that election campaigns have gradually become more professionalized and that campaign commercials gained in importance (their amount increased from twelve in 1957 to 63 in 1998).

By her formal and content analysis of 417 selected campaign commercials from twelve different parliamentary elections, Holtz-Bacha illustrates the quantitative distribution of her coded formal categories with regard to the parties and to the single elections. In doing so, she aims to reveal certain trends and developments in the visual arrangement of the campaign commercials, e.g., presentational form, production techniques, and the orientation towards the candidate.[9] In the case of the relatedness of the meanings of text and images,[10] what shows up is a strong focus on the language and an understanding of audiovisual images as mere depictions and illustrations of what is said. In this light, both are considered as static and separated entities and not in view of their mutual interplay and dynamic unfolding. Subsequent works examine similar aspects and extend the scope of analysis to European elections, but they do not come to new conclusions except for the hypothesis that the parties did not make huge efforts in the conception of the TV campaign ads (see Esser, Holtz-Bacha, and Lessinger 2005).

In contrast to the various studies on the content of campaign commercials, studies dealing particularly with their effects are hitherto rare in Germany. They focus on their general range by means of audience ratings[11] as well as concentrate on the impact of the TV campaign ads on thoughts, attitudes, or behavior of the viewers. The latter mostly work with experimental designs and surveys in order to gain insights into the effects of the TV campaign ads. Semetko and Schoenbach (1994), for instance, argue that due to their strong presence in television they can strengthen the interest of citizens in a current election campaign. They also examine potential agenda-setting effects of the topics from the campaign commercials on the voters but do not find explicit evidence for that. On the other hand, Holtz-Bacha and Kaid (1993, 1996) intend to reveal the change of

---

9 Nevertheless, the subcategories are not consistent and mix up different levels of analysis: for instance, Holtz-Bacha subsumes both testimonials and montage under 'presentational form'.

10 Similar to previous studies, this reveals a taken-for-granted existing message whose emergence for the viewer in the process of watching is not examined. Furthermore, this suggests an implicit separation of both levels and their static instead of a dynamic understanding.

11 Holtz-Bacha (2000, 82) has pointed out in this regard that audience rating provides no sufficient basis to draw conclusions because it says nothing about the viewers' attention to the ads.

candidate images with the spectators after having watched campaign commercials by means of evaluative surveys before and after the TV campaign ad. They conclude by stating that the viewers are at least in the short term influenced by the presented image of the candidate. It should be pointed out that, compared to the actual process of watching, the viewers' evaluation of the candidate (i.e., appraisal) amounts to another level of abstraction and a higher level of consciousness that involves more factors than his or her staging in the campaign commercial. Furthermore, the use of surveys and the quantitative focus of most effect studies only allows for general and abstracted evaluations that do not rely on direct causalities but rather on the interplay of several factors that are hardly reconstructable (see, e.g., Podschuweit 2007 for another quantitatively-informed approach).

Recent research seeks to broaden the perspective, such as Dörner and Schicha's edited volume (2008) on campaign commercials from an interdisciplinary point of view. Proceeding from selected TV campaign ads from the German parliamentary elections in 2005, analyses are carried out from various disciplines by means of different approaches, including regarding aesthetic aspects. In this respect, Prümm (2008, 184) argues that major parties work with a cinematographic code because they are using specific narrative conventions and structural elements as well as camera technology.[12] In doing so, they refer to 'something' beyond their situated context of television: to cinema. According to Prümm, the parties want to take advantage of cinema's affect-mobilizing potential and thus use cinematic elements within their campaign commercials, wherefore he refers to them as 'micro drama'. On the basis of four selected campaign commercials from the 2005 elections, he detects narrative schemes, establishing shots, or continuity montage and concludes that cinematic aesthetics is a suitable means for the parties to fill vacuums and cover up contradictions (Prümm 2008, 188). In saying so, he takes up the negative understanding of film and audiovisual staging as a distraction from issues and mere content-free images.

In summary, it can be stated that German research on campaign commercials has focused primarily on single content-related and formal aspects by adopting primarily hypotheses like Americanization, personalization, and image-orientation from American research in this field. What is most striking is that

---

12 Riedel (2008) puts forward a similar line of argument. Proceeding from a historical poetics of campaign commercials, he aims to illustrate that they make use of aesthetic patterns and strategies from television, film, and Internet and thus draw on viewers' established visual experiences. Among others, he gives the example of image segmentation as used by the German party The Left. According to Riedel (2008, 198), this technique is widely known from the opening credits of American TV series.

the media specifics of the TV campaign ads as audiovision has not sufficiently been taken into account and if it was, single parts or elements were taken out of context and described with regard to the represented content. Argumentation analyses subordinate, if not completely disregard, the audiovisual to the narrative or argumentative level. Finally, the majority of studies display a quantitative focus whereby no insight into the concrete form and role of the single aspects in the respective campaign commercial can be gained.

Compared to the state of research on campaign commercials in Germany, the number of Polish studies in this field is even smaller. They have predominantly dealt with the impact of campaign commercials on the voter's attitudes and behavior but did not come to new conclusions than those of previous German or American studies. In their comparative analysis, Cwalina, Falkowski, and Kaid (2000) aimed to investigate the influence of TV campaign ads on the candidate's image in Germany, France, and Poland. For this purpose, the authors conducted a perception study that consisted of three steps: a pre-test, the presentation of the campaign commercials, and a post-test. In the pre and post-test, the study participants had to evaluate their perception of the candidates by means of a scale with word pairs of personal traits. On the basis of similar or varying results among these questionnaires, the authors concluded the extent of impact the campaign commercial had on the respondents and came to the conclusion that they could strengthen existing preferences, weaken them, or have no impact at all. Apart from the problem of basing the results exclusively on the campaign commercials in terms of a cause-effect relationship, the notion of perception as a subjective evaluation (in terms of appraisal) again amounts to a higher level of consciousness that is not only to be due to the actual reception process and involves more influencing factors.

Mazur (2005) focuses especially on the impact of negative campaign commercials in the 2000 Polish presidential elections and the 2001 parliamentary elections. In his case study, he examines negative elements in speech and audiovisual staging in two TV campaign ads that he conceives of as influential factors on spectators' perception. In doing so, however, he separates the two main modalities from each other, extracts single aspects from their media context, and thus subscribes to a static understanding of meaning-making that he considers primarily tied to language and visually depicted by audiovisual images. Focusing exclusively on the plotline on the level of audiovisual representation, Mazur takes meaning for granted, as did previous analyses of campaign commercials, and disregards the processuality of the perception process that he is actually interested in.

A similar but more large-scale approach is taken in Cwalina, Falkowski, and Roznowski's (1999) analysis of 81 campaign commercials from the 1995 Polish presidential elections. By means of content analysis, the authors examine among others production techniques, sound design, verbal and non-verbal behavior in order to infer possible viewer impact. Such a quantitative analysis generates at best a distributional list of single elements among the campaign commercials that remain, however, abstracted and separated from their respective media context. Cwalina, Falkowski, and Roznowski's conclusion that Polish TV campaign ads do not differ from those in the USA or other West European countries thus remains rather superficial, as it does not provide insights into their concrete audiovisual staging. This seems primarily to be due to the authors' economic and marketing perspective of audiovisual media, which entails an immanent level of abstraction and predetermined viewing of the material. Therefore, comparative studies claiming that campaign commercials of the Western European countries and the USA are more or less similar might lead in the wrong direction.

As became apparent, Poland has hitherto rarely been an object of research for comparative studies of campaign commercials. One attempt to bring comparable empirical data especially from Poland and Germany together has been made by Musiałowska (2008), who compares political communication in both countries from the perspective of the media and of political parties between 1997/1998 and 2005. In the case of campaign commercials, she proceeds from pre-formulated hypotheses that she seeks to confirm or refute by means of quantitative content analysis. Among others, she assumes that German campaign commercials are more professional, emotional, leader-focused, and positive than Polish ones. The variables she relies on in order to categorize the TV campaign ads according to these attributes are however heterogeneous and rather random: for example, for the degree of professionalization the coders should analyze the "overall impression", thereby making recourse to underlying music, cutting rate, and the use of special effects (Musiałowska 2008, 122f.). Apart from the fact that these aspects appear to be insufficient in order to make a point on the overall impression of the campaign commercial, they are moreover not consistent to some extent when it comes to their coding. Thus, in the case of music, the coders should judge "e.g. whether it sounded amateur or whether it was tailored to the spot's dynamics etc." (Musiałowska 2008, 122f.). Such an evaluation is highly subjective and non-reliable. As in previous studies, Musiałowska's analysis furthermore primarily draws on language and representation[13] in order to reconstruct particular attributes like negativity or emotion. As a result, meaning-making that emerges from the temporal interplay of both main modalities in

---

13 The term "visual level" that Musiałowska is using in the context of campaign commercials suggests that she considers them primarily as a static depiction of verbal content instead of a dynamic medium of movement-images.

a non-verbal and non-representational manner is not taken into consideration. Finally, Musiałowska comes, among others, to the hardly substantiated conclusion that Polish campaign commercials are less professional, emotional, and leader-oriented than German ones.

In summary, it can be stated that social sciences research on campaign commercials is strongly dominated by assumptions, methodologies, and findings from American exploratory work and examines their content as well as their effects. In both respects, the focus of analysis is on language and audiovisual representation, neither of which are considered in their mutual interplay but separately from each other. Whereas language is conceived of to play the major role in conveying a particular meaning, audiovisual images are held to play a supporting role primarily in terms of visual depictions of single elements from the verbal level. Along these lines, the result of particular impressions, images, and emotional reactions is attributed to single features and aspects in both modalities which are in most cases only used with regard to their presence or absence – but not in their interplay with other modalities in the temporal course – in order to describe and categorize the campaign commercials. On this basis, the analysis ultimately leads to general evaluations of the impact and effectiveness of TV campaign ads, which are the result of subjective assessment rather than of reliable criteria. As will be shown in the following overview of the state of cognitive-linguistic research on figurativity in political communication, this phenomenon of lacking reliability and connection to the concrete context reappears with regard to the claimed persuasive impact of metaphor and metonymy.

2.2 Political Metaphor as Pervasive and Persuasive Tool

Linguistic research on figurativity in the context of political discourse – just as in other contexts of use – is characterized by a strong focus on metaphor and a disregard of metonymy. In practice, the latter should actually have at least an equal role with its principle of one kind of thing standing for 'another', contiguous one (e.g., the flag for the country or the head of state for the people). After the publication of his composite work together with Mark Johnson, George Lakoff himself has quickly extended his scope of research to politics and tried to detect basic patterns, i.e., conceptual metaphors, in the conceptualization of politics as detectable in language. Behind this, both for him and for other metaphor scholars, is the argument that metaphors make complex and abstract issues clear and concrete. As politics revealed a high degree of abstractness in their structures, processes, and relationships it is regarded as self-evident that metaphors are used in speaking about politics (e.g., Musolff 2004,

Stenvoll 2008). As such, they contribute to the greater understanding of the political sphere while also purposefully communicating a particular simplified version of a complicated reality (see Androshchuk 2014, Goatly 2007, Mio 1997). The latter understanding amounts to the same phenomenon of an exclusive orientation to manipulation and persuasion of the addressee while lacking a reliable empirical basis that equally characterizes social sciences research on campaign commercials. Related to this, the impact of metaphor in most political communication research is in the majority of cases explained by itself without taking its concrete form and unfolding in a situated context of use into consideration. Rather, respective studies proceed from overarching mental meaning structures (top) that shall be verified in selected linguistic data (down).

George Lakoff is an exponent of such a top-down approach. In his book *Moral Politics* (1996/2002), he puts forward the existence of two contrasting cognitive models that underlie and pervade American right (i.e., Republican) and left-wing (i.e., Democratic) political rhetoric: the Strict Father model and the Nurturant Parent model. Lakoff suggests that these two models represent different conceptualizations of a family, its members, and their hierarchy and role within the family that amount to opposing worldviews shaping right respectively the left-wing political thinking.

The Strict Father model is associated with the right-wing worldview and is characterized by a hierarchical power structure, i.e., a father as the family patriarch who wields authority and to whom the wife and children have to obey. Concomitant with such a clear-cut distribution of roles, the prevailing rules and values that are communicated and executed by the father likewise exhibit a clear distinction of right and wrong. On that basis, the children are supposed to become independent and autonomous people wherefore strength plays a significant role for the family life. On the other hand, the Nurturant Parent model that is considered as characteristic of left-wing values exhibits no hierarchical, but a horizontal power structure. In respect to such a collaborative understanding, Cienki has pointed out that the term 'family' does not exclusively refer to the family in the narrow sense of the word but covers several possible structures that work together as a group (Cienki 2005, 3). Contrary to the Strict Father model, caring and empathy are suggested to be of major significance for the Nurturant Parent model: it does not aim at executing power and rules onto the children but focuses more on letting them grow up and accompanying and caring for them during their phase of exploration.

Lakoff argues that these two distinct models that shape the understanding of what a family is and how it functions give rise to different moral values: "The assumption is that each way of thinking about which kind of family structure is the 'right' kind serves as a basis for structuring one's understanding of behavior and how to evaluate it – in short, one's views of morality." (Cienki 2005, 3) In concrete terms, the Strict Father model is considered to be shaped by moral conceptual metaphors such as MORALITY AS STRENGTH, AUTHORITY FIGURES AS PARENTS, and RIGHTS AS PATHS. By way of contrast, the Nurturant Parent model is conceived of being shaped by conceptual metaphors such as MORALITY IS EMPATHY, MORAL ACTION IS NURTURANCE, or SOCIAL TIES ARE CHILDREN NEEDING CARE. As a result, from both models arise different ideas of the nation and along with them different assumptions about the role of government and president, which Lakoff among others seeks to verify by reference to governance, the political agenda, and political decisions.

Cienki (2004, 2005) has tested the debates between George W. Bush and Al Gore in 2000 for these models and their respective metaphors and concludes that they are rather rarely manifested in the language of the two candidates. His findings indicate that the top-down approach to the examination of metaphor in political discourse, i.e., the prioritization of presumed mental models (systems level) against the level of use, carries the risk of formulating hypotheses of overarching meaning structures and thereby losing sight of the actual context of use. For his study, Cienki has used the transcripts of the TV debates and coded them for verbal metaphorical expressions of the conceptual metaphors proposed by Lakoff (1996/2002). In doing so, he lays a strong focus on the spoken word, but he additionally considers speech-accompanying gestures as a further articulatory modality of the expression of metaphorical meaning. It is Cienki's merit to have explicitly drawn attention to the "[t]wo different directions of research [...]: the testing of proposed models against data, and the deduction of models (or at least relations between metaphorical expressions) from data" (Cienki 2005, 14) as well as to their different perspectives and results. In doing so, he addresses the necessity of differentiating between the often confused systems level and the level of use.

Another systems level-informed work to metaphor in political communication is Lakoff's and Elisabeth Wehling's (introductory) book *Auf leisen Sohlen ins Gehirn. Politische Sprache und ihre heimliche Macht* (2008). The conception of metaphor that becomes apparent through the title is informed by the CMT idea of an entrenched and pervasive cognitive principle that guides and shapes human reasoning in an unconscious manner. This way, metaphor is commonly ascribed a manipulative and virtually insidious character that some make use of (by learning it, for instance, from spin doctors), and others are subliminally influenced by; a contradiction that has mostly gone unquestioned. Lakoff and Wehling follow a similar line of argument as Lakoff and Johnson in *Metaphors we live by* (1980): they broadly explain human understanding, the conceptualization of and thinking about politics, and how politics can influence it. In this respect, all assumptions are formulated with the claim that they are collectively real, i.e., they are suggested to account for how 'we' make sense of the world. However, this 'we' is neither clarified nor empirically substantiated. In this regard, linguistic research on figurativity in political communication displays a similar taken-for-granted manipulative power of metaphor, as is the case in social sciences research on campaign commercials. Lakoff explains this by making recourse to frames as deeply entrenched mental networks shaping human cognition and classifying metaphor as one kind or strategy of framing (Lakoff and Wehling 2008). According to him, the verbal metaphorical expression of political measures or programs leads through recurrent use in media and language use to its entrenchment in human thinking and understanding and as such to a subtle deception. Lakoff names examples like the Clear Skies Act of 2003, the Bush tax cuts, or Death Tax for the Estate Tax, suggesting that these Republican designations highlight particular positive or negative aspects of what they refer to, and equally hide other, probably unpleasant or problematic, ones.[14] As the most prominent example of such a verbal creation Lakoff mentions the "War on Terror" that George W. Bush introduced to denote and justify the international military campaign in response to the September 11 attacks.

Following up on his idea of two distinct worldviews, Lakoff argues that Republicans were politically more successful because they had a consistent conservative frame that Democrats mostly attacked but did not offer another, new perspective from within their progressive worldview. In conclusion, Lakoff and Wehling argue the case for irrational politics that rely less on issues and instead rather on labels and images (see also Wehling 2016). In this respect, their conception of figurativity in political communication is similarly fatalistic as social sciences research of campaign commercials. On the basis of this finding, Lakoff formulates concrete instructions for Democrats to communicate more offensively about political topics, i.e., to shape political discourse by introducing their own Nurturant Parent model and its corresponding moral values in order to win sympathy and votes. Like Lakoff's *Moral Politics* (1996/2002), Lakoff and Wehling (2008) display a rather general approach to the problem of metaphor in political communication and put forward broad assumptions that are barely empirically substantiated. This is especially true as the claim of metaphor's unconscious manipulative power remains under discussed and under applied to real-world contexts.

---

14 As such, the Clear Skies Act sounded like a program that aimed at the reduction of air pollution when it was actually a legitimization of polluters. Only big income earners benefited from Bush's tax relief which barely became apparent as its designation drew primarily attention to the aspect of easing the burden of taxes.

Jonathan Charteris-Black's work on metaphor in political communication (2004, 2005, 2013) aims to fill this empirical research gap. He has examined British party political manifestos, American presidential inaugural speeches, press and financial reporting, religious discourse, and speeches by various political actors, including Winston Churchill, Martin Luther King Jr., and Tony Blair, for the use of verbal metaphors in order to account particularly for how they influence convictions, attitudes, and values. In respect to this question, Charteris-Black follows Lakoff's line of argument and proceeds from the assumption that language evokes unconscious emotional associations: "These associations may not be ones that we are fully conscious of because they have an emotional basis." (Charteris-Black 2005, 13f.) He considers this connection between metaphor and emotion the decisive factor for appraisal and thus ultimately for persuasion:

> I have argued that metaphor has a very important persuasive role in evoking strong emotional responses that may prioritise one interpretation of a text over another. It is this persuasive role that constitutes the ideological and rhetorical basis of metaphors. I have illustrated this with the sort of associations evoked by words from the lexical field for conflict and other words such as 'blood'. [...] In these cases figurative uses of language were very important in evoking a particular emotional response on the part of the hearer/reader. In the case of 'shed blood', agents are negatively evaluated while objects are positively evaluated. (Charteris-Black 2004, 41–42)

What is remarkable in this quote is that Charteris-Black neither differentiates between association, emotional response, and evaluation nor clarifies their mutual relation. Apart from that, his assumption that words by default inhere particular associations displays a confusion of the systems level and the level of language use. Not least of all, he does not provide empirical evidence for the "emotional response on the part of the hearer/reader" claimed by him.[15]

It is Charteris-Black's merit to have conducted (corpus) research on metaphor in various contexts of political discourse. However, he exclusively draws on written text: the speeches he is analyzing are investigated in their transcribed form. Of course, this focus on verbal language facilitates the corpus analytical work, but it equally leaves out the concrete multimodal context of use, i.e., further articulatory modalities like speech-accompanying gestures, prosody, or body movements. As Charteris-Black is looking for instantiations of conceptual metaphor, he is from the outset biased with regard to particular expressions and formulations (top-down approach) wherefore a qualitative analysis of the dynamic and emergent unfolding of figurative meaning is impeded. Indeed, he primarily

---

15 Charteris-Black does not clarify what he refers to by "emotional response", i.e., if he means a neurological, a bodily, or a psychological reaction.

generates quantitative outcomes, i.e., statistical accounts of the number of particular verbal metaphorical instantiations in a certain corpus. It has to be mentioned, however, that the amount is not able to provide insight into the concrete realization and role of the metaphor in the respective speech, reporting, or manifesto at the particular point where it occurs.

Andrew Goatly (2007) follows a similar line of argument as Charteris-Black's Critical Metaphor Analysis that brings together cognitive-linguistic accounts of metaphor and critical discourse analysis. Suggesting that metaphor plays a fundamental role in establishing and handing down ideology, he proceeds from a broad understanding of the term in van Dijk's sense as allowing "people, as group members, to organize the multitude of social beliefs about what is the case, good or bad, right or wrong, *for them* and to act accordingly" (van Dijk 1998, 8). Thus, Goatly is interested in "metaphorical patterns in the vocabulary and grammar of English for representing and shaping ideologies and social practices" (Goatly 2007, 2). He provides a diachronic insight into the emergence and scope of application of metaphor themes in various realms of everyday life based on lexical data from the database Metalude (listing conventional, lexicalized metaphors) and argues that they shape human thinking and social behavior.

Goatly's extensive approach has an added value as it looks comparatively at how metaphorical themes are distributed in different fields of social life and what kinds of implications they have for the understanding of certain issues. Furthermore, he relates selected metaphorical themes to the theoretical thinking of philosophers, such as Thomas Hobbes, Adam Smith, and Charles Darwin in order to reconstruct how they used and elaborated them in their "ideological tradition" and to finally reveal how they have recently become the "basis for New Right thinking" (Goatly 2007, 7). His attempt of a Critical Metaphor Analysis again exclusively focuses on metaphor as a manipulation and deception of the human mind and pursues the goal to uncover presumed entrenched and unconscious lines of thought in people's thinking and acting. As a result, he first and foremost "paint[s] an unduly pessimistic view of the effects of metaphor in social life" (Goatly 2007, 4), thereby pursuing a downright educational goal:

> [...] I have selected the themes by way of warning. The world faces a number of pressing crises [...] to which neo-conservative thinking, dependent upon the metaphorical patterns themes I analyse, seems to have no answer. If this book can make a tiny contribution to raising awareness of the dangers of acting out these metaphors it may be modestly successful. (Goatly 2007, 5)

By proceeding from overall mental patterns that guide human thinking and acting, Goatly puts forward the same line of argument as did Lakoff and Johnson, namely to deduce universal mental patterns (i.e., how 'we' think, how 'we' act, etc.) from recurrent lexical units that he takes from a dictionary and not from real-world usages. Müller (2008a) has elaborated on the problem of equating the systems level (of a dictionary) and the level of use in detail and has pointed out that the assumption of overarching mental patterns is difficult to empirically verify. Moreover, she has put forward a dynamic view of metaphoricity that might be highly activated for a language user in one given moment of time while being low for another one (Müller 2008a).

Apart from Lakoff's and Goatly's broad approaches to English-speaking data, Bohdan Androshchuk (2014) has conducted a comprehensive case study of metaphor in political communication in Germany. He has examined the metaphorical target domain of the family in a corpus of political manifestos and Bundestag debates of various parties (CDU/CSU, SPD, FDP, the Greens, the Left) during the 16th legislative term of the Bundestag in order to find out which metaphors are used to describe and structure the family and family politics. In so doing, he aims to empirically account for the reality structuring and manipulating role of political metaphor, to reconstruct ways of thinking that are typical for particular groups in a certain time period, and to reveal similarities and differences among different groups (Androshchuk 2014, 23). On that basis, he ultimately intends to measure the veracity of metaphorical meaning and to deduce its persuasive potential.

Androshchuk from the outset suggests that metaphor defies actual reality (amounting to a semantic anomaly) and thereby implicitly subscribes to a speech act conception of metaphor (Searle [1979] 1993). On that basis, metaphor is considered a rhetorical strategy that intentionally activates ideological references to elicit a particular reaction on the part of the addressees. For Androshchuk, this persuasive potential results from metaphor's ability to make issues vital and graspable as their particular connotations and associations are transferred from the source to the target domain that thereby becomes emotionally charged (Androshchuk 2014, 97, 100). These emotions evoke a particular line of thinking on the part of the addressee and, as a result, a particular behavior. Apart from the question for the empirical evidence of these claims, Androshchuk reasons in a contradictory manner by arguing elsewhere that metaphor comes up with an ambivalence that does not provide the recipient with a clear semantic and cognitive orientation (Androshchuk 2014, 270). Just as in the case of social sciences research on campaign commercials, Androshchuk's focus is exclusively on the (potential) persuasive effects of metaphor but not on the upstream process of meaning-making, whereby a fatalistic account of metaphor in political discourse becomes apparent.

Though examining only one particular type and thematic aspect of political discourse, Androshchuk takes a broad approach to the metaphorical expressions identified and analyzed by subsuming them under overarching, seemingly conceptual labels. This step of abstraction, however, leads to a diversion from the actual expression in a situated context of use that in various cases is poorly substantiated.[16] Contrary to Androshchuk's attempt to provide a quantitatively informed overview of factional and cross-party metaphors, the labels are in their generality not able to offer any insight into the actual emergence, contextual use, and development of individual expressions. Furthermore, it has to be mentioned that his consideration of both political manifestos and verbal statements in debates of the German Bundestag is problematic insofar as it equates two fundamentally different communicative contexts, i.e., written and spoken language,[17] in which metaphorical meaning might play out and unfold quite differently. While manifestos are elaborated and redacted over a longer period of time, verbal statements during debates exhibit a higher degree of spontaneity whereby metaphors come up dynamically from the flow of communication. Further, manifestos do not necessarily represent the opinion of each and very party member, while the individual statements of single politicians do not have to be shared by their entire party.

Contrary to Androshchuk, Andreas Musolff (2000, 2004, 2012, 2016) has examined political metaphor in a corpus of public discourse. Criticizing Lakoff's (1996/2002) "small basis of empirical data" (Musolff 2004, 3), he calls for a corpus-based analysis in order to verify the cognitive-linguistic hypothesis of metaphorical political worldviews. One of his objects of study is European Union politics from 1989 to 2001 as dealt with in 28 German and British broadsheet newspapers and magazines. For Musolff, politicians' direct statements, e.g., in interviews and debates are not the only starting points for investigating metaphorical expressions of "attitudes towards Europe" (Musolff 2000, 2004): "Rather, the whole ensemble of texts produced in public by politicians and media commentators can be assumed to form a coherent whole [...]" (Musolff 2004, 5). Going against previous studies, he does not merely present a status quo but looks also for stabilization processes and diachronic patterns of particular metaphors in the corpus (Musolff 2004, Chapters 6 and 7). This amounts to a more dynamic view that takes the respective context of use and the development of metaphorical meaning into account. In so doing, Musolff exceeds a mere quantitative overview of conceptual metaphors by moreover describing and analyzing them

---

16 For instance, Androshchuk (2004, 197) categorizes the metaphorical expression "at the children's cost" [*auf Kosten der Kinder*] as one instantiation of the conceptual metaphor FAMILY/ CHILDREN ARE OBJECTS OF PRESSURE [*Familie/Kinder sind Objekt des Druckes*].

17 It should be mentioned here that Androshchuk's treatment of the politicians' verbal statements as if they were written due to relying on stenographic reports of the debates runs the risk of missing metaphors that are expressed in gestures but not in words.

qualitatively with regard to their concrete form and dynamics. When discussing the question of deceptive metaphor, he comes to a balanced conclusion based on a detailed qualitative analysis that political metaphors can establish rather open or closed scenarios (Musolff 2004, 173–177). Their linguistic analysis provides insight into the presuppositions these scenarios present, while in the end, "[i]t is up to the users to judge whether they accept an analogical warrant or not" (Musolff 2004, 175).

Musolff's studies are a notable exception from the majority of cognitive-linguistic research on metaphor in political communication where it is often from the outset equated with manipulation and ideology,[18] whereby the main interest is on its intentional use by a producer while the addressee is conceived of as a passive recipient deciphering the message and being influenced by it (for a critical discussion of such an understanding of metaphor in political discourse, see Gehring 2015). Another recurrent feature in most research is a strong focus on written language although spoken discourse is often the object of investigation. In these cases, however, it is analyzed in written, i.e., transcribed form and not with regard to its multimodal realization (e.g., in gesture, prosody, body movements). As a result, it is likely that certain metaphors that are not verbally expressed are missed. In general, the focus on verbal metaphor in the context of political communication amounts to a traditional, language-informed view and, in a way, to a reduction of the phenomenon. On the other hand, the concrete metaphorical expressions in language are mostly neglected as against their presumed superordinate conceptual structures. As such, they are considered as their instantiations and merely serve as evidence for the existence of conceptual metaphors. This manifests in case studies focusing on special topics and research questions of metaphor in political communication too.

Kathleen Ahrens (2011), for instance, deals with Lakoff's (1996/2002) two cognitive models of the Strict Father and the Nurturant Parent and intends to provide evidence for their reality in the ideology of four different U.S. presidents. For this purpose, she investigates the speeches of Ronald Reagan, George W. Bush Sr., Bill Clinton, and George W. Bush Jr. by means of lexical frequency patterns that she considers related to the two models. On the basis of four selected words that she suggests to be the "top two metaphors for each model" (Ahrens 2011, 170), she tests them together with their selected sense and direct hypernyms for

---

18 The term 'ideology' suggests the psychological reality of a particular fixed worldview (see, e.g., van Dijk 1998). However, it is problematic to consider metaphorical expressions as immediate reflections of such mental patterns that are shared by entire groups of political actors as it undermines the dynamic emergence and unfolding as well as the specificity of metaphorical meaning on the part of a language user in a particular context.

their frequency in the corpus. As becomes apparent, Ahrens takes a top-down approach: due to such a pre-selection of words standing for the respective cognitive model ('strength' and 'authority' for the Strict Father model, 'nurturance' and 'empathy' for the Nurturant Parent model), the analysis is from the outset biased and less open to metaphorical meaning as it emerges dynamically in the particular data.

Another problematic issue is the lack of differentiation between the cognitive level and the level of language use that results from CMT: the assumption that verbal metaphorical expressions one-to-one instantiate an overarching fixed model negates the creativity and subjectivity of language users. Unlike Androshchuk, Ahrens reflects on the context-boundedness of metaphor: analyzing Radio Addresses and State of the Union Addresses, she comes to the conclusion that the presidents seem to adapt their use of metaphor to their target audience in each case.

With her case study of "metaphors common in political and journalistic discourse in Malta with regard to EU-membership" (Petrica 2011, 143) Monica Petrica (2011) examines a context of use apart from the otherwise strong US-American research focus. She too subscribes to CMT and aims to "disclose potential culture-specific conceptual metaphors" (Petrica 2011, 143) in a corpus of English-language press in Malta between 2000 and 2008 while also highlighting similarities with conceptual metaphors prevailing all over Europe. Such conclusions on a broad cultural level are problematic as they suggest an overarching and static conception of culture. Moreover, the deduction of general cultural conceptual worldviews from media coverage amounts to cultural reduction and stereotyping. The recurrent focus on conceptual metaphors whose existence is to be verified by means of verbal instantiations in media products prioritizes the cognitive level towards the level of actual use and does not sufficiently differentiate between the two.

In summary, it can be stated that linguistic research on figurativity in political discourse bears largely on social sciences research on campaign commercials in that it 1) strongly focuses on spoken or written language, 2) displays a rather pejorative conception of the claimed persuasive impact of figurativity on a presumed passive recipient, and 3) most often abstracts from the concrete context of use to higher-order frameworks. Furthermore, it primarily investigates metaphor while taking insufficient account of metonymy. Most conducted research in the field displays a broad approach and corpus-based analysis that first and foremost provides a quantitative overview of the frequency of particular (conceptual) metaphors, but not of their concrete form and how they play out in a particular context of use. The following section describes the added value of a dynamic approach to audiovisual figurativity in its application to campaign commercials with regard to the two outlined fields of research.

2.3 The Dynamic Perspective: Active Spectators and Varieties of Audiovisual Figurativity

With its research focus on audiovisual figurativity in campaign commercials, this book aims to bring together the mainly separately analyzed levels of language and audiovisual staging. In so doing, it intends to put forward an understanding and scientific examination of campaign commercials as a particular genre of political discourse that needs to be considered and analyzed with regard to its media specificity instead of being conceived of as an audiovisual illustration of verbal content. Being qualitatively oriented, this study aims to put forward an alternative way of examining campaign commercials with the objective of providing insights into how meaning emerges dynamically from the interplay of language and audiovisual staging in the process of watching TV campaign ads.

On the one hand, it intends to fill a research gap of cognitive-linguistic research on figurativity in political discourse that so far has primarily focused on the analysis of written (and in the case of spoken – transcribed) texts. On the other hand, it is to contribute to social sciences research on campaign commercials that hitherto has particularly taken account of their potential effects but barely asked for the upstream process of meaning-making through experiencing the TV campaign ads.[19] By the descriptive sequence-analytical proceeding to the question how and what kind of meaning emerges throughout the campaign commercials, it puts forward a take that is as open-minded and close to the material as possible. This implies that the analysis does not proceed from presumed overarching conceptual metaphors or metonymies in order to verify them by means of verbal and audiovisual instantiations in the respective campaign commercials (i.e., top down). Instead, the examination "starts from the bottom up and remains close to the experiential level of the data" (Müller and Schmitt 2015, 322), whereby figurative meaning is reconstructed as it is considered to emerge from the situated media context of the corresponding TV campaign ad. For this purpose, the analysis and findings shall be made transparent by means of reliable criteria (with the three aspects of dynamics leading the way; see Chapter 5), whereas subjective evaluations of the campaign commercials are to be avoided.

On this basis, the question for the affective potential of both campaign commercials and figurativity is addressed from a different perspective. It is not taken for granted in terms of a default feature of certain words, audiovisual images, or mental concepts but is considered an inherent feature of audiovisual figurativity

---

19 Moreover, in a third respect, advertising in general and campaign commercials in particular are hitherto a neglected issue within film studies – a research gap that this book equally aims to draw attention and contribute to.

and the situated media context itself. As such, the affective appeal to viewers through figurativity and campaign commercials is suggested as being not a product but an ongoing process that they are going through bodily while watching the TV campaign ad. The analyses carried out in this book aim to provide insight into how this process is playing out dynamically by taking the respective data in their entirety, i.e., in their temporal unfolding, into account instead of extracting single elements or aspects from their situated media context. Such a processual conception of affective appealing leads to a shift in focus towards the concrete audiovisual 'material' and its inextricable link with an experiencing viewer without whom meaning-making and affective experience is impossible. From this it follows that the producer is not in the center of attention as was mostly the case in previous social sciences research on campaign commercials and cognitive-linguistic research on figurativity in political communication. Instead, the analyses with their dynamic view of audiovisual figurativity address the process rather from the viewers' perspective. In doing so, viewers are no longer considered as passive recipients and decipherers of pre-established meaning but rather as active participants of the meaning-making process. By conceiving of affective experience as an inherent and fundamental feature of the emergence of meaning, its rather pejorative account in most research is brought into question.

It is the advantage of this study's small selection of empirical data that it is possible to account for the nuances and variant forms of figurativity in each and every campaign commercial to be analyzed. Previous, above all quantitatively informed corpus-analytic research (both in the social sciences and in cognitive linguistics) has edited its findings in tables of how frequent particular aesthetic arrangements or superordinate conceptual patterns occur and thereby disregarded the concrete process of the emergence and unfolding of (figurative) meaning. Through in-depth comparative analyses of four selected campaign commercials, this study is able to illustrate and reconstruct how similar figurative verbal expressions or imagery through the respective interplay of language and audiovisual staging can emerge and unfold completely different and give rise to a highly specific image of a candidate. This suggests that (figurative) meaning-making in campaign commercials does not play out in a uniform but in a varying manner that in turn has an impact on the emergent meaning of the candidate. Therefore, this study intends to stimulate further qualitative research and detailed analysis (both by the social sciences and cognitive linguistics) of campaign commercials and figurativity in audiovisual media formats to shed more light on these variant forms and nuances.

3 Cognitive-Linguistic Perspectives on Figurativity

The research field of figurativity still enjoys great popularity in cognitive linguistics. Metaphor especially has been the subject of extensive discussion and research in various contexts of use (cf., e.g., Forceville and Urios-Aparisi 2009, Gibbs 2008, Hampe 2017, Musolff and Zinken 2009, Semino and Demjén 2017), e.g., in face-to-face communication (e.g., Cameron 2007, 2008a, 2008b, 2011, Cienki and Müller 2008a, Müller 2008a, Müller and Cienki 2009, Müller and Tag 2010), advertising (e.g., Forceville 1996, 2002, 2008a, 2008b, Urios-Aparisi 2009, Yu 2009), film (e.g., Eggertsson and Forceville 2009, Urios-Aparisi 2014), or political discourse (Androshchuk 2014, Charteris-Black 2004, 2005, 2013, Lakoff 1996/2002, 2008, Musolff 2004, 2016). By contrast, metonymy is – except for a limited set of studies (especially Littlemore 2015, Mittelberg 2006, 2008, 2010, 2013, Mittelberg and Waugh 2009, 2014; see also Catalano and Waugh 2013, Urios-Aparisi 2014, Yu 2009) – far from being extensively examined, especially as an individual topic of research, i.e., without metaphor.

The dynamic approach to be developed in this book is not intended to deepen this disequilibrium but to take account of and refer to metaphor and metonymy in equal measure. It proceeds from the same basic assumption as the cognitive theory of metaphor and metonymy in that it conceives of both as parts of human everyday speaking, thinking, and understanding grounded in experience (Radden and Kövecses 1999, 18). In order to differentiate between the two, the study is not intended to go into the cognitive-linguistic theoretical debate about their differences, but to proceed from "how each makes different connections between things" (Gibbs 1999a, 62). In this respect, the basic received understanding is that metaphor involves two *different* experiential realms (in CMT terms, a cross-domain mapping), while metonymy involves two things that are (factually or pragmatically) linked within the *same* experiential realm (cf. Barcelona 2000, Croft 1993, Gibbs 1999a, Mittelberg and Waugh 2014, Radden 2000). In other words, both are considered as processes of experiencing and understanding one kind of thing in terms of another; yet, metaphor connects these things through the principle of similarity and metonymy connects them through the principle of contiguity (cf. Croft 1993, Jakobson [1956] 1990, [1965] 1987, Mittelberg 2010, Peirce 1960).

Unlike in most studies that stand in the tradition of the cognitive theory of figurativity, the audiovisual figurative meanings to be analyzed in the campaign commercials will not be deduced from assumed pre-existing patterns of figurative thought. In this regard, the dynamic approach as proposed here is in line with Gibbs (1999a, 74) who has warned against equating figurativity in language use

https://doi.org/10.1515/9783110578782-003

and figurativity in thought. This study, therefore, clearly focuses on concrete and situated cases of metaphorical and metonymical meaning-making in the campaign commercials and does not intend to draw conclusions from them about potential superordinate conceptual patterns.

The investigation of figurativity in audiovisual media as compared to, e.g., face-to-face communication is at an early stage and only gradually progressing. In regard to this topic, it is notable that respective studies still stand very much in the tradition of Lakoff and Johnson's conceptual metaphor theory and seek to verify audiovisual instantiations of conceptual metaphors and metonymies in films and commercials. Although there is agreement about Marshall McLuhan's (1964, 23–35) claim of the medium being the message in that "as soon as one changes the medium via which a message (including both its factual and emotive aspects) is conveyed, the content of this message is changed as well" (Forceville 2009a, 21), it seems that this insight has barely affected the understanding of figurativity itself. Forceville's remarks make this quite clear:

> Each medium – here defined as a material carrier and transmitter of information – communicates via one or more signaling systems. The medium of non-illustrated books, for instance, exclusively draws on the mode of written language; [...] and post-silent film on visuals, written language, spoken language, non-verbal sound, and music. If, as is argued here, each of these signaling systems (which will henceforward be called "modes") can cue, independently or in combination, metaphorical targets as well as metaphorical sources, a full-blown theory of metaphor cannot be based on its verbal manifestations alone, since this may result in a biased view of what constitutes metaphor. (Forceville 2009a, 21)

Apart from the exclusive reference to metaphor (the explanation likewise applies to metonymy all the same), what is striking is the understanding of different media as material information carriers and transmitters: it entails the implicit assumption of pre-existent meaning that can manifest in varying ways and thereby affects the content it is conveying. As a result, one fundamental aspect is completely disregarded, namely that a medium is not merely a carrier but that it first and foremost *creates* the message, i.e., it makes meaning. The focus on the transmitting function basically restores the vicious circle of CMT as it proceeds top down from assumed higher-order mental patterns to their audiovisual instantiations and is thus biased from the outset. Furthermore, the majority of studies on figurativity in audiovisual media still take spoken or written language as a starting point for their analysis, what in turn can be ascribed to the fact that different media are not considered with regard to their media specificity and role in figurative meaning-making. Audiovisual images are thus conceived of as mere depictions or illustrations of verbal content within cognitive linguistics. As a result, the implications of being exposed to, of viewing, and experiencing audiovisual movement-images that unfold dynamically in space and time are entirely neglected. This is the reason why the dynamic approach to audiovisual figurativity as proposed in this book draws on a transdisciplinary connection of a cognitive-linguistic approach to the *activation of metaphoricity*[1] (Müller 2008a, 2008b, Müller and Tag 2010) and a film-analytical approach to *cinematic expressive movement* (Kappelhoff 2004, Kappelhoff and Bakels 2011; see also Kappelhoff and Müller 2011, Müller and Kappelhoff 2018, Scherer, Greifenstein, and Kappelhoff 2014).

This chapter aims to both give an outline of previous approaches to audiovisual figurativity from a cognitive-linguistic perspective and to concomitantly develop an individual perspective through recourse to theoretical and practical works that lend themselves to a dynamic approach to audiovisual figurativity as put forward here. Thereby, it will not proceed chronologically but systematically both by bringing together scholars and approaches with similar assumptions and by arranging the individual sections according to the implications of investigating figurativity in audiovisual media. In this light, the notion of multimodality will be initially introduced and discussed: starting from the assumption that figurativity is not a matter of verbal manifestations alone, the term multimodality emerged and became established during the last decade in order to account for manifestations of metaphor and metonymy apart from language (among others in gesture, static and moving images, and sound). As will be shown, the thereby developed distinction of mono- and multimodal figurativity is hardly compatible with the dynamic approach to audiovisual figurativity as it reduces the phenomenon and its dynamics.

Based on the assumption of figurativity's fundamental modality independence (cf. Müller 2008a), the subsequent section deals with the question of how this affects the actual act of figuration, i.e., if metaphorical and metonymical meaning is to be considered a product or a process. According to whether scholars hold a CMT-informed view or not, they tend to consider figurativity in audiovisual media, face-to-face communication, or pictures as static modal instantiation of conceptual patterns or as an ongoing process of meaning-making. In the following section, a closer look shall be taken on the forms that figurativity assumes in multimodal contexts of use and how this affects its meaning. Proceeding from the fact that figurative meaning in a situated media context unfolds dynamically and 'bottom up', its particular form of expression opens up a methodological access to the identification of audiovisual metaphor and metonymy. Subsequently, the aspect of experience (either of something in terms of something else or

---

1 Müller's (2008a) notion of 'metaphoricity' that refers to a language user's cognitive, affective, and interactive process of seeing one thing in terms of another is thereby extended to metonymy.

something contiguous) that plays a central role in figurative meaning-making will be addressed. The consideration of further modalities apart from language provides insights into the emergence of figurative meaning from embodied experience and its role for understanding on the part of a speaker, listener, or viewer. In this regard, approaches will be introduced that conceive of experience as rather cognitive and those that link it to a speaker's, listener's, or viewer's actual experience. Finally, the last section summarizes the main assumptions and insights and relates them to each other in terms of a comprehensive dynamic account of multimodal figurativity.

3.1 Materialized Conceptualization: Figurativity and Multimodality

In his cyber course in pictorial and multimodal metaphor, Charles Forceville prefaces:

> A complete theory of metaphor cannot ignore the non-verbal. The cognitivist paradigm insists that verbal metaphors are manifestations rather than reduplications of thought, and thereby forcefully suggests that thought can give rise to non-verbal or multimodal metaphor. (Forceville 2007a)

The background of this remark is that CMT-informed research on metaphor and metonymy has long focused exclusively on written and spoken language in order to draw conclusions about human cognition and meaning-making (cf. Engelke 2013, 171, Forceville 2009a, 21). The problem of such reasoning is a perpetuating circle "in that it [i.e., cognitive-linguistic research] starts with an analysis of language to infer something about the mind and body which in turn motivates different aspects of linguistic structure and behavior" (Gibbs and Colston 1995, 354; see also Cienki 1998, Deignan 2010, Müller 2008a, Ritchie 2010). Lakoff and Johnson have directed attention to the fact that metaphor and metonymy are more than mere rhetorical and poetic devices, namely basic cognitive principles of human thought pervading ordinary language and interaction (Lakoff and Johnson 1980, 3, 1999).[2] However, their line of argument rests upon constructed linguistic expressions that should prove the existence of conceptual metaphors and metonymies and vice versa. From such a perspective, figurativity in written and spoken language is nothing but a surface reflection of pre-existing conceptual networks,

---

2 Lakoff and Johnson were not the first in taking this view. Before, Andrew Ortony (1979) pointed out that metaphor is an important tool of cognition and communication.

whereby its individual and on-the-spot emergence and unfolding in language use is completely disregarded. The aim to overcome CMT's circular reasoning and concomitantly to prove its central assumption of figurativity being "a mode of thought" (Lakoff 1993, 210) was a main reason for the increasing importance of the notion of modality and multimodal metaphor or metonymy. Accordingly, cognitive linguists began to investigate other possible forms of their materialization, such as in pictures, audiovisual media, or in gesture (e.g., Cienki and Müller 2008a, Eggertsson and Forceville 2009, Forceville 1996, Forceville and Urios-Aparisi 2009, Littlemore 2015, Mittelberg 2006, Mittelberg and Waugh 2009, 2014, Müller 2008a). The variety of studies carried out clearly suggests that figurativity is "modality-independent" (Müller 2008a, 32), i.e., that it occurs in mono- as well as in multimodal forms.

Cognitive linguistics is not alone in this important finding: natural sciences as well as other disciplines of the humanities have also come to the general insight of the multimodality of information, i.e., that meaning is conveyed in different signifying systems simultaneously (Forceville and Urios-Aparisi 2009, 3; see also Bucher 2012 and Schmitt 2015).[3] According to Bucher (2012, 54), the term implies two forms of usage: as an empirical notion, it takes account of the development of new technologies and the concomitant changes of media communication and thus focuses on new types of communicative manifestations, e.g., Social Networks or digital newspapers on demand. In terms of categorical understanding, on the other hand, multimodality amounts to the fundamental feature of all forms of communication that meaning is always constituted by means of various semiotic resources (Bucher 2012, 55), which is why their respective impact on and their mutual interplay for meaning constitution has to be considered in greater detail. As self-evident as this might sound, it is a highly controversial and fiercely discussed issue as a general definitional clarification of what constitutes a modality or a mode could hitherto not be developed.[4]

In cognitive linguistics, scholars have first drawn a distinction between monomodal and multimodal metaphor or metonymy[5] in order to distinguish

---

3 Bucher has called this shift the "multimodal turn" [*multimodale Wende*] (2012, 54) in media history (see also Kress and van Leeuwen's (1998, 186) statement that "[a]ll texts are multimodal").
4 For a detailed discussion of the term multimodality from a cognitive-linguistic perspective, see Forceville (2009a, 22–25). Although he neither can establish a final definition, Forceville has discussed possible criteria of modality and their consequent implications for the analysis of multimodal metaphorical manifestations. For a juxtaposition of multimodality and multimediality from a semiotic perspective, see Fricke 2008, 39–50.
5 Forceville and Urios-Aparisi's edited volume *Multimodal Metaphor* (2009) demonstrates that both terms are used in cognitive-linguistic analyses of various forms of communication.

between materializations with source and target exclusively in one modality and those with source and target "each represented exclusively or predominantly in different" modalities (Forceville 2009a, 24). Neither differentiation, however, answers the question of what a modality or mode actually is. Hitherto, no exhaustive and set definition has been developed and most scholars investigating multimodal figurativity avoid a comprehensive differentiation of criteria. Instead, they take for granted the modalities that are relevant for their own focus of research. The following remarks by Forceville can be considered representative for many scholars who examine multimodal metaphor and metonymy. Forceville provides a preliminary list of modes on the basis of an open determination of the term with mixed criteria, i.e., sensory, medial, and semiotic aspects, and concludes:

> In short, it is at this stage impossible to give either a satisfactory definition of "mode," or compile an exhaustive list of modes. However, this is no obstacle for postulating that there are different modes and that these include, at least, the following: (1) pictorial signs; (2) written signs; (3) spoken signs; (4) gestures; (5) sounds; (6) music (7) smells; (8) tastes; (9) touch. (Forceville 2009a, 23)

With regard to former studies of multimodal metaphor, it seems that most cognitive-linguistic scholars so far have tacitly agreed about this list of possible modalities, although it is problematic. Forceville has pointed out that in some contexts it might be difficult to subsume a particular materialization (of metaphorical or metonymical meaning) strictly under one of these modes, e.g., when it comes to the distinction of music from sound in audiovisual contexts.[6] Moreover, the mode of pictorial signs appears to be imprecise, as it does not differentiate static from moving images. Thus, the mixed criteria underlying Forceville's preliminary list of modes seem to be too inconsistent. However, a definition based on consistent factors likewise presents issues. For example, an exclusively sensory-informed understanding of mode "lumps together spoken language, music, and non-verbal sound" under the sonic mode, while "both written language and gestures would have to be part and parcel of the visual" (Forceville 2009a, 22). From a cognitive-linguistic point of view, a differentiation between spoken language and music, or written language and gesture, is highly significant, not least due to completely different processes of semiosis.

Admittedly, the "the common linking of 'mode' with sensory modalities" (Bateman and Schmidt 2012, 77) seems to fit perfectly in the case of moving images, as Schmitt has indicated, "at least at first glance, since *audio-visuals* is commonly used as a synonym due to the two senses those images prominently

---

6 Also typeface would be problematic to categorize, as it could belong to different modalities like pictorial signs, written signs, or even to both (Forceville 2009a, 22–23)

address" (Schmitt 2015, 309–310). Nevertheless, the dynamic approach to audiovisual figurative meaning-making as taken in this book is not compatible with such an understanding of audiovisual media as an adding up of articulatory modes that represent and communicate contents (see also Müller and Kappelhoff 2018, Schmitt forthcoming/2019). The notion of mode or modality implicitly rests upon the assumption that meaning is existent in advance, and audiovisual media function as a channel or carrier transmitting it. Such a conception underlies the majority of previous cognitive-linguistic studies on audiovisual figurativity in different formats and genres, such as feature films, commercials, or TV news (e.g., Forceville 2009b, Eggertsson and Forceville 2009, Urios-Aparisi 2009, Yu 2009). Most of them still stand strongly in the tradition of Lakoff and Johnson's CMT and basically follow the same circular reasoning as in the examination of figurativity in written and spoken language, where it is considered a surface reflection of pre-existing conceptual networks. In this respect, the notion of modality or mode and multimodal figurativity in principle plays a role to prove the existence of conceptual meaning, while the media-specific properties of audiovisual movement-images are of no significance.

This is clearly reflected in Forceville's definition of mono- and multimodal metaphor (or metonymy): while monomodal manifestations have their "target and source exclusively or predominantly rendered in one mode", multimodal ones' "target and source are each represented exclusively or predominantly in different modes" (Forceville 2009a, 23, 24). From such a point of view, figurativity is schematized and made into a product that can be divided into individual components. It presupposes first of all a clear determination and assignment of the source and the target domain (not to mention the concomitant assumption of a unilateral transfer of meaning) both of which have to be attributable to different modes in order to build a multimodal metaphor or metonymy. Certainly, this schematization issues from the endeavor to provide a consistent basis and reliable approach to the study and analysis of figurativity in varying contexts of use.[7] Nevertheless, the processuality and emergence of figurative meaning is thereby completely excluded from consideration. What is more, the schematic conception leads to the deconstruction of the dynamic totality of the inherently multimodal audiovisual medium. That is to say that the "complex orchestrations of mappings between source and target, which imply various articulatory modalities, like

---

7 In this respect, see also Engelke's (2013) remarks that Schmitt (2015, 309) has concisely summarized as follows: "Against the background of scientific differentiation and post-structuralism, a need for regaining a lost holistic perspective has evolved: 'a perspective that grasps cognition and meaning in the entirety of their perceptive, semantic, semiotic, discursive, and cultural dimensions'".

visual composition, sound design, editing, acting and so forth" (Kappelhoff and Müller 2011, 122) in their mutual interplay are mostly reduced to selected single articulatory modalities of audiovisual staging separated out of their temporal and compositional context.

A short outline of one example from the Polish Law and Justice party's (PiS) campaign commercial (see Section 8.2) shows how this approach is questionable: in its first half, the commercial presents a scenario of a group of people standing in front of a glass building, being excluded from political participation. Inside, a group of businessmen-like politicians have sealed themselves off from the people outside. The contrast between having access and being inside as compared to having no access and being outside that makes political participation and involvement experience- and understandable cannot simply be attributed to acting, sound design, or montage alone. Instead, it is their spatio-temporal interplay as a dynamic process that gives rise to this emergent meaning. By contrast, the deconstruction of figurativity and audiovisual media from a schematic conception generates single manifestations in terms of entities. This amounts to an abstraction from how figurative meaning is made in various contexts of use, i.e., in terms of going from one metaphorical or metonymical instantiation to the next instead of going through a process in which meaning is constantly flowing and unfolding.

Audiovisual images are hitherto being conceived of as mere depictions or illustrations of verbal content within cognitive linguistics. The analyses of figurativity carried out in audiovisual media seem to be strongly guided by conceptual metaphors and metonymies that have been formulated and verified by means of constructed linguistic expressions. Consequently, audiovisual media in the context of figurativity is first and foremost described and analyzed on the level of audiovisual representation.[8] How figurative meaning emerges through the interplay of various articulatory modalities of audiovisual staging, either together with or without language, is thus not taken into consideration. As a result, the supposed object of study is from the outset taken for granted and is only retroactively confirmed. However, in order to arrive at a full picture of audiovisual figurativity it is necessary to take sufficient account of the media-specific features of moving images. Ventola, Charles, and Kaltenbacher (2004, 1) have suggested that the combination and interplay of various modes force scholars "to think about

---

8 Forceville's study about "[t]he role of non-verbal sound and music in multimodal metaphor" (2009b), for example, suggests that both can cue a source domain or trigger mappable connotations of a source domain in commercials and films. His analyses, however, refer to the level of audiovisual representation of music and sound and thus already entail culturally-rooted interpretations (see Section 1.3).

the particular characteristics of these modes and the way they [...] function and combine in the modern discourse worlds". This is still a desideratum in cognitive-linguistic research on audiovisual figurativity because it considers audiovisual images as static pictures and mere illustrations of language.

On these grounds, the notion of multimodality in terms of a product that can be taken apart and attributed to a source and a target domain of figurativity provides a less suitable and fruitful basis for the analysis of audiovisual figurativity in this book. It should be noted that audiovisual media is considered inherently multimodal due to its numerous articulatory modalities of audiovisual staging (cf. Scherer, Greifenstein, and Kappelhoff 2014, 2085). The emergent figurative meaning in campaign commercials that will be reconstructed and analyzed in this study with regard to its emergence and unfolding will not, however, be termed as multimodal, but as audiovisual in order to dissociate it from the static and schematized conception of meaning-making inherent to the notion of multimodality. Instead, it follows a conception of modality as Schmitt has put it forward:

> By *mode*, I suggest to focus on various layers of imagery that are assumed to interact in the spectator's perception of audio-visual images: expressive movement figurations – i.e., the gestural dimension of audio-visual images – and verbal articulations (be they spoken or written) as well as represented (i.e. depicted, in German 'dargestellt') visible or audible elements (such as objects, actors, landscapes, etc.) that are given expression within these audio-visual gestures. Those modes I conceive of as varying aggregate phases of embodied perceptual scenarios unfolding in audio-visuals. (Schmitt 2015, 314)

By considering these aspects as equal and with regard to their mutual and dynamic interplay over the course of time, the resulting perspective does not conceive of audiovisual figurativity as a static entity but as an emergent and ongoing process of meaning-making as will be shown in the subsequent section.

3.2 Enactive Conceptualization: Figurativity and Situatedness

The majority of research on multimodal figurativity in audiovisual media has primarily focused on manifestations of conceptual metaphors and metonymies, most often in films and commercials. By taking pre-existing general concepts as their starting point, respective studies tend to explain figurative meaning-making mainly on a collective, but not on the individual, usage level. The underlying explanation for the suggested and not another understanding of a film is based on the assumption that everybody possesses these conceptual networks and therefore immediately detects and understands them. As a result, the claim of a process of understanding that 'all' are sharing is not at issue and the question for the concrete configuration and form of figurative meaning is not relevant. The abstracted labels of the conceptual metaphors and metonymies solely give some indication of the existence of a corresponding manifestation in the respective audiovisual data. Yet how the self-same concretely unfolds for the viewers, how it fits in for them in the particular film or commercial, and which role it thereby plays for them remains unclear.

In his analysis of an educational Chinese commercial for nonverbal and multimodal manifestations of metaphors and metonymies, Ning Yu (2009) concludes that it is primarily based on the two conceptual metaphors LIFE IS A JOURNEY and LIFE IS A STAGE. It is striking that he extrapolates the latter primarily from the underlying verbal message ("In everyone's heart there is a big stage"), while inferring the former predominantly from audiovisual representation (i.e., a young woman dancing in different places). It seems that Yu, by committing himself to these two conceptual metaphors, subordinates to them all content-related aspects that he is dealing with in the analysis. Many of his findings thus appear to be read into the commercial from this top-down perspective. This is primarily due to the fact that Yu derives meaning from the audiovisually represented content[9] and the explicit expression in language, which he takes for granted. Thereby, it is not made clear what kind of status the figurative meanings that he puts forward have: not being related to each other, they amount to a conglomeration of meanings that is suggested to be active and processed by all viewers.

A similar premature preference for pre-existing concepts instead of an analysis of the actual audiovisual context and its temporal unfolding can be detected in a study of Eggertsson and Forceville (2009). The authors have investigated the existence of a systematic "structural metaphor" of HUMAN VICTIM IS ANIMAL in various horror films. In so doing, they proceed from an allegedly existing conceptual metaphor, which shall be verified by their examples. From such a point of view, the analysis is biased from the beginning and tends to rashly consider certain elements or aspects of audiovisual representation as manifestation of a collective conceptualization. Thus, the authors do what Forceville actually had been rejecting for the analysis of metaphors in their context of use, i.e., to conceive of them as mere "*reduplications* of thought" (Forceville 2007a). Yu as well as Eggertsson and Forceville present surface appearances of assumed pre-existing conceptualizations and thereby restrict figurativity's potential of situated and

---

9 As for multimodal metonymies, he names among others the clothing style standing for culture. This, too, displays an exclusive focus on represented content and a bias by contextual knowledge (e.g., that the commercial aims at promoting public welfare and influencing the thinking of people).

dynamic meaning-making in audiovisual media. For them, audiovisual figurative meaning exists prior to the situation of a spectator watching a film, an advertisement, or a campaign commercial. It is considered to be on the one hand amodally present as conceptual meaning and, on the other hand, 'contained' in the images (independent of a viewer constructing it). This way, the contextual situatedness of meaning-making as well as the understanding and experience of the viewer play no role at all. As a result, the studies rarely exceed a recital of single audiovisual instantiations of assumed conceptual metaphors, and the interrelatedness or possible coherences between these separate metaphors are not taken into consideration.[10]

The reason for this might be that research on multimodal figurativity, in its turning away from language, has initially focused on static images. Here especially Forceville's work is to be mentioned. He has examined figurativity predominantly in pictorial advertising (later on also in cartoons, comics, and animes; see, e.g., Abbott and Forceville 2011, Bounegru and Forceville 2011, Forceville 2011, 2017). In this respect, he has developed a typology of different forms of metaphor in language and/or static images for which he has coined the superordinate term of 'pictorial metaphor' (Forceville 1996). The thereby characteristic interplay of static images and language or the constitution of metaphorical meaning through the static visual depiction alone has – due to the absence of spatio-temporal dynamics – promoted an understanding of figurative meaning in terms of a product that is paradigmatically transferred to audiovisual movement-images. This results in two implications that are linked with each other and appear problematic for a dynamic understanding of figurativity: figurative meaning is considered as being objectively contained in the image, i.e., as being visually represented, and is thus reduced to a global and synthetic display of mental content. Concomitantly with this exclusive focus on the semiotic properties of the medium, the spectator and equally the actual process of figurative meaning-making become insignificant for "experiencing and understanding one kind of thing in terms of another" (Lakoff and Johnson 1980, 5). The consequence of these two implications is a static conception of figurativity in audiovisual contexts of use, namely in terms of a fixed and pre-existent product.

Other multimodally-informed studies have explicitly suggested and underlined the dynamics and emergence of figurative meaning. In this regard, the

---

10 Urios-Aparisi (2009) displays rudiments of a more context-sensitive approach in his four case studies of multimodal metaphors in TV commercials by taking the interplay of metaphor and metonymy in the course of one TV ad into account: "Each metaphor builds on the previous one and relates to the first metonymy." (Urios-Aparisi 2009, 110) However, he proceeds top down, i.e., he exclusively focuses on manifestations of conceptual metaphors.

examination of verbo-gestural metaphor and metonymy is to be mentioned because it has put forward the central role of the speaker(s), the processuality, and the interactivity of figurative meaning-making in face-to-face communication. One important representative of such a dynamic account is Lynne Cameron's Discourse Dynamics approach based on dynamic systems theory (2010, Cameron et al. 2009, Gibbs and Cameron 2008). She has suggested that verbal figurative expressions in face-to-face interactions express how a person conceptualizes, feels, and evaluates something. Based on what the speakers communicate, they thus provide insight into how they make sense of a particular issue, situation, or topic and build a bridge for mutual understanding. Cameron has examined such a dynamic and reciprocal negotiation process through a reconciliation talk between an IRA assassin and a relative of one of his victims and illustrates how by metaphors and metonymies they try to explain themselves, understand the other, and negotiate opinions and attitudes (Cameron 2007, 2011). In doing so, she puts forward an understanding of figurative meaning-making that is inextricably linked with the people expressing and developing it: "In interactional situations, metaphors are negotiated and coconstructed across speakers" and give "evidence of thinking and perspective" (Cameron 2007, 200). Her approach is "mainly inductive or 'bottom up', with metaphors emerging from the data" (Cameron 2007, 205) as they are used for the purpose of exchanging and negotiating ideas with a co-participant in a particular interactive situation instead of reproducing mental representations top down:

> As I have argued elsewhere [...], emergent and evolving sets of connected metaphors gathered from actual discourse events are not necessarily the same constructs as the fixed and stable 'conceptual metaphors' of cognitive metaphor theory, and may be more appropriately labelled 'systematic metaphors'. (Cameron 2007, 201)

With her recourse to the dynamics and contextual situatedness of figurativity in face-to-face interaction, Cameron provides an important foundation for the examination of figurativity in audiovisual media (see also her notion of 'metaphorizing' in Cameron 2018). As she locates it in social interaction and with people who through it construct reality, express a particular perspective, and develop mutual understanding, figurativity comes into view as a lived process of meaning-making. In this respect, further studies that take speech-accompanying gesture as another articulatory modality apart from language into consideration put forward a similar line of argument. Proceeding from the assumption that communicative movements of the hands are performed spontaneously, they are considered an appropriate means to substantiate the claim that figurative meaning is found ad hoc in the moment of use instead of being a reproduction of pre-existing concepts (e.g., Cienki and Müller 2014, Kolter et al. 2012, Müller 1998,

2013, Müller and Ladewig 2013, Müller and Tag 2010). The gestural depiction of the source domain of a verbal metaphorical or metonymical expression (cf. Müller 2013, 206–207, Cienki 2013, Cienki and Müller 2008a, 2008b), thus displays its subjective and vital conceptualization on the part of a speaker. In other words, metaphorical or metonymical gestures "are not simple reflections of something out there in the real world. Instead, they are mediated by processes of conceptualization, interaction, and the depictive possibilities of visible bodily movement" (Müller 2013, 209).

Mittelberg (2006, 2008, Mittelberg and Waugh 2009) has investigated this with regard to the interplay of metonymy and metaphor from a cognitive-semiotic perspective and suggests that from the interpreter's perspective metonymy leads the way into metaphor.[11] She concludes that speech-accompanying gesture "can shed light on the externalization, or "*ex*-bodiment" [...] of mental imagery and internalized structures and practices" (Mittelberg 2008, 148) because the "human body functions as the locus where cognitive-semiotic processes *take shape*, linking knowledge, linguistic expression, and visible action in the formation of utterances" (2008, 149; emphasis mine). Here, a clear connection becomes apparent between multimodal figurativity and its situated context of use in which it takes a particular (bodily) form and shape.

As straightforward as the emergence and dynamics of figurativity in face-to-face interaction might be – in the case of audiovisual media no such interactive context seems to be given, which might be why the idea of a static and fixed entity persists. Yet the dynamics of figurative meaning-making *is* not fed by but instead *is* the media context in which it occurs. Lakoff and Johnson's (1980) famous definition of "experiencing and understanding" characterizes it as an active operation that is linked to a language user, i.e., it is inherently and necessarily tied to someone who is experiencing and understanding one thing in terms of another. In order to be able to speak of audiovisual figurative meaning, a viewer thus has to go through the process of seeing as, namely in the process of viewing, that therefore can only be considered an interactive one between the spectator and audiovisual compositions. From such a dynamic perspective, audiovisual figurative meaning-making amounts to an *enacted* process (instead of a mere passive deciphering). The theoretical approach of enactivism emphasizes such an interrelatedness of body and mind with regard to the organization and acquisition of knowledge (see De Jaegher and Di Paolo 2007, Fuchs and De Jaegher 2009, Jensen

---

11 More precisely, it is the metonymical mapping between the hand (source) and an imaginary object (target) that constitutes the prerequisite for a metaphorical mapping between the self-same object (source) and the abstract idea (target) it represents (Mittelberg and Waugh 2009).

2017, Varela, Thompson, and Rosch 1991). According to that, cognition is not sol-ipsistic but inherently tied to the body's interaction with its environment and emerges on the basis of action, perception, and experience.[12] Applying such a point of view to audiovisual figurative meaning-making entails that understand-ing something in terms of something else involves the cognitive and experien-tial participation of the viewer that results in the activation of figurativity (see Section 3.3 and the notion of 'doing metaphor' in Gibbs 2018 and Jensen 2017).

In summary, previous cognitive-linguistic research on audiovisual figurativity has hitherto primarily been focused on its cognitive processing in terms of uncon-scious deciphering and assigned the viewer a rather passive role in the mean-ing-making process. Therefore, these studies struggled with an explanation for the effectiveness of metaphor and metonymy in audiovisual media, i.e., their psy-chological reality for and persuasive impact on a spectator. By contrast, research on multimodal figurativity in face-to-face communication has suggested that it emerges ad hoc within the scope of its ongoing context of use, unfolds dynam-ically, and thereby creates systematic, interactively-created patterns of thinking (e.g., Cameron 2007, 2011, Cienki and Müller 2008a, 2008b, Müller and Tag 2010). Also considering audiovisual figurativity as a dynamic phenomenon brings the process of viewing and experiencing audiovisual movement-images to the fore. In this respect, it is the "temporal and multimodal structure of the unfolding film" (Greifenstein and Kappelhoff 2016, 190) that constitutes the situated ground for the emergence and unfolding of figurative meaning on the part of the viewer. As will be argued in the following section, such a dynamic and bottom-up approach to audiovisual figurative meaning-making likewise opens up methodological access to the identification of audiovisual metaphor and metonymy.

3.3 Highlighted Meaning: Activation of Figurativity

In his study on pictorial and multimodal metaphor in commercials, Forceville (2008b, 298) addresses and discusses the question of how spectators are "alerted that a metaphor must or may be construed in the first place, i.e., how do they know that one thing (the 'target') is presented in terms of a thing from another category (the 'source')". He first of all links the identification of a metaphor on the part of a spectator to the recognition of source and target domain; therefore,

---

12 In his sociocultural theory, Lev Vygotsky (1978) has pointed out the significance of interper-sonal and environmental interaction as the basis for the development of higher mental functions with children.

the detailed examination of modalities in which the two can be "represented" and "cued" is of utmost relevance. Only on the basis of a clear modal assignment of the two domains is the spectator in a second step able to relate them to one another and, thus, to make metaphorical meaning. Forceville's explanations are characterized by a traditional language-informed understanding of metaphor that he applies to other modal contexts of use, in this case an audiovisual one.

Concerning the question of the recognition and the actual processing of figurative meaning, he draws on a longstanding discussion within research on figurativity, especially metaphor studies, that is hitherto a controversial matter, namely "what exactly is activated when a metaphor is used and is active for a given speaker or writer" (Müller 2008a, 62). There are different approaches to deal with this question: either, metaphor and metonymy scholars restrict the validity of their findings by arguing from the outset that figurative meaning is potentially processed by or activated with speakers, listeners, or viewers (e.g., Cameron 2007, 2011, Pragglejaz Group 2007, Steen et al. 2010). The second option is that scholars suggest or negate the dynamic activation and processing of metaphors and metonymies and differentiate between activated and non-activated, in other words, between dead and alive ones (e.g., Black 1993, Lakoff and Turner 1989, Ricœur 1986, Searle 1993; see also Steen's notion of 'deliberateness' 2006, 2011). This "basic and commonly held assumption" (Müller 2008a, 1) that is still advocated by many metaphor scholars distinguishes metaphors according to the criteria of conventionalization, novelty, transparency, and consciousness (Müller 2008a, 178–209) into those that are recognized as such by language users (alive) and those that are not recognized anymore and therefore powerless (dead). In traditional views, only novel and poetic metaphors belong to the first category, while conventionalized and non-transparent metaphors are assumed not being processed consciously anymore and therefore not being metaphors any longer (e.g., Black 1993, Ricœur 1986). Conceptual metaphor theory has challenged this assumption by turning the argument upside down: especially conventional metaphorical expressions of ordinary language, i.e., the most entrenched ones, were the most vivid and active ones because they are processed most effortlessly and unconsciously (Lakoff and Johnson 1980, Lakoff and Turner 1989, 130).

It seems that this perspective shapes research on audiovisual figurativity in large part to date. The conceptual metaphors LIFE IS A JOURNEY and LIFE IS A STAGE that Yu (2009) has identified in his analysis of a Chinese educational commercial are not at all questioned with regard to their recognition by the viewer and their relevance for his or her figurative meaning-making process because they are held to be collectively shared mental models that are effortlessly noticed and processed below the level of consciousness. Eggertsson and Forceville's (2009) study on the structural metaphor of HUMAN VICTIM IS ANIMAL in horror films follows a similar line of argument. It is cognitively informed, i.e., the activation of metaphoricity is considered a primarily conceptual phenomenon. Such a static perspective that locates metaphoricity on the level of the language system is not able to differentiate with regard to the level of language use, which is shaped by the concrete situation and temporality of use as well as the involved users.

As Müller (2008a, 60–61) has, however, suggested, "language needs to be processed internally and needs to be adapted to specific contexts of use". In order to overcome the problem of equating the systems level and the level of use[13] in the examination and analysis of figurativity, she has drawn on "qualitative analyses of spontaneous language uses" (Müller 2008a, 62), primarily on speech and gesture, in order to argue the case for a selective and gradual activation of metaphoricity by a given speaker at a given moment in time (Müller 2008a, 2008b, 2011, Müller and Tag 2010). With that said, she is in line with Gibbs who has argued: "Many figurative-language theorists make the mistake of assuming that a theory constructed to explain one temporal moment of trope understanding can easily be generalized to account for *all* aspects of understanding" (Gibbs 1993, 256). Though Müller's understanding of metaphoricity as a dynamic feature of metaphors in language use has initially been developed on the basis of face-to-face interaction, it is suited to likewise apply to audiovisual contexts, as it – in contrast to previous studies – proceeds from the situated context of use (of audiovisual figurative meaning-making) and concomitantly from the role of the viewer as active meaning-maker.

What distinguishes Müller's dynamic approach to the activation of metaphoricity from experimental settings (such as priming studies or surveys) and corpus-linguistic research dealing with figurative meaning-making is that it exceeds single units and moments and instead accounts for the "dynamic structures of metaphors" (Müller and Tag 2010, 89) over longer stretches of time.[14] It is exactly this processual conception that previous cognitive-linguistic research on audiovisual figurativity almost completely lacks. First steps towards a more context-sensitive approach only show up in Urios-Aparisi's (2009) case study of four TV commercials with regard to the interplay of multimodal metaphor and metonymy for the persuasive purpose of the advertisements. Though he also proceeds from underlying conceptual metaphors that are activated in the commercials, he nevertheless considers the temporal unfolding of metaphorical meaning and

---

13 Müller (2008a, 2008b, 2011) has extensively dealt with the activation of metaphoricity in respect of the systems level and the level of use as well as the corresponding theoretical and practical implications and argues the case for a differentiation instead of an equation of the two levels.
14 For a more detailed discussion of this problem, see Müller and Tag 2010, 89.

its interrelatedness with metonymy in the course of the TV ads: "Each metaphor builds on the previous one and relates to the first metonymy." (Urios-Aparisi 2009, 110) In so doing, he overcomes the mere enumeration of separate metaphorical 'moments'. However, he still sticks to the idea that audiovisual images instantiate superordinate conceptual metaphors and does not differentiate between the systems level and the level of use.

Müller conceives of metaphorical meaning-making in whatever context of use as being inextricably linked with a language user (i.e., a speaker, listener, viewer, etc.) who goes through the cognitive process of "experiencing and understanding something in terms of something else" (Lakoff and Johnson 1980, 5). CMT-informed approaches share this assumption; however, they assume that entire mental concepts and models are activated for a speaker each and every time he or she uses a linguistic metaphorical expression based on it (cf. Lakoff and Johnson 1980, 3, Müller 2008a, 63–76). Müller casts doubt on such an assumption[15]: "It just seems highly implausible that, under normal conditions of language production, each and every time such a metaphor is used, activation would have to run through the entire system" (Müller 2008a, 68). Instead, she puts forward a selective cognitive activation of metaphorical meaning that is strongly tied to its particular context of use and the corresponding processing demands (cf. Cameron 1999, 4). In this light, she subscribes to conceptions of Leonard Talmy (2000, 2007), Wallace Chafe (1994, 1996), Ronald Langacker (2001), and Todd Oakley (2009) who have emphasized the dynamic nature of conceptualization and the interplay between conversational interaction and other cognitive processes, such as attention.[16]

> In a speech situation, a hearer may attend to the linguistic expression produced by a speaker, to the conceptual content represented by that expression, and to the context at hand. But not all of this material appears uniformly in the foreground of the hearer's attention. Rather, various portions or aspects of the expression, content, and context have differing degrees of salience [...]. (Talmy 2007, 264)

This draws attention to the 'material' of language use, i.e., its form, compositional structure, and content that are assumed to reflect the interlocutors' interactively negotiated flow of attention (Müller and Tag 2010, 93) or, in Cameron's terms (2010, 20), the "talking-and-thinking" in interaction.[17] Consequently, the

---

15 Gibbs also argues (1998, 92): "[T]his does not mean [...] that these metaphorical schema are ordinarily accessed each and every time a metaphor is read and heard".

16 For a summary of cognitive-linguistic approaches to attention, see Croft and Cruse 2004.

17 By this term, Cameron relies on Dan Slobin's (1996) "thinking for speaking" as well as on Vygotsky's sociocultural theory ([1934] 1986) that stresses the inseparability of cognitive and communicative processes.

activation of metaphoricity for one or various speakers is suggested as being linked with their interactive behavior, which is considered an access to the intrapersonal and interpersonal flow of attention in conversational interaction. Put more simply, interlocutors are assumed to express and negotiate interactively what is individually salient for them in a given moment of time (Müller and Tag 2010).[18] If a speaker puts metaphorical meaning into the focus of attention, then it is most likely cognitively activated for him (Müller 2008a, Müller and Tag 2010). Within the context of the communicative event, this act of expression is however not considered an end in itself but is always directed towards an attending co-participant, who constitutes meaning on this basis (Müller and Tag 2010, 95). Therefore, Müller and Tag (2010, 89) suggest that the foregrounding of metaphoricity by a speaker for an attending interlocutor probably points to the likewise activation on his part. Due to the continuous progress of mutually directing attention, the interacting participants create an observable and perceivable salience structure that can be used as an empirical source of information for the emergence and dynamic unfolding of metaphorical meaning (Müller and Tag 2010, 85).

The basis for the description and analysis of this salience structure (and thus the activation of metaphoricity) is, according to Müller and Tag, an additional communicative effort that is made to make metaphorical meaning salient.[19] This effort becomes, among others, noticeable in verbal elaborations, speech-accompanying gestures, or pictures that express metaphorical meaning in addition to a verbal metaphorical expression (Müller 2008a, 2008b, Müller and Tag 2010).[20] Put another way, multimodal metaphors indicate that metaphoricity is activated, or waking, for a given speaker at a given moment in time. As gestures are not

---

18 Karl Bühler also ([1934] 1990) pointed implicitly to the interactive negotiation of salient aspects in communication. By his principle of abstractive relevance, he argued that sign users are able to differentiate between (phonetic) relevant and irrelevant information.

19 Cameron has similarly argued this in her Discourse Dynamics approach to metaphor. Drawing on empirical data, she suggests that metaphors emerge and develop dynamically over the course of a conversation. She calls this phenomenon 'metaphor shifting' (Cameron 2010, 89) and distinguishes various possible manifestations, such as repetition, relexicalization, explication, or contrast of the metaphor vehicle (i.e., the source domain). Each of these cases displays an increase of metaphorical instantiations, either by mere repetition or by the semantic elaboration of the source domain, and "may reflect" (Cameron 2010, 92) their cognitive reality for the user. Due to the fact that Cameron exclusively draws on transcriptions of face-to-face conversations, she is however reliant on "other types of evidence" (Cameron 2010, 92) besides speech to substantiate this claim.

20 Müller and Tag (2010, 94–95) call this the "Iconicity Principle of: *More material indicates more meaning*".

conventionally linked to a given word or sentence but are produced spontaneously, verbo-gestural metaphor strongly suggests that metaphoricity in language use is activated selectively and gradually (Müller and Tag 2010, 92, Müller 2008a, 2008b). On this basis, Müller argues that not only novel, but also conventionalized linguistic metaphors can be cognitively activated – or 'waking' in her terms (Müller 2008a)[21] – for a user, as far as he or she displays it interactively. Metaphoricity is thus no static feature of single conceptual or lexical units on the systems level of language, but a dynamic property that is inherently linked with at least one given participant within an interactive context of use (Müller and Tag 2010, 93; see especially Müller 2008a).

With such a conception, the dynamic view of metaphor as theoretically developed by Müller (2008a) and methodologically elaborated by Müller and Tag (2010) provides an alternative and novel access to the examination and analysis of audiovisual figurativity as against previous cognitive-linguistic studies. For one thing, the act of viewing audiovisual media no longer appears as a passive reception process but as an interaction between the audiovisual 'material' and the spectator by analogy to face-to-face communication. Admittedly, it is no mutual interaction in the sense that the viewer responds to the audiovisual 'interlocutor' to the same extent. Nonetheless, it can be suggested as an interactive situation (cf. Kappelhoff and Müller 2018) inasmuch as a film, TV ad, music clip, or campaign commercial always addresses somebody: the viewer. As such, audiovisual compositions can be said to exhibit a perceptible salience structure that organizes and shapes the viewer's flow of attention with regard to their form, their temporal and structural arrangement, and content. On this intersubjectively foregrounded basis, the viewer can be considered to make figurative meaning to a similar extent as a speaker does through gesture and speech in face-to-face communication.

Nevertheless, due to the fact that audiovisual media does not display the same degree of spontaneity as face-to-face interaction, the question remains of whether audiovisual figurativity has been planned by the producers of audiovisual formats. This problem does not fall within the scope of this book because it clearly takes a recipient-oriented perspective. Admittedly, it can be suggested that skillful acting, staging, production, and editing of audiovisual media are always oriented to a particular effective effect and resonance on the part of the spectator. Yet this consideration has misled cognitive-linguistic as well as film studies' research about audiovisual figurativity to conceive of it exclusively as an artistic tool of a producer, who is assumed to instantiate it purposefully

---

21 For a detailed account of the dynamic view, see Müller 2008a.

(e.g., Carroll 1996, [1994] 2001, Forceville 2008b, 2009b, Whittock 1990, Yu 2009 see especially Chapter 5). Such a conception, however, makes figurativity a meaningful entity that a producer has at his disposal and that a viewer processes passively and unwittingly, i.e., the emergent process is reduced to a static pre-existent product.

A dynamic view instead embeds figurative meaning-making as an active and lived process with an "experiencing and understanding" user into a situated context of use and thereby opens up methodological access to the identification of audiovisual metaphor and metonymy. Although Müller and Tag's (2010, 89) "cognitive-linguistic and sequential-analytical approach" to reconstruct the cognitive processes of figurative meaning-making in the flow of attention is theoretically motivated, it nevertheless amounts to a context-bound method that "starts from the bottom up and remains close to the [...] data" (Müller and Schmitt 2015, 322). In doing so, it avoids the equation of the systems level and the level of use as well as the concomitant abstraction from the situated media context and instead reveals how figurative meaning for a viewer emerges from a vital experience. This orientation towards activated audiovisual figurative meaning amounts to a selective consideration from the total of all forms of potential figurative meaning (e.g., potential unconsciously processed conceptual metaphors or metonymies). Such a selection of vitalized conceptualizations against sleeping metaphor and metonymy is substantiated through the focus of this book on the viewer's situated process of figurative meaning-making. By taking these highly specific conceptualizations as a starting point for the reconstruction of figurative meaning-making, the "images, sensory qualities, or motives" (Schmitt, Greifenstein, and Kappelhoff 2014, 2105) that ground them come to the fore. As will be argued in the subsequent section, the previous cognitivist conception of figurativity's experientially based source domain is from this point of view hard to maintain.

3.4 Experiential Grounds: Figurativity and Embodiment

As self-evident as it might seem that figurative meaning and bodily experience are strongly interrelated (Lakoff and Johnson 1980, 1999), what it actually means and where it is to be 'located', especially in multimodal contexts of use, is rather vague. Metaphor has primarily been referred to as the form of thinking that makes abstract ideas comprehensible by understanding and experiencing them in concrete, physical terms: "*In actuality we feel that no metaphor can ever be comprehended or even adequately represented independently of its experiential basis.*" (Lakoff and Johnson 1980, 19) Scholars who examine metaphor and metonymy in multimodal contexts tend to adopt this assumption in its generality but do not get to the bottom of it. Yu, for instance, subscribes to "the cognitive linguistic view [that] conceptual metaphors emerge from the interaction between body and culture: they are grounded in bodily experience, but shaped by cultural understanding" (Yu 2009, 121). Regarding the conceptual metaphors and metonymies he has identified in the Chinese educational commercial, he locates embodied experience in the inferences and entailments of their mappings (Yu 2009, 127–137).[22] As such, it is considered to be entrenched and subconscious knowledge that is cognitively stored and has coalesced with a more abstract domain to form a neural connection that guides human thinking and action (see Lakoff and Johnson 1980, 1999).[23] Eggertsson and Forceville argue along similar lines with regard to their structural metaphor of HUMAN VICTIM IS ANIMAL:

> The metaphor is a highly embodied one [...] in exploiting the mapping of very physical actions (shaving, hunting, trapping, caging, slaughtering, killing) directed against animals, but also has cultural dimensions [...] inasmuch as it highlights behaviors toward animals that are sanctioned or even encouraged by mainstream society (Eggertsson and Forceville 2009, 445)

What becomes obvious from these two studies is a cognitivist understanding of the experiential basis of figurativity that amounts to a by-default and subconsciously processed piece of information whose reality and effectiveness is justified by the same argument that CMT uses for conceptual metaphors: what is most entrenched is most powerful (Lakoff and Turner 1989, 129). Such a cognitive notion of embodiment comes up with a dissociation of actual experience from the body (and abstracting it in the human mind). Though Lakoff and Johnson (1999) argue the case against a separation of body and mind, they basically consider embodiment a static, fixed, and standard property of cognitive models and conceptual structures. As such, it serves as a justification and evidence for the existence of conceptual metaphors and metonymies as Lakoff and Johnson suggest them.

As the majority of cognitive-linguistic studies on audiovisual figurativity subscribe to CMT and its cognitive notion of embodiment, research on verbo-gestural figurativity in face-to-face interactions again provides a more dynamic and less systems-informed approach to addressing the question of embodied experience

---

22 Among others, Yu enumerates entailments of EXPERIENCE IN LIFE IS TRAVEL OF JOURNEY, such as EASY TRAVEL is GOOD EXPERIENCE or FAST MOTION is FAST PROGRESS (Yu 2009, 128).
23 For a full exposition of Lakoff and Johnson's considerations with regard to the embodied mind, see Lakoff and Johnson 1980, 1999.

in the context of figurative meaning-making. In this respect, Mittelberg's notion of ex-bodiment (Mittelberg 2006, 2008, 2013, Mittelberg and Waugh 2009) is useful: according to her, speech-accompanying gestures are "a means to express, reify and show to interlocutors both imagined and sensed dimensions of mental imagery" and "may lend a perceptible gestalt to concepts, ideas and memories" (Mittelberg 2013, 756). As such, they do not merely convey an activated conceptualization of speakers but concomitantly express what it looks and feels like for them, i.e., how they conceive of it (Müller 1998, 2013, 2014, Müller and Ladewig 2013, Müller and Tag 2010). In the case of figurative meaning, gestures most often 'exbody', i.e., display, the experiential realm as a concrete and vital conceptualization that is made tangible for the speaker himself and for an interlocutor (cf. Cienki 2013, Cienki and Müller 2008a, 2008b, Müller 2008a, 2008b, 2013, Müller and Tag 2010). Thus, gesture indicates empirically observable evidence for the experiential basis of figurative meaning. Furthermore, it suggests that this experiential basis is nothing abstract but highly specific due to being inextricably linked to a speaker's subjective conceptualization.

Due to her cognitive-semiotic perspective, Mittelberg's notion of exbodiment is, however, similar to Lakoff and Johnson's notion of embodiment. Her scholarly interest is in how "cognitively entrenched patterns of experience – arisen from visual perception, navigation through space, tactile exploration, and other practices of bodily interaction with the sensorial and social world – may motivate gestural sign formation and interpretation" (Mittelberg 2013, 756). Despite considering that it takes a concrete shape, she conceives of embodied experience as a feature of conceptual structures that materializes in the gestural modality. This way, the focus is on single moments of activated figurative meaning, wherefore its emergence and dynamic unfolding in the context and dynamics of the situation of use do not come into view. Along with this, the possibility of a bodily experience in terms of an actual sensation that comes up with the gestural enactment is not considered.

Yet, Müller and Tag have argued that the activation of metaphoricity is not restricted to the cognitive level alone but "also implies an embodied experience of metaphor and thus activation comes with an affective or experiential quality" (Müller and Tag 2010, 85). By shifting the focus to "felt qualities of meaning"[24] (Johnson 2007, 17), Müller and Tag do not principally locate the embodied basis of figurative meaning on the conceptual level but in the very process of activation through lived gestural realization in a particular context of use:

---

[24] "You must look at the felt qualities, images, feelings, and emotions that ground our more abstract structures of reasoning." (Johnson 2007, 17)

> The very fact that a speaker *embodies* part of his utterance transforms this utterance into a sensory experience for both the speaker and the addressee. This sensory experience entails conceptualizations, points of view but also affective qualities inherent to these embodiments of meaning (Müller and Tag 2010, 114).

With this, not only does the individual gestural form and the concomitant subjective conceptualization and understanding of figurative meaning become the focus of attention, but so does an inherent feature of gesture as a medium of expression itself: "[W]henever I [i.e., a speaker] perform a gesture this performance comes along with a feeling of movement and is immediately perceived as movement" (Müller and Ladewig 2013, 301). Proceeding from these movement qualities as the basis for figurative meaning constitutes a fundamentally different take on its embodied dimension. It does not look for generalized experiences but for the situational settings in which subjective experiences become a vital source for figurative meaning-making.

Müller (2008a, 2008b; see also Müller and Tag 2010) illustrates that by means of a speaker who summarizes her first relationship and characterizes its course as a path that went up and down, however with an overall tendency downward (Müller 2008a, 204–208). Over the course of her explanations, she puts increasing communicative effort into conveying her subjective experience and conceptualization of her first relationship to her interlocutor. Initially, she introduces it with a downward movement of the head and elaborates it subsequently with an additional downward hand gesture. Due to lacking ratification by her interlocutor, she finally reformulates and elaborates the up and down of her relationship while simultaneously performing a large drawing gesture "which starts high and ends low" (Müller and Tag 2010, 101). As Müller and Tag suggest, the movement qualities of the speaker's various downward head and hand gestures come up with a sensory-motor experience of the experiential realm (i.e., the up and down), both for the speaker and for the interlocutor (Müller and Tag 2010, 114). That is to say, the speaker's particular way of performing this movement provides the experiential basis for her subjective understanding of the love relationship and for her interlocutor to share it.

It is such a situationally embedded and phenomenological understanding of embodiment (for a detailed exposition, see Müller and Kappelhoff 2018) that Gibbs is alluding to by arguing:

> We need not talk of metaphor as only part of our mental representations for concepts (e.g. anger), or as expressed by language (e.g. *She bursted with anger*). Metaphor is a kind of tool that arises from body-world interactions, which we can 're-experience' in an embodied way, and is not simply accessed from long-term memory, in different ways in different real-world situations. (Gibbs 1999b, 156)

Theoretical accounts and empirical findings within the cognitive sciences support the phenomenological assumption of a closely linked bodily experience and word meaning (cf. Müller and Ladewig 2013, 300). Lawrence Barsalou's cognitive-psychological theory of grounded cognition (2008), for instance, proceeds from the assumption that memorizing, speaking, or abstract reasoning do not rely on amodal symbols but on formerly directly perceived multimodal information that is cognitively stored. Therefore, he refers to them as perceptual symbols.[25] In the case of usage, "perceptual, motor, and introspective states acquired during experience with the world, body, and mind" (Barsalou 2008, 618–619) are considered to be simulated. Pulvermüller (1999) and Wilson and Gibbs (2007) have found that sensory-motor experience and language processing inform each other in that processing action or object words activates the respective sensory-motor brain areas, and that a sensory-motor experience facilitates the understanding of metaphorical expressions.

These findings suggest generalized patterns of experience that a qualitative analysis of verbo-gestural or audiovisual figurativity cannot address. However, it can account for closer insights into the "individual, subjective, and dynamic level of experience that characterizes any ad hoc uses" (Müller and Ladewig 2013, 300) of figurative meaning-making, and this refers both to production and comprehension. This idea becomes notably evident through the example of verbo-gestural figurativity. Expressing, for example, a verbo-gestural metaphor in a conversation, a speaker observably activates the experiential realm as a vital sensory-motor experience and thereby displays his or her subjective conceptualization of what he or she refers to metaphorically. This individual perspective is affective not only by virtue of what is depicted in the gesture, but also by how it is performed. In this regard, the respective quality of gestural performance expresses the speaker's subjective experience of the topic referred to (cf. Müller 1998, 2013, Kappelhoff and Müller 2011, 125).[26]

> [M]ovement *creates* the qualities that it embodies and that we experience; thus it is erroneous to think that movement simply takes place *in* space, for example. On the contrary, we formally create space in the process of moving; we qualitatively create a certain spatial character by the very nature of our movement – a large, open space, or a tight, resistant space, for example. (Sheets-Johnstone 2011, 124)

---

25 For a detailed explanation of Barsalou's understanding of grounded cognition and his theory of Perceptual Symbol Systems (PSS), see Barsalou 1999, 2008.

26 Drawing on Bühler's "*organon model*", Müller (2013, 200) considers gesture to fulfil the same three basic functions as language. With the example of a gesture that imitates drawing, Bühler implicitly touches upon this assumption. According to him, performing it one time joyfully and another time in a frightened or angry manner, the speaker in each of the named cases expresses a different attitude towards the act of drawing (cf. Bühler 1933, 39).

Maxine Sheets-Johnstone's quote clearly suggests that the qualitative experiential aspect is no pre-existing formal feature associated with a certain movement. To the contrary, it only emerges due to the dynamic unfolding of movement in its respective situational context. Applied to verbo-gestural figurativity, this suggests that metaphors and metonymies do not entail a specific affective or experiential quality ex ante. Instead, it is the emergent result of dynamic and embodied figurative meaning-making in a particular context.

Such a constructive account of embodied figurative meaning-making appears self-evident for face-to-face communication. In the case of audiovisual figurativity, however, it seems to be not so straightforward. Admittedly, audiovisual media neither displays comparable reciprocal conditions of interaction as does face-to-face communication, nor similar spontaneous or ad hoc uses of figurative meaning. From the viewers' perspective and with regard to their process of meaning-making, however, audiovisual compositions in their spatio-temporal unfolding can be considered analogous to gestures (cf. Müller and Kappelhoff 2018, Scherer, Greifenstein, and Kappelhoff 2014). They, too, give figurative experiential realms a perceptible form gestalt and thus 'express' an embodied experience that comes with an affective quality. Müller and Schmitt have illustrated this in a case study of a German political TV report on winners and losers of the financial crisis:

> [W]hile a voice-over is saying, "Business runs brilliantly" ("Die Geschäfte laufen glänzend"), a group of consultants is lifting sparkling glasses of champagne. Here, the sparkling glasses of champagne present the verbalized source domain of shimmering diamonds, and with this visual presentation of the metaphoric source domain, a highly specific sensory-motor experience of how "brilliant" businesses feel like is being evoked. (Müller and Schmitt 2015, 321)

From this perspective, the experiential ground of audiovisual figurative meaning is explicitly linked with the concrete media context and a viewer's experience in the process of watching than with generalized and dis-embodied experiences of conceptual structures. Proceeding from the particular interplay between the verbal level and the audiovisual composition or, more precisely, "between what is being said and how this is being staged audio-visually" (Müller and Schmitt 2015, 321), allows for reconstructing how audiovisual figurative meaning is activated and vitalized on the basis of embodied conceptualizations. Activation of figurativity thus provides a form-analytical access to how audiovisual compositions guide the viewer's attention towards those embodied conceptualizations that seem to be relevant for meaning-making in the respective audiovisual data.

3.5 Conclusion

The systematic overview of cognitive-linguistic perspectives on figurativity has shown that research on audiovisual figurativity is hitherto strongly informed by conceptual metaphor theory and thereby still struggles with the problem of circular reasoning (top down from assumed superordinate conceptual structures to their linguistic and audiovisual manifestations to inferences about the mind and body). Along with that, a differentiation between the levels of language as a system and of language use has not been made, and there has been just as little consideration of the media-specific properties of audiovisual compositions. Instead, audiovisual figurativity has primarily been treated as another piece of evidence for the existence and effectiveness of conceptual metaphor and metonymy, however, without reasonable empirical substantiation.

It can be noted that there is still a strong focus on language in cognitive-linguistic research on audiovisual figurativity and a persisting understanding of audiovisual images as mere illustrations or depictions. As a result, the audiovisual movement-image is considered in terms of a (static) image that is not at all questioned with regard to how it creates meaning but is instead reduced to its represented content. Along with this static understanding, audiovisual figurative meaning is regarded as a fixed product that is constituted by the sum of source and target domain (e.g., Forceville 2009a, 2009b, 2017). Both are suggested to be objectively instantiated in a particular modality, e.g., in language and audiovisual compositions, from which figurative meaning can thus be objectively extracted in terms of single elements (Forceville 2007b, 2008a, 2008b, 2009b, Eggertsson and Forceville 2009, Urios-Aparisi 2009, 2014, Yu 2009). Audiovisual figurative meaning-making is therefore not considered an enactive process on the part of the viewer but amounts to a rather passive – mostly even unconsciously defined – recognizing and processing of underlying and entrenched networks of meaning. This applies both to the cognitive aspect of comprehension and the affective aspect of embodied experience of (audiovisual) figurative meaning. Due to such a static conception of metaphor and metonymy, neither their temporal and multimodal unfolding over the course of a film or commercial, nor the involvement of the viewer in the establishing of figurativity, and thus as active constructor of meaning, are taken into account.

Therefore, theoretical approaches and empirical studies of figurativity from the realm of face-to-face communication provide a link with the investigation of audiovisual figurativity because they put its dynamic and constructive character at the heart of their examination (e.g., Cameron 2007, 2008b, 2010, 2011, Kappelhoff and Müller 2011, Müller and Ladewig 2013, Müller and Tag 2010). In this context, figurative meaning-making has turned out to be an ongoing process that emerges and unfolds over the course of time, across various interlocutors and articulatory modalities. Instead of drawing on static pre-existing prototypical sets of mental imagery, speakers are suggested to create figurative meaning ad hoc and within a concrete situation of use and continually elaborate it in speech and gesture as well as through interactive negotiation. The gestural embodiment of figurativity's experiential realm indicates vital subjective conceptualizations (cf. Cienki 2013, Cienki and Müller 2008a, 2008b, Müller 2008a, 2008b, 2013). In this respect, the quality of gestural performance suggests a specific sensory-motor experience of the experiential realm that makes figurative meaning available, i.e., present and vitalized (Kappelhoff and Müller 2011, Kolter et al. 2012, Müller and Ladewig 2013).

It seems that this dynamic and constructive account of figurative meaning-making has not found its way into cognitive-linguistic research on audiovisual figurativity, because the act of viewing audiovisual media is not considered as interactive as face-to-face communication. Nonetheless, figurative meaning-making in audiovisual media from a spectator's perspective plays out as a spatio-temporal experience in a similar manner to how it does for participants of a face-to-face interaction. The transfer of this dynamic and constructive account to audiovisual media thus allows for a reconstruction of the situated process of figurative meaning-making as it unfolds for the 'user', i.e., the viewer, and close to the situation of use, i.e., the audiovisual data.

Apart from cognitive linguistics, film and media studies as the pertinent disciplines for the investigation of meaning-making in audiovisual media in general have been concerned with figurativity. They also have a longstanding and far-reaching tradition of dealing with metaphor and metonymy, however, by displaying the same tendency towards prioritizing the former at the cost of the latter. The subsequent chapter will give a systematic overview of pertinent film-theoretical work and compatible perspectives on audiovisual figurativity. As will be shown, the majority of film-theoretical studies – in common with cognitive-linguistic research – exhibit a recurrent missing consideration of the media specifics of audiovisual images and instead display a strong focus on language.

4 Film-Theoretical Perspectives on Figurativity

In his cyber course on pictorial and multimodal metaphor, Charles Forceville (2007a Lecture 1, 11) states that "[w]hat constitutes a metaphor [...] is partly affected by the medium in which it occurs". Thereby, he is touching upon the question of media specificity with regard to figurative meaning-making. In this respect, audiovisual images had "more ways to establishing" similarity between "two things" compared to, for example, static images (Forceville 2007a Lecture 4, 2). Yet, it seems that what has been disregarded when it comes to the theoretical discussion of metaphor and metonymy in film is precisely film's media-specific properties. Concretely, previous as well as recent film-theoretical and media studies approaches have mostly drawn on linguistic theories of metaphor and metonymy or conceptual metaphor theory in order to define the two and their particularities in audiovisual media. In this context, they most often proceed from contrasting film with language, and figurativity in film with figurativity in language respectively.

This chapter gives an outline of different approaches to audiovisual figurativity from a film-theoretical perspective. Thereby, it will not proceed chronologically but systematically both by bringing together approaches with similar assumptions and by arranging the individual sections according to their degree of media specificity (from low to high). In this light, semiotic and rhetorical accounts will be initially introduced and discussed. They conceive of metaphor and metonymy as general principles of figuration in film or as rhetorical devices serving a film's elocution and thus do not take into account the specificity of the medium of film. The subsequent section presents approaches that predominantly draw on relevant linguistic and cognitive theories of metaphor and metonymy. The side effect of such application of figurativity in language to film is that the film's media specificity is disregarded or limited to the level of audiovisual representation. In contrast, the following section addresses approaches looking at figurativity in the context of temporality, movement, perception, and experience in the medium of film. In so doing, they exceed mere representation and also include the media-specific aspect of the spectator's film experience. On this basis, the last section concludes with recent approaches that relate meaning-making in film decidedly to the modulation of affects. They thus not only display an outstanding degree of media specificity but also of compatibility with the notion of multimodal figurativity that has been outlined in the previous chapter.

https://doi.org/10.1515/9783110578782-004

4.1 Figuration and Illocution: Figurativity and the Film Code

Semiotic film theory displays a fairly broad understanding of metaphor and metonymy. In order to explain meaning constitution in film, Christian Metz, as one of the prominent representatives of film semiotics, has "sought to locate the process of understanding not at the level of the image, but at the level of the syntactic structure of a film text." (Kappelhoff and Greifenstein 2016, 185) In order to get to the heart of this structure, he draws on key notions and assumptions of structuralism, in particular Roman Jakobson's bipartite model of language (see Metz [1975] 1982, 174–182). In asking for what makes communication behavior and linguistic and non-linguistic messages meaningful, Jakobson ([1956] 1990) refers to Saussure's two axes of paradigm and syntagm. However, he himself deals with them in terms of the two fundamental operations of sign formation and their combination to larger units: selection and combination. While the selection of signs refers to interchangeable units that are associated through the principle of similarity, the combination of signs involves the successive and/or simultaneous connection of elements that are associated through the principle of contiguity (Jakobson 1990, 119–120; cf. Mittelberg 2010, 121). Jakobson relates these different modes of association, similarity and contiguity, to metaphor and metonymy:

> The development of a discourse may take place along two different semantic lines: one topic may lead to another either through their similarity or through their contiguity. The metaphoric way would be the most appropriate term for the first case and the metonymic way for the second, since they find their most condensed expression in metaphor and metonymy respectively. (Jakobson 1990, 129)

In saying so, Jakobson makes clear that he conceives of metaphor and metonymy not only as rhetorical devices, but most of all as two poles between which meaning emerges. According to him, however, "[t]he alternative predominance of one or the other of these two processes is by no means confined to verbal art. The same oscillation occurs in sign systems other than language" (Jakobson 1990, 130).

This is what Metz aims to address. In his work *The Imaginary Signifier* (1982), he follows Jakobson's focus on metaphor and metonymy of all figures "because [...] they are felt to exemplify more clearly than the others the 'pure' principles of similarity and contiguity respectively – that is, precisely those involved in the paradigm/syntagm distinction" (Metz 1982, 176). Like Jakobson, Metz is not concerned with "localised metaphors or metonymies that could be isolated" but rather with "metaphorical and metonymic operations" (Metz 1982, 151). For him, they are the fundamental figurative processes of signification in film, which is why "[...] producing an immediate list of the principal cinematic figures is not part of my aim" (Metz 1982, 172). Pursuing a psychoanalytic approach, he relates metaphor and metonymy to Freud's categories of 'condensation' and 'displacement' in order to explain how film projects the unconscious. This idea was already expressed by Jakobson himself (1990, 132) and was further developed by Lacan's ([1957] 1995) thesis that the unconscious is structured like a language. In the metaphorical formula of 'one thing in terms of another', condensation is at work as one significant is superimposed onto the other (Pagel 1989, 47–50, cf. Metz 1982, 235–244). Although meaning is thereby hidden and repressed, it nevertheless remains in its absence latently present: this is a moment of contact between primary and secondary processes (Pagel 1989, 47–50). On the other hand, the metonymical combination of elements along the signifying chain is displacement as it allows for saying something other than what is apparently at one's disposal (Metz 1982, 266–273). It is only in the constant movement from one signifier to another that meaning emerges instead of being present at a particular point in the chain (Lacan [1966] 1977, 153ff).

While Metz in the wake of Jakobson's theory still conceives of metaphor and metonymy as being equal and not super- or subordinated to each other, other semiotic approaches exclude metonymy from further examination in favor of metaphor. Thereby, in some cases even metaphor loses its single status and is categorically mixed with other figures of similarity. Jacques Gerstenkorn (1995), for instance, deals with metaphor only in the context of a 'metaphorical field' which encompasses operations being unified by the principle of creating resemblance. According to this view, Gerstenkorn (1995, 18, 86) subsumes different forms of analogy under the term metaphor, e.g., syllepsis, plays of echo, various kinds of comparison of actually incongruent things, entire films or film parables. Broadening the concept of metaphor in film to such an extent levels its specificity and turns it into a rather vague matter that is hardly distinguishable.

A counterapproach of the other extreme is Jean Mitry who argues that metaphor in film actually could not exist. As it was based on substitution, it would be impossible to occur in the case of concrete objects presented in a film: "In language, genuine or lexicalised metaphors only exist because words deal with concepts. Images deal with objects, however, with concrete facts which cannot take each other's place, but can only undergo a change of meaning." (Mitry 2000, 197) According to Mitry, metaphor is only to be found as a cognitive product on the part of the spectator.

> Film does not establish its significations with metaphors. It *builds* them by contrasting facts and actions in juxtapositions, created most often in editing and whose connotations always have to be deciphered. The metaphor is not *presented*; it only exists as such (its meaning) in the mind of the audience. (Mitry 2000, 197)

In these remarks, what is noticeable is the mention of the audience in the context of figurative meaning-making in film. The so far presented semiotically driven approaches have predominantly focused on how film signifies. In the wake of such a view, they consider figurativity as a structural element of film itself and thus implicitly suggest that meaning is constituted on film's own terms. This is to say that metaphor and metonymy are primarily located on the level of the filmic 'text' and of audiovisual representation respectively. At this point, Mitry brings in the spectator as an important factor involved in this process. Through his formulation of 'deciphering', however, a perspective on figurative meaning-making in film shows up that strongly focuses on the intention of the producer.[1] This aspect is a core argument of rhetorical accounts of figurativity in film that are subsequently introduced.

In contrast to the broad understanding of metaphor and metonymy put forward by the previous semiotic approaches, rhetorically-oriented conceptions focus on concrete instantiations, i.e., single figures. Roy Clifton's treatise *The Figure in Film* (1983), for instance, discusses metaphor, simile, metonymy, antithesis, etc. in different films in terms of rhetorical devices that are intentionally used and implemented by a filmmaker. When discussing metaphor in particular, he conceives of the vehicle as a director's comment, referred to as gloss, on the tenor, which is referred to as image (Clifton 1983, 87). By the notion of image, Clifton links metaphor (and also metonymy) in film explicitly to the level of audiovisual representation. The audience plays a role for figurative meaning-making in that it has the task to "complete the metaphor" (Clifton 1983, 87), i.e., to detect the director's gloss on the image. The marking of the figure is for Clifton both an indicator for its intentional implementation in film and an argument for its recognition by the viewer: "I merely assume that [...] a director has deliberately assembled what we see in the frame [...]." (Clifton 1983, 101) Accordingly, "the viewers must make the metaphor: they are given cement and gravel, but they must mix the concrete" (Clifton 1983, 87).

From these considerations, a hierarchical structure arises: as figurative meaning-making is primary linked to a director or producer of a film,[2] the viewer is first and foremost assigned a passive role as a recipient of meaning. This becomes particularly evident in Klaus Kanzog's (2001) remarks: he equates film with speech and defines it as a "visual speech act" (Kanzog 2001, 15) that addresses the viewer

---

1 Moreover, the notion of 'deciphering' implies that figurative meaning is objectively pre-existent in the audiovisual material before being recognized by the viewer. Such an understanding of film and other media as mere a packaging and transmitter of pre-existing messages (see Shannon and Weaver's 1949 outlined sender-receiver model of communication) both separates 'contents' from their mediality, and rules out the active participation of viewers in meaning-making.

2 The problem of if one single person acting as a film's producer can even be taken for granted will not be discussed here in great detail. For a critical remark on that question, see, e.g., Joost 2008, 85.

for the purpose of persuasive effects. Due to this rhetorical focus, the film's objective and meaningful existence is taken for granted beyond its situated experience by a spectator. In line with this, Kanzog refers to signification in film as meaning identification [*Bedeutungsfindung*] (Kanzog 2001, 14) and understanding on the part of the addressed recipient. As a result, he focuses exclusively on the level of audiovisual representation. This becomes particularly evident in his quotation of Hermann Barth who argues that in filmic discourse, verbal and iconic sign complexes are subject to rhetorical speech which is why the analysis should focus on what is conveyed and how it is represented (cf. Barth 1990, 16).

In this respect, i.e., concerning the manner of representation, Kanzog introduces metaphor and metonymy as elements of style elocution that shall shape the viewer's perception. As becomes apparent, his understanding of figurativity in film is clearly informed by speech act theory, especially when he writes that all images first of all have to be detected in their original meaning and only then are recognized according to their contextual situatedness (Kanzog 2001, 112). In saying so, Kanzog follows Searle's (1993) conception of a false, non-literal use of language in the case of figurative meaning resulting in a discrepancy that has to be decoded by an addressee in a meaningful way. As there is no lexicon for film, Kanzog argues that montage or camera work could establish figurative meaning by putting together two different objects. In order to be recognized and understood by the viewer, these combinations have to stand out as a particular mode of perception through camera work, editing, and montage (Kanzog 2001, 114f.).

This rather static and intentionally informed conception of audiovisual figurativity reappears in other rhetorical approaches to film, such as Gesche Joost's (2008), where it is elaborated with respect to the persuasion of the viewer. Joost aims at applying general rhetoric to film and outlining the respective film-specific communication techniques of an audiovisual rhetoric. As a result, her approach entails a clear focus on the production side and its intended effects on the viewer in terms of a tripartite communication process playing out between the rhetor, the medium, and the addressee (Joost 2008, 31). Metaphor and metonymy play a double role in Joost's approach: on the one hand, they are broadly defined as meaning-making operations (in Jakobson's sense) and reinforce her claim that film is fundamentally rhetorical, i.e., with regard to its structure (Joost 2008, 54–55). On the other hand, they are considered rhetorical figures in film, deliberately used by the filmic rhetor,[3] that evoke an intended effect on the spectator. As such, metaphor and metonymy

---

3 Joost (2008, 86–93) emphasizes that she does not conceive of the rhetor as an empirical person to whom one could individually ascribe specific intentions. Rather, the rhetor results from the sum of deliberate decisions taken by the people involved in the process of film production with respect to its intended effects on the viewer.

belong to a secondary system of argumentative and aesthetic patterns that the rhetor disposes of for successful communication (Jost 2008, 148–149).[4]

Joost's approach encapsulates the set of problems of all semiotic and rhetorical approaches to audiovisual figurativity that have been introduced in this chapter. Their focus on film's syntactic structure and the producer's intention as core parts of meaning constitution and affective resonances basically leaves the viewer out of the meaning-making process. Understood in a broad sense as basic figurative processes of meaning constitution in film, the conception of metaphor and metonymy is extended so much that it lacks media specificity. In the narrow sense, on the other hand, metaphor and metonymy are considered static elements of a catalog or cultural canon of forms. As a result, the temporal, attentional, and affective dynamics of figurativity do not come into view, which is also due to the fact that it is located on the level of audiovisual representation. It is precisely the static conception and the attribution to audiovisual representation that recur as characteristic features of approaches informed by linguistic and cognitive theories of figurativity which are subject of the following section.

4.2 Artistry and Cognitive Principle: Figurativity and Message Deciphering

In contrast to a broad and structural understanding, film- and media-theoretical approaches to be discussed below point to endeavors to justify audiovisual figurativity in the narrow sense and as a concept on its own. While insisting on the difference between its manifestation in audiovisual media and in language, many authors nevertheless draw on pertinent linguistic or cognitive theories of metaphor and metonymy in order to claim their audiovisual specificity. In the following, some selected exponents of this mentality will be introduced and outlined. Regardless of their respective theoretical orientation, all of the following share some recurrent central assumptions:

- their almost exclusive focus on metaphor over metonymy is mostly conceived of as an adjunct or secondary component of the former;
- audiovisual media settings are considered as unidirectional and intentionally informed communication, i.e., transfer of meaning from a filmmaking sender to a watching receiver;

---

4 Arne Scheuermann's (2009) account of film as a rhetorical design follows a similar line of argument: he conceives of audiovisual figurativity as an intentionally used tool of a filmmaker in order to elicit affective reactions on the part of the viewer.

– figurative meaning is ascribed to the level of audiovisual representation as a combination of two actually incompatible elements (reminiscent of rhetorical metaphor theory);
– figurativity's spatial and temporal fixation is understood in terms of a signifying unit.

Taken all together, figurative meaning is considered to be contained in audiovisual images in an objective form and is thus existentially independent of its perception by the viewers. This strong focus on form is due to the fact that the approaches to be discussed in the following still cling to the idea of metaphor and metonymy becoming manifest in words which is transferred to audiovisual images.

In his work *Metaphor and Film* (1990), Trevor Whittock tries to undertake a comprehensive theoretical discussion of what he calls 'cinematic metaphor'. The definition he gives at the beginning of his book already reveals the objective understanding outlined above: "Metaphor is usually defined as the presentation of one idea in terms of another, belonging to a different category, so that either our understanding of the first idea is transformed, or so that from the fusion of the two ideas a new one is created." (Whittock 1990, 5) Apart from the generalizing claim ("our understanding") that Whittock expresses at that point, what is remarkable is the notion of category. Obviously fed by the language-based idea of a lexicon of fixed significants and significates, it suggests a correspondence of audiovisual representation and 'reality', thereby disregarding both the level of use as against the systems level and the mediatization process in audiovisual media settings.

At another point, however, Whittock explicitly mentions it when justifying metaphor's existence in film: "Metaphor is encapsulated within the very film image itself" as a "clash between the object filmed and the manner of its filming" (Whittock 1990, 29, 35). In order to pre-empt the reproach of levelling metaphor's specificity as against other reasoning processes through such a broad definition, Whittock adds as sine qua non that metaphor has to "involve some transformation", i.e., the seeing as of the tenor in terms of the vehicle[5] (Whittock 1990, 5, 126). By saying so, he suggests a dynamic understanding of metaphorical meaning-making as a process based on a triadic structure: the emergence of

---

5 Whittock relies on Ivor A. Richards' (1936) terms 'vehicle' and 'tenor' as metaphor's two constitutive parts.

a mediating third entity on the basis of perceiving and conceiving one thing in terms of another.[6]

Metaphor, as "both [...] an operation of thought and [...] an artistic occurrence" (Whittock 1990, 129), still remains first and foremost tied to the filmmaker. Having translated his own cognitive seeing as into an "appropriate [film] image", he is the decisive factor for a receiver's successful interpretation of the metaphor by "[choosing] whether to accentuate the metaphor or to keep it discreet" (Whittock 1990, 29, 42). Due to such a complete focus on the producer and the psychological understanding of the process Whittock's conception of cinematic metaphor persists in the language-based (literary) idea of figurativity as intentional "artistic creativity" (Whittock 1990, 3). Coming up with ten "formulas", an overview of the varieties of cinematic metaphor, he moreover subsumes different figures of analogy under the label of metaphor, among others metonymy, synecdoche, or juxtaposition (Whittock 1990, 49–69). In doing so, he blurs metaphor's – and likewise metonymy's – particularity.

Noël Carroll's ([1994] 2001, 1996) reflections on film metaphor – he makes no mention of metonymy at all – display similar assumptions. Justifying its occurrence in film, he implicitly refers to the manifestation of metaphorical meaning in audiovisual images and the process of deciphering and identification by a spectator as put forward by Whittock: "[T]here are some *visual images* that function in the same way that verbal metaphors do and *whose point is identified* by a viewer in roughly the same way that the point of a verbal metaphor is identified by a reader or a listener" (Carroll 2001, 347; emphasis mine). Carroll even goes a step further and subordinates film metaphor to visual metaphor, arguing that both of them bring together two elements that in reality are physically incompatible. In this light, he looks to find a visual equivalent for the "grammatical devices" (Carroll 1996, 812) that create identity between the two elements in verbal metaphor. This visual counterpart of 'A *IS* B' in film is "homospatiality", i.e., the visual fusion of disparate elements "in one, spatially bounded, homogeneous entity" (Carroll 2001, 354). Carroll's primary focus on the visual manifestation ignores the inherent movement and temporality of audiovisual images[7] and thereby reduces metaphor in film to a spatially bound, static device that he claims to

---

6 This appears to be in line with what Müller (2008a, 23–32) calls the cognitive process of establishing metaphoricity. Whittock understands it in a similar way, yet without the dynamic aspects of temporal unfolding and changing degree of activation.

7 Notwithstanding his awareness of this neglect of media specificity, he states: "I see no reason to expect that film metaphors will possess some uniquely cinematic features that distinguish them from visual metaphors in other arts." (Carroll 1996, 821)

be "a central case – if not the most central case – of film metaphor" (Carroll 1996, 809).

Like Whittock, he conceives of metaphor in film from the perspective of an intentionally acting producer, the filmmaker. In order to be recognized and comprehended, metaphor's two disparate elements have to be visually perceptible and the filmmaker has to make them salient in order to draw the spectator's attention to them (Carroll 1996, 814). The correct consideration of the filmmaker's intentions concerning the meaning of the metaphor is, according to Carroll, primarily fed by the viewer's comparison between filmic context and reality: perceiving a semantic contradiction between the two necessarily precedes the context-bound, non-literal meaning. In that regard, Carroll's conception is reminiscent of Searle's (1979) pragmatic metaphor theory. This reference to pragmatics is reinforced by the set of felicity conditions – originally established by Austin (1962) and Searle (1969) for speech acts in general – that Carroll (1996, 815–817) develops for matching filmmakers' and viewers' assumptions in respect to metaphorical meaning in film. Viewed in this light, the process disappears behind a list of conditions whose cognitive reality and entire processing contrasts with Carroll's claim of a recognition "simply by looking, rather than [...] some process of reading, decoding or the like" (Carroll 1996, 814).

While Whittock's and Carroll's approaches to – primarily – metaphor are still strongly informed by classical linguistic conceptions and theories of figurativity, most recent film-theoretical accounts address it especially in the light of the embodied cognition theory. Starting from the question of how meaningful content beyond the spoken word is conveyed in film, they are especially interested in – again primarily – metaphor's property to express abstract and complex meaning on the basis of embodied experience. It is, among others, strategies of medial emotionalizing that these approaches seek to explain and for that refer to cognitive theories of figurativity. The tenet of conceptual metaphor theory serves as their key reference: human thought and action is fundamentally structured by conceptual metaphors and metonymies that make abstract things – such as emotions – understandable in terms of concrete images and experiences (Lakoff and Johnson 1980, 1999, Lakoff and Turner 1989, Kövecses 2000). The following approaches rely on audiovisual manifestations of such conceptual structures in order to explain processes of nonverbal meaning-making and emotionalizing in film.

By her concept of audiovisual metaphor (2005, 2008, 2010, 2016) Kathrin Fahlenbrach intends to account for the activation of feelings on the part of viewers watching a film. She conceives of metaphorical meaning-making as an intermediate process that cognitively fuses impressions from perception, thought, bodily experiences, and feelings evoked by the film to a coherent meaning (Fahlenbrach 2010, 69). According to her, film techniques, such as camera, sound, or montage, stage conceptual metaphors by audiovisually activating associative schemes and stimulus-response patterns that underlie these conceptual metaphors (Fahlenbrach 2007, 332, 339). They are recognized by the spectators instinctively and activate on an unconscious level the respective (cultural) metaphorical meaning pattern with its inherent "bodily and cognitive associations" (Fahlenbrach 2008, 86). As such, Fahlenbrach argues that the famous staircase scene from Stanley Kubrick's THE SHINING (UK/USA 1980) instantiates the emotion metaphor of FEAR IS AN OPPONENT IN A STRUGGLE[8]: while Wendy, stammering and screaming in a high-pitched voice, backs away from Jack, he, yelling at her aggressively, quietly and insistently propels her through the room and upstairs (Fahlenbrach 2008, 94). Fahlenbrach furthermore brings in the constant camera shifts between point-of-view shots of Jack's face, expressing total insanity, and Wendy's face, expressing mortal fear, in order to substantiate the consistent audiovisual manifestation of the underlying conceptual metaphor. This contrasting audio- and visual juxtaposition of Jack and Wendy through audiovisual techniques is suggested to give the pre-symbolic conceptual metaphor a perceptible gestalt that elicits all its associative schemata, stimulus-response patterns, and symbolic meanings. As a result, the corresponding deeply rooted conceptual metaphor is activated immediately on the part of the viewers and can therefore take its full cognitive, perceptual, and emotional effect on them (Fahlenbrach 2010, 281).

With her cognitive model, Fahlenbrach adopts central assumptions and thus also problematic aspects of CMT: she prioritizes the conceptual systems level against the level of actual use. The embodied meaning she is alluding to thereby amounts to cognitively stored experiences (in contrast to Johnson's "felt qualities of meaning" [2007, 17]). This priority of the conceptual system makes metaphor a symbolic instantiation of superordinate cognitive deep structures. Following CMT, Fahlenbrach looks for these manifestations as reifications on the level of audiovisually represented bodies and spaces. Due to her top-down perspective, her subjects of interest are 'common' and often used conceptual metaphors in film as well as 'typical' patterns of their audiovisual manifestation (Fahlenbrach 2010, 43). This necessarily entails that the identified audiovisual metaphors remain as broad formulations that are rather abstract with regard to their meaning for the film and the viewer.

---

8 Fahlenbrach traces this metaphor back to the ontological metaphor of EMOTIONS ARE THINGS and to the force-schema, defined by Kövecses (2000) as the basic structure in all emotion concepts (Fahlenbrach 2010, 85).

The viewer as an agent is not the main area of interest for Fahlenbrach's idea of metaphorical meaning-making. She develops her argument on the basis of unconsciously effective meaning structures and associative networks that film producers use intentionally to evoke particular emotions and to trigger a particular understanding of things or characters in the film. Maarten Coëgnarts and Peter Kravanja (2012, 2014, 2015) put forward a similar line of argument when they align themselves with David Bordwell's (2008) theoretical concept of the poetics of cinema and his key issue of "how [...] filmmakers use the aesthetic dynamics of the film medium to achieve particular effects on spectators" (Coëgnarts and Kravanja 2012, 2). Based on this unilateral directedness of meaning-making in film, metaphor for them is a fixed and representational object that the filmmaker can intentionally apply in order to convey an abstract meaning of issues and actions to the spectator.

Coëgnarts and Kravanja (2012, 2014) draw on Lakoff and Johnson's postulate that people systematically conceptualize abstract domains by means of mappings from concrete, bodily-based domains and therefore take up the idea of image schemas in order to transfer them to film. According to them, metaphorical meaning-making in film is grounded in recurrent basic schemata about which people have sensory-motor experiences and bodily knowledge. This knowledge in turn is extended to higher-order, disembodied categories that lack concrete features in order to understand them. For instance, in Michelangelo Antonini's film THE PASSENGER (IT/FR/ES 1975), Coëgnarts and Kravanja (2012) identify the PASSAGE OF TIME IS MOTION IN SPACE metaphor as a solution to the problem of innovatively conveying a flashback to the spectator. According to them, Antonini uses a lateral movement of the camera[9] for activating the SOURCE-PATH-GOAL schema that underlies the conceptual metaphor of TIME IS MOTION IN SPACE. Due to this deeply entrenched concrete meaning structure,[10] they argue, the spectator is enabled to make full sense of the respective scene when the protagonist switches his identity. This meaning-making process is caused by the filmmaker and his intention: he aimed at conveying and representing the passage of time in this way (i.e., as motion in space) and thereby shapes the spectator's understanding of time in a particular manner.

---

9 Thereby, the movement from an initial point A to an ending location B serves as the source for the target domain 'passing of time' (Coëgnarts and Kravanja 2012, 5).

10 Coëgnarts and Kravanja adopt Lakoff and Turner's (1989, 129) argument that it is conceptual metaphor's and metonymy's entrenchment that makes them most effective: "Because of the strong connection with our bodies and daily lives, these schemas are often left unnoticed, applied without contemplation or even awareness. As preconceptual, highly schematic Gestalts, they function beneath the level of consciousness and prior to theoretical reflection." (Coëgnarts and Kravanja 2012, 15)

All approaches that have been introduced in this section are informed by linguistic or cognitive theories of figurativity, giving rise to minor nuances in their respective conception. While Whittock focuses on artistic creativity and Carroll stresses figurativity as a pragmatic proposal of some way of seeing, both Fahlenbrach and Coëgnarts and Kravanja highlight its cognitive basis as a central and universal principle that makes felicity conditions redundant. Notwithstanding this, all of them share the idea of audiovisual figurative meaning becoming manifest and reified on the level of audiovisual representation. This constricted perspective makes a static meaningful entity the typical case and disregards film's inherent temporal, attentional, and affective dynamics. In contrast, the following section addresses approaches looking at figurativity in the context of temporality, movement, perception, and experience in the medium of film.

4.3 Intellectual Shock and Affective Fusion: Figurativity and Viewers' Participation

Even though the approaches to be discussed in this section rarely mention metonymy and instead focus on metaphor, they nevertheless apply to both of them as they deal with the principle of bringing two kinds of things together in a situated context. In doing so, they take primarily a view that focuses on the qualitative experience of temporally unfolding movement. In contrast to static and fixed entities of figurative meaning that were put at the heart of the afore-outlined approaches, the following conceptions shift the focus to meaning-making in the media-specific experience of temporally unfolding audiovisual compositions. Starting from the basic question of how a movement sensation in film emerges from successively running images, provides a remarkable and fruitful springboard as it applies to both film in general and figurativity in particular.

In his essay *A Dialectic Approach to Film Form*, the Soviet film director and theorist Sergej Eisenstein ([1929] 1951a, 45) puts forward a "dynamic philosophy of things: Being – as a constant evolution from the interaction of two contradictory opposites. Synthesis – arising from the opposition between thesis and antithesis". Just as "[i]n nature we never see anything isolated, but everything in connection with something else [...]",[11] Eisenstein argues, the sensation of movement in cinema does not result from perceiving two immobile images next to each other, but on top of one another (Eisenstein 1951a, 45, 49). In saying so, he

---

[11] This is a quote from Johann Wolfgang von Goethe that precedes Eisenstein's explanations with regard to the dialectic principle.

suggests that meaning in film is not ex ante entailed in cinematic representation, but that it emerges from the formal composition of the film through montage. The process of meaning-making thus arises from the viewer's experience of the two images' mutual relatedness in terms of movement: instead of following each other separately, they dynamically superimpose onto one another in the process of film-viewing.

This makes implicit reference to the establishing of a triadic structure in figurative meaning-making, i.e., seeing one kind of thing as another with "two concepts or domains [...] activated in parallel" (Müller 2008a, 26). Like Eisenstein has done in regard to the sensation of movement from two images,[12] Müller clearly distinguishes the triadic process of seeing as from a unilateral transfer of meaning. In this respect, there appear clear correspondences in the dynamic and processual understanding of meaning-making between Eisenstein's montage theory and the dynamic approach to audiovisual figurative meaning-making put forward here.

Eisenstein's remarks on montage furthermore already hint at – albeit in regard to the temporality of audiovisual images – the rejection of an exclusive focusing on the level of audiovisual representation:

> The movement within these building-block shots, and the consequent length of the component pieces, was then considered as rhythm. A completely false concept! This would mean the defining of a given object solely in relation to the nature of its external course. (Eisenstein 1951a, 48)

He employs this line of thought explicitly on audiovisual figurativity in his essay *Dickens, Griffith, and the Film Today* ([1944] 1951b). Informed by his strong focus on the dialectic principle of dynamics, Eisenstein orients his entire theoretical thinking on montage to conflict. For him, it is only the "collision of independent shots – shots even opposite to one another" (Eisenstein 1951a, 49) that makes for the emergence of new meaning. This is the essence of Eisenstein's theory of intellectual montage, and it also shapes his understanding of figurative meaning-making in film.[13] In his discussion of David W. Griffith's parallel montage, Eisenstein criticizes him for having misunderstood "that the region of metaphorical and imagist writing appears in the sphere of *montage juxtaposition*, not of

---

12 What is more, Eisenstein's differentiation implicitly spells out the difference between metaphor and simile that has often been confused by some theorists (see Section 4.1): instead of comparing two things in the sense of putting them *next* to each other and thereby maintaining their differences, metaphor conflates particular aspects of both and on that basis creates – via *superimposition* – a "new, higher dimension" (Eisenstein 1951a, 49).
13 With that said, he however restricts the phenomenon formally.

representational montage pieces" (Eisenstein 1951b, 241). In Eisenstein's eyes, Griffith is at fault for having translated the metaphor in "an isolated picture" and not in "the structure, nor [...] the harmonic recurrence of montage expressiveness" (Eisenstein 1951b, 241).

Clearly dissociating metaphor from the level of audiovisual representation,[14] Eisenstein's account likewise contrasts with various recent (cognitively-informed) approaches of audiovisual metaphor and metonymy, e.g., Forceville (2017), Fahlenbrach (2016), or Coëgnarts and Kravanja (2014). Instead of a pre-established meaningful entity, he considers figurative meaning-making as an emergent process that is based on the spectator's experience of audiovisual compositions in the process of film-viewing. This dynamic account and the consideration of media specificity make him compatible with the dynamic view on metaphor as proposed by Müller (2008a, 2011). With metaphor's formal restriction to the "*juxtaposition of shots*" as making for "*an arrangement of a new qualitative element, a new image, a new understanding*" (Eisenstein 1951b, 245), he however disregards the multiple forms and patterns of audiovisual figurativity to play out.

In respect of the relevance of Eisenstein's montage theory for the conception of audiovisual figurativity as put forward in this book, it is important to note that his thoughts on intellectual montage are a further development of his montage of attractions (or expressive montage; see Eisenstein [1924] 1982). In this regard, he has primarily emphasized the attentional and emotional impact of the "juxtaposition of facts" on the viewers. This emotional effectiveness of the movement of collision is informed by theater: Eisenstein conceives of the expressive movements of actors at the theatre and of expressive movements of the montage of attractions in film as equal because both address the audience affectively. As such, they are both expression and affective experience at the same time: "[T]his montage of movements as a whole also produces [...] the visual effect of the emotion supposedly experienced." (Eisenstein 1982, 19) The "new image" and "new understanding" (Eisenstein 1951b, 245) resulting from the juxtaposition of shots can thus be conceived of as being grounded in its affective expressivity.

It is this conflation of experiencing and understanding that the French philosopher Gilles Deleuze elaborates on in the chapter "Thought and Cinema" of his book *The Time-Image* ([1985] 2008) in relation to meaning-making in film and metaphor. Drawing on Eisenstein's dialectic account, he outlines the two already mentioned aspects in greater detail as two moments of the interaction (or 'circuit'

---

14 "[F]or the *imagist* and *extra-life-like* (or *sur*realist) 'manipulation' of film-shots there must be *an abstraction of the lifelike representation.*" (Eisenstein 1951b, 242) in Deleuze's terms) between the audiovisual movement-image and the viewer.[15] "According to Eisenstein, the first moment goes from the image to thought, from the percept to the concept." (Deleuze 2008, 152) The perceptual experience of distinct images or components within the image that manifests itself as a shock has an intellectual effect; it forces the spirit to think. The process unfolds from the "I FEEL" to the "cinematographic I THINK: the whole as subject" (Deleuze 2008, 153). This first moment is what Eisenstein has referred to as new image or new understanding – the intellectual, or cognitive process. The second moment concerns the inverse direction of the first one: "[It] goes from the concept to the affect, or [...] returns from thought to the image" in order to re-provide the intellectual process with an "affective charge" (Deleuze 2008, 154). Deleuze underlines that both moments are inextricably linked with each other and that both are of equal rank:

> The organic has as correlate the pathetic. The highest form of consciousness in the work of art has as correlate the deepest form of the subconscious, following a 'double process' or two coexisting moments. In this second moment, we no longer go form the movement-image to the clear thinking of the whole that it expresses; we go from a thinking of the whole which is presupposed and obscure to the agitated, mixed-up images which express it. (Deleuze 2008, 154)

This second moment that Deleuze has also referred to as an "internal monologue, a drunken monologue working through figures, metonymies, synecdoches, metaphors [...]" (2008, 154), indicates the affective impact of montage expressiveness as outlined by Eisenstein. In a third step, Deleuze brings together the two mentioned moments in the context of discussing metaphor. Firstly dissociating himself from a language-informed understanding of the cinematic image and pointing out its nature as a movement-image,[16] he argues the case for cinema's capacity for metaphor. For him, this capacity is not constituted through the technical superimposition of two distinct images, but through their affective fusion due to shared harmonics (Deleuze 2008, 155). Apart from this form, cinema is however also able to give rise to metaphors in the image and without montage. At this point, Deleuze again refers back to Eisenstein and his ideas on affective

---

15 According to Deleuze (2008, 152), his analysis of Eisenstein's dialectic account can be considered to be valid for the entire cinema of the movement-image.
16 A detailed discussion of Deleuze's concept of the movement-image in the light of a media-specific theoretical framework for cinematic metaphor is given by Müller and Kappelhoff (2018, Part 1).

composition, and differentiates between extrinsic and intrinsic[17] metaphors (Deleuze 2008, 156).

Regardless of its form, what remains the same and of importance in both cases is: "[T]he composition does not simply express the way in which the character experiences himself, but also expresses the way in which the author and the viewer judge him" (Deleuze 2008, 156). It is this conflation of intellectual and affective processes that leads Deleuze to the insight that metaphor "integrates thought into the image" (Deleuze 2008, 156). In this way, the circuit between the film and the spectator is fully established:

> The complete circuit thus includes the sensory shock which raises us from the images to conscious thought, then the thinking in figures which takes us back to the images and gives us an affective shock again. Making the two coexist, joining the highest degree of consciousness to the deepest level of unconsciousness: this is the dialectical automaton. (Deleuze 2008, 156)

Metaphor thus represents or inheres the "identity of concept and image", i.e., "[t]he concept is in itself in the image, and the image is for itself in the concept" (Deleuze 2008, 156). Deleuze relates this principle of bundling affective experience and meaning-making in metaphor also to film in general, as art of the masses: it "posits the unity of nature and man, of the individual and the mass" (Deleuze 2008, 157).

Two aspects in Eisenstein's and Deleuze's theoretical thoughts on metaphor in film are of key importance for the dynamic approach to audiovisual figurativity put forward in this book: the media specificity and – strongly linked to it – their take on the affective dimension. By their dissociation of the level of representation and of equating the cinematic image with a verbal utterance, Eisenstein and Deleuze focus on audiovisual images as movement-images that induce an immediate experience of movement. In doing so, an aspect comes up for the subject matter of audiovisual figurativity that is still highly underrepresented, not only in cognitive-linguistic approaches, but also in film-theoretical accounts. Though Eisenstein and Deleuze refer their remarks to metaphor in particular, they can be conceived of as likewise being applicable to metonymy. In their understanding, figurativity as a fixed product of a translation to audiovisual representation is abandoned and gains processual nature as a becoming that is nowhere contained objectively but occurs and unfolds in the circuit between viewer and film. In this respect, Eisenstein and Deleuze account for the temporal dynamics of audiovisual figurativity (and audiovisual movement-images in general).

---

17 "[...] where a single image captures the harmonics of a different image which is not shown" (Deleuze 2008, 156)

Their dynamic perspective involves conceiving of the perceptual experience of audiovisual images as an affecting process that takes place on the part of the spectator in the process of film-viewing, and they relate this affective dimension to metaphor. Among other things, Deleuze underlines that he considers affective and cognitive processes to be at work in metaphor in equal measure. Thereby, he is consistent with Lakoff and Johnson's (1980) definition of an interplay of "experiencing and understanding" that cognitive metaphor theories often modified in terms of prioritizing understanding towards experiencing. Moreover, Eisenstein and Deleuze put forward a very specific take on affectivity that arises from the concrete experience of audiovisual movement-images and on the part of the viewer. Such a conception contrasts with the idea of cognitively stored disembodied emotional schemata as held especially by cognitive theories of metaphor and metonymy and is rather in line with Johnson's embodied account of "felt qualities of meaning" (2007, 17). As such, Eisenstein's and Deleuze's ideas provide the interface for film-theoretical perspectives (on figurativity) that focus on the aspect of meaning-making through embodied affective experience and will be the subject of the following section.

4.4 Double Vision and Cinematic Expressivity: Figurativity and Embodied Experience

The interplay of affective and cognitive processes in audiovisual figurativity brought up by Eisenstein and explicitly emphasized by Deleuze is based on the conception of audiovisual images as movement-images that – in their temporal unfolding in the process of film-viewing – are realized as subjective bodily sensations on the part of the viewers. In this regard, the aspect of affectivity in audiovisual images and its role for the emergence of meaning come into play from a film-theoretical perspective. The question regarding the link between affective and meaning-making processes provides an interface for audiovisual figurativity in particular and meaning construction in audiovisual media in general:

> If metaphor links two different realms of experience, then the processes of forming metaphors should open up a way to access the processes of fictionalization as arrangements of film experiences, which spectators concretely traverse in the process of seeing and hearing. (Kappelhoff and Greifenstein 2016, 184)

The approaches that are to be introduced and discussed in the following are consistent with the dynamic approach to audiovisual figurativity proposed in this book in that they conceive of meaning to emerge through the interplay of various expressive modalities, unfolding as a temporal process whose expressive qualities are perceived and embodied. Even though these approaches may not always refer explicitly to figurativity itself, they nevertheless apply to it by their idea of a strong intertwining of sensuousness and meaningfulness, experiencing and understanding.

The starting point is the stronger orientation of film and media studies towards research regarding emotion and embodied cognition over the last years. The central question is, among others, which kind of interrelation exists between the affective impact of audiovisual media and the representations or contents emerging in the process of viewing. What thereby comes into view is an actively involved spectator who constructs meaning on the spot, i.e., in the very encounter with audiovisual images. Cognitively informed approaches link such a 'poiesis of film-viewing' (Müller and Kappelhoff 2018) first and foremost to universal schemata of everyday perception, neuronal operation processes, and causal-logical conjunctions in terms of stimulus-response patterns (Kappelhoff and Greifenstein, 185–186). In contrast, embodiment and immersion approaches suggest a physiological sensation of audiovisual images that becomes manifest as viewers' concrete bodily experience and thereby only gives rise to meaningfully arranged audiovisual representations.

The cinema and media theorist Vivian Sobchack (1990, 1992, 2004) advocates such an embodied approach to meaning-making in audiovisual media. She, too, highlights the dynamics of the audiovisual image that Eisenstein (1982) has touched upon in his montage theory and that Deleuze (2008) elaborates on with his notion of the movement-image. Clearly distinguishing the difference between the mechanic conditions for the emergence of a movement impression from the integral dynamic experience of cinematic movement, she stresses: "The always presently inscribing and intentionally mobile cinema [...] can never only objectively or transcendentally Be for us – because it is also always subjectively and existentially Becoming before us." (Sobchack 1990, 24) In order to clarify this process of constant becoming that unfolds between viewers and film, Sobchack makes extensive reference to Maurice Merleau-Ponty's *Phenomenology of Perception* ([1945] 1962). When she refers to the process of film-viewing as the "dialectics of double vision" (Sobchack 1990), she is adopting his idea of the bodily here-and-now situatedness within the world and transfers it to cinema. Merleau-Ponty's conception turns explicitly against a solipsistic, logical, and disembodied idea of meaning-making. Instead he proceeds from the assumption that human beings are always related to their environment in a bodily manner and that therefore making (literally) sense of the world precedes higher-order cognition and logic.

Applied to the process of film-viewing, this means that the spectator's perceptual experience is related to and intimately linked to cinematic movement, i.e., the temporal unfolding of audiovisual images. That is to say, in the moment of watching a film the spectator is not considered a passively receiving subject, separated from the film object. Instead, Sobchack attributes a body both to film[18] and to the spectator and defines the process of film-viewing as their intersubjective and intercorporeal encounter from which meaning emerges. According to her, film articulates a specific view and sense of the world that becomes bodily real for the viewer as if it were his or her own experience[19]:

> We can *see* the visible and objective body of another who is *looking* at the world or ourselves, and *understand* that objective body as also a body-subject – whose *sight* is as intentional and meaningful as our own. What is so unique about the cinema's "viewing view," however, is that it presents and represents the activity of vision not merely as it is *objectively seen* by us, but also as it is *introceptively lived* by another. (Sobchack 1990, 25)

It is this dialectics of film experience that Sobchack is alluding to when she writes: "Watching a film, we can see the seeing as well as the seen, hear the hearing as well as the heard, and feel the movements as well as see the moved." (1992, 10) This dialectics that she has above formulated characteristically as conflation of *seeing and understanding* provides a parallel to figurative meaning-making[20]: in the sensation of a world "as immediate experience mediated by an 'other'" (Sobchack 1992, 10), in cinema's foreign view that is experienced as if it were one's own, resides the essence of metaphor described by Lakoff and Johnson (1980, 5) as seeing something *as if* it were something else (cf. Kappelhoff and Greifenstein 2016, 188). Note that Sobchack's conception of embodied experience differs fundamentally from the cognitive understanding of embodiment as pre-existing mentally stored perceptual schemata and experiential patterns. The concrete bodily conflation of two distinct sensations that Sobchack is referring to is the emergent outcome of a dynamic process of double vision, no schema that is being processed as a result of recognition and cognitive understanding. That is to say, Sobchack puts experiencing first, i.e., before understanding, as did Merleau-Ponty. Such a grounding of meaning-making in bodily experience is in

---

18 "The 'film's body' is not visible in the film except for its intentional agency and diacritical motion. It is not anthropomorphic, but it is also not reducible to the cinematic apparatus (in the same way that we are not reducible to our material physiognomy); it is discovered and located only reflexively as a quasi-subjective and embodied 'eye' that has a discrete – if ordinarily prepersonal and anonymous – existence." (Sobchack 2004, 66)

19 Merleau-Ponty (1962) has recognized this reciprocity, i.e., the conflation of expression and experience, also in the expressive behavior of interlocutors in face-to-face communication.

20 Elsewhere, Sobchack has explicitly pointed out the link between cinematic experience and figurative meaning-making: "This relation between the literal sensible body and metaphor as sensible figure is central to both our understanding of cinematic intelligibility and of the cinesthetic subject who is moved and touched by going to the movies [...]" (Sobchack 2004, 68).

accord with Müller's (2008a, 2011) dynamic view on metaphor and the dynamic approach to audiovisual figurativity proposed in this book.

Other exponents of a dynamic and embodied account of meaning-making in film (e.g., Barker 2009, Marks 2000, Voss 2011) follow Sobchack's line of argument and extend it theoretically and analytically. In this light, Hermann Kappelhoff's (2004) concept of *expressive movement* is of particular relevance as it addresses the embodied perception and intersubjectivity of cinematic movement in greater detail. Starting from a cultural historical perspective, he has extensively examined and developed it for the theoretical and analytical description of film experience. In brief, he traces expressive movement back to the melodrama of the late eigtht-eenth century, to classical film-theoretical accounts (Balázs [1924] 2010, Eisenstein 1982, Münsterberg [1916] 2002), to psychological, linguistic, and anthropological theories, and to concepts from philosophical aesthetics and the theory of arts (e.g., Bühler 1933, Plessner [1941] 1970, Simmel 1995). According to Kappelhoff, what all of these share is the idea of the close interrelation of movement perception and affective experience. As he suggests, aesthetic and acting theories of the eigthteenth century have initially attributed this interplay to the actors and their expressive bodily behavior: through facial expression, gesture, and body movements of the actors on the stage spectators were considered to be moved affectively (Kappelhoff 2004, 63–83; see also Greifenstein and Kappelhoff 2014). Hence, this affective quality does not inhere in the characters or in the plot presented on stage but in the becoming visible of sentiments, moods, and atmospheres in the movements of the actors. By the rational aesthetic construction and performance of actors' move-ments along with the visualization of affect in the act of perception, the audience becomes bodily addressed and reacts with real tears (Kappelhoff 2004, 63–83).

As Kappelhoff demonstrates, classical film theory later on applies the concept of expressive movement also to the aesthetic composition of film scenes. Compared to the human being in everyday life, Hugo Münsterberg underlines that film has exten-sive possibilities of emotionalizing beyond the body: "While the human individual [...] has hardly any other means than the bodily expressions to show his emotions and moods", film disposes of the "additional expression of the feeling through the medium of the surrounding scene, through background and setting, through lines and forms and movements" (Münsterberg 2002, 102, 103). As a result, expressive movement encompasses not only "dynamics of obvious movement (e.g., movement of actors and objects on screen, camera movement)" but also "more complex forms of transformation (e.g., lighting, rhythmic arrangements of shot lengths, acoustics)" (Bakels 2014, 2052). Both are conceived of as aesthetic means that "aim at shaping the feelings of a heterogeneous and anonymous audience" (Bakels 2014, 2051).

On that extensive historical basis, Kappelhoff (2004) makes the process of embodied experience in film-viewing that Sobchack refers to theoretically and analytically graspable and useable through the concept of *cinematic expressive movement*. Through his conception of the perceptual experience as a dimension of cinematographic or cinematic movement that unfolds temporally he takes an aspect into account to which Sobchack has been paying little attention: time. She indeed has underlined the dynamics of cinematic movement as being inherent to the medium of film, but does not follow up on this idea with regard to the aspect of time. However, it is through and within the temporal unfolding that cinematic expressive movement and the affective experience of viewers take shape. Drawing on Bela Balázs, who already in 1924 had pointed to the link between affective experience and the experience of the temporal structure of the cinematic image, Kappelhoff explains: "Only in the film image, do the movements [...] become the entirety of an expressive movement" which in turn "refers to the time in which the transformations of the cinematic image structure the unfolding perceptive sensations on the part of the spectator" (Kappelhoff and Müller 2011, 136).

Although in Kappelhoff's (2004) concept of cinematic expressive movement there is no explicit mention of figurative meaning-making, it nevertheless displays fundamental points of contact. It does not conceive of the audiovisual image as a represented world of objects but first and foremost as a medial staging and structuring of a specific perceptual experience. That is to say, it considers embodied affective experience as the basis for the emergence of meaning in film. It thus shows clear references to Deleuze's and Eisenstein's dynamic understanding of figurativity in film and its inherent interplay of affective and cognitive processes. At the same time, the dynamic and embodied conception of meaning-making corresponds to cognitive-linguistic dynamic views on metaphor as proposed by Müller (2008a, 2008b, 2011, Müller and Tag 2010) and Cameron (2007, 2010, 2011). With its strong focus on embodied experience as the basis for meaning constitution, the concept of cinematic expressive movement conveys what Lakoff and Johnson (1980) have defined as the essence of metaphor: experiencing and understanding one thing literally *in the sense* of something else.

In this regard, the embodied film-theoretical approaches that have been discussed in this section align with the conception of multimodal figurativity as it was previously developed (see Chapters 1 and 3). The developed relevance of the temporal dynamics, processual emergence, and embodied grounding of figurative meaning-making finds a fruitful correspondence in the concept of cinematic expressive movement (Kappelhoff 2004) in order to be applied to the analysis of audiovisual figurativity. As a result, the process of the audiovisual activation and making present of metaphorical and metonymical experiential realms in its temporal unfolding is conceived of as inhering affective qualities that are bodily experienced by viewers. This combined way of thinking seems especially interesting with regard to political campaign commercials as with their short-term and persuasive character, they aim at the highest possible degree of intelligibility, appeal, and addressability.

4.5 Conclusion

The systematic overview of film-theoretical perspectives on figurativity has shown that the impact of media-specific properties on figurativity as postulated by Charles Forceville (2009a) is – similar to cognitive linguistics – only marginally taken into consideration in film and media studies. The audiovisual image is considered either language-like as an utterance or picture-like as a sequence of static images from which figurativity can be objectively extracted in terms of single elements. Film appears no better than a communication tool of a filmmaker in order to convey particular ways of seeing and thinking or effects to the recipient. For this purpose, figurativity seems to be an appropriate stylistic device that – if properly implemented by the filmmaker, and correctly recognized and deciphered by the spectator – can have an extensive intellectual and affective impact. Hence, also from a film-theoretical perspective, metaphor and metonymy remain static meaningful entities in a filmmaker's hands. That way, dynamic aspects of figurative meaning-making are not considered in the first place: neither its temporal and multimodal unfolding, nor the involvement of the viewer and his or her situatedness in the context of film experience are taken into account.

In semiotic and rhetorical accounts, metaphor and metonymy are conceived of as general principles of figuration in film (Metz 1982, Mitry 2000) or as rhetorical devices serving a film's elocution (Clifton 1983, Kanzog 2001) whereby they are extended in such a way or associated with other stylistic devices that they lose their specificity. As such, they appear as stylistic elements of persuasive communication at the filmmaker's disposal in order to convey his own perspective or particular idea of an issue to the spectators. As a result, figurativity in audiovisual media is recurrently located on the level of representation; a conception that persists in approaches based on cognitive and linguistic theories of metaphor and metonymy (such as Carroll 1996, 2011, Coëgnarts and Kravanja 2012, 2014, Fahlenbrach 2010, 2016). Respective accounts rather disregard metonymy and focus mainly on audiovisually contained metaphor, which they consider either as an intentional artistic occurrence of a filmmaking sender or as an audiovisual instantiation of universal cognitive schemata. Thereby, figurativity serves as a fixed message of a producer in a unilateral communication process, in which the passive role of the spectator consists in decoding a pre-existent meaning contained in audiovisual images.

A crucial change in perspective was found in classical film theory, in particular in Eisenstein's theory of montage (1982) and in Deleuze's (2008) philosophical and image-theoretical reflections on the movement-image. Both conceptions of figurativity exceed mere audiovisual representation and focus especially on the temporal dynamics of the cinematic image, which they relate to the spectator's experience. As such, figurative meaning-making is considered a process that arises from the experience of two images' mutual relatedness in terms of movement instead of being objectively contained in the audiovisual image. In this experience of the figurative "juxtaposition of facts" (Eisenstein 1951b), affective and cognitive processes intertwine, and figurative meaning emerges through the concrete perceptual experience in the circuit between spectator and film.

Phenomenologically-informed approaches (e.g., Barker 2009, Sobchack 1992, 2004) have elaborated this aspect in greater detail, however not explicitly in relation to figurativity. In the experience of audiovisual movement-images they consider cinematic expression, perception, and affective experience as being interrelated and therein the basis for viewers' meaning-making. The idea of making present and developing a sense of something foreign through one's own body (i.e., as if it were one's own) in the act of perceptual experience is a bridge leading to figurative meaning-making. The concept of cinematic expressive movement (Kappelhoff 2004; see also Kappelhoff and Bakels 2011) makes this process of the embodiment of meaning graspable as a movement dimension that orchestrates the perception of spectators.

By bringing together multimodal figurativity and audiovisual compositions through this film-analytical approach and the cognitive-linguistic dynamic view of multimodal metaphor (Müller 2008a, 2008b; Müller and Tag 2010), the activation and concretization of metaphorical and metonymical experiential realms becomes reconstructable in its affective grounding and processual emergence. The theoretical and practical implications of such a transdisciplinary approach (Kappelhoff and Müller 2011, Müller and Kappelhoff 2018, Scherer, Greifenstein, and Kappelhoff 2014) will be developed in greater detail in the following chapter.

5 Implications of a Dynamic Approach to Audiovisual Figurativity

In his book *The Meaning of the Body* (2007), Mark Johnson clearly argues the case for a dynamic, embodied, and emergent understanding of meaning-making: "We are not making our world of objects, but we are instead *taking up* these objects in experience. In other words, objects are not so much *givens* as they are *takings*." (Johnson 2007, 75) Proceeding from the central role that aesthetic experience plays for making sense of art, Johnson also comes to the conclusion that everyday human reasoning and understanding is inextricably linked with bodily experience, i.e., "how something shows itself to us, [...] how something feels to us" (Johnson 2007, 70). It is the self-same aspect that is at the heart of the dynamic approach to audiovisual figurativity as proposed in this book and that has so far received only little recognition both in pertinent cognitive-linguistic and film-theoretical approaches. "How something feels to us", therefore, refers to the embodied experiential dimension that brings together multimodal figurativity and audiovisual compositions. It does not, however, allude to the embodied experience in terms of pre-existing mental schemata and patterns that are unwittingly decoded and processed, but rather in terms of concrete, situated bodily sensations that arise from the intersubjective encounter of viewers and audiovisual images.

In this case, three central points of contact between multimodal figurativity and audiovisual compositions are successively introduced: temporal dynamics, attentional dynamics, and experiential dynamics. From a theoretical point of view, these three aspects serve as condensed synopses of those concepts and ideas that result from the theoretical overviews of both disciplines in the Chapters 3 and 4 and are relevant for and compatible with the dynamic approach to audiovisual figurativity proposed here: the cognitive-linguistic dynamic view of metaphor (Müller 2008a, 2008b, 2011, Müller and Tag 2010) and the film-analytical concept of cinematic expressive movement (Kappelhoff 2004, Kappelhoff and Bakels 2011).[1] From a practical point of view, the three aspects are conducive to making analytically accessible the audiovisual figurativity within the campaign commercials to be discussed in this book. That is to

---

[1] The transdisciplinary approach to metaphors in audiovisual media as combining these two theoretical concepts (see especially Müller and Kappelhoff 2018) originates from the interdisciplinary project "Multimodal Metaphor and Expressive Movement" ("Multimodale Metaphorik und Ausdrucksbewegung", 2009–2013), headed by Hermann Kappelhoff and Cornelia Müller, at the interdisciplinary research center *Languages of Emotion* (Freie Universität Berlin) and was further developed at *Cinepoetics*, Center for Advanced Film Studies at the Freie Universität Berlin.

https://doi.org/10.1515/9783110578782-005

say, based on the theoretical implications of both disciplines, a transdisciplinary method (Kappelhoff and Müller 2011, Müller and Kappelhoff 2018, Müller and Schmitt 2015, Scherer, Greifenstein, and Kappelhoff 2014) is developed that will be applied in the analyses.[2]

The chapter concludes with reflections on different forms of figurativity that are considered to result from particular dominance phenomena among the two dimensions of audiovisual figurative meaning-making (i.e., the activation of figurativity and the affective experience of cinematic expressive movement) in the campaign commercials. These variant forms of audiovisual figurativity are made analytically accessible through a sequential microanalysis of the two dimensions. In so doing, the specific temporal, attentional, and experiential profile of audiovisual figurative meaning-making as it unfolds in a particular campaign commercial becomes reconstructable. Depending on whether the profile displays either a predominance of language, audiovisual staging, or a balanced interplay among the two, different focal points are suggested to occur with regard to the content-related orientation and the candidate image formation in the respective campaign commercial. On this basis, a more nuanced differentiation is possible that no longer discriminates purely issue- and image-focused campaign commercials as usual in social sciences and media studies research, or puts forward qualitative evaluations of professional and unprofessional TV campaign ads. Instead, different variant forms of audiovisual figurative meaning-making come to the fore that are grounded in the particular interplay of language and audiovisual staging in a situated media context.

5.1 Temporal Dynamics of Audiovisual Figurativity

Campaign commercials should make political candidates as comprehensible as possible within their available time frame; they should bring them 'near' to the viewers. No matter if they do so in a straightforward or a modest manner, they have to take the viewers along in the process of conveyance in order to come up with a vital idea. However, the question of a beforehand intended impression or

---

2 The transdisciplinary method (CineMet) that constitutes the basis for the analyses of audiovisual figurativity in this book is an outcome of longstanding transdisciplinary work of film studies together with linguistics on metaphors in audiovisual media and face-to-face interaction in the interdisciplinary project "Multimodal Metaphor and Expressive Movement" and at *Cinepoetics*, Center for Advanced Film Studies (for an outline of the method, see Müller and Kappelhoff 2018). For the purpose of this study and its particular focus on the temporal, attentional, and experiential dynamics of audiovisual figurativity, it has been further developed.

message in this or that form is not the main concern of this study.[3] Rather, it is all about the process of meaning-making as it unfolds temporally on the part of the viewer in the interaction with the campaign commercial, i.e., how he or she makes meaning in the situated process of viewing.

In this respect, applied and cognitive-linguistic research on the use of metaphor and metonymy – especially in face-to-face communication – has indicated that figurative meaning-making is a process that plays out temporally, interactively, and multimodally (e.g., Cameron 2008a, 2011, Kolter et al. 2012, Müller 2008a, 2008b, Müller and Ladewig 2013, Müller and Tag 2010). Not only can figurative meaning emerge, condense, extend, or change in the course of one conversation or stretch of talk (Cameron 2008b, 2010, Müller 2008a, Müller and Ladewig 2013, Müller and Tag 2010) but it can also do so across single conversations and over longer periods of time (Cameron 2007, 2011). In this process, the expressive modalities of figurative meaning are also subject to constant change (between mono- and multimodality), always according to the affordances of the respective context of use. This relates to what Johnson refers to above when he describes objects as being takings instead of givens: rather than emerging suddenly, figurative meaning in face-to-face interaction instead develops dynamically. For example, a conventionalized figurative verbal expression can become activated and elaborated in gesture and, through such a concretization of its experiential realm, give rise to further related or verbal expressions (Müller 2008a, 2008b, Müller and Tag 2010). This way, figurative meaning, i.e., the bringing together of two adjacent or distinct realms, can be considered as constantly in progress rather than something that is fixed and still standing. Schmitt, Greifenstein, and Kappelhoff (2014) underline this idea in their notion of 'mapping in time'. Analogous to its temporal-dynamic unfolding in face-to-face interactions, figurative meaning in audiovisual media emerges from the temporal and multimodal interplay of language and audiovisual compositions in the concrete media context instead of being instantiated and processed in an isolated and schematized manner:

> Mapping as term thus is not meant to find already established similarities in semantic fields or conceptual domains beyond a situated media context, but as making interactions possible, constructing similarities ad hoc through images, sensory qualities, or motives. (Schmitt, Greifenstein, and Kappelhoff 2014, 2105)

---

3 Undoubtedly, strategic aspects as well as the expertise of the specialists who are responsible for the conception and production and strive for maximum comprehensibility and appeal play a role for the staging of the campaign commercials and thus also for the meaning-making process. However, equating meaning-making and intentional actions or subordinating the former to the latter, simplifies the complexity of the meaning-making process in audiovisual media to a unilateral information processing.

Thereby, literal audiovisual illustrations of verbal figurative expressions that have been commonly conceived of as a standard case of audiovisual figurativity are only one possible form or stage among others in a whole trajectory (for the notion of metaphor trajectory, see Cameron 2010, 2018): figurative meaning might initially emerge and be further elaborated in language singularly, before it is multimodally activated through audiovisual images. Another possible form is the unfolding of a figurative scenario on the level of audiovisual representation alone and its later verbal concretization. Through the temporal reconstruction of the ongoing progress of figurative meaning-making in and across language and audiovisual images, a trajectory becomes visible of how a metonymical or metaphorical experiential realm are vitalized and concretized over shorter or longer, condensed or extended stretches of time. Thus, the dynamic temporal focus brings the concrete and situated 'how' of figurative meaning-making to the fore instead of the mere 'what' in terms of abstract formulas. In other words, by sticking closely to the respective data, it becomes possible to reconstruct the temporal unfolding of the meaning-making process as it plays out for a spectator in the process of viewing.

This temporal specificity of figurative meaning-making provides a link to film-theoretical research on (figurative) meaning-making in audiovisual compositions. While most works that deal with metaphor explicitly are informed by a static and conceptually-anchored conception, approaches proceeding from the cinematic image as a movement-image emphasize the situated and temporal unfolding of meaning on the part of the viewers (e.g., Deleuze 2008, Eisenstein 1951a, Kappelhoff 2004). In so doing, they suggest a becoming of meaning instead of an objectively given one that only has to be processed and decoded in terms of pictorial content. Likewise, figurative meaning in audiovisual media cannot be considered a static product that is contained in isolated pictures and is deciphered from them. Instead, it is conceived of as being closely linked to an experiencing viewer in a temporal process of relating things to each other on the basis of their configuration as dynamically unfolding composition. The spectator is thus not passively receiving and decoding pre-existing meaning but creates it by establishing the triadic structure (Müller 2008a), the seeing as, in the particular temporally unfolding experience of audiovisual media.

This particular temporality is inextricably linked to the respective audiovisual images in the concrete process of being viewed and experienced by the spectator. As such, it brings into being a highly specific meaning instead of standardized or abstract meaning patterns. This situated how of meaning-making, i.e., its concrete temporal form, can be made visible by means of the film-analytical concept of cinematic expressive movement (Kappelhoff 2004, Kappelhoff and Bakels 2011). Just as multimodal figurativity is suggested to unfold following a particular trajectory of different forms and stages, audiovisual compositions are considered to play out in a specific rhythmic course that is composed of different movement configurations and patterns. These configurations (i.e., cinematic expressive movements) display a distinctive temporality that orchestrates an affective experience on the part of the viewers. In their overall temporal arrangement, they thus unfold as a specific affective course (or trajectory) that spectators go through in the process of viewing and on whose basis they make meaning. Similar to multimodal figurativity, the particular temporal arrangement and succession of cinematic expressive movements can play out differently: in longer audiovisual formats, they tend to unfold more complex and extended patterns, while shorter formats display rather straightforward and short-termed patterns (Scherer, Greifenstein, and Kappelhoff 2014, 2089). Such temporal arrangements in different audiovisual media are conceived of as "highly relevant for how spectators experience them affectively" (Scherer, Greifenstein, and Kappelhoff 2014, 2089) and on that basis make meaning.

Based on the outlined correspondences between multimodal figurativity and audiovisual compositions with respect to their temporal dynamics both can be theoretically related to each other. Subsequently, methodological tools for analysis can be developed from this transdisciplinary theoretical model. In this connection, Müller's (2008a) concept of the activation of metaphoricity (also applying to metonymicity) provides an analytical access to audiovisual figurative meaning as it emerges as an actual vital and embodied conceptualization of viewers watching a campaign commercial. This focus on activated (and not on potential) figurativity is due to the interest in the spectator's concrete process of figurative meaning-making in the very act of viewing a campaign commercial. This, however, does not imply claims about the psychological reality of figurative meaning for a given spectator (cf. Müller and Schmitt 2015, 314, Müller and Tag 2010, 88–89). Instead, the approach to activated figurativity is theoretically motivated and based on the empirically accountable foregrounding of figurativity through the elaboration of its experiential realm in a situated context (Müller 2008a, Müller and Tag 2010). This is the *first dimension of audiovisual figurative meaning-making* (cf. Müller and Schmitt 2015).

As such, figurative meaning-making becomes accessible as a process of seeing one kind of thing in terms of another in a given (media) context: through the interplay between language and audiovisual staging, i.e., what is being said and how it is being staged, a concrete embodied conceptualization of the figurative experiential realm becomes visible. When, for instance, Angela Merkel's voice-over in the Christian Democratic Union's (CDU) 2009 campaign commercial refers to the German reunification as "unity" [*Einheit*], while simultaneously showing scenes of East and West Berliners in November 1989 together in front of and on the Berlin wall, then the audiovisual staging creates a vital idea of this unity in terms of the togetherness of a huge mass of people. Alternatively, when Donald Tusk's voice-over speaks of a "plan of building a strong and rich Poland" [*plan budowy silnej i bogatej Polski*] in the 2011 campaign commercial of the Polish Platforma Obywatelska (PO) while he is shown shaking hands with people who shovel sand in bags, then the metaphor's experiential realm of building is made present as a concrete embodied idea.

As described above, the presentation of verbally expressed experiential realms through audiovisual staging is not the only possible form of activating figurativity. By semantic elaboration over the course of time, a figurative realm can also be activated monomodally, i.e., on the verbal or on the audiovisual level. For example, the scenario of the building project of a strong and rich Poland in the PO campaign commercial develops successively through various verbal metaphorical expressions (see Section 7.2) and thereby evokes a concretization and activation of the experiential realm. Such mono- and multimodal activations indicate an "embodied and dynamic conceptualization" (Müller and Schmitt 2015, 322) of figurative meaning on the part of a viewer and thus reveal how audiovisual figurative meaning emerges and unfolds temporally over the course of a campaign commercial.

The concept of cinematic expressive movement also allows for the reconstruction of how audiovisual figurative meaning unfolds qualitatively in the temporal course of campaign commercials. Developing as temporal movement patterns, cinematic expressive movements unfold in their composition a flow of experience that the spectators go through and that can be made analytically accessible.

> It is the reconstruction of such an experience, such a kind of 'feeling', which our analysis of cinematic expressive movement targets – an immediate affection through the dynamic orchestration of audio-visual compositions as temporally-organized forms of movement experience [...]. (Müller and Schmidt 2015, 321)

Such an affective course – composed of one or various cinematic expressive movements – is considered to become the experiential grounds for the emergence of audiovisual figurative meaning. This is the *second dimension of audiovisual figurative meaning-making* (cf. Müller and Schmitt 2015). In other words, through the flow of affective experiences of audiovisual compositions, seeing and understanding 'in terms of' obtains its experiential basis.

In order to reconstruct this flow of experience in the campaign commercials analytically, they are segmented into temporal units: cinematic expressive movement units (emu). These emus are "not distinct and isolated temporal units" (Scherer, Greifenstein, and Kappelhoff 2014, 2088) but analytical tools: as perceptual experiences, they merge into one another. A cinematic expressive movement is composed of various "articulatory modalities of audio-visual staging" (Scherer, Greifenstein, and Kappelhoff 2014, 2085), i.e., "film techniques, such as camera movement, montage, sound design, acting, visual composition, etc." (Müller and Schmitt 2015, 320) that develop movement patterns organizing the viewer's perception process. The viewer realizes this shaping of time as a bodily experience in the process of viewing (Kappelhoff 2004, Scherer, Greifenstein, and Kappelhoff 2014, Schmitt, Greifenstein, and Kappelhoff 2014). In this regard, cinematic expressive movements provide the affective grounds for figurative meaning-making in audiovisual media (cf. Kappelhoff 2004, Kappelhoff and Müller 2011, Müller and Kappelhoff 2018, Schmitt, Greifenstein, and Kappelhoff 2014). As a result, their analysis by means of expressive movement units allows for insights into the emergence and temporal unfolding of audiovisual figurative meaning in campaign commercials.

In summary: temporal dynamics play a fundamental role for both multimodal figurativity and cinematic expressive movement. Bringing the two together in a dynamic approach to audiovisual figurativity allows for reconstructing trajectories of figurative meaning-making in campaign commercials. Through the analytical exploration of the interplay between the verbal and the audiovisual level over the course of time, and of the temporal arrangement of expressive movement units, these trajectories become graspable in terms of a specific intersubjective encounter between viewers and campaign commercial. Hereby, the temporal unfolding of audiovisual figurative meaning is not conceived of as something separated from the viewer but instead as a temporal structure that is created by and through him. This structure is composed of various stages that make figurative meaning a constant becoming.

It should be noted, however, that the temporal dynamics of multimodal figurativity and cinematic expressive movement are not considered as being separated from each other. It is for reasons of transparency that they have been outlined separately. Taking account of both and relating them to one another, "makes it possible to document how metaphoric [and metonymical] meaning emerges dynamically over the course and along with the flow of the audio-visual composition" (Müller and Schmitt 2015, 322). The activation of figurative meaning and the modulation of affective experience over time are closely connected with the attentional dynamics of audiovisual figurativity: concomitant with the temporal trajectory, a salience structure is established that guides the viewer's flow of attention. This aspect of dynamics will be discussed in the following section.

5.2 Attentional Dynamics of Audiovisual Figurativity

In discussing the different temporal extensions of activated figurative meaning, it was previously mentioned that their expressive modalities too are subject to constant change between mono- and multimodality. In the context of audiovisual compositions, the two main modalities through which figurativity dynamically emerges, unfolds, and changes are language and audiovisual staging. In this regard, audiovisual figurativity not only displays a temporal profile but also an expressive or salience profile on whose basis the spectator makes situated sense in the process of viewing. That is to say, in the temporally orchestrated activation and concretization of the experiential realm (first dimension) and in the modulation of affective experience (second dimension) the spectator is sensorily addressed and thereby guided in his flow of experience and attention. As a result, "not all of this material appears uniformly in the foreground of the [...] [viewer's] attention. Rather, various portions or aspects of the expression, content, and context have differing degrees of salience" (Talmy 2007, 264).

In her discussion of the common static categorization of verbal metaphors as either dead or alive in linguistic and cognitive metaphor theories, Müller (2008a) argues the case for a dynamic categorization from the perspective of language use. According to her, the selective activation of metaphoricity, i.e., the establishing of a triadic structure by seeing C in terms of B, "in a given speaker/ listener or writer/reader at a given moment in time" (Müller 2008a, 195), suggests that metaphoricity is a gradual property. While in one given moment in time activation can be low, in another it can be high. Müller differentiates such cases by means of her newly developed dynamic category of sleeping and waking metaphors:

> Sleeping metaphors are metaphors that are realized in an utterance or written text and have metaphoric potential (determined from the analyst's point of view); waking metaphors are metaphors whose metaphoric potential is activated online during speaking (determined from the user's point of view through activation indicators, i.e., activation is *empirically observable* through elaboration, specification, and a *metaphoricity that crosscuts modalities*). (Müller 2008a, 196–197; emphasis mine)

The temporal unfolding of figurative meaning in the campaign commercials can be qualitatively differentiated through this dynamic categorization. Müller links the individual cognitive activation of metaphoricity for a user to its concrete modal expression and unfolding as observable in the situated context of use.[4] Proceeding from the assumption that activated metaphoricity and metonymicity

---

4 Note that such a formal descriptive perspective does not claim the psychological reality of figurativity in terms of consciousness (Müller and Tag 2010) but is a theoretically motivated claim for taking account of the phenomenon observed by Raymond Gibbs and Gerard Steen that "[m]etaphors may not always be activated when people immediately comprehend metaphorical language" (Gibbs and Steen 1999, 3).

are empirically observable in their situated media context, figurativity in audiovisual media can display varying degrees of activation:

> [T]he more instantiations of a source domain or image-offering field, the higher the degree of activation in a given speaker at a given moment in time. [...] The more "material" is used to express metaphoricity, the more salient this metaphor is for a listener or reader – and hence the more active it is for a speaker/writer. (Müller 2008a, 201–202)

With regard to audiovisual compositions, the most straightforward form of activated and salient figurativity seems to be the audiovisual illustration of a verbal figurative expression's experiential realm. At the same time, the monomodal verbal or audiovisual elaboration (on the level of audiovisual representation) of the experiential realm amounts to "more material" that expresses figurativity and foregrounds it in a spectator's perception (cf. Müller and Tag 2010; see also Cameron 2008b, 2010). In the process of viewing, i.e., in the interaction between audiovisual compositions and a spectator, a "multimodal salience structure" (Müller and Tag 2010, 85) or particular attentional profile of figurative meaning emerges over the course of time. Just as in a face-to-face interaction, this attentional profile is no object without any relation to the viewer, but an emergent outcome of the dynamic interaction between him or her and the audiovisual movement-image. As such, the dynamic foregrounding of figurative meaning in the course of a campaign commercial goes along with the viewer's constantly moving focus of attention (cf. Müller and Tag 2010). In addition to the temporal dynamics that allow for insights into the linear temporal unfolding of audiovisual figurativity, the attentional dynamics thus provide insight into its simultaneous unfolding in a campaign commercial (cf. Müller and Tag 2010).

The aspect of the simultaneous unfolding is also relevant with respect to audiovisual compositions that organize the spectator's process of viewing in terms of audiovisual movement patterns. It regards the distinctive compositional structure of these movement patterns as formed by the articulatory modalities of audiovisual staging (Scherer, Greifenstein, and Kappelhoff 2014, 2085). Unlike multimodal figurativity, which can roughly be broken down into isolated moments for analytical reasons, an audiovisual movement pattern cannot be segmented into instants in time because it "refers to the time of the unfolding of movement itself" (Kappelhoff and Müller 2011, 135). Thus, when addressing the simultaneous unfolding of audiovisual movement patterns this refers to the composition of articulatory modalities that orchestrate a specific perceptual experience. This is not conceived of as a vertical arrangement of the single modalities of audiovisual staging that in sum result in a particular movement quality. Instead, this quality always emerges in the temporal unfolding of the movement pattern itself (i.e., as a viewer's bodily experience), and thereby likewise in relation to other movement patterns (cf. Kappelhoff and Bakels 2011, 85, Scherer, Greifenstein, and Kappelhoff 2014, 2082, Schmitt, Greifenstein, and Kappelhoff 2014, 2098).

Nevertheless, it is possible to speak of a meaning being profiled here: namely, in the spectator's flow of experience that is constantly modulated in the process of viewing by embodying the movement qualities as felt experiences (cf. Kappelhoff and Bakels 2011, 85, Kappelhoff and Müller 2011, 137, Schmitt 2015, 313). This process of being literally moved (Scherer, Greifenstein, and Kappelhoff 2014, 2083) organizes how the spectator's attention flows from certain felt experiences to others. In this regard and following Talmy, it can be suggested that in audiovisual compositions too, "various portions or aspects of the expression, content, and context have differing degrees of salience" (Talmy 2007, 264). Here, salience does not refer to content in terms of the level of representation, but to the movement qualities that are staged through each and every movement pattern and resonate as a viewer's affective experience. In contrast to Müller's gradation from high to low activation on the basis of the amount of material that is used to express figurative meaning, no particular quantity of articulatory modalities is mandatory for the attentional dynamics of audiovisual compositions. What plays a role in this regard is rather the interaction and arrangement of expressive movement patterns among themselves. This clearly shows how closely the temporal and the attentional dynamics of audiovisual compositions are related to one another.

Based on the outlined theoretical correspondences, the attentional dynamics of multimodal figurativity and audiovisual compositions can be integrated into the transdisciplinary methodological framework put forward here. In order to reconstruct the interactive foregrounding of metaphorical meaning – and thus to make visible different degrees of activated metaphoricity – in face-to-face communication, Müller and Tag (2010) have combined a sequential analytical approach and a descriptive analysis of foregrounding strategies. This way, the analysis covers two dimensions: "a simultaneous one and a linear one" (Müller and Tag 2010, 93). While the aspect of simultaneity refers to how figurative meaning is expressed and thus to its degree of activation for a given speaker at a given time,[5] the aspect of linearity includes the temporal pattern of activation over the course of the conversation in terms of steps and clusters (Müller and Tag 2010, 94–97). Müller and Tag (2010, 97) propose a three-step procedure starting with the identification of multimodal (activated) metaphors and looking for further modal expressions of their experiential realms, then finding cues that

---

5 Müller and Tag (2010, 94–97) mention the amount of modal instantiations of the metaphor's experiential realm and the number of salience markers pointing towards figurative meaning as empirically observable foregrounding strategies that follow different principles.

mark metaphorical meaning, and finally tracing the evolving and unfolding of foregrounded metaphors over the course of time. The results of the analysis are visualized in a diagram with the simultaneous strategies on the y-axis and the linear steps on the x-axis. As the accumulation of different kinds of foregrounding strategies is assumed to increase the degree of activation, they are depicted as icons on top of each other (i.e., adding up to low or high activation).

The foregrounding strategies that have been formulated for verbo-gestural metaphors in face-to-face communication are hardly transferable to audiovisual media.[6] However, the first and the last step of Müller and Tag's procedure provide a useful methodological tool to identify activated metaphors and metonymies in language and audiovisual images and to trace their distribution over the course of a TV campaign ad (*first dimension of audiovisual figurative meaning-making*). In doing so, figurativity that is considered being low and non-activated is admittedly disregarded. Following Müller and Tag's argumentation and also Talmy's notion of attention phenomena, this means, however, an orientation towards the flow of attention as it (from a descriptive analytical perspective) emerges interactively and situated between the viewer and the campaign commercial. Due to the transdisciplinary perspective that is taken here, language is considered as one possible form of figurative meaning-making among others in audiovisual media.

> Moreover, analysing metaphors in audio-visual media shows that linguistic metaphors are only the tip of the iceberg regarding the multitude of ways in which metaphoric meaning-making can occur. It is by locating metaphoric meaning-making in a process of seeing and feeling one type of thing in terms of another that we extend the scope of metaphor from the realm of language to a realm in which multiple modalities interact (Müller and Schmitt 2015, 315)

In order to get a more profound idea of the attentional dynamics of audiovisual figurativity, the flow of attention as informed by multimodally activated metaphors and metonymies is to be complemented by the flow of attention as orchestrated by the movement patterns of audiovisual compositions. The analysis of cinematic expressive movement by means of expressive movement units provides access to reconstruct this flow of attention. They can be descriptively analyzed by means of a set of articulatory modalities of which the most relevant are camera (shot size, camera movement and perspective), montage, sound design (music, sounds, voice), and visual composition (visual arrangement and staging of figures and

---

6 Müller and Tag (2010) address, among other points, the large performance and central position of a gestural metaphorical expression as salience makers. Being inherently multimodal, audiovisual compositions cannot be broken down in such a manner.

objects, color, light, graphic forms) (cf. Müller and Schmitt 2015, 320). However, it should again be stressed that cinematic expressive movements are perceived as holistic temporal gestalts, not in terms of isolated articulatory modalities adding up. Accordingly, the description by means of articulatory modalities is considered an analytical tool in order to make the movement qualities as articulated through cinematic expressive movement reconstructable. In this regard, the attentional dynamics of audiovisual compositions are closely linked with their experiential dynamics (see Section 5.3).

Not all articulatory modalities of audiovisual staging are necessarily fore-grounded at the same time: when "perceptively [merging] to and within expressive gestalts" (Müller and Schmitt 2015, 320), some of them can be more dominant than others (which, then, are subdominant) (see Kappelhoff, Bakels, and Greifenstein forthcoming/2019, Kappelhoff et al., *Empirische Medienästhetik*: "eMAEX – a standardized method of analyzing qualities of filmic expression") for the spectator, i.e., in his or her focus of attention in the process of film-viewing. For instance, in the CDU's 2009 campaign commercial (see Chapter 6), camera, visual composition, and music play a dominant role in unfolding and foregrounding the (cinematic expressive movements') experiential qualities of gravitas, balance, and dominance. Naturally, montage and acting also contribute to this experience, e.g., through a moderate cutting rate and through the protagonist Chancellor Angela Merkel's appearance. Nevertheless, it is in the temperate camera movement, the clear visual arrangement and staging of figures and objects, and the musical quality in which the pattern of the cinematic expressive movement finds its expression in the most pervasive and marked manner.

As such, the descriptive analysis of dominants and subdominants serves to reconstruct how a specific movement pattern is formed (as cinematic expressive movement) and unfolds a particular experiential quality. This simultaneous aspect likewise provides the basis for reconstructing the linear unfolding of these perceptually salient gestalts over time, i.e., the temporal arrangement of cinematic expressive movements. In doing so, the affective course that a viewer is going through is made analytically accessible. It provides insight into the experiential grounds for the emergence of audiovisual figurative meaning through the flow of affective experiences of audiovisual compositions (*second dimension of audiovisual figurative meaning-making*).

In summary: attentional dynamics play a fundamental role for both multimodal figurativity and audiovisual compositions. Bringing the two together in a dynamic approach to audiovisual figurativity allows for a closer look at the different forms in which figurative meaning plays out in the campaign commercials to be analyzed. Using activation as an identification method leads to a reconstruction of where and how figurative experiential realms become salient for the viewer as vital ideas and experiences, and which steps and clusters this process unfolds. Concomitantly, cinematic expressive movements structure the viewer's flow of perception whereby they bring particular movement qualities to the fore that – as felt experiences – can become the source of vital figurative meaning themselves (Müller and Schmitt 2015, 314). The attentional dynamics of audiovisual figurativity thus establish a "multimodal salience structure" (Müller and Tag 2010, 85) by which figurative meaning-making is graspable and reconstructable as a process of vitalized experiential realms through embodied experience. In this respect, the concretization of figurative meaning as orchestration of the viewer's flow of attention and experience is closely connected with the experiential dynamics of audiovisual figurativity: as a consequence of the temporal trajectory and the salience structure, an affective course is established that modulates the viewer's affective experience.

5.3 Experiential Dynamics of Audiovisual Figurativity

In the case of speech-accompanying gestures that embody the figurative source domain, it seems to be self-evident to suggest that the activation of figurative meaning implies an "affective or experiential quality" (Müller and Tag 2010, 85): the gestural movements present the metaphorical or metonymical experiential realm as "felt qualities of meaning" (Johnson 2007, 17). To speak of an embodiment of figurative meaning in the case of audiovisual media, on the other hand, seems less obvious at first glance. Following the methodological argument in this chapter, however, audiovisual figurativity inherently comes with an embodied experiential aspect, namely in a twofold respect:

> [A]udio-visual metaphors involve 'experience' in a double sense: an immediate affection through the dynamic orchestration of audio-visual compositions, i.e., a temporally organized form of movement experience [...], and a sensory-motor experience of metaphoric source domains, i.e., as activation of metaphoricity [...]. (Müller and Schmitt 2015, 313)

In contrast to cognitive metaphor theories (e.g., Grady 1997, Kövecses 2000, Lakoff and Johnson 1980, 1999, Lakoff and Turner 1989), the embodied affective dimension of figurativity is thus not explicitly considered as mentally stored information that is instinctively accessed and schematically processed. Due to its close link to a concrete context of use, figurative meaning is considered to always emerge in a highly specific and situated manner. Embodied experience is thus not conceived of as a side effect of pre-existing figurative meaning but rather as its concrete grounding. This is what Müller and Schmitt (2015, 336–337) have tentatively called "understanding through experience".

Müller's (2008a) dynamic categorization of sleeping and waking metaphors according to their degree of activation in language use suggests that articulatory modalities beyond language not merely serve as co-channels for conveying figurative meaning, but that they substantially and processually shape it. By means of verbo-gestural metaphors, Müller has suggested that gesture conveys aspects of meaning that are not expressed verbally, and that these aspects can give rise to elaborations of metaphorical expressions in turn (see, e.g., Cienki and Müller 2008, Kappelhoff and Müller 2011, Kolter et al. 2012, Müller 2008a, 2008b, Müller and Cienki 2009, Müller and Ladewig 2013, Müller and Tag 2010). She considers gestures to make visible and draw attention to how somebody sees, feels, and imagines something in terms of something else. This kind of sensory visualization and concretization mostly refers to the experiential source domain (Müller 2013, 206–207, Müller and Cienki 2009) that is gesturally enacted by means of different modes of representation (drawing, modeling, acting, representing; see Müller 1998, 2014). Even highly conventionalized metaphorical expressions can be vitalized and become waking metaphors in this way. Müller (2008a, 204–208) has demonstrated this through the example of a woman talking about her first love relationship by using the metaphor of an up and down [ein Auf und Ab]. This conventional German metaphorical expression becomes activated through a simultaneously performed downward head movement and a downward moving hand gesture: its imagery, i.e., "the metaphoricity of these seemingly dead metaphors [was] quite active" (Müller 2008a, 206) for the speaker at that moment in time. Moreover, the gestural concretization displays the speaker's subjective, embodied conceptualization (Müller and Ladewig 2013, 301) of figurative imagery as a vital sensory-motor experience, i.e., what it looks like and how it feels for her (cf. Müller and Tag 2010, 114, Cienki and Müller 2014).

Multimodal figurativity thus clearly suggests that the cognitive process of seeing C in terms of B is modality-independent (Müller 2008a, 2008b), and that metaphor's or metonymy's experiential realms can be activated as a vital scenario with experiential qualities that "transcends language, involves gestures, bodily movements, and routine motor programs that are habitually associated with a certain everyday pattern of action" (Müller 2008a, 94). Making figurativity salient through the thereby used communicative effort provides an empirically observable anchor point for reconstructing the sensory-motor experience of figurativity's experiential realms, both at a given moment in time and with regard to its elaboration over the course of time.

This close nexus between the attentional and the experiential dynamics also applies to audiovisual compositions: the composition and merging of various articulatory modalities to temporally organized movement gestalts not only organizes the spectators' flow of attention but also their flow of experience in the process of viewing. The composition of dominants and subdominants foregrounds, on the one hand, objects, spaces, and figures on the level of representation in their qualitative nature. Describing a sequence from William Wyler's melodrama JEZEBEL (USA 1938), Kappelhoff and Müller (2011; see also Müller and Kappelhoff 2018) explain how mise-en-scène and visual composition stage a straight, focused movement when the protagonist Julie dynamically and energetically enters her house in order to welcome her guests. At the end of the sequence when Julie is faced with her guests, this dynamic movement is stopped and turns into a static quality. In this light, Kappelhoff and Müller (2011, 139) point to the role of the cast members' costumes: "[...] the [...] invitees turn towards Julie, merging to form a barrier; the ball dresses and costumes thereby move so close to another that they become a wall". Through the interplay of mise-en-scène and visual composition, the material features of the "women's light-coloured, wide crinoline dresses and the consistent black and white silhouettes of the men" (Kappelhoff and Müller 2011, 140) come to the fore as sensory-motor experiences.

On the other hand, such foregrounded objects, spaces, and figures turn into parts of the movement composition: "All levels of what is represented on the screen have become elements of the temporal presentation of the movement-image." (Kappelhoff and Müller 2011, 140) The formation of the costumes as a human barrier that Julie is facing in the mentioned sequence is part of the closure of the movement pattern staging a straight and focused movement that is stopped. As such, the represented objects, spaces, and figures also have a second experiential dimension that is articulated in the temporal unfolding of the cinematic expressive movement. Hence, the movement pattern of straight and focused movement that ends in a halt, as staged and foregrounded in the mentioned sequence, is considered to resonate as affective experience on the part of the viewer (Kappelhoff and Muller 2011; see also Kappelhoff 2004, Scherer, Greifenstein, and Kappelhoff 2014). The temporal arrangement of such movement patterns over the course of time thus not only organizes the viewers' flow of attention from those felt qualities to others but also modulates their flow of experience.

Finally, the experiential dynamics of multimodal figurativity and audiovisual compositions display obvious theoretical correspondences and can be integrated into the transdisciplinary methodological framework. By using Müller's concept of activation as an analytical access for identifying audiovisual figurativity, not only does a multimodal salience structure of foregrounded metaphoricity and metonymicity in the campaign commercials become reconstructable, but so too does the flow of experience on the part of the spectator. By paying particular attention to verbal metaphorical and metonymical expressions and to how they are being staged, it becomes possible to detect salient moments of figurative meaning-making in the campaign commercials to be analyzed. Taking a closer analytical look at the interplay between words and audiovisual images as well as the manner of staging provides insights into the concrete sensory-motor experience and conceptualization of figurative experiential realms (*first dimension of audiovisual figurative meaning-making*).

Considering the situated media context and describing in detail the respective audiovisual concretization of the experiential realms has the advantage to not run the risk of attributing generalized and disembodied qualities to figurative meaning (see, e.g., Androshchuk 2014). This way, the analysis "starts from the bottom up and remains close to the experiential level of the data" (Müller and Schmitt 2015, 322). Extending the scope of analysis to the temporal unfolding of audiovisual figurativity in such a context-bound manner allows for insights into how figurativity's imagery is experientially explored, elaborated, and further specified over the course of a campaign commercial. Likewise, similar or contrastive vitalizations and concretizations of the experiential realm among the different campaign commercials can be made transparent. And, not least the sensory concretization can transcend its instantaneous experiential quality and become a pattern of its own within the overall composition of the campaign commercial. In the 2009 CDU TV campaign ad, for instance, several activated audiovisual metonymies emerge throughout over its entire course. Due to their regular frequency and consistent form, they transcend the experiential qualities of the respective experiential realms and form a repetitive pattern that foregrounds the principle of metonymical meaning-making – contiguity – itself as an experience of cohesion (see Section 6.2).

The transdisciplinary perspective taken here considers verbal language as one possible form of figurative meaning-making in audiovisual media (Müller and Schmitt 2015, 315). Accordingly, the sensory-motor experience of activated figurative imagery is conceived of as being related to and complemented by a second dimension of experience: the "immediate affection through the dynamic orchestration of audio-visual compositions" (Müller and Schmitt 2015, 313), i.e., cinematic expressive movements. The segmentation of the campaign commercials into cinematic expressive movement units (emu) – that make the temporal and attentional dynamics of audiovisual compositions analytically graspable – allows for reconstructing their experiential dynamics. As such, it is the distinctive movement gestalt realized by the spectator as a felt experience that gives rise to the temporal units. This clearly shows that the temporal, attentional, and experiential dynamics of audiovisual compositions are basically not separable from each other. Through the detailed description of the compositional structure of cinematic expressive movements as formed by the articulatory modalities of audiovisual staging, the affective experience of the viewer becomes reconstructable in each and every emu.

In their exemplary analysis of two emus in a scene from the Classical Hollywood war film bataan (Tay Garnett, USA 1943), Scherer, Greifenstein, and Kappelhoff

(2014) visualize the results of their analysis in a diagram that relates the level of narration, the description of each movement pattern, and the affective experience throughout the entire scene to one other. This form of visualization of the analytical results will also be applied to the analysis of campaign commercials carried out in this study. It allows for both the simultaneous view on the experiential qualities as staged in a single emu, and the linear view on the affective course as created by the unfolding and interplay of various emus over the course of time. Both views provide the background for the analytical reconstruction of how audiovisual figurative meaning is grounded in affective experiences evoked by the composition of audiovisual movement-images (*second dimension of audiovisual figurative meaning-making*). In the campaign commercial of the Polish Law and Justice Party (PiS) from 2011, for instance, it is the transformation from a dynamic straight movement being halted to a focused, dynamically flowing movement (unfolding in one emu) that provides a vital experience of the equal chances promised by the candidate Jarosław Kaczyński. More precisely, "the audio-visual composition spells out a specific manner of experience" (Müller and Schmitt 2015, 325), namely how having both unequal and equal chances actually feels (see Section 8.2).

In summary: the experiential dynamics of multimodal figurativity and audiovisual compositions display fundamental correspondences and points of contact. Bringing the two together in a dynamic approach to audiovisual figurativity allows for more comprehensive insights into the experiential grounds of figurative meaning-making in the campaign commercials to be analyzed. Making the candidates and their political goals vivid and comprehensible through figurative meaning is thus not restricted to the mere audiovisual depiction of its imagery, but implies its sensory vitalization and affective experience for a viewer in the process of viewing. In this regard, the experiential dynamics of multimodal figurativity and of audiovisual compositions are not conceived of as being ontologically distinct; they are only separated for analytical reasons. Both are suggested to go hand in hand with one another in a dynamic interplay so that audiovisual figurative meaning is continuously shaped and elaborated by a flow of experiences.

This, in turn, makes it hard to grasp its emergent nature by a concise 'A IS B' formulation. In the subsequent concluding section, the outlined temporal, attentional, and experiential dynamics are brought together in order to propose a way of spelling out and qualifying emergent figurative meanings on a micro level, i.e., within the campaign commercials, and on a macro level, i.e., in terms of an overall figurative theme that encompasses the campaign commercial as a whole. For this reason, different variant forms of audiovisual figurativity (ranging from rather explicit to subtle) are differentiated and outlined in greater detail on the basis of the three aspects of dynamics.

5.4 Variant Forms of Audiovisual Figurativity

Throughout the previous three sections highlighting the single dynamics it has become increasingly clear how closely linked they are with and among each other. Activated figurativity draws attention to itself compared to non- or low-activated figurativity and thereby establishes a multimodal salience structure that unfolds over the temporal course of a campaign commercial and comes with sensory-motor experiences of the activated imagery (*the first dimension of audiovisual figurative meaning-making*). Cinematic expressive movements emerge through the composition of articulatory modalities as movement patterns that orchestrate the flow of attention as well as the flow of viewers' experience and thereby frame and ground figurative meaning (*the second dimension of audiovisual figurative meaning-making*).

In that regard, the three aspects of each of the two dimensions will not be considered separately, but will always be discussed as interrelated integral features of a dynamic approach in a cohesive manner. The analytically motivated distinction of the two dimensions of audiovisual figurative meaning – the activation of figurative meaning through vitalizations of experiential realms and the affective experience of cinematic expressive movement – will be maintained in order to allow for the systematic clarification and description of its complex processuality and constant flow. In this light, the methodological approach to the analysis of the campaign commercials follows the transdisciplinary method (CineMet) developed through longstanding collaborative work of film studies and linguistics and systematically spelled out by Müller and Kappelhoff (2018; see also Greifenstein and Kappelhoff 2016, Kappelhoff and Müller 2011, Müller and Schmitt 2015, Schmitt 2015, Schmitt, Greifenstein, and Kappelhoff 2014).

> [W]hat is reconstructed are metaphoric mappings from the experiential qualities staged in each and every scene. This allows to formulate emergent metaphoric meanings not within a typical "A = B" structure, but rather by spelling them out in descriptive sentences, which include both experiential qualities as well as metaphoric conceptualizations. Metaphor emergence is indicated by *small letters in italics*, while overall metaphoric themes evoked by those emerging metaphors are represented by *CAPITAL LETTERS IN ITALICS*. This procedure allows to exemplify in great detail how the interplay between the audio-visual composition and the verbal is orchestrated and how, through this interplay, metaphoric meaning is activated as embodied and dynamic conceptualization. (Müller and Schmitt (2015, 322)[7]

The hereby-formulated emergent figurative meanings have their grounding in the descriptive analysis (together with illustrating diagrams) of activated figurativity

---

7 Whenever mention is made of 'metaphor' or 'metaphoric', it is considered to likewise refer and apply to metonymy in the context of this book.

and the composition of cinematic expressive movements. However, the analytical succession of the two dimensions of audiovisual figurativity is not conceived of as fixed but will be handled flexibly according to their respective form and unfolding in each and every campaign commercial. Finally, both dimensions are correlated with one another by formulating an overall figurative theme for each campaign commercial. This figurative theme has a similar status as Cameron's *systematic metaphor*: it is a "construct of the researcher, [...] created to help condense the [...] data, and to summarize metaphorical ways of expressing ideas, attitudes and values" (Cameron, Low, and Maslen 2010, 128). It is the analytical attempt to find a concise wording for a complex dynamic and emergent process. As such, the figurative theme is not claimed to represent the psychological reality or physiological processes of individual spectators (cf. Müller and Schmitt 2015, 337). Instead, it is considered a theoretical tool that summarizes and merges various intertwining forms of audiovisual figurative meaning in the campaign commercials and is thereby likewise conducive to the findings' clarity, comprehensibility, and reliability.

It is worthwhile to carefully examine the respective interplay of the two dimensions of audiovisual figurative meaning-making in this final correlation that completes the analysis. Due to its bottom-up perspective and the concomitant closeness to the data, the interplay between activated figurativity and the affective experience of cinematic expressive movement that gives rise to the figurative theme is considered to play out differently in each campaign commercial. This becomes most apparent when Karl Bühler's ([1934] 1990) *organon model* of language is used as a basis of comparison. In this regard, the interplay of the two dimensions of audiovisual figurativity can be considered in terms of the interplay of the three communicative functions of language that he has spelled out. According to Bühler (1990, 35), the linguistic sign can realize three functions in a concrete speech event: it can be representation,[8] expression, and appeal. He explains that these three functions are, however, not mutually exclusive but that all of them are always co-present in a communicative situation, with varying degrees of dominance. That is to say that Bühler conceives of language to usually realize one function in a dominant manner while the other two are indeed also present but less in the fore. These respective dominance phenomena put a particular mark on meaning-making and communication in the concrete context of use, for instance, with a greater focus on representation in scientific language, on expression in lyric poetry, or on appeal in the case of rhetoric (Bühler 1990, 39).

---

8 Müller has pointed out that "the English term representation is misleading here: the German word *Darstellung* entails the idea of presentation or depiction, it does not imply the idea of re-presentation" (Müller 2013, 204).

The same principle will be suggested to hold for the interplay of activated figurativity and the affective experience of cinematic expressive movement in the process of audiovisual figurative meaning-making: it can play out in terms of various dominance phenomena and thus give rise to variant forms of audiovisual figurative meaning-making. This idea is already rudimentarily outlined with regard to the comparative investigation of cinematic expressive movements in different media formats. Scherer, Greifenstein, and Kappelhoff (2014, 2088–2089) indicate variations in respect to two aspects here: the temporal and the multimodal articulation. In the first case, what is at stake are varying degrees of complexity of the cinematic expressive movement patterns concerning the length of the format. While feature films display a more complex temporal arrangement with longer and varying structures, shorter formats such as commercials show rather short-termed and more concise ones. The second and more relevant case at this point is that of multimodal articulation referring explicitly to "distinct types of intertwining images and sounds" (Scherer, Greifenstein, and Kappelhoff 2014, 2089), in which 'sound' refers to the spoken word. Though the observations made do not specifically refer to the format under discussion in this book, they are nevertheless highly relevant for the argument subsequently presented.

> In television news reports, *speech predominates over audio-visual staging*, with the effect that the visuals often are perceived as mere illustrations, as doublings of the spoken word. Fiction films, on the other hand, tend to *make the audio-visual orchestration salient*, whereof dialogue is only one compositional element. This is however rather a matter of genre and presentational form and format. The way a fiction film aims at establishing temporal gestalts through different articulatory modalities can differ decisively as well: The breathless use of language in screwball comedies differs drastically from the use in taciturn westerns or in musicals where every utterance or sound can initiate the next song and dance act. (Scherer, Greifenstein, and Kappelhoff 2014, 2089; emphasis mine)

These differences with regard to the interplay or the reciprocal dominance of language and audiovisual staging are remarkable because they seem to give the respective genre and format a particular perceptual and experiential shape that comes up with a specific manner of meaning-making.[9] Although the authors

---

9 Remarkably enough, Bühler has already touched upon that correlation when he discusses dominance phenomena among the three functions of language:

> "'Expression in language' and 'appeal in language' are partial objects for all of language research, and thus display their *own specific structures* in comparison with representation in language. To put it briefly, lyric poetry and rhetoric have something specific to themselves that distinguishes them from each other, and also (remaining in the literary realm) something that distinguishes them from epic poetry and drama; and their structural laws are even more obviously different from the structural law of scientific representation." (Bühler 1990 [1934], 39; emphasis mine)

do not elaborate on this correlation, their remarks on various ways of affective addressing of spectators in different audiovisual formats nevertheless provide a starting point for that assumption. Proceeding from their observation that "[c]ommercials in television tend to modulate strong, unambiguous affective experiences most explicitly through both dialogue and audio-visual staging" (Scherer, Greifenstein, and Kappelhoff 2014, 2089), the differentiation between three forms of audiovisual figurativity as proposed in the following is to be regarded as its elaboration and further development.[10] The question of if these three forms are specific to the genre of campaign commercials or might also apply to commercials in general, transcends the scope of this book and should be subject to further investigation.

Following Scherer, Greifenstein, and Kappelhoff's (2014) idea of distinct types of intertwining language and audiovisual staging, the interplay of these two main modalities gives rise to three different forms of audiovisual figurativity on the *macro level* of a campaign commercial. It should be noted that these three forms are conceived of as gradual dominance phenomena, i.e., they are not to be understood as clearly defined either-or types, but rather in terms of ranges merging into one another within a continuum with the following endpoints:

I. Audiovisual figurative meaning-making through the activation of verbally expressed experiential realms (*first dimension*)

II. Audiovisual figurative meaning-making through the affective experience of cinematic expressive movement (*second dimension*)

Of course, both dimensions are always present in the campaign commercials, and the activation of figurative imagery is in effect always embedded into cinematic expressive movement. However, how the two dimensions are distributed within and among the TV campaign ads, how they play out, and how strongly they are represented determines which of the three variant forms of audiovisual figurativity on the macro level is in the end dominant. The argument is theoretically motivated. In this regard, the quantifying distinction serves a better comprehensibility of the (qualifying) assignment of a campaign commercial to one of the three forms on the macro level.

In the case of the first dimension (I), audiovisual figurative meaning-making primarily proceeds from a verbal figurative expression that is activated through a

---

10 The analyses carried out in the following are to go beyond the mere reconstruction of "experiences through both dialogue and audio-visual staging". As such, they aim at a greater differentiation of emergent phenomena based on the concrete markedness of the self-same interplay.

verbal or audiovisual presentation of its imagery. Its temporal dynamics can vary from condensed to extended, e.g., when the experiential realms of a figurative expression is semantically elaborated within a short period of time (unfolding an entire scenario) or recurrently taken up over the course of the campaign commercial with pauses or interruptions in between. Concerning the attentional dynamics, foregrounding is high (and so is activation) in the case of an audiovisual or verbal activation of an experiential realm, and it can persist or possibly increase through an extended elaboration. Depending on whether the temporal and attentional dynamics are condensed or extended, the experiential dynamics of activated figurativity – i.e., the sensory-motor experience of the figurative imagery – likewise can play out in a concentrated (e.g., through a one- and short-time activation) or prolonged manner (e.g., through a semantic elaboration that unfolds over a longer stretch of time).

In the case of the second dimension (II), audiovisual figurative meaning-making primarily proceeds from the affective experience of cinematic expressive movement that becomes the source of understanding something in terms of something else. As may be the case, this affective experience can additionally be made explicit through verbal figurative expressions. Its temporal dynamics are – due to the legally prescribed length of the campaign commercials and as compared to fiction films – of relatively short duration. Therefore, a campaign commercial is suggested to usually consist of one or two cinematic expressive movements. The attentional dynamics can vary from strong to weaker foregrounding of the movement quality according to the interplay of dominants and subdominants. Here, too, foregrounding can increase through extension in time. Depending on whether the temporal dynamics play out in one or various cinematic expressive movements, their experiential dynamics might vary from a simple to a composite affective course gone through by a viewer.

According to which one of the two dimensions predominates quantitatively in a campaign commercial, a particular tendency arises towards either one of them or – in the case of quantitative balance – to an intermediate form. The predominance of activated figurativity is linked with a higher degree of explicitness of audiovisual figurative meaning, whereas in the case of predominant non-verbalized affective experience of cinematic expressive movement, a higher degree of subtlety of audiovisual figurative meaning prevails. If no clear tendency towards either one of the dimensions shows up, a close mutual interplay of explicit and subtle figurative meaning-making is assumed in the campaign commercial. It should be noted again that the predominance of one dimension of audiovisual figurative meaning-making towards the other does not mean that the latter is not present or relevant, let alone that there is no interplay between the two. Instead, the three variant forms are considered – in line with Bühler – dominance phenomena of the interplay of both dimensions in a situated media context. Furthermore, the boundaries and transitions between them are conceived of as fluent. That is to say, they are rather forming a specter within which audiovisual figurative meaning can emerge, unfold, and change, even within the same campaign commercial. This is illustrated by the continuum below (Figure 2).

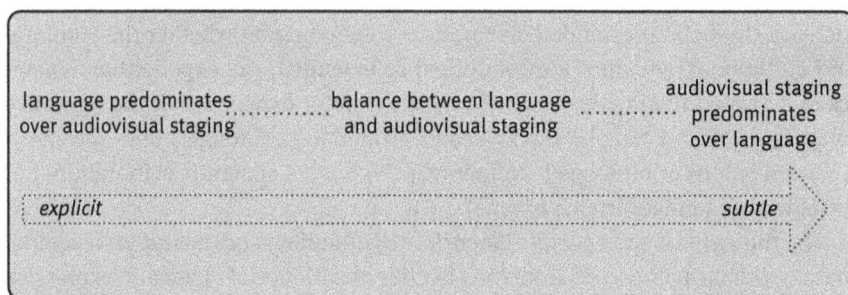

Figure 2: Three variant forms of audiovisual figurativity

In summary, by means of the cognitive-linguistic concept of the activation of metaphoricity (Müller 2008a, 2008b, 2011, Müller and Tag 2010) and the film-analytical approach to cinematic expressive movement (Kappelhoff 2004, Kappelhoff and Bakels 2011, Scherer, Greifenstein, and Kappelhoff 2014) multimodal figurativity and audiovisual compositions meet in three aspects of dynamics: temporal, attentional, and experiential. In this connection, their transdisciplinary combination in a dynamic approach provides methodological tools for analyzing the two dimensions of audiovisual figurativity – the activation of figurativity and the affective experience of cinematic expressive movement – in detail. On that basis, three variant forms of audiovisual figurativity are proposed and specified that are due to the respective dominance – or balance – of the two main modalities language and audiovisual staging. These three dominance phenomena "display their own specific structures" (Bühler 1990, 39) with regard to the temporal, attentional, and experiential dynamics. One main aspect in which the variant forms are assumed to be reflected is the explicitness or subtlety of the emergent figurative meaning and, as a consequence, different focal points with regard to the conceptual and content-related orientation of the campaign commercials. In the following chapters, two campaign commercials from German and Polish parliamentary elections each will be analyzed. The focus of the analysis will be on the respective interplay of the two dimensions of audiovisual figurative meaning-making, how this affects the meaning-making process, and what kind of image it creates of the respective candidate.

6 Angela Merkel, a Sovereign With Civil Roots

In his examination of campaign commercials of the 2005 parliamentary elections for the German Bundestag, Karl Prümm (2008) suggests that their medial professionalism is used as an indicator for the political competence and agency of the parties and their candidates, in short, their capacity to govern. In this respect, he sees parallels to TV product advertising as campaign commercials made use of indirect modes of presentation coming from an 'apolitical sign repertoire', i.e., the 'cinematic code'. Through specific narrative conventions and structural elements, image and camera technologies, the TV campaign ads pointed beyond their situated presentational context, i.e., TV, to the cinema (Prümm (2008, 184) Prümm dissects techniques of cinematic staging as well as motivic reminiscences of cinematic models from campaign commercials of the Christian Democratic Union (CDU), the Social Democratic Party of Germany (SPD), and The Greens. According to him, the campaign commercials appropriate them in order to integrate the candidates into an aesthetic and narrative space that provides them with a framework, a role, a story, a feeling, and thus also with a right to exist and to govern whereby they are made evident.

In this respect, the campaign commercial of the CDU for the 2009 German parliamentary elections constitutes a paramount example of a cinematic staging and film-like composition. It reveals that not only metaphor plays a significant role in the orchestration of meaning-making but also another figurative mode: metonymy. Informed by an intricate interplay of the two, the CDU's TV campaign ad can thus be considered a case of what Louis Goossens has termed *metaphtonymy* in the sense of a "mere cover term which should help to increase our awareness of the fact that metaphor and metonymy can be intertwined" (Goossens 1990, 323). In the case of the CDU campaign commercial, these two figurative modes find their expression in one of the two dimensions of figurative meaning-making so that metonymical meaning predominantly plays out as multimodally activated figurativity, while metaphorical meaning is primarily grounded in sensations evoked by cinematic expressive movement. The campaign commercial is therefore a prime example for the complex interplay between both metaphor and metonymy and between language and audiovisual staging in respect to audiovisual figurative meaning-making. Both activated metonymical meaning in language and emergent metaphorical meaning through audiovisually orchestrated affective experience unfold continuously in time but are brought together and interrelated on the part of the spectator in the process of viewing.

The CDU campaign commercial that entirely focuses on the party's leading candidate, the incumbent chancellor Angela Merkel, is remarkable because its

https://doi.org/10.1515/9783110578782-006

overall figurative theme emerges gradually and without any verbal expression that would have induced it explicitly. The following analysis demonstrates that various audiovisual metonymies (activated by audiovisual specifications of experiential realms) recurring over the course of the TV campaign ad in a similar audiovisual form, unfold a repetitive pattern that exceeds the 'local' meaning of the single metonymies. This pattern foregrounds the principle uniting all metonymies, i.e., contiguity, which in turn is mapped onto the relation between Merkel the German people. On the other hand, the audiovisual staging activates affective qualities that immediately appeal to the viewers and give them a feeling of Merkel's majestic power. As will be shown, due to the constant flow and interplay of metonymy and metaphor, an image of Merkel emerges that brings together qualities, associations, and meanings of both figurative modes in a highly interesting synthesis: the image of a monarchic sovereign who considers herself as somebody with civil roots and thus standing for the people.

6.1 The Image of a Monarch: Angela Merkel as Political Message

In its September 9, 2013 edition, the German news magazine *Der Spiegel*'s cover portrayed Angela Merkel regally wearing a baroque dress, a sash, a necklace in German national colors, and a crown-like headgear (Figure 3 left). The picture is staged within a frame, suggesting that it is a museum object, with a title label below that reads: "Angela the Great" [*Angela die Grosse*]. The corresponding caption on the picture reads: "The new complacency of Angela M." [*Die neue Selbstgefälligkeit der Angela M.*]. It is supposed to represent an ironic adaption of a "Portrait of Catherine II [i.e., the Great] in front of a mirror" (1762–1764), painted by Vigilius Eriksen (Figure 3 right).[1]

In the corresponding article, the author René Pfister criticizes Merkel's manner of electoral campaigning for the parliamentary elections in September 2013. He blames her for avoiding the debate on complex, difficult, or unpleasant topics as well as for avoiding statements regarding the country's future. The campaign message she is communicating instead, according to Pfister, linked the stable welfare of the country to her own person: 'Her message is a message of reassurance: If you vote for me, then you get four good years again.' (Pfister 2013,

---

1 On taking office in 2005, Angela Merkel announced that she would put a portrait engraving of Catherine the Great on her desk (Holm 2005).

24; translation mine) In his article, Pfister seeks to illustrate the ironic message of the cover picture, i.e., of a complacent monarch Merkel, on the basis of the CDU election campaign in 2013.

Figure 3: Cover picture of *Der Spiegel* (left) and extract of V. Eriksen's "Portrait of Catherine II in front of a mirror" (right)

As an example, he mentions a huge election poster that was attached next to Berlin's main station at the beginning of September 2013 showing solely the well-known Merkel diamond (or rhombus) next to the slogan "Germany's future in good hands" [*Deutschlands Zukunft in guten Händen*] (Figure 4). Due to regular usage, the gesture has become a kind of trademark of Merkel, a fact that the poster has taken advantage of for campaign purposes. The concentration on Merkel's gesture as a visually recognizable motif and central campaign message is remarkable as thereby meaning emerges through a close interplay of metonymy and metaphor. The gesture as such is sufficient to stand as a part for the whole person. Simultaneously, the depicted hands activate the imagery of the written metonymical expression that 'something is in good hands' where too a part of the body stands for the whole person bearing responsibility. It is only on that basis that Germany's future that is said to be in good hands is metaphorically understood as a touch- and manageable object that somebody has at his or her command. The interplay of metonymical and metaphorical meaning evokes an image of Angela Merkel as a powerful and qualified decision maker on the basis of a gesture expressing power and balance.

Figure 4: CDU election poster in Berlin during the 2013 parliamentary elections (© dpa)

For Pfister, these circumstances of the 2013 election campaign reveal the height of the CDU's exclusive focusing on its party leader and the concomitant rejection of programmatic contents. The campaign commercial to be analyzed in this chapter suggests that the CDU already during the 2009 election campaign retreated completely in favor of staging Merkel alone. In this light, it is remarkable that the TV campaign ad over its entire course neither mentions nor shows the name of Merkel's party. Only at the very end, the logo of the CDU is shown briefly. Apart from that exception, the whole campaign commercial solely revolves around Merkel in the true sense of the word with a camera focusing on her and thereby making her the center of each shot and sequence. Such an unquestioned centering of a person as a party's political profile and flagship message exhibits strong parallels to the exclusive orientation of a state towards its sovereign in the age of absolutism. This analogy might have motivated the juxtaposition of Merkel and Catherine the Great as absolutistic monarchs on the *Spiegel* front cover.

The CDU campaign commercial for the parliamentary elections in 2009 seems to take up and play with that image of Merkel as a monarch (although it was produced much earlier). However, it does not examine it in the critical manner as Pfister does in his article, instead constructing it according to an understanding in Merkel's favor. The TV campaign ad was released in the beginning of September 2009 and was telecasted several hundred times over the period of three weeks until September 25 on public and private television. It was produced by Kolle Rebbe, a Hamburg advertising agency, that specializes in promoting consumer goods for, e.g., Gauloises, Olympus, or Otto. Before, the CDU had cooperated for decades with the agency Von Mannstein and only in 2001 changed its strategy by employing McCann-Erickson, an international branding expert, in order to modify and enhance its public image (Bialek 2007). Kolle Rebbe was entrusted with the task of managing the entire promotional and communicative appearance of the party in autumn 2007. When asked for the major tasks his agency had to fulfill in the campaign, the Executive Director Stephan F. Rebbe answered that he considers the creation of images and metaphors a key point. According to him, they are able to convey complicated political issues in a straightforward manner by boiling the message down concretely (Kolle Rebbe 2007).

In the medial perception, the campaign commercial seems to have achieved this goal. The journalist Robin Meyer-Lucht (2009), for instance, refers to it as the most professional TV campaign ad of the 2009 election campaign at that point, because it was able to not only make statements but to 'translate' them into images. By staging Merkel as being both inside, i.e., powerful and successful, and outside, i.e., understanding of people's needs, the campaign commercial had found a metaphor for her political style the way she wanted it to be perceived (Meyer-Lucht 2009).[2] By attributing the translation of statements into images to audiovisual metaphor, the static understanding of figurativity in audiovisual media becomes manifest again, suggesting that figurative meaning was pre-existing content that could be packed into moving images.[3] Instead of conceiving of metaphor and metonymy solely from an abstracted product perspective, the subsequent analysis of the CDU campaign commercial is aimed at reconstructing the processual emergence of figurative meaning. From this perspective, Meyer-Lucht's observation of Merkel's staging as powerful officeholder inside and expert on people's needs outside is not conceived of as the result of recognizing metaphorical expressions translated into images. Rather it is considered an emergent outcome of a dynamic interplay between metaphorical and metonymical meaning-making: metonymy unfolds a repetitive part- or aspect-for-whole pattern throughout the campaign commercial, while articulatory audiovisual modalities provide a vital metaphorical imagery on the basis of felt qualities of gravitas, power, and balance.

---

2 In the campaign commercial, Angela Merkel is in the first half shown looking out of her chancellery's window on which recollections of German historical events as well as of her professional history are projected and thus appear as outside, and in the second half in a walk through different rooms of the chancellery, i.e., inside.

3 Forceville's formulation that "commercials *contain* a multimodal metaphor" (2007b, 20; emphasis mine) suggests that audiovisual images are containers that could be 'filled' with figurative content by a producer who intends to elicit audiovisual figurative meaning on the part of the viewers in the way he or she wants it.

6.2 'I Am You': Angela Merkel as Representative of the German People

In the case of the CDU campaign commercial, the two dimensions of audiovisual figurativity (i.e., multimodal activation of figurativity and affective experience of cinematic expressive movement) correspond to metonymical and metaphorical meaning-making. First the commercial will be briefly outlined and summarized. What is particularly noticeable is its baroque-seeming style of framing the candidate Angela Merkel, providing the viewer with an apparently exclusive insight into the separated world ('behind the scenes') of a powerful ruler. Merkel is presented as contemplatively looking out of the semi-reflecting windows of her chancellery, on which recollections of German historical events as well as of her professional history show up as ephemeral projections. This image of recollection is complemented by her voice-over commenting on her thoughts. It is superseded by Merkel's walk through the chancellery that is thematically associated with future political objectives (which are – in a similar manner to the recollections – illustrated and specified through picture-in-picture fade-ins). At the end, Merkel walks straight up to the camera and announces her central message, summed up in the election slogan: "We have the power" [*Wir haben die Kraft*]. Ultimately, the campaign commercial creates the image of an empress who is both a powerful and successful office holder (inside) and at the same time understands what people are concerned with (outside).

Angela Merkel's state of recollection that comprises the first 50 seconds of the TV campaign ad is permeated and characterized by audiovisual metonymies referring to central aspects in her voice-over statements. For example, the utterance "We have shown that we can decrease the number of non-workers, strengthen families, advance education and research" [*Wir haben gezeigt, dass wir die Zahl der Arbeitslosen senken, Familien stärken, Bildung und Forschung voranbringen können*] is complemented by the following projections on the transparent window in front of which she is standing: the families are depicted by a dissolve of a baby being held in an adult's arms, while a young man writing equations on a transparent board represents sophisticated education and research. Words and audiovisual images thereby bring together entities that are "linked within the same experiential domain [...] or frame [...]" (Mittelberg and Waugh 2014, 1748). By the audiovisual depiction, one of these elements "is profiled, allowing inference of the other element(s)" (Mittelberg and Waugh 2014, 1748). In the mentioned utterance, the dissolve of a baby relates to and evokes the verbally expressed families by virtue of being one adjacent aspect of the latter. In a similar manner, the shown researcher writing math formula refers to the verbally expressed education and research by embodying a pragmatic implication belonging to the same frame. In so doing, the metonymical principle of a contiguous entity or aspect standing for the respective entire idea brings in a particular perspective on the addressed topic. This feature or effect of metonymy has been referred to as "domain highlighting" by Croft (1993, 348) and is considered an outcome of "the point of view of the speaker's concerns" (Ruiz de Mendoza 1997, 164).[4] In this respect, metonymy (just as metaphor) is considered to imply the "manipulation of experiential domains in understanding and communication" (Croft 1993, 354).

In order to grasp this effect of metonymy in more depth, it is necessary to look beyond the general observation that audiovisual images solely represent verbally expressed content and instead take a closer look at the respective dynamic interplay of words and audiovisual images. Audiovisual metonymies of the kind described above occur throughout the entire CDU campaign commercial: in its first two-thirds as ephemeral projections on the transparent window showing Merkel's recollections of the past, in the last third as picture-in-picture fade-ins presenting associations of future objectives. Due to this recurrence, the metonymical principle of contiguity unfolds in terms of a repetitive pattern over the campaign commercial's course, thereby strongly foregrounding metonymical meaning in a multimodal manner.

This argument opens up a link to the theoretical concept of activated metaphoricity. The activation of metaphoricity is conceived of as a dynamic and temporally organized process that finds expression in an "expressive effort that speakers [...] employ to mark metaphoricity as a salient object of attendance in the flow of a conversation" (Müller and Tag 2010, 111; see also Müller 2008a, 2008b). One possibility of such a foregrounding is the employment of different modalities to convey metaphorical meaning: "Using more than one modality to express a metaphor foregrounds metaphoricity in the ongoing utterance and it follows the iconicity principle of: More material indicates more meaning." (Müller and Tag 2010, 94) The audiovisual presentation of close and adjacent aspects of Merkel's mentioned ideas amounts to the (additional) expressive effort of a speaker using gesture in order to convey metaphorical meaning in face-to-face interaction.[5] By giving it a multimodal form, it makes the metonymical

---

4 Dirven (2002, 80) presents similar comments on the effect of metonymy: "Metonymy, therefore, is a cognitive process reflecting the speaker's intentions."

5 Müller and Tag (2010, 111) themselves point out that "these foregrounding strategies are not restricted to foregrounding metaphoricity". Instead, "the foregrounding principles as well as their respective strategies [...] are to be conceived of as first steps towards a cognitive-linguistic and micro-analytic methodology that reconstructs the temporal and dynamic orchestration of meaning in multimodal utterances".

imagery salient in the viewer's attention and thereby increases metonymy's domain-highlighting effect: the selection of certain parts, aspects, or features complemented by their particular audiovisual concretization makes the specific profiling of the whole idea particularly obvious. In the following, the emergence and multimodal foregrounding of metonymical meaning in the CDU campaign commercial will be explained in greater detail. It will be shown that by unfolding a repetitive pattern, metonymy draws the viewer's attention to the adjacency and closeness of the entities it is linking to one another, most notably of Merkel and the citizens.

The first 20 seconds of the TV campaign ad provide the initial and central link between Merkel and the German people by bringing together her political development and the recent German history in the event of the reunification. Merkel and the Berlin Reichstag building are closely linked to each other by constituting a fixed, twofold visual ground in relation to the faded faded-in projections that never cover it completely. Being shown in a dissolve montage with a high-angle shot of the Reichstag behind her in the first shot, Merkel's voice-over says: "I was not born a chancellor" [*Ich wurde nicht als Kanzlerin geboren*]. Thereby, the verbally uttered 'chancellor' and the image of the Reichstag building are related to one another and create an audiovisual metonymy by linking her, the German head of government, to the seat of the government. Subsequently, the image of the Reichstag is partly covered by scenes of the fall of the Berlin wall. People climbing and standing on the wall and in front of it in November 1989 are shown while Merkel's voice-over says: "But then came one of the greatest moments of happiness for our country, the unity" [*Aber dann kam einer der größten Glücksmomente unseres Landes, die Einheit*].[6] The choice of the word 'unity' in order to refer to the event of the German reunification is remarkable for it semantically highlights the aspect of togetherness and closeness. The audiovisual concretization further foregrounds and specifies this impression by presenting groups of people holding out their hands to each other and standing crowded together, complemented by the audible shout of the Monday demonstrators, "We are the people" [*Wir sind das Volk*]. As a result, another audiovisual metonymy emerges, linking the verbal reference object 'unity' [*Einheit*], i.e., the German turnaround, to one of its adjacent and pragmatic implications, i.e., the re-gained togetherness of the people. Subsequently, a cut shows Merkel from a wider angle in front of the window following a cyclist passing by on the Berlin wall and in front of the Brandenburg

---

6 The translations are as literal as possible in order to arrive at a clear picture of the "specific experiential dimensions and foci" of the metonymical imagery and of the concrete "interplay between what is being said and how this is being staged audio-visually" (Müller and Schmitt 2015, 321).

gate, almost entirely covering the Reichstag building in the background. The cyclist, organically arising from the crowd of people (through a dissolve montage) and riding freely along the wall, on the one hand stands metonymically for the reunified citizens. Simultaneously, he becomes a metonymy for Merkel who, as one of the reunified, purposefully sets off for the future which, in her case, is her political career. The dissolve of the bicycle ride to a now rather frontal image of the Reichstag and Merkel's comment "I wanted to serve Germany" [*Ich wollte Deutschland dienen*] link the cyclist's path with her personal development: the event of the turnaround becomes the birth of her political career and she a representative of the people.

By returning to the visual ground of Merkel and the Reichstag at this point, the building is conflated with the verbally expressed 'Germany', i.e., the seat of the German government stands metonymically for the residents of the country it is politically representing. Thereby, the audiovisual metonymy from the beginning has changed: it has turned from an image of political representation to an image of popular representation through the historical event of the turnaround. In other words, the German reunification functions as a connecting element between the person of Merkel and the people. Through these means, the campaign commercial creates a subjective perspective on her personal background as well as her recent political position and lays the ground for the central metonymy of the campaign commercial: *Merkel stands for the people.*

The choice of pronouns on the verbal level supports this link: it changes from 'I' to a more including we ('our') and ends with 'I' again. While in the first sentence, Merkel refers exclusively to herself ("I was not born a chancellor") with regard to her personal background and political career, she extends the scope of reference in her second utterance ("one of the greatest moments of happiness for our country") and thereby links herself to the German citizens. She thereby constructs a shared period of history as the common ground for herself and the people.[7] On that basis, she returns again to her personal story ("I wanted to serve Germany"), however, now with the background of being related to those she wants to serve. Figure 5 depicts the dynamic interplay of verbal utterances and audiovisual staging, resulting in the audiovisual metonymical meanings described above that connect Angela Merkel with the German people.

---

7 The adversative conjunction 'but' [*aber*] preceding her sentence about the German reunification presents the historical event as a moment of vocation for Merkel having led her to take the path of politics. Thereby, the turnaround of the Berlin wall constitutes both the beginning of a new era for German society and the birth of Merkel's political career.

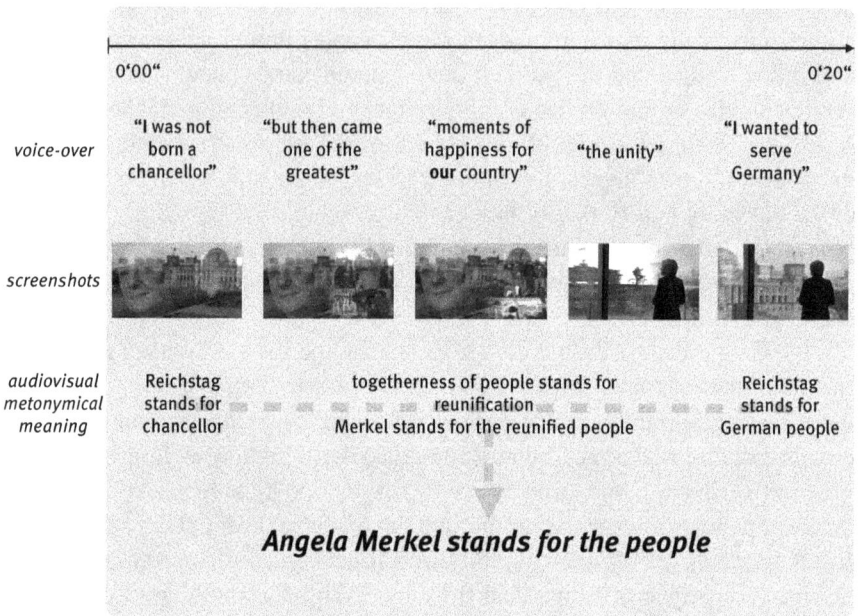

Figure 5: Metonymical links giving rise to the metonymy *Angela Merkel stands for the people* (ANGELA MERKEL)

The fact that Merkel and the German people are linked with one another in this manner during the first 20 seconds of the campaign commercial does not imply that they are on the same level. This might be primarily attributable to the particular contiguity relation underlying the audiovisual metonymies just outlined: the link between the Reichstag and Merkel, the togetherness of the people and the reunification, or the connection between the Reichstag and the German people is not that of an internally motivated *pars pro toto*. Instead, these entities are connected by closeness, contact, and adjacency to one another as they belong to the same semantic frame (Fillmore 1982; cf. Mittelberg and Waugh 2014, 1754–1755). These considerations draw on Roman Jakobson's distinction between synecdoche and metonymy proper[8]:

---

8 Within the field of gesture studies, Mittelberg (2006, 2010, 2013) has revisited Jakobson's distinction in order to account for the cognitive-semiotic principles that motivate gestural meaning as well as to draw attention to the role of metonymy for the emergence of metaphorical meaning in verbo-gestural contexts.

To show the hands of a shepherd in poetry or the cinema is not the same as showing his hut or his herd, a fact that is often insufficiently taken into account. The operation of synecdoche, with the part for the whole or the whole for the part, should be clearly distinguished from metonymic proximity. (Jakobson and Pomorska 1983, 134)

Jakobson's emphasis on the differentiation between these two forms of contiguity relations seems to be of relevance for the analysis of the central metonymy. The metonymical pattern throughout the entire campaign commercial primarily consists of external metonymies (or metonymies proper in Jakobson's terms) that on the one hand emphasize the closeness and (adjacent) togetherness of Merkel and the people. On the other hand, they simultaneously foreground a particular perspective on the frame (and thereby their different *status*) both belong to: the perspective of political representation and leadership. Merkel's words confirm this overtone: starting from her initial sentence that she was not born a chancellor, she professedly distances herself from the ancient image of hereditary nobility, i.e., gaining political power consequently by birth, and instead emphasizes her civil background (and closeness to the people). Nevertheless, the fall of the Berlin wall became her initial moment to set out for a political career ("But then came one of the greatest moments of happiness"), that is to say, to become the first among equals in order to "serve Germany". This way, she nevertheless affirms the aforementioned image of herself as a monarch, however, in a modified manner that amounts to her own understanding: a monarch legitimated by her civil roots and vocation and not by hereditary nobility.

This particular image of a civil sovereign is strengthened and extended in the further course of the campaign commercial by an emerging metonymical pattern: Merkel's voice-over interacts with audiovisual images that present adjacent aspects of what is expressed verbally. What is audiovisually shown, therefore, does not merely refer to itself but stands exemplarily for something to which it is related by (external) contiguity. Such a multimodal concretization highlights the metonymical imagery as well as the particular perspective on the superior frame and puts it into the viewer's line of focus. Saying that she finally became the German chancellor, Merkel's voice-over is complemented by an audiovisual image of her inauguration oath. In the further course of the campaign commercial, the audiovisual concretizations keep substantiating the verbal metonymical expression while giving them a perceptible form by adjacent aspects: families through a baby, education and research by a researcher, excitement by jubilating people and a cheering Merkel. Figure 6 depicts these stages of audiovisual metonymical meaning from 0'20" to 0'53" that further strengthen the central metonymical link between Angela Merkel and the German people.

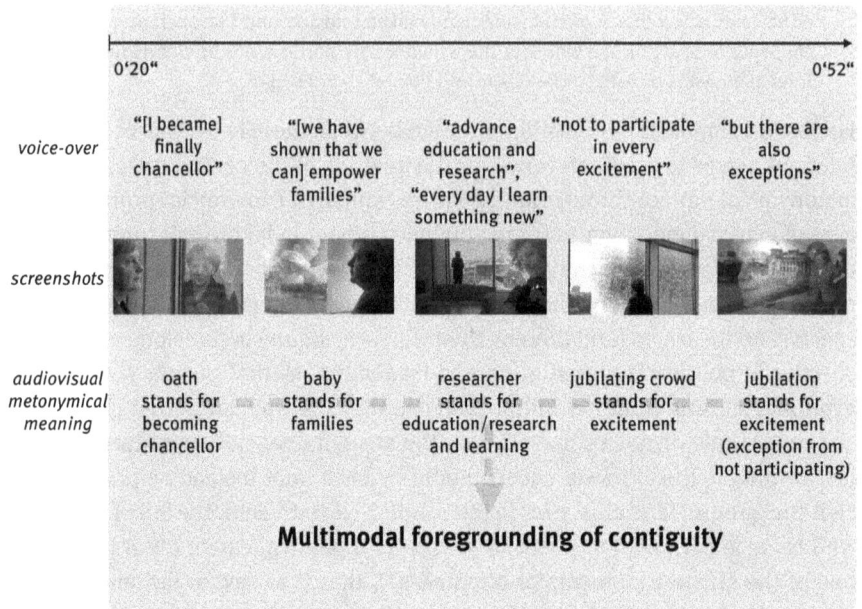

	0'20"				0'52"
voice-over	"[I became] finally chancellor"	"[we have shown that we can] empower families"	"advance education and research", "every day I learn something new"	"not to participate in every excitement"	"but there are also exceptions"
screenshots					
audiovisual metonymical meaning	oath stands for becoming chancellor	baby stands for families	researcher stands for education/research and learning	jubilating crowd stands for excitement	jubilation stands for excitement (exception from not participating)

Multimodal foregrounding of contiguity

Figure 6: Emerging repetitive metonymical pattern and foregrounding of contiguity (ANGELA MERKEL)

The prominent foregrounding of contiguity serves as an effective basis for Merkel's final statement at the end of the campaign commercial: "Together we can achieve a lot. We, all together." [*Gemeinsam können wir viel erreichen. Wir, alle zusammen.*] The entire TV campaign ad or, more precisely, its composition, amounts to this verbal declaration that explicitly highlights closeness and togetherness. So far, the metonymical pattern has rather structurally foregrounded the contiguity relation between Merkel and the people by constantly associating two adjacent elements from the same frame or realm. Now, at the end, the central metonymy is additionally taken up and presented semantically by the use of various collective expressions ('together', 'we all') in spoken language. Furthermore, the metonymy is foregrounded by Merkel's gaze into the camera and her direct address of the viewer when she speaks of 'we' as well as by the presentation of 'WE' in a third modality, namely in written language.

Such an additional communicative effort that makes metonymical meaning more explicit suggests that the degree of activated metonymicity on the part of the viewer noticeably increases at the end of the campaign commercial. Before that final statement, i.e., during the last 36 seconds of the campaign commercial, the metonymical pattern continues in the same manner as in the first 53 seconds by audiovisually presenting adjacent aspects of what Merkel is talking about. For instance, the mention of the weak that need protection is complemented by the image of a leg being washed. Figure 7 gives an overview of the audiovisual metonymies during the last 36 seconds of the TV campaign ad that finally culminate in the highly activated central metonymy of the campaign commercial.

In summary, the detailed analysis of the interplay between what is being said and how it is being staged audiovisually has shown that the campaign commercial of the CDU is permeated and structured by numerous audiovisual metonymies. All of them are attributable to the dimension of figurative meaning that is grounded in the activation of figurativity through vitalizations of experiential realms (first dimension). The particular repetitive pattern of metonymical meaning that emerges and unfolds in the CDU TV campaign ad displays the following profile: its temporal dynamics are extended by the recurrence of various audiovisual metonymies throughout the whole campaign commercial that are characterized by the same audiovisual form. The extendedness does not result from a semantic elaboration of one scenario but from the structural foregrounding of the metonymical principle of contiguity. The attentional dynamics are characterized by a strong foregrounding due to the verbal and audiovisual articulation of the single metonymical meanings. This foregrounding indicates a high degree of activation because the audiovisual staging makes the metonymical imagery available as vital sources of experiences. In their dynamic unfolding as a repetitive pattern, the degree of activation is thus constantly high and even increases at the end through the additional articulation of metonymical meaning in written language. The experiential dynamics are temporally condensed from one activation to the next. However, it seems that the sensory-motor experiences of the respective single experiential realms play a minor role due to the unfolding of metonymical meaning as a repetitive pattern. Instead, the experience of contiguity and closeness between the two related experiential realms inherent in every sensory-motor experience of the emergent metonymies orchestrates the experiential dynamics in an extended and comprehensive manner.

Arising from the interplay of language and audiovisual vitalizations and unfolding as a recurrent pattern, metonymical meaning is productive in eliciting and strengthening a positive image of Merkel as a politician who is associated with her citizens through inherent closeness and pragmatic contiguity. Most importantly, the detailed reconstruction of how this central metonymy emerges and the profile of the metonymical pattern on the basis of the three aspects of dynamics clearly suggests that metonymical meaning-making is as dynamically characterized as is metaphorical: it emerges and unfolds in the course of time, in the flow of attention, and in the flow of the viewers' experience. A metonymical mapping as the outlined one between Merkel and the German people is,

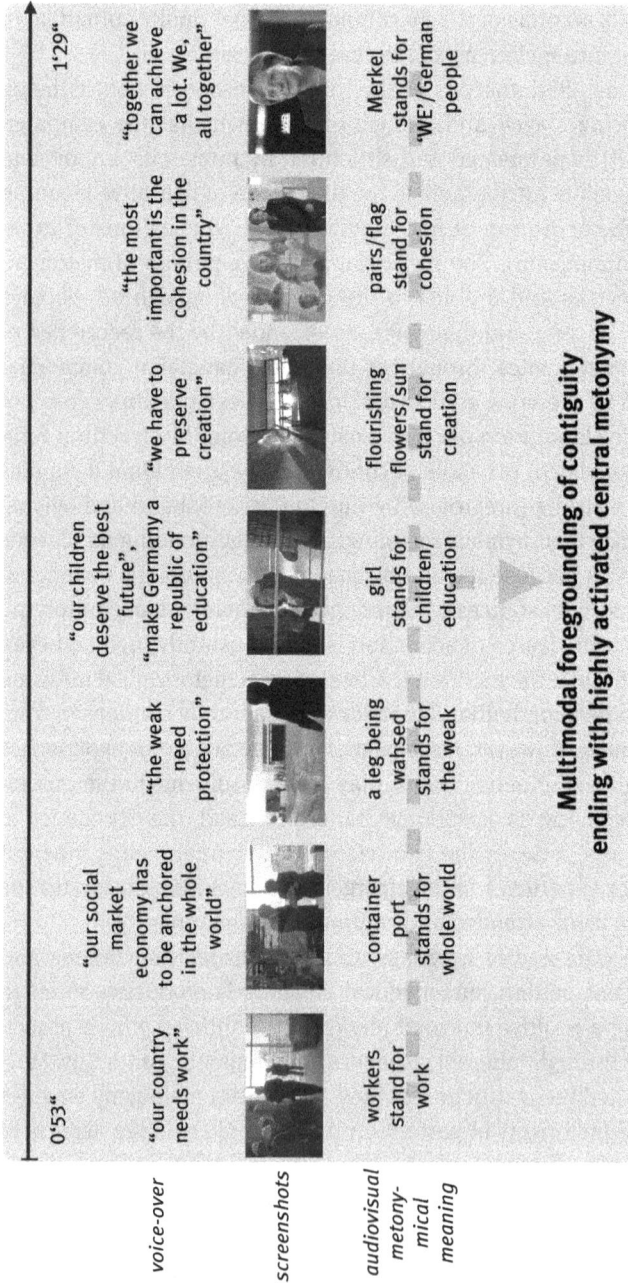

Figure 7: Unfolding repetitive metonymical pattern (ANGELA MERKEL)

according to Mittelberg and Waugh (2009, 329), an essential "prerequisite for the metaphorical mapping" in that it provides a semiotic basis that "leads the way into metaphor" (Mittelberg and Waugh 2009, 347). Before analyzing the interplay between metonymical and metaphorical meaning in the CDU campaign commercial, the following section will focus on metaphorical meaning-making from the affective experience of cinematic expressive movement.

6.3 The Experience of Gravitas: Angela Merkel as Center of Power

The window that Merkel gazes out of separates and connects. On the one hand, it divides the space by creating a visible boundary between an inside and an outside. Thereby, it clearly distances Merkel (in front of it) from the social reality on the other side and creates a separate, private, and interior space for her. This boundary between a public outside and a private inside is, on the other hand, transparent and thus indicates at least a point of contact between the two spaces and the potential for their mutual link. In this respect, the transparent windowpane seems to be an adequate realm of experience for the metaphorical understanding of Merkel's political style:

> She is thereby simultaneously inside (powerful, successful office holder) and outside (understanding what people are concerned with). With this, the campaign commercial has found a metaphor – a metaphor for the political style of Merkel as she wants it to be seen. (Meyer-Lucht 2009; translation mine)

Meyer-Lucht's conclusion seems to semantically correspond to the emergent metonymical meaning (the link between Merkel and the people) outlined in the previous section. However, what is striking in his formulation of the metaphor are the qualitative features he's attributing to Merkel's political style in respect to the two sides of the windowpane. Proceeding from the established cognitive-linguistic understanding of metaphor in audiovisual media, i.e., as a fixed entity that translates a statement into an image, one does not get very far as the qualitative features of success and power are neither expressed verbally nor contained visually. From the dynamic approach to audiovisual figurativity taken in this book, these qualitative attributes are considered to be grounded in experiential qualities that are evoked by audiovisual staging, more precisely, by cinematic expressive movement. As such, it is in line with Mark Johnson's notion of "immanent or embodied meaning [...] that lie[s] beneath words and sentences" as "felt qualities, images, feelings, and emotions that ground our more abstract structures of meaning" (Johnson 2007, 17). Thereby rejecting exclusively conceptually and propositionally-informed approaches to the emergence of (figurative) meaning, Johnson argues the case for the fundamental role of aesthetics for reasoning and understanding: "In the visual arts, it is images, patterns, qualities, colours, and perceptual rhythms that are the principal bearers of meaning" (Johnson 2007, 234).

This section demonstrates that the experiencing and understanding of Angela Merkel as a successful and powerful office holder is not primarily grounded in the image of the transparent windowpane but above all in the affective experience of cinematic expressive movement (Kappelhoff 2004, Kappelhoff and Bakels 2011, Müller and Kappelhoff 2018). This targets the second dimension of audiovisual figurative meaning-making. The CDU campaign commercial is composed of two expressive movement units (emu) that correspond to the division of topics into past achievements during its first two thirds (0'00" to 0'52"), and things to achieve in the future during its last third (0'53" to 1'29"). Their respective experiential qualities evoke a particular sensation of power and dominance that viewers experience bodily and attribute to Merkel. It is this sensation that provides the experiential ground for understanding Merkel in terms of something else, namely of a powerful, even absolutistic, sovereign.

In order to make clear the difference between audiovisually represented content and cinematic expressive movement, the analysis starts from a short outline of what is shown during the TV campaign ad's first 52 seconds. It begins with Angela Merkel approaching a window from an interior perspective and observing the Reichstag building staged as her background behind the windowpane.[9] This initial image of literally observing something subsequently transforms metaphorically into an act of recollection,[10] whereby the observation of things outside becomes an observation of mental images of recollections. The outside perspective of the window is partly covered by appearing and disappearing fragments and impressions of the historical event when the Berlin wall fell in 1989. Subsequently, Merkel's contemplative thoughts change towards her political career and the achievements of her previous period of governance (from 2005 to 2009), finally returning to herself as an adaptive, principled, and down-to-earth person.

---

9 It is noteworthy that this view from the chancellery to the Reichstag building as the seat of the German government is not in accordance with reality. It is an aesthetic arrangement experienced in the process of viewing and, as such, is ascribed to Merkel as an as authentic one: "[T]here is no action disclosed to the spectators in an objectively given world, rather there is a subjective world of experience, experienced in concrete ways of perception and forms of sensation" (Müller and Kappelhoff 2018, 182).

10 This perceptual experience is strengthened by the fact that Merkel's verbal comments come (as a voice-over) from the offstage, i.e., she does not move her lips during the whole campaign commercial, except right at the end (1'20" to 1'24") when she is directly addressing the viewer.

After this rough introductory outline of the represented content (the 'what'), the focus in the following will be on how it is brought about through audiovisual articulatory modalities. The first 52 seconds of the TV campaign ad are characterized by only a few, slow camera movements and a visual repetitive structure: Merkel standing in front of the window is the recurring motif of each shot. Neither she nor the camera is moving in a remarkable manner, evoking a calm and moderate atmosphere. When movement is part of the shot, e.g., when Merkel approaches the window or when the faded-in projections of the reunification show people climbing the wall, it is – due to slow motion technique – nevertheless always experienced in a temperate manner. The duration of the shots corresponds to this calm and moderate atmosphere. They are not changing quickly but provide adequate time for their represented content (i.e., Merkel in front of the window) to unfold as a tableau before being followed by the next one.[11] The picture-in-picture fade-ins are composed in the same manner: although their duration is shorter, they all follow one another in a tempo that does not disturb the calm atmosphere. The reason for this is the rhythmic alignment and interplay between fore- and background, i.e., between the tableau and the fade-ins. They change regularly, thereby never competing with each other for the viewer's attention, and interact harmoniously by being interrelated (e.g., through lines of sight) and thus rather compose to one image (see Figure 5 and 6).

Through the balanced composition of the Merkel tableaus with an elongated duration of time and the fade-ins alternating in quicker, but regular, succession, a consistent order is established that fits the sense of tranquility. This foregrounding of regularity and balance matches the visual composition: the recurring Merkel tableaus and the fade-ins clearly divide the audiovisual image into a deep foreground and a flat surface in the background, a visual pattern that lasts for the whole campaign commercial. On the basis of this visual arrangement within the frame, Merkel appears as the central element and vanishing point of each shot. This is primarily achieved by lighting: Merkel (and the foreground in general) appears darker – as if she was standing in front of a screen –, sharper, and clearer than the rest of the image. In contrast, the fade-ins are rather blurred and fuzzy images. This aesthetic opposition contributes to the differentiation between the here and now and the recollections on the semantic level. Furthermore, Merkel is mainly shown in close-ups and medium-close-shots whereby she is evidently in the foreground as against the other parts and objects within the frame. This visual composition contributes to the regularity and balance outlined above.

---

11 This is also due to invisible editing, especially motivated cuts and dissolves between subsequent shots.

The coordinated interplay between a mainly calm foreground and a slightly moving background is also evoked by the underlying music: rhythmic and cheerful violin notes in the background are overlaid by slow legato piano and violin notes in the foreground. By analogy with the visual composition, these two components are characterized by a remarkable interplay. While the cheerful and playful melody in the background brings in a slightly moving and lilting quality, it is not strong enough to dominate the temperate and solemn melody in the foreground. On the contrary, its dynamics lap around the dominant legato notes that call the tune: there is no tonal eruption or irregularity, but a well-ordered structure that is only moving slightly. The interplay of the musical dominant and subdominant as a constant pattern over the course of the campaign commercial thus brings about an experience of regularity and temperateness. The solemn, grave, and moderate character of the underlying music corresponds to court baroque pieces of music that were used for the purpose of sovereign representation and demonstration of power and supported the sequence of determined fixed steps while dancing. This recourse to baroque majesty matches the visual motif of Merkel in front of the window that evokes the impression of an illustrious empress or commander observing her empire.

In summary, camera, visual composition, and sound design compose to a distinctive movement pattern or, more precisely, an expressive movement unit (emu) that brings about an *experience of temperateness, balance, and gravitas*. Through its temperateness and gravitas, it grounds the recollection image by unfolding a contemplative atmosphere. The experiential qualities of the emu are attributed to Merkel as an office holder and make her appear as a majestic and dignified ruler. Figure 8 depicts selected shots from the first emu in order to provide visual and thematic reference points for the outlined experiential qualities.

Along with the represented (i.e., Merkel looking out of the window, observing past events) and the verbal content (i.e., historical and political achievements in the past), these experiential qualities unfold a quiet and contemplative atmosphere with Merkel in the first emu. In contrast, the second emu (from 0'53" to 1'29") evokes a more dynamic atmosphere that has changed from the previous recollection to an action image. This shift is characterized and experienced by a transformation of the qualities outlined above. However, not all of them are changing completely. For instance, the balanced arrangement of elements within the frame persists as well as Merkel's position as the visual vanishing point and stable dominant figure of each shot. What complements these features and merges with them to a different movement composition is the modest dynamization, evoked by movement within the frame, of the camera, and of the music. Therefore, the second emu is not perceived as strong contrast or disruption of the previously staged experience of temperateness, balance, and gravitas but as a consistent development or transition between two connected successive parts.

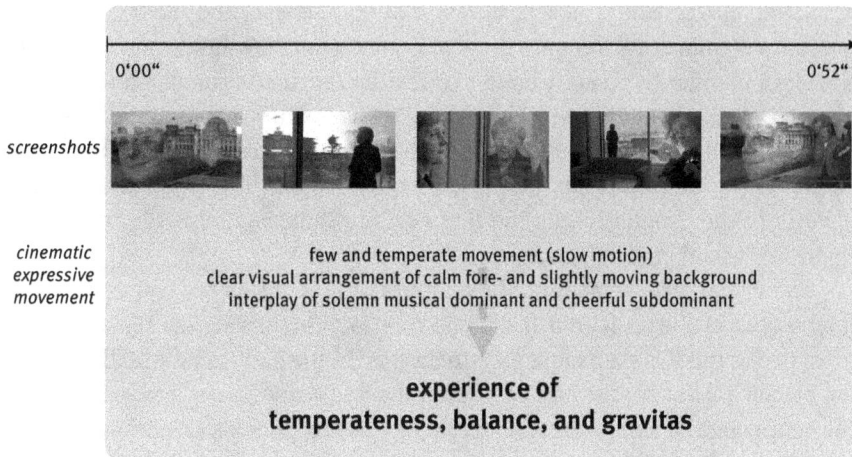

Figure 8: Experiencing temperateness and gravitas (ANGELA MERKEL)

The second emu starts with a turnaround: Angela Merkel turns her back on the window (and on her reflection of the past) and strides into the depth of the room towards the camera, enumerating measures that have to be taken in the future. The mentioned actions are again audiovisually depicted by picture-in-picture fade-ins. The camera follows Merkel through the chancellery, where she meets a group of visitors and a little girl waving at her. Merkel's stride ends in front of the camera, now addressing it as well as the viewer directly by saying the final slogan: "Together we can achieve a lot. We, all together." [*Gemeinsam können wir viel erreichen. Wir alle zusammen.*] The word 'we' appears capitalized and in bold type in front of a small German flag. In the following dissolve to a black screen, the word becomes the beginning of the final slogan: "WE HAVE THE POWER. CDU" [*WIR HABEN DIE KRAFT. CDU*].

The staging of this represented content during the last third of the campaign commercial is primarily characterized by an increase of movement and dynamics. Merkel is still the recurring motif of each shot. Yet, she is not standing still anymore but striding powerfully into the depth of the room now, accompanied by a camera that circles around her at moderate speed. In doing so, the dynamics of her movement is even more foregrounded and increased. But Merkel's walk is shown in slow motion and the circling movement of the camera is also slow, wherefore the viewer does not experience a strong dynamization but one in moderation. In this way, the dynamics of the second emu are linked to the first one in a twofold manner: they differ from it due to a higher degree of dynamics, but simultaneously build on it by advancing and accelerating its few, calm, and temperate movements. The shot duration of the tableaus and the fade-ins does not differ significantly from the first emu: generally, they follow one another in a smooth manner by dissolves and in a regular tempo. As compared to the first emu, it is striking that in the middle of the second emu (i.e., approximately from 1'06" to 1'20") the shot duration is marginally shorter than at its beginning and end, evoking the impression of a slight intensification. The temperateness and balance of the dynamics from the first emu are thus maintained in the second (more active and energetic) one.

The visual arrangement of Merkel and the fade-ins as the two central and interrelated elements within the frame that foregrounds her as the vanishing point of each shot is even more prominent than in the first emu due to the widening of space. Merkel's turning away from the flat windowpane and striding into the depth opens a half-rounded room she is entering after leaving her office. This semicircle embraces her and puts her evidently in its center. The camera that continuously circles around her creates the same effect: Merkel is the unquestioned focal point of each shot. As in the first emu, lighting and field size also contribute to this highlighting by making her appear darker, sharper, and clearer than the rest of the audiovisual image. This principle of a well-ordered, balanced arrangement within the frame corresponds to the power and temperateness evoked by the movement dynamics and further qualifies it by dominance.

Corresponding with the movement dynamics within and evoked by the shots, the underlying music slightly intensifies and dynamizes, too. The previously prevailing gravitas and solemnity through dominating slow legato piano and violin notes persists. However, the pitch of the whole melody rises remarkably as compared to the first emu. Moreover, the melodic line is more notably structured by means of sforzandos that recur regularly and lead to a clear dominance of and concentration on one single note that sets the tone with respect to the remaining notes. Through this accentuation as well as by a slight increase of its tempo, the playful melody interacts with the solemn one on equal grounds and thereby evokes the experience of an intensification heading for a point of culmination. This culmination is no eruption, though, but the clear return of dominance of the solemn over the playful melody, fading harmoniously away as a decrescendo at the end of the campaign commercial. Although the music dynamizes and intensifies in this second emu, its regularity and well-ordered structure never get lost. As in the first emu, the melodies are moving temperately but never irregularly or unexpectedly. Thus, music's controlled powerful swelling with a dominant accentuated center corresponds to the visual composition.

In summary, it is again the interplay of camera, visual composition, and sound design that dominates the movement composition of the second emu which is why its experiential qualities are so closely related to the first emu. In the second emu, they are persisting, intensifying, or elaborated and evoke an *experience of dominance, balance, and power*. As with the first emu, it grounds the action image by unfolding a progressive atmosphere. These experiential qualities are attributed to Merkel as an office holder that make her appear as a powerful ruler who holds everything under control and in balance. The selection of shots depicted in Figure 9 serves as visual and thematic reference points for the experiential qualities.

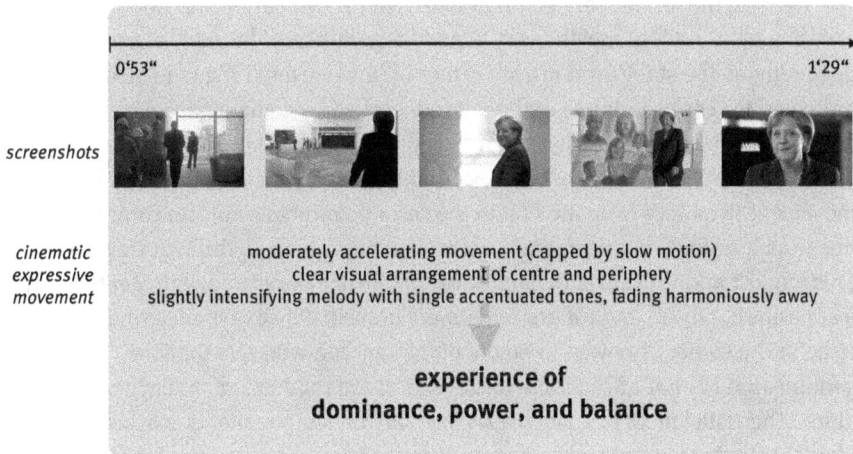

Figure 9: Experiencing dominance and power (ANGELA MERKEL)

Cinematic expressive movements are not considered as distinct temporal units (Scherer, Greifenstein, and Kappelhoff 2014, 2088; cf. also Kappelhoff 2004, Kappelhoff and Bakels 2011, Müller and Kappelhoff 2018, Müller and Schmitt 2015). Instead, they amount to viewers' flow of experience in the process of viewing reconstructed through their analysis in terms of individual expressive movement units. Therefore, the two previously analyzed emus of the CDU campaign commercial are not regarded as separate but as being interrelated. As such, they orchestrate the whole TV campaign ad by "creating an affective course that the spectators go through experientially by watching it" (Scherer, Greifenstein, and Kappelhoff 2014, 2088; see also Kappelhoff and Bakels 2011, Müller and Kappelhoff 2018). That is to say, viewers feel the gravitas, the dominance, and the power that are orchestrated by the audiovisual compositions of the two emus and attribute these qualities to Merkel. They go through the transformation from the initial rather contemplative atmosphere that subsequently dynamizes and intensifies to an action image. As both emus are also closely interrelated with regard to their experiential qualities, this transformation does not represent a disruption in the flow of experience but a consistent unfolding and development: the interplay of gravitas, temperateness, and balance of the first emu and dominance, power, and balance of the second emu brings about an affective experience of stability that grounds the 'metaphorizing' (see Cameron 2018) of Angela Merkel, i.e., of experiencing and understanding her in terms of something else. This emergent metaphorical meaning that arises from the affective experience of cinematic expressive movement can be formulated as follows: *Angela Merkel is experienced and understood as an (absolutistic) sovereign who is the center of power.*

Wearing the formal pant suit that makes her stand out in each shot, and either standing nearly still or moving very temperately, Merkel is introduced from the very beginning as the stable and mighty center of power everything is related and subordinated to. The orderliness and regularity evoked by camera, visual composition, and the arrangement and rhythm of music provide the ground to conceive of her as a self-controlled and dignified office holder. The increase and intensification of movement dynamics from the first to the second emu does not run contrary to this image as it unfolds in a temperate, controlled manner (e.g., through slow motion). This modest and restrained dynamization is directly associated with Merkel's political position, power, and influence: viewers immediately experience what it means to be in the center of power, to be the dominant one who sets the tone. This emergent meaning is not attributable to the expressive qualities of audiovisual staging alone. The visual motif of an empress observing her empire that is activated through Merkel's staging in front of the window as well as the classification of the underlying music as baroque court music complement the emergent metaphorical conceptualization and create a consistent image of Merkel. Such an interaction of various levels is in line with Schmitt's notion of multimodality in regard to metaphorical meaning-making in audiovisual media as integrating "verbal utterances, represented audiovisual elements and the figuration of an expressive movement" (Schmitt 2015, 321).

Remarkably enough, the metaphor of Angela Merkel as a (absolutistic) sovereign is neither contained in the language, nor in the audiovisual representation of the campaign commercial. Instead, it emerges dynamically in the flow of experience the viewers go through when watching the TV campaign ad, i.e., while being moved by experiential qualities that are evoked by the two emus. The bodily experience of gravitas, dominance, and power provides viewers with the experiential ground for an image of (sovereign, absolutistic) power that is associated with Angela Merkel. Within the affective experience of stability that unfolds through the interplay of emu 1 and emu 2, an (post-hoc) activation of metaphoricity takes place at the very end of the campaign commercial. The campaign slogan "We have the power" makes the sensation of stability explicit by putting it into a word ('power') and at the same time concretizing its imagery ('we'). This concretization seems to be contradictory because the experiential quality is on the level of audiovisual representation actually attributed to Merkel, whereas now it is verbally extended to a collective 'we'. However, by bringing together the multi-modal activation of figurativity and the affective experience of cinematic expressive movement and, concomitantly, metonymical and metaphorical meaning, in the following section it will be demonstrated that the extension of the experiential quality (i.e., power and stability) from Merkel to a collective 'we' is by no means a contradiction. It instead paves the way for Merkel's central political message.

6.4 "We Have the Power": Angela Merkel and a Sense of Commonality

Strictly speaking, the metonymical and the metaphorical meaning in the campaign commercial are inconsistent with one another. While the emergent metonymical meaning foregrounds Merkel's civil affiliation and closeness to the people, the audiovisually evoked sensation of stability make her experience- and understandable as a powerful (downright absolutistic) sovereign in control. The image of a citizen who belongs to the collective of civil society and the image of a head of state who is outranking all other individuals are strict opposites and do not seem to be compatible in a consistent image or political message. On the other hand, Meyer-Lucht (2009) considers the campaign commercial the most professional TV campaign ad of the 2009 election campaign which brings about a "lulling at the highest stage". If the campaign commercial was indeed contradictory and inconsistent with regard to its central message, Meyer-Lucht (2009) could hardly rate it as a "bravura piece of political persuasive communication' that 'achieves its communicative objective very efficiently". It seems that the viewer does not feel any semantic inconsistency between the metonymical and metaphorical meaning by watching the campaign commercial, i.e., between Merkel as one of the people and Merkel as a downright absolutistic sovereign. One possibility to clarify this issue might be the recourse to a principle that Mittelberg and Waugh (2009) have called "metonymy first, metaphor second" in order to describe the structural interplay of both figurative modes. In the case of the CDU campaign commercial, metonymy indeed leads the way into metaphor by providing an obviously more basic and intuitive connection between Merkel and the people as suggested by the cognitive theory of metaphor and metonymy:

> The grounding of metonymic concepts is, according to Lakoff and Johnson (1980: 39), "in general more obvious than is the case with metaphoric concepts, since it usually involves physical or causal association". Hence, metaphors which are grounded in metonymy are more basic and natural than these which do not have a metonymic basis: with these, metonymy provides an associative and motivated link between the two conceptual domains involved in metaphor. (Radden 2000, 93)

The distinct basicness of metonymical meaning is due to the fact that it brings together two entities from the same experiential domain (e.g., Barcelona 2009) or frame (Fillmore 1982) that are either linked through an inner contiguity relation (e.g., part for whole) or an outer contiguity relation (i.e., by being pragmatically linked) (see Mittelberg 2006, 2010, 2013 for the differentiation of internal and external metonymy in verbo-gestural contexts of use). Merkel's metonymical relation with the civil society is actually general knowledge that is moreover made explicit when Merkel's voice-over says, "I was not born a chancellor" and thereby implicitly distances herself from sovereignty by birth. However, the metonymical link between Merkel and the German people emerges and unfolds dynamically over the course of the entire campaign commercial in the form of a repetitive pattern foregrounding the principle of contiguity.

This link is established and highly foregrounded at the beginning of the campaign commercial, namely in the historic event of German reunification. In doing so, the campaign commercial actually does not draw on the mere fact that Merkel is a citizen like others. She even implicitly disagrees by her utterance "I was not born a chancellor" with a basic connection of herself by birth. Through her verbal utterance "But then came on of the greatest moments of happiness for our country, the unity" she makes the event of the turnaround the birth of her political career. At the same time, the use of the collective personal pronoun 'we' opens up a point of contact with the German people. In other words, the German reunification provides the ground for an outer contiguity relation between Merkel and the people. Both are connected by the pragmatic context of having experienced the same historic event. This metonymical link persists through the multimodal foregrounding of contiguity that strengthens Merkel as one of the people, her civil roots, and her proximity to people's concerns. As such, it builds an evident ground for metaphorical meaning that, in turn, brings about the image of a sovereign ruling everything. However, the audiovisual metaphorical meaning that makes Merkel experienceable as a stable center to which everything is related and clustered around, does not run contrary to her metonymical closeness to the people. Through the interplay of metonymical and metaphorical meaning, an overarching figurative theme of the TV campaign ad emerges that can be formulated as follows: *ANGELA MERKEL IS EXPERIENCED AND UNDERSTOOD AS A POWERFUL SOVEREIGN WITH CIVIL ROOTS WHO IS CLOSE TO THE PEOPLE.*

The reason for why the two facets of the campaign commercial's figurative theme are not contradictory becomes particularly apparent through the written statement at the very end of the campaign commercial: "We have the power". Due to the ongoing metonymical foregrounding of contiguity between Merkel and the people this 'we' cannot be referred to Merkel's party, the CDU. Indeed, her party is not once mentioned throughout the entire campaign commercial except for its faded-in logo at the very end in the lower right corner. Thus, the extension of the mentioned power, which viewers over the course of the entire campaign commercial have solely experienced with Merkel, to her party is unlikely, as the latter has hitherto played no role.[12] Instead, everything has been oriented towards Merkel: she has the power because she is always in the center, because everything is subordinated to her, because she sets the tone. Now, at the end, the metonymical link between her and the German people becomes verbally explicit ("Together we can achieve a lot. We, all together") and is thereby highly activated. Through the final slogan "We have the power" the experience of Merkel's power is thus retrospectively extended to the people, the citizens, and thus also to the viewers. They are allowed to feel themselves incorporated into this stable center of power – a literal sense of commonality (see Kappelhoff 2018). Put differently, Merkel's power is the people's, or viewers', power. She gives them the feeling of stability and balance. Therefore, she is entitled to stand and speak for the people: "We, all together".

In this respect, the emergent figurative theme *ANGELA MERKEL IS EXPERIENCED AND UNDERSTOOD AS A POWERFUL SOVEREIGN WITH CIVIL ROOTS WHO IS CLOSE TO THE PEOPLE* is consistent with the metaphor of the transparent window for Merkel's political style that Meyer-Lucht (2009) has mentioned in his article. According to him, the window locates her both inside, i.e., as a powerful and successful office holder, and outside, i.e., understanding people's concerns. This twofold presence of a political and a civil or social, as well as of a private and a public self, on the level of audiovisual representation fits into the figurative theme of the campaign commercial. Such emergent figurative meanings are, however, not exclusively attributable to visual motifs and audiovisual representation, but primarily emerge from the dynamics of activated metaphoricity or metonymicity and of audiovisually orchestrated affective experiences.

To conclude, the developed figurative theme of the campaign commercial clearly indicates that the *Spiegel* cover picture of Angela Merkel as Catherine the Great is consistent with Merkel's self-understanding and her party's understanding of her as staged in the 2009 TV campaign ad. What Pfister (2013) had criticized with regard to the CDU's 2013 election campaign, namely the party's exclusive focus on the person and competence of its chancellor, proves itself already in the campaign commercial of 2009. Merkel sends a message of reassurance to the citizens (Pfister 2013, 24): as long as she is in the center, has control, sets the tone, and ensures stability and balance, the citizen is entitled to be included in this power and safety.

---

12 Admittedly, Merkel is potentially metonymically linked to the CDU through the fact of her party affiliation.

It is Merkel's sovereignty, her position as the supreme monarch who has her eye on everything that is the central message and justification for her re-election: 'Because *I* am the center of power, i.e., because *I* am the queen, *we* will succeed.'

6.5 Conclusion: Metaphor and Metonymy as Interrelated Meaning-Making Processes

The analysis of the CDU campaign commercial clearly indicates that both metaphor and metonymy contribute to the emergence of the overall figurative theme in equal measure. The exclusion of either would amount to extracting a crucial aspect of the TV campaign ad's overall statement and completely change it. Without the metonymical link of Merkel with the people through the pragmatic context of the German reunification, the experiential quality of monarchic and stability-providing power remained restricted to her. Without it and thus solely with the metonymical connection of 'I am one of you', in turn, the campaign commercial would lack the decisive sensation of stability and power that provides Merkel with an affective contour and makes her experientially palpable. Due to that intricate interplay of metaphor and metonymy that Goossens (1990) has aptly termed by the notion of metaphtonymy, an exclusive focus on metaphor might overlook crucial processes and aspects of audiovisual figurative meaning but also of figurative meaning in general. In line with its dynamic understanding of audiovisual figurativity, the analysis documents the dynamic nature of not only metaphor but also of metonymy. As such, it is likewise considered a process of meaning-making that unfolds in time and that can be cognitively and affectively activated, e.g., through audiovisual vitalizations of its imagery. Thereby, it provides evidence that Müller's (2008a) concept of activation of metaphoricity and Müller and Tag's (2010) analysis of the foregrounding of metaphoricity are equally applicable to metonymy; clearly illustrated by how the activated metonymies in the campaign commercial and their temporal unfolding as a repetitive pattern make the principle of contiguity salient.

In the analysis, metonymical as well as metaphorical meaning have turned out not to be isolated representational contents that are instantiated or contained in words and audiovisual images.[13] Rather, it is clearly indicated that they emerge and unfold as ongoing processes through the flow of time, attention, and experience.

---

13 However, they interact with audiovisually depicted visible or audible elements (such as objects, actors, landscapes, etc.) (cf. Schmitt 2015, 314). Hitherto, previous cognitive-linguistic studies have too one-sidedly focused on only this form of figurative meaning-making in audiovisual media and thereby completely ignored other, dynamic forms.

In the CDU campaign commercial, metonymy and metaphor each play out in the two dimensions of figurative meaning-making (see Chapter 5). Metonymical meaning emerges through the audiovisual concretization, i.e., the activation of mainly verbally expressed experiential realms and thus in a rather explicit manner. Metaphorical meaning, on the other hand, arises from the affective experience of cinematic expressive movement and thus in a subtler manner. The interplay of both brings together the contiguity between Merkel and the people (the more explicit form of figurative meaning) and the majestic power of an empress (the subtler, rather felt form of figurative meaning) in equal measure. This intricate mutual relatedness in the process of audiovisual figurative meaning-making reminds of Johnson's phenomenologically informed take on meaning-making in general:

> [M]eaning is a matter of relations and connections grounded in bodily organism-environment coupling, or interaction. The meaning of something is its relations, actual and potential, to other qualities, things, events, and experiences. In pragmatist lingo, the meaning of something is a matter of how it connects to what has gone before and what it entails for present or future experiences and actions. (Johnson 2007, 265)

On the macro level of figurative meaning-making, the CDU campaign commercial thus displays a balanced interplay of the two dimensions of figurative meaning and also of language and audiovisual staging. This balanced form brings about the overall theme and political message that the viewer associates with Angela Merkel. In this manner, the aesthetic arrangement and narrative structure make obvious recourse to film and cinema. Instead of a clear predominance of language over audiovisual staging (as it is assumed to be typical for television news reports), the CDU campaign commercial tends to "make the audio-visual orchestration salient, whereof dialogue is only one compositional element" (Scherer, Greifenstein, and Kappelhoff 2014, 2089). Moreover, its composition of the two expressive movements amounts to an elaborated affective dramaturgy (cf. Scherer, Greifenstein, and Kappelhoff 2014, 2089) that orchestrates a transition from a recollection image to an action image. In doing so, Merkel is integrated into an aesthetic and narrative space that provides her in a film-like manner with a framework, a role, and a story. In other words, by telling Merkel's political story, the TV campaign ad at the same time creates a story about Merkel that makes her palpable, comprehensible, and ultimately evident. On the one hand, it creates the image of a powerful sovereign that is not of hereditary nobility but of civil origin and therefore close to the people. On the other hand, the well-established metonymical pattern extends the qualities of power associated with Merkel to the people she is standing for and thereby evokes a feeling of stability and security. Viewers conceive of her as being powerful and competent because they feel her gravitas, power, and dominance as experiential qualities in their own bodies.

7 Donald Tusk, a Leading Builder Under Pressure

In the 2011 Polish parliamentary elections, the Polish Prime Minister Donald Tusk was in the same situation as Angela Merkel in the 2009 German parliamentary elections: after four years as Prime Minister he stood for re-election.[1] Proceeding from this position of the incumbent, both the campaign commercial of his party, the Civic Platform [*Platforma Obywatelska*] (PO), and the entire election campaign focused foremost on the achievements of the government under Tusk's previous leadership (Kolczyński 2012, 44). This content-related orientation is a parallel between Tusk's and Merkel's TV campaign ads.

The selected PO campaign commercial is simply called PREMIER DONALD TUSK (advertising agency mindshare) and concentrates solely on Tusk as officer holder and head of government. In terms of its content, Kolczyński has summarized it as pointing out three thematic motives: (1) naming successes of the government (past); (2) presenting images from Tusk's campaign (present time); and (3) expressing the belief in the well-being of Poland (future) (Kolczyński 2012, 46). With that said, the PO campaign commercial displays clear analogies to the CDU TV campaign ad.[2] Moreover, it parallels it in terms of the aesthetic arrangement and audiovisual staging a metonymical pattern relates single shots that merge into one another through dissolves to short captions. In the CDU campaign commercial, this connection is provided between spoken language and picture-in-picture fade-ins. Furthermore, Tusk is presented via voice-over throughout the entire campaign commercial, commentating on what is shown and contextualizing it on a higher level with regard to its national and international relevance. As in the CDU campaign commercial, he also ends looking to the future of the country that concerns all. During all this, Tusk at no time addresses the spectator directly on the level of audiovisual representation as does Merkel at the end of the CDU campaign commercial. He, on the other hand, addresses the Polish citizens directly verbally at the beginning in the personal and informal plural form of address 'you' [*wy*].

---

1 Unlike the office of the German chancellor, the Polish Prime Minister is not elected but nominated and appointed by the President of the Republic of Poland. This nomination is, however, oriented to the majority situation in the Sejm (the lower house of the Polish parliament) and the Senate (the upper house of the Polish parliament) resulting from the parliamentary elections and the coalition that is formed on this basis.

2 One difference is that Merkel's election campaign plays no role in it, instead images of her in various situations are shown that underline different roles and personal facets (e.g., jubilating during the World Cup in 2006, meeting the staff in her office, or being in eye-contact with a little girl from a visiting group in the chancellery).

https://doi.org/10.1515/9783110578782-007

The following analysis of audiovisual figurative meaning-making in the PO TV campaign ad will demonstrate that, despite various content-related and aesthetic analogies, it gives rise to a completely different image of its candidate and a contradictory message as compared with the CDU campaign commercial. It will be reconstructed how the PO's TV campaign ad evokes an image of its protagonist and incumbent Prime Minister, Donald Tusk, as a leading builder who is under pressure (overwhelmed and overloaded) with regard to finishing his project of building the house of a prosperous Polish state. With this, figurativity in campaign commercials is shown to play out temporally, attentionally, and especially experientially differently in each case in spite of the potential recourse to similar motifs or a comparable use and arrangement of articulatory modalities of audiovisual staging. The fact of using one and the same technique, object, or element gives no evidence about its status and role within the situated media context into which it is embedded (i.e., the campaign commercial as a whole).

Accordingly, one reason for the major difference between the CDU and the PO campaign commercial is the respective configuration and the mutual interplay between the two dimensions of audiovisual figurative meaning-making. Contrary to the CDU's campaign commercial, figurative meaning in the PO campaign commercial is much more language-induced, i.e., it emerges from activations of imagery by verbal elaborations, and from audiovisual concretizations of an entire scenario. The affective experience through cinematic expressive movement subordinates to this dimension and qualifies the figurative scenario affectively, which as such emerges primarily multimodally. Because the audiovisual staging takes a backseat with respect to language, while both dimensions had a balanced status in the case of the CDU campaign commercial, no such film-like style unfolds with Tusk. Instead what is presented is an argumentative and openly promoting style that reminds of classical product and campaign advertising. Admittedly, it is not only the interplay of the two dimensions, but also the particular figurative imagery with its audiovisual staging and verbal elaboration that unfolds a dramatic atmosphere with an overwhelmed protagonist in the PO TV campaign ad.

A detailed analysis of the two dimensions of audiovisual figurativity clarifies and reconstructs how this image and understanding of Tusk emerges in the process of viewing. After some introductory remarks on the PO's election campaign for the Polish parliamentary elections in 2011, the verbal and audiovisual activation of the figurative experiential realm to a complete vital experiential scenario is illustrated and subsequently complemented by an analysis of the cinematic expressive movement. Finally, both dimensions are brought together with regard to their interplay for the emergence of an overall figurative theme.

7.1 Highlighting an Ongoing Process: "Poland Under Construction"

The election campaign before the 2011 Polish parliamentary elections was characterized, among other things, by the legal and political debate about the prohibition of paid campaign commercials on the radio and television. In February 2011, the lower house of the Polish parliament, the Sejm, attempted to change the electoral law by an amendment that would interdict the broadcasting of paid forms of presentation or political advertising in electronic media, such as radio and television (Kolczyński 2012, 34). The initiator of this amendment was the ruling party, the Civic Platform (PO). The background of its attempt was the wish to qualitatively change the campaign and to make alternative (and more direct) communicative forms apart from campaign commercials more attractive for the parties (Kolczyński 2012, 34). The Sejm further explained this step by citing the need for a balance of power between big and small political parties in view of their unequal financial budget (Dziok 2011). However, the Polish Constitutional Tribunal declared it (after the contestation by parliamentarians of the Law and Justic party) to be not in conformity with the parties' and politicians' freedom of speech and expression as well as with the voters' right to information gathering ("TK: Dwudniowe wybory i zakaz," 2011). It was therefore rendered inoperative in July 2011 (Kolczyński 2012, 35), one month before it would have been effective and three months before the parliamentary elections took place.

Contrary to previous declarations, the PO became the party that spent the most money on the broadcasting of TV-advertising and that displayed the largest share of purchased minutes (Peszyński 2012, 186). As compared with the 2007 parliamentary elections, the PO increased the percentage of its costs for campaign advertising in the field of television enormously (in private even more than in public service television), while the proportion for radio broadcasts remained almost unchanged. In the run-up to the October 9 elections, the PO dominated electoral advertising (Kolczyński 2012, 39). According to the department of supervision for the Office of the National Council of Broadcasting and Television [*Biuro Krajowej Rady Radiofonii i Telewizji*], the proportion of the PO's expenses for the broadcasting of paid announcements amounted to 41.4% of the total spent by all parties (Kolczyński 2012, 39).[3] Compared to the 2007 parliamentary elections, this was tantamount to an increase of nearly 17% (Kolczyński 2012, 40).

---

3 Comparing the PO's percentage of expenses with that of Jarosław Kaczyński's party Law and Justice [*Prawo i Sprawiedliwość*] (PiS) which amounted to 26% (Kolczyński 2012, 39), illustrates the PO's dominant presence during campaigning.

Apart from the PO, other parties' election committees, however, purchased relatively few minutes and spent significantly less money for this purpose in 2011 than they had during the previous two parliamentary elections, a possible result of the unclear legal framework. In turn, more use was made of the medium of the Internet, also for the dissemination of audiovisual reports and programs (Peszyński 2012, 198–199). The decision of the Constitutional Tribunal concerning the legal admissibility of paid campaign commercials on the radio and on television was taken in July and thus fairly late for the parties in order to reframe the original campaign conception (Kolczyński 2012, 35).

As a result, the initial condition before the elections was favorable to the PO and its coalition partner, the Polish Peasants' Party [*Polskie Stronnictwo Ludowe*], who had been in office since 2007.[4] The PO's nominated candidate, Bronisław Komorowski, won the 2010 presidential elections and became the President of Poland. According to public opinion surveys, the PO was from the beginning of 2011 ahead in favor with the population (Kowalczyk 2012, 255). In this light, the PO strategically focused mainly on its achievements of the terminating office term to keep favor (Kolczyński 2012, 44, Peszyński 2012, 188). As a keystone of the its communicative strategy for the election campaign, Kolczyński (2012, 45) mentions two promotional cycles in order to present the work of the political leader Tusk as concrete successes: "Poland under construction" [*Polska w budowie*], consisting of seven TV campaign ads that were also available on the Internet, and "Poland is changing" [*Polska się zmienia*], comprising of six Internet campaign commercials. The first cycle was primarily characterized by the format of the man on the street, i.e., statements of normal people, who reported on investments and achievements owing to the initiative of Tusk's government (Kolczyński 2012, 45, Kowalczyk 2012, 267). During the second cycle, primarily single party politicians were at the fore, who emphasized successes in acquiring funds from the European Union and their future use for national concerns and problems (Kolczyński 2012, 45).[5]

---

4 Winning the 2011 parliamentary elections, the PO was the first (and so far the only) incumbent governing party in post-communist Poland that was re-elected and reappointed in office (Szczerbiak 2013, Turska-Kawa and Wojtasik 2012).

5 Often, a third type of PO campaign commercials is mentioned that is reminiscent of negative campaigning. It is a campaign commercial that was broadcasted shortly before the election day and shows rampaging hooligans and aggressive proponents of the cross (in commemoration of the former Polish President Lech Kaczyński, who was killed in an accident) and ends with the following faded-in words: "They will go to the polls, and you?" [*Oni pójdą na wybory, a Ty?*] This indirect attack on the PiS party is considered the only exception from a predominantly positive 2011 election campaign (Kolczyński 2012, 47, Kowalczyk 2012, 267–268).

The campaign commercial to be analyzed is from the first cycle ("Poland under construction"). However, this particular commercial varies from the format of the man on the street and focuses entirely on the head of government, Donald Tusk. Apart from reporting on the successes of the previous office term and his vision of a future strong and prosperous Poland, Tusk is also presented as an ordinary man who is on an equal footing and close to the people. In this respect, the campaign commercial draws on one central element of the PO election campaign, namely Tusk's tour through Polish cities and villages in order to be in touch with the citizens, thereby displaying his presence and awareness of their needs. The commercial shows scenes of his encounters with adults and children in their homes or at public places as well as with workers and soldiers. It also shows Tusk in the context of his work as Prime Minister, interacting with other politicians from home and abroad in order to illustrate Poland's political stability and international reputation. Additionally, Tusk's status as a political leader is brought to the foreground by naming successes he has achieved during his past term of office and visions he has in mind for Poland's future.

These two aspects of closeness to the people as well as successful political leadership also play a role in the CDU campaign commercial of Angela Merkel. However, the image of a powerful sovereign who guarantees stability and balance and is close to the people, as was the case with Merkel, does not emerge with Tusk. This is predominantly due to the slogan "Poland under construction" that permeates the campaign commercial. Its substantial focus is on an ongoing process, i.e., a still running project that is unfinished. The formulation 'under construction' strongly foregrounds this intermediate stage, whereas the final product and the potential successful completion of this process recedes into the background.

The metaphor of a Poland (still) under construction is from the beginning the central subject of the campaign commercial PREMIER DONALD TUSK. Far from being contained into one (audiovisual) image, it instead unfolds over the course of time as a vital experiential scenario: the interplay of words and audiovisual staging, along with audiovisually represented content, develops it step by step. If any of these temporary figurative stabilizations were conceived of as an isolated entity, they would not be perceived belonging to the construction scenario.

The analysis reconstructs on how the imagery of the construction process is audiovisually activated as a concrete and vital experiential scenario and which kind of image of this construction scenario emerges. On that basis, light is shed on the concrete audiovisual staging of the slogan of "Poland under construction" that is central for the campaign commercial. The TV campaign ad has a strong foregrounding of the construction process, wherefore the final product, the building of the Polish state, is not present. By contrast, the work in progress, the activity of building it, and the incompletion are constantly highlighted. This particular audiovisual figurative concretization of "Poland under construction" is linked to Tusk who, in its context, becomes the leading builder and the person responsible for the fragmentary, unfinished state of work. The scenario is complemented and rounded out by a cinematic expressive movement that evokes tension, pressure, and disorganization. As a result, the interplay of both dimensions of audiovisual figurative meaning-making (multimodally activated figurativity and affective experience of cinematic expressive movements) does not bring about the image of a powerful sovereign but of an overwhelmed leading builder who is under pressure and begs for a deadline extension in order to finish his project. In view of the favorable initial conditions of Tusk and his PO during the 2011 election campaign, this overall figurative theme seems inconsistent, even contradictory. In Section 8.4 and Chapter 9, this issue will be taken up and discussed in comparison with Angela Merkel's emergent candidate image as well as with regard to its implication for the notion of incumbent strategies.

7.2 An Unfolding Construction Scenario: Donald Tusk as Leading Builder of a Future Poland

Instead of establishing a contemplative recollection image as in the CDU TV campaign ad, Donald Tusk's campaign commercial gets immediately to the point. The first shot shows the bus, with the sign *Premier Tusk,* on which he traveled around Poland for canvassing purposes in the run-up to the parliamentary elections (Chodakowski 2012). The bus moves dynamically, quickly crossing the image field from right to left. This image is partly dissolved into a transparent Polish flag, slightly fluttering in the wind, suggesting the journey's destination. The two motives of Tusk's bus and the Polish flag anticipate central thematic aspects of the campaign commercial: as metonymies for the head of government and the Polish state or society, they connect the two whose concrete (figurative) form is going to be elaborated over the course of the TV campaign ad. Thematically and on the level of audiovisual representation, these two aspects are reflected by national and international political as well as social successes of Tusk's term in office, and various shots showing Tusk amidst citizens to whom he is close, with whom he is talking and shaking hands. In the following, how they merge to an overall figurative theme through multimodally activated figurativity and the affective experience of cinematic expressive movement will be reconstructed.

As the PO campaign commercial makes extensive use of another modality apart from spoken language and audiovisual staging, it makes meaning on two levels: first and most directly, through the interplay of audiovisual staging and written language (faded-in short commentaries in the lower part of the screen) and secondly, through relating this interplay furthermore to spoken language (Tusk's voice-over). This twofold relatedness of the audiovisual image (to written and spoken language) entails a more complex starting point for the reconstruction of audiovisual figurativity than in the case of the CDU campaign commercial. Simply put, what is shown audiovisually is metonymically taken up and specified through faded-in written commentaries expressing nationally and internationally relevant political achievements of Tusk's government from 2007 to 2011. This is demonstrated, for example, in the following pairings: a woman pushing a child on a swing connects with the caption "200,000 new places in kindergartens" [*200 tys. nowych miesc w przedszkołach*], Donald Tusk amidst a group of children is linked with the caption "law against domestic violence" [*ustawa przeciw przemocy w rodzinie*], or Tusk walking together with his wife is complemented by the caption "extension of maternity leave" [*wydłużenie urlopów macierzyńskich*].

Each of these audiovisual metonymies emerges because what is shown is adjacent to what is written: childcare for the kindergarten, children (potentially affected) for the law, and Tusk's wife for motherhood. This way, a metonymical pattern unfolds throughout the course of the campaign commercial that functions as an illustration for the written successes of Tusk's term of office. What is remarkable is that it does not foreground the principle of contiguity in the same way as was the case in the CDU TV campaign ad. This is due to the high-grade extended activation and elaboration of metaphorical meaning through the interplay of spoken language and audiovisual representation. Tusk's voice-over provides the metonymically depicted success with a personal meta-comment on a more general level: he thanks the Polish people for their trust in him, highlights Poland's position within the European Union, points out that a continuation of harmonious work together will make the future of Poland the fulfilment of ancient dreams, and ends with the observation that Poland still needs some years of quiet to finally succeed. In saying so, the voice-over rates the achievements of his government as successes, and at the same time suggests that there is still more work to do. It is exactly this issue that the campaign commercial unfolds as an emergent figurative scenario of construction.

The imagery of construction is introduced at the very beginning of the commercial in a literal way. The caption "More than 1,400km of roads under construction" [*Ponad 1400 km dróg w budowie*] appears together with an aerial shot of the Rędziński Bridge in Wrocław: the words relate metonymically to what is shown (i.e., the finished bridge standing for the other building projects) and present it as one of Tusk's achievements during his past term in office. Although the bridge was finished and opened in August 2011, this is not exactly what is expressed verbally: the faded-in caption foregrounds an ongoing process as a state of affairs ("under construction"), not the completion. Admittedly, such a contrastive relation between language and audiovisual image[6] does not prevent the activation of metonymical meaning but provides it with a quality of incongruence and tension: despite the written mention of construction, what is seen and perceived is stagnation. This literal introduction of the construction scenario is verbally elaborated some seconds later when Tusk's voice-over points out that "Today, Poland is constructed [i.e., established] as a model throughout Europe" [Dziś *Polska jest stawiana za wzór w całej Europie*]. Although the perfective participle form of the verb foregrounds the end of a process and a finished product, the Polish word *wzór* has a basic meaning of draft or sketch, i.e., something that is only theoretically finished, mostly as a reduced representation or preliminary form of the intended final product. In this regard, Tusk's sentence entails a substantial contradiction between the verb and the implication of incompleteness through the noun *wzór*. Nevertheless, this verbal expression relates Poland to the context of construction and extends the previously figurative scenario to a metaphorical one.

Tusk's voice-over presents the second part of his already started sentence with the adversative conjunction 'but' [*ale*]: "but what for us is most important and unchangeable are the basic values on which we build our joint future" [*ale to co jest dla nas najważniejsze i niezmienne to podstawowe wartości na których budujemy naszą wspólną przyszłość*]. Through the conjunction, both parts of the sentence are formally connected with each other. More importantly, however, the word 'build' semantically relates to the earlier 'model' [*wzór*], evoking a consistent image of Poland that already exists as a draft version and still needs to be built. This way, the focus shifts towards the ongoing and not yet finished action that is moreover linked to the future of the Polish people ("on which we build our joint future"), also with regard to the moment of its completion. Furthermore, speaking explicitly of the foundation of the house to be built ("basic values") foregrounds in particular the start of the construction. This brings about the image of a building project of Poland that has just started and still has much left to be done.

In the following verbal utterances, the construction scenario is further elaborated. Tusk's voice-over says, "If we continue to work in unity and harmony" [*Jeżeli będziemy dalej pracować w zgodzie i harmonii*]. Due to the fact that the verb 'work' [*pracować*] directly follows on the successively activated construction scenario of Poland, it is semantically related to it as bodily work. In addition, the

---

6 A similar case of contrastive relation has been found in a report of the German TV newscast *Tagesschau* (see Kappelhoff and Greifenstein 2016, Müller and Kappelhoff 2018, Schmitt, Greifenstein, and Kappelhoff 2014).

verbal expression entails an explicit focus on processuality and incompleteness: due to the adverb 'further' [*dalej*] and its implication that the reference action is in full play but not yet effectively finished. At the same time, the verb 'work' is conjugated in future tense [*będziemy pracować*], thereby – especially in conjunction with the word 'futher' [*dalej*] – emphasizing the fact that the action is not yet finished in the here and now.

Immediately afterwards, a shot shows Tusk walking along a row of construction workers with whom he is shaking hands. Their clothing, i.e., the building-site helmets, the reflective safety vests, and the overalls, connects to the before verbally expressed image of bodily (construction) work and exertion and transfers it now observably into the context of a construction site. This way, the image of the construction workers both retrospectively activates the verbal expression of (bodily) 'work' by showing its professional agents,[7] and likewise elaborates the construction scenario of Poland by presenting Tusk in terms of a leading builder[8] who is in close contact with his workers. Neither the process of active working nor the product of a finished building object is shown. The audiovisual representation therefore rather evokes a static atmosphere: the workers are standing relatively motionless closely together in a row in front of Tusk who is the only moving person in this scene.

To give a preliminary overview of the emergent figurative meaning in the PO campaign commercial: Poland is experienced and understood as a construction project under the direction of Donald Tusk that already exists as a model and is currently being realized. It, however, is still at an early stage (whereby the aspect of an ongoing process comes up with incongruence and tension) and with much still left to be done. This description is an analytical tool in order to approximately summarize the inherently dynamic unfolding of emergent figurative meaning over the course of time from bottom up. What is remarkable is that the activation of the imagery plays out primarily in spoken language, i.e., monomodally, whereby the scenario nevertheless successively takes shape.[9]

---

7 However, it does so in a contrasting way because the verbal expression reads "continue to work". What is shown, however, is no continuation but stagnation.

8 This is evoked through the fundamental different clothing (in contrast to the workers, Tusk wears a suit) and through the represented action: while the workers stand rather passively in a row, Tusk passes them one after another and shakes hands with them.

9 In research on audiovisual figurativity, this phenomenon has hitherto largely been disregarded in favor of paradigmatic multimodal forms. First studies on the monomodal unfolding of figurative meaning, especially in face-to-face contexts of use, have been carried out by Cameron (2008a, 2008b, 2010), Müller (2008a), and Müller and Tag (2010).

In the second part of the sentence "If we continue to work in unity and harmony", the construction scenario is linked with and elaborated by ancient dreams and wishes. Continuing, "the future of our country can be the fulfilment of our age-old dreams" [*przyszłość naszego kraju może być spełnieniem naszych odwiecznych marzeń*], Tusk's phrase foregrounds the state of incompleteness through the connection between the future completion of the building project (Poland) and the fulfilment of ancient dreams. Subsequently, the so far primarily verbally elaborated construction scenario becomes explicit: Tusk's voice-over declares that "four difficult years are too little in order to realize the plan of building a strong and rich Poland" [*cztery trudne lata to za mało żeby zrealizaować plan budowy silnej i bogatej Polski*]. In saying so, the expression gets to the heart of the previously foregrounded building project of Poland in its incompleteness, and equally elaborates it by qualifying the future product and adding a reason for its unfinished state.

As a result, a future Poland that is strong and rich is experienced and understood in terms of a building that is not yet finished because the construction period was too short. This way, the audiovisual metaphorical meaning, whose degree of activation has gradually increased, reaches its peak in an explicit verbal labeling. Furthermore, it is audiovisually presented and thus additionally foregrounded: two women are shown in front of a sand heap with a shovel and sandbags as Tusk shakes hands with them.[10] This scenario complements the verbally highly activated metaphorical imagery of a future Poland in terms of a construction site where people are still working. In the shot, there is again an obvious focus on the incompleteness of the undertaking. In contrast to the previous shot with Tusk and the building workers, the scenario now appears less organized and professional: the two women are dressed in everyday clothes and stand in the midst of the sand while they are shaking hands with a casually dressed Tusk. The object to be built is nowhere to be seen, the setting is rural, and the construction site appears unorganized and unprofessional. Thereby, the scenario of a site inspection that comes up on the level of audiovisual representation evokes a rather chaotic atmosphere that is underlined by the wobbly camera movement. In this manner, the mentioned 'difficult years' are audiovisually made tangible.

The subsequent shots showing the Polish troops in Iraq keep this impression up by their grainy outdoor setting with blown up dust and sand that makes

---

10 The women maintain protective measures and operations during the flood in Poland in 2010. This is suggested through the caption, which reads: "help for flood victims" [*Pomóc powodzianom*]. However, due to the high-grade activation of metaphorical meaning through explicit verbal labeling, the shown scene is related to the verbally expressed construction context.

it difficult to discern anything. The image of Tusk talking with a commander is therefore a recurring motif of inspection through its similarity to the shots with the two women and the building workers. This clearly demonstrates the elaboration of the experiential construction scenario through the dynamics of viewing: considered in isolation and exclusively on the level of audiovisual representation, the shots of Tusk with the troops would probably not be regarded as being associated with a construction scenario. However, in and through the spectators' process of viewing, their similar motif and staging as well as the previously strongly foregrounded and unfolded construction scenario are contextualized and interrelated.

The highly activated construction metaphor whose focus is so clearly on the incompleteness is finally taken up indirectly at the end through a verbally expressed prospect to its completion: "Some years of quiet [i.e., peace] are still necessary so that Poland finally succeeds" [*Potrzeba jeszcze kilka lat spokoju żeby Polsce wreszcie się udało*]. Here, completion and accomplishment are verbally foregrounded in a twofold manner: by means of the adverb 'finally' that points to an end or completion (that, however, is not yet achieved), and by means of the verb 'succeed' in terms of a successfully finished action or realized plan. Likewise, the future state is foregrounded through the conditional form of the verb [*żeby się udało*].

The final sentence of Tusk's voice-over is remarkable for another reason. It elaborates the construction scenario qualitatively by linking 'quiet' in terms of peace with completion: the last necessary condition for the building of Poland to succeed and to be completed are some "years of quiet". Thereby, the (previous) construction process is qualified as not being quiet but as turbulent, troubled, and restless instead. This is reflected by the variety of different audiovisual metonymies, the concomitant number of diverse topics that are addressed in the campaign commercial, the contradictive activations of the construction scenario, and not least of all by the previous verbal expression "four difficult years". These four years have brought to Tusk's attention many things to be done and have made him go through different settings and situations of a huge and heterogeneous construction site. The message he is expressing is that he is still right in the middle of the whole process, and the building of Poland is not yet completed. Therefore, his final sentence comes across like a request for another term in office in order to finish it, thereby implicitly assuring: more time means an end of the restlessness; it brings the constant being-in-motion, the ongoing and lasting process gradually to a halt and transfers it into a (final) state of affairs, i.e., the finished building of Poland. Figure 10 gives an overview of the major stages of mono- and multimodal metaphor activation and elaboration over the just outlined course of the campaign commercial.

0'00"   0'45"

voice-over

"Poland is constructed as a model" — "on which we build our joint future" — "continue to work" — "four difficult years are too little in order to realize the plan of building a strong and rich Poland" — "some years of quiet are still necessary so that Poland finally succeeds"

screen-shots

captions

"roads under construction" — "more than 700,000 new jobs"

audio-visual metaphorical meaning

Poland as (unfinished) construction project at an early stage of realization — Tusk as leading builder — Poland as unfinished building due to a too short and turbulent construction period — completion of project as another (quiet) period

foregrounding of stagnation — foregrounding of incompleteness — foregrounding of stagnation — foregrounding of stagnation

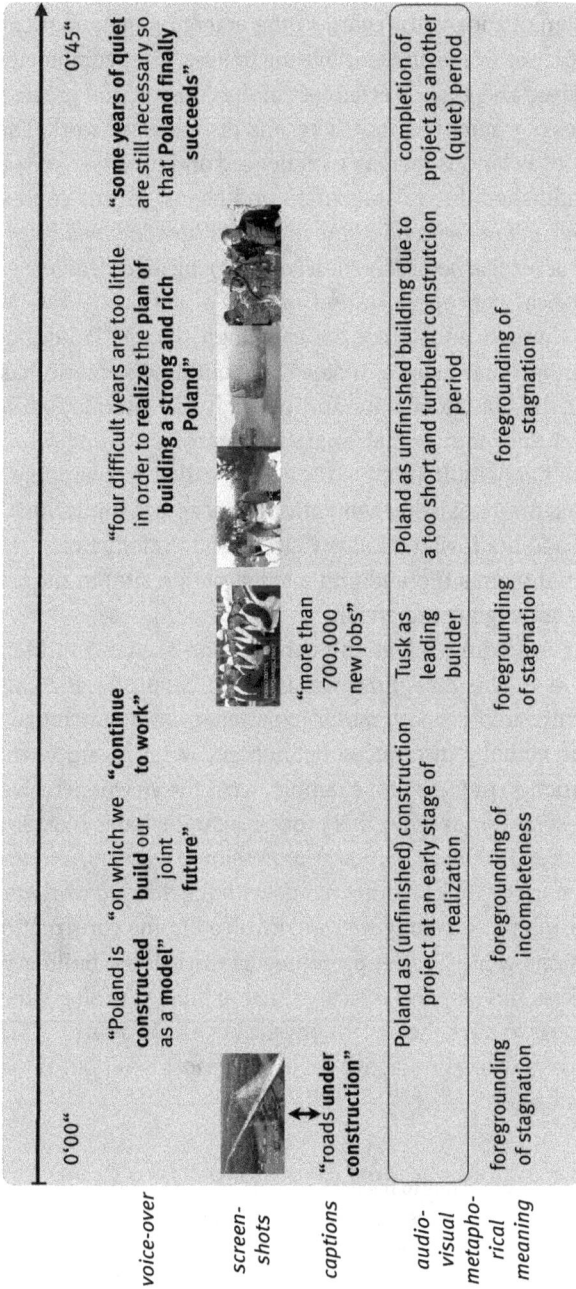

Figure 10: Emergence and unfolding of a construction scenario (PREMIER DONALD TUSK)

In summary, the verbally elaborated and thereby strongly foregrounded image of a construction process is only a few times complemented and concretized by audiovisual specifications in the campaign commercial. Therefore, these moments take on greater significance with regard to the emerging metaphorical meaning through the interplay of words and audiovisual images. They complement the verbally evoked progress and goal-directedness of the construction process with heterogeneous images of stagnation, inactivity, and disorganized work. The progress and development of Poland is thereby experienced and understood as a building project that is unfinished due to stagnation and chaos. In this context, *Donald Tusk is experienced and understood as the responsible leading builder of the future Poland, which is not yet finished, wherefore he is begging for a deadline extension.*

The metaphorical conceptualization of Tusk's work as Prime Minister is not simply there through translating the campaign slogan "Poland under construction" into audiovisual images. Instead, the outlined scenario has emerged dynamically over the course of time and through the interplay of verbal language (voice-over) and audiovisual images, thereby unfolding what Schmitt, Greifenstein, and Kappelhoff (2014, 2104) have called a "mapping in time". Instead of assumed or pre-existing semantic or conceptual similarities, the interplay of language and audiovisual images gives rise to interactions between two present experiential realms (Poland and a construction site) in the context and course of the PO campaign commercial.

This dynamic unfolding brings the construction scenario to life and gives it a shape and a face. This face, however, is a particular one, it comes up with a certain perspective and sensory-motor experiences that concretize and elaborate the scenario verbally introduced beforehand. With regard to the verbally expressed 'construction process', for example, what the viewer perceives through audiovisual representation is what this process actually looks like: as an undertaking that implies skilled workers,[11] non-professional workers, and actual physical labor.[12] The image of Tusk shaking hands with the dressed workers moreover reveals that those who rate among the 'we' involved in the construction process do not have the same work: Tusk is presented as the leading builder who meets the building workers and inspects the construction process or site, whereas those he is meeting appear to have the task of physical work. As a result, this concretization of the imagery evokes no active building atmosphere, but rather a representative and static one.

---

11 At least, this image is evoked due to the professional clothing of the workers.
12 The clothing of the workers evokes the image of people undertaking the hard physical work of constructing entire buildings from the ground up, e.g., pouring the foundation, carrying steal beams, laying bricks, etc.

By contrast, the image of Tusk shaking hands with the two women in the midst of sand and sandbags rather evokes the atmosphere of a busy construction site, albeit an unprofessional and unorganized one. Due to the absence of a building object and active work, it also brings an experience of stagnation. There is no technical equipment to be seen but only a shovel beyond two working people that are neither appropriately nor professionally dressed for the purpose of building. The exclusive prominence of sand in the shots of the women and the troops evokes a sensory-motor experience of its granular and crumbling materiality, thereby coming with an experience of instability rather than of stability and progress that are necessary for a construction process.

Compared with this, through the use of the present tense for the continuation and progress of the building process and the use of future- and goal-related expressions ('future', 'fulfilment', 'will succeed'), verbal language makes salient an image of something in motion that is on the way to its goal. In doing so, sensory-motor experiences are also activated. For example, the use of verbs that entail bodily activity, e.g., 'constructed as a model', 'build our joint future', or 'continue to work', comes with an experience of power and progress with regard to the construction process. Metaphorical expressions such as, "fundamental values on which we build" or "building a strong and rich Poland", evoke a sensory-motor experience of the stability and solidity of the building object. Finally, the statements, "the fulfilment of our age-old dreams" and "so that Poland finally succeeds" activate an experience of completion and accomplishment. As a result, the sensory-motor experiences that are evoked through the verbal and audiovisual concretizations of the imagery of construction display a discrepancy that was already noted for the multimodal activations of metaphorical meaning: in the contrasting interplay of speech and audiovisual images, the processuality of the construction process comes up with a quality of incongruence and tension.

The following section illustrates how this tension in the metaphorical conceptualization of Poland as a construction project in progress is reflected in the affective experience of cinematic expressive movement (the second dimension of audiovisual figurative meaning-making). The audiovisual composition orchestrates a feeling of tension that the viewer ascribes to Tusk as a pressed and overwhelmed leading builder, who has not finished his project. Through an affective experience of tense pressure and breathless hurry, the PO campaign commercial makes the Polish Prime Minister during one term in office tangible as a leading builder with a heavy workload. In doing so, cinematic expressive movement affectively complements and comments on the metaphorical construction scenario.

7.3 Feeling the Workload: Donald Tusk as Being Overwhelmed with Duties

The audiovisual metonymical pattern throughout the PO campaign commercial not only vitalizes the respective achievements of Donald Tusk's terminating office term, but also in its entirety, gives a vivid idea of the variety and number of things that he has begun and achieved: the creation of 200,000 new kindergarten places, 1,400 kilometers of streets under construction, a law against domestic violence, the abolition of military service, economic growth in spite of the economic crisis, more than 700,000 new jobs, the termination of the mission in Iraq. In spite of the considerable number of successes, Tusk nevertheless has to finally admit that he did not succeed in making his overall goal, i.e., the building of Poland, completely into reality during his four years as Prime Minister: "Four difficult years are too little in order to realize the construction plan of a strong and rich Poland". This statement, however, does not link this failure to Tusk's capacity or incapacity. The limited time frame as Prime Minister and its characterization as a difficult period are the circumstances that hindered Tusk in his endeavor to fully realize the undertaking. As such, the audiovisual metonymies not only serve as evidences for the achieved successes of the ending office term but also (in their sum) as a justification for failing to finish the building of Poland. Over the course of the PO campaign commercial, the spectator experiences what this means concretely for Tusk by going through the dramatics and consequences of the leading builder's situation: in terms of sensations of being strained and constricted, under tension and pressure. Therefore, he ends by saying: "Some years of quiet [i.e., peace] are still necessary so that Poland finally succeeds'. Although the verbal expression is impersonal ('sth. is necessary/needed' [*potrzeba*]), this 'quiet' refers to Tusk's needs: he needs a new completion deadline, an additional construction period that buys him time and latitude in order to successfully finish the building project.

Strictly speaking, the PO campaign commercial displays a similar content structure as that of the CDU. It is about the candidate's (and incumbent's) successful achievements during the previous term of office and it concerns what shall be achieved in the future. In the case of Angela Merkel, it is her sovereign dominance and power that arranges everything in a particular order around her, i.e., the unquestioned center of gravity. Donald Tusk's case is different: his achievements, their settings, and the people surround and press him. In contrast to Merkel who keeps others at distance and claims the center of attention for herself alone, Tusk appears hardly as a sovereign head of government but rather as an overwhelmed, surrounded person beaten by the amount of his tasks. On the one hand, this seems rather surprising in view of what is verbally expressed at first of a positive image of a house of Poland that is under construction and will be completed in the not too distant future. On the other hand, the tense atmosphere links to the few audiovisual concretizations of the construction scenario that presents it as a rather stagnating and disorganized situation (see Section 7.2). The image of Tusk as an overwhelmed leading builder is especially grounded in and complemented by the campaign commercial's audiovisual composition, which evokes the sensation of being overpowered, under stress and pressure as an affective experience on the part of the viewer. In contrast to the CDU campaign commercial, the PO's TV campaign ad unfolds this experience within one expressive movement unit (emu) that encompasses its entire length of 45 seconds.

The most striking feature of the commercial's audiovisual composition is the amount of different and heterogeneous topics, images, and shots that alternate in close succession and appear to be rather loosely arranged. As a result, viewers not only understand the amount of Tusk's successes or tasks but also experience them in their quantity. Already during the first ten seconds that address the achievements of the ending term of office, six dissimilar shots follow each other (Figure 11 below): Tusk's election bus together with a faded-in transparent Polish flag, then a mother pushing a child on a swing, the same child in a sand box turning to the camera, subsequently an aerial shot of the Rędziński Bridge in Wrocław, Tusk among a group of children, and finally Tusk patting a boy's head within the circle of a group of people. The shots relate to their faded-in captions, thereby creating audiovisual metonymies of Tusk's achievements in his previous term of office.

This is similar to the CDU campaign commercial (except for the fact that Merkel's successes are expressed verbally by her voice-over). However, the staging of the successes is entirely different. In the CDU campaign commercial, they are presented as picture-in-picture fade-ins within the larger image of Merkel in front of the window. As such, the audiovisual metonymies have a frame that creates cohesion among them and puts them – despite their heterogeneity – into the wider context of Merkel's recollections. In the PO's TV campaign ad, there is no such frame or motif. The audiovisual image as a whole presents the success, and it changes quickly into the next one. As a result, the heterogeneity of the single images (Figure 11 below) is perceived and experienced more intensively and evokes an atmosphere of restlessness, rush, and tension. The camera work contributes to these experiential qualities through a variety of perspectives, field sizes, zooms, and movements from one shot to the next. The shots within the mentioned first ten seconds of the campaign commercial are exemplary for the entire ad and clearly illustrate this fact. While the camera shows Tusk's bus at the beginning in a close-up and slightly low angle shot, it changes in the following to a medium-long-shot on eye-level that shows the mother with her child as well as the child in the sand box, subsequently transforming into an extreme long shot with a high angle showing the Rędziński Bridge, and finally turning into medium (close) shots of Tusk among groups of people in slightly high and low angles. Over the course of this, the camera also changes from being static to moving, e.g., through zooms, pans, and tilts. Such a remarkable alternation of shots that obviously display no overarching pattern comes additionally along with a sensation of disorder and chaos (Figure 11).

	0'00"			0'10"
voice-over	"today, I want to say to all Poles"	"I am thankful to you for your trust and that I can care about our common matters"		"it is my task as a Prime Minister"
screenshots				
captions		"200,000 new places in kindergarten"	"more than 1,400km of roads under construction"	"law against domestic violence"
audiovisual metonymical meaning		child at playground stands for kindergarten places	motorway and bridge stand for built roads	children stand for victims of domestic violence

Figure 11: Heterogeneous topics, camera perspectives, and field sizes (PREMIER DONALD TUSK)

The montage that connects this heterogeneity of topics, images, and shots by means of dissolves intensifies the sensation of rush and disorder even more. Although the transitions between the shots are not experienced too abruptly, they nevertheless mark disruptions and bring about a flow of various impressions that unfolds continuously. This is further supported by the relatively short (and varying) duration (one or two seconds on average) and quick succession of the shots, which leads to a perceived flood of heterogeneous and highly inconsistent images on the part of the viewer. As a result of such a montage and along with the outlined camera work, a highly dynamic and arrhythmic movement pattern emerges over the course of the PO campaign commercial, which brings about an overwhelming experience. In other words, viewers not only see but actually feel what an overload of impressions of topics, things, and images feels like: a rush that approaches them head-on in a quick and accumulative manner and pushes them back by its forceful dynamics.[13]

The quality of the campaign commercial's underlying music parallels this experience in an evident manner. Its minor tonality as well as its pressing forward and

---

[13] This is also to be due to the twofold relatedness of audiovisual images to written and spoken language, which entails a higher degree of complexity for the process of perceiving and processing in the process of viewing.

dramatically rising style that culminates in a final chord unfold a tense atmosphere that gradually intensifies. The interplay of drums, trumpets, and violins establishes a floating and very prominent minor chord at the beginning that increases in volume and intensity. As the music continues, it develops into a melody that is heading towards a crescendo. This increasing momentum forward is additionally intensified by the underlying rhythm of the drums. As such, it grows into a flow that gains in strength and intensity and carries the viewer away by its unfolding force dynamics.

Together with the camera and montage, the sound design thus merges to a particular movement gestalt that brings about an experience of breathless hurry and tense pressure. This movement gestalt becomes graspable as one cinematic expressive movement unit (emu) that pervades the whole TV campaign ad (i.e., 45 seconds). Different from the CDU campaign commercial with two emus, the PO TV campaign ad does not display a perceptible closure of its qualitative duration as in the case of the transition from Merkel's recollection to the action image. The movement pattern in the PO TV campaign ad is characterized by constantly rising dynamics, i.e., intensity and tempo, that only run out at the very end of the campaign commercial when it reaches its peak and enters into relief. The intonation of Tusk's voice-over underlines the holistic character and expressive quality of the movement pattern: it extends over the course of the entire campaign commercial with no remarkable pause or halt but a constantly increasing speaking rate. Likewise, the incessant succession of shots does not interrupt or end at any point in the campaign commercial. All articulatory modalities of the audiovisual composition, i.e., camera movement, montage, and sound design merge to the emu and evoke an experience of tension and pressure that increasingly intensifies and escalates. Figure 12 depicts the unfolding of the outlined movement pattern over the course of the campaign commercial.

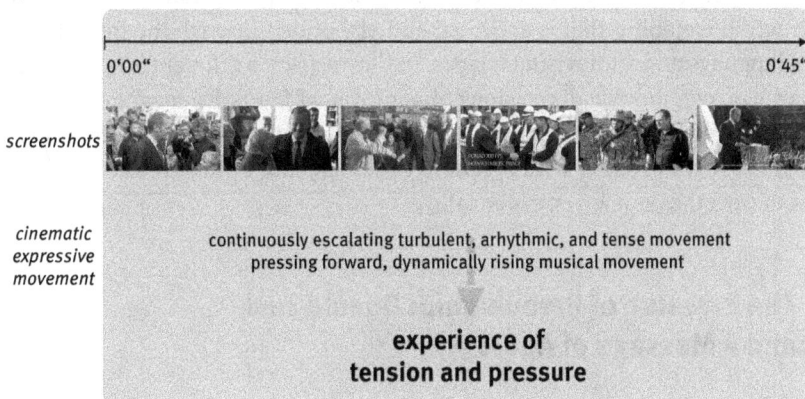

Figure 12: Experiencing breathless hurry and tense pressure (PREMIER DONALD TUSK)

This experience is firstly associated with the multimodally staged achievements and implementations of Tusk's outgoing term of office that follow each other in close and inconsistent succession throughout the campaign commercial. It is their sum, interplay, and order that in its inherent diversity and heterogeneity evokes the experience of pressure, tension, and stress. Due to this affective grounding, their multitude and variety are brought to the foreground and their characterization and understanding as achievements and successes of Tusk's governmental work fade into the background. They thus make tangible the Prime Minister's workload, i.e., they are the experiential basis (and justification) for how busy Tusk has been, how many things he has had to deal with. Basically, it is therefore not only what the audiovisual images represent that is relevant and meaningful, but also their staging and composition. As such, they orchestrate a feeling of being confronted and pushed back by tasks and duties that are expected from one, which are mounting up one after another, thereby increasingly accumulating and overwhelming their addressee. In this manner, the emu makes Tusk's emotional state and personal situation before the elections tangible: as an affective experience of being confronted, overloaded, and pushed back by a flood of things to do and to manage as the head of government. As a result, *Tusk is experienced and understood as being pressed and overwhelmed by an amount and variety of duties and tasks during his outgoing term of office.*

The affective course orchestrated by the cinematic expressive movement in the PO campaign commercial indicates a fundamental difference from the emergent meaning in the CDU TV campaign ad. The latter's two emus stage a sensation of power and stability that, in addition to the multimodal activation of figurativity, can be considered to equally contribute to the overall figurative theme. In contrast, the affective experience unfolded within the one emu of the PO TV campaign ad complements and underpins the experiential scenario of the construction metaphor that is activated and elaborated through the interplay of verbal language and audiovisual images. In this respect, a different interplay and relation between the two dimensions of audiovisual figurative meaning-making becomes apparent. Before discussing it in the concluding section, both dimensions are brought together with regard to the emergence of the overall figurative theme of the PO campaign commercial.

7.4 The Pressure of Premiership: Donald Tusk and a Message of Apology

Strictly speaking, the PO campaign commercial could be considered the figurative visualization of Donald Tusk's office term as Prime Minister. Its short duration and the large number of shots[14] provoke a sensation of stress and tension when viewing it. As such, the spectator embodies what Tusk is staged to have gone through over the terminating period of Premiership. In this respect, the message of the campaign commercial comes across very clearly. Forty-five seconds for so many images and shots is too short. Likewise, four difficult years for so many tasks cannot be sufficient. The contrast between the time frame and what it has to cover thus provides the link between the viewer's perceptual experience by watching the campaign commercial and the complex issue of a Prime Minister's incumbency. It feels too short and limited for the amount of responsibilities, duties, and things to implement and brings about a tension and stress that are pressing Tusk and pushing him back. Likewise, the viewer is overwhelmed by the amount of shots, images, and topics. In this manner, the flood of images of political obligations carries both of them away and transfixes them. In this state, the Prime Minister is in need of what releases the tension and stress and brings in peace: he needs an extension of time in order to finish his project building the house of Poland. This scenario is neither exclusively contained on the verbal or audiovisual level, nor in the form of a one-to-one correlation between a verbal metaphor and a corresponding audiovisual image. Instead, it is the emergent epiphenomenon of the interplay between the two dimensions of audiovisual figurative meaning-making over time that results in the activation, elaboration, and concretization of a construction scenario. However, this interplay is characterized by a predominance of multimodally activated figurativity, i.e., of language.

The experiential realm of a construction scenario is introduced, activated, and elaborated predominantly on the level of language through Tusk's voice-over, and thus monomodally. Throughout the campaign commercial, his underlying commentaries dynamically unfold a vital scenario of Poland as an ongoing construction project under his direction, however at an early stage and with several things still to be done. Nevertheless, the aspect of an ongoing process comes up with inconsistency and tension through semantic contradictions in individual expressions. This tension intensifies through contradictive multimodal activations of the construction scenario by audiovisual images of professional construction workers, two women shoveling sand, and the Polish troops in a sandy environment in Iraq. These audiovisual concretizations foreground stagnation and disorganization instead of work and progress. Through Tusk's explicit utterance that four difficult years were too short in order to realize the building of a strong and rich Poland, the metaphorical construction scenario reaches its peak of activation. It ends with another elaboration that links its future state of

---

14 In total, the campaign commercial consists of 22 shots over a course of 45 seconds. This amounts to an average shot length of two seconds.

completion with 'quiet' in terms of peace, whereby the construction process is in turn qualified as turbulent, troubled, and restless. In this context, *Donald Tusk is experienced and understood as the responsible leading builder of the future Poland, which is not finished yet, wherefore he is begging for a deadline extension.*

The inconsistency and tension that inherently resonate with the mono- and multimodally activated and elaborated construction scenario take shape in the audiovisual staging of the campaign commercial. In other words, the movement pattern that unfolds over the entire campaign commercial (within one emu) concretizes the implicit contradictions of the experiential realm as an embodied experience of breathless hurry and pressure. It is predominantly the interplay of camera, montage, and sound design that forms this movement pattern through an incessant succession of heterogeneous shots (e.g., with different camera perspectives, field sizes, and camera movements), short duration and quick succession of shots, and underlying music with a steadily raising and swelling minor melody that creates tension. Viewing the campaign commercial, spectators thus go through a flood of extremely heterogeneous images (and topics) that approach and pass them by in a highly dynamic manner. The force dynamics of this flood resonate in the viewers' experience as a sensation of being overwhelmed by something that incessantly accumulates. This affective experience unfolding within one emu makes Tusk's workload as Polish Prime Minister tangible: as being confronted, overloaded, and pushed back by a flood of things to do and to manage. As a result, *Tusk is experienced and understood as being under pressure and overwhelmed by an amount and variety of duties and tasks during his outgoing term of office.*

Of course, these two dimensions of audiovisual figurativity are neither experienced nor conceived of as distinct processes or temporal units but as intertwined aspects of the emergence of an overall figurative theme throughout the PO campaign commercial. Donald Tusk's work as Prime Minister is experienced and understood in terms of leading the ambitious building project of a prosperous Poland that is still under construction due to a too short time frame through multimodally activated figurativity. At the same time, the audiovisual staging makes the construction process affectively experienceable with regard to its complexity and magnitude. In this respect, the interplay of the two dimensions not only brings about a vital experience of a construction process of a house to be built but also provides the argumentative basis for the central message of the campaign commercial.

The conceptualization of a future prosperous Poland in terms of a building that is still under construction is thus not the focus of attention. Instead, the TV campaign ad is centered on the implications and consequences of this scenario for the leading builder Donald Tusk. The heterogeneity and variety of facets as well as sub-tasks are presented as being too much for him within the limited time frame of four years, thus serving as the explanation and justification for why Tusk could not finish the building in time. A successful completion of the building project, therefore, requires more time (verbally concretized as a time of 'quiet'), i.e., another office term. As a result, through the interplay of language and audio-visual staging, an overall figurative theme emerges that can be formulated as follows: *DONALD TUSK IS EXPERIENCED AND UNDERSTOOD AS A PRESSURED LEADING BUILDER OF THE UNCOMPLETED CONSTRUCTION PROJECT OF POLAND, ASKING FOR AN EXTENSION OF THE DEADLINE FOR COMPLETION.*

The construction scenario in its particular multimodal concretization (through spoken language and audiovisual images) and affective qualification (through sensations evoked by cinematic expressive movement) thus brings about a message of apology. It justifies his failure as a vital experience of a stressful and demanding job that viewers experience first hand, i.e., bodily by watching the campaign commercial. By such an experiential alignment between Tusk and the viewers, his workload is made tangible and evident. On this basis, the TV campaign ad accounts for the necessity of Tusk's re-election. If the viewers wish to stop and calm down the rush, pressure, and tension that they are going through, they have to give Tusk more time, i.e., another term of office. This image of the candidate Donald Tusk differs fundamentally from Angela Merkel's in the CDU campaign commercial. While Merkel strides across her stately home, letting the faded-in successes stand as evidence for her sovereignty and her competence, Tusk's achievements run as a pressing flood of tasks that pressure him. There is no sign of Merkel's sovereign power and monarchic dignity with Tusk; he is the stressed leader who is running after his own plan and now asks for a second term of office.

This dissimilar experience and understanding of the two politicians comes along with a different interplay and relation between the two dimensions of audiovisual figurative meaning-making: instead of an equal contribution of both to the overall figurative theme and a film-like style as in the CDU campaign commercial, the construction scenario in the PO TV campaign ad primarily emerges and unfolds in spoken language and through single audiovisual activations in a rather explicit and argumentative style. The implications of such a predominance of language over audiovisual staging are discussed in the subsequent concluding section.

7.5 Conclusion: The Interplay of Language and Audiovisual Staging as Rhetorical Design

The image evoked of the candidate Donald Tusk in the analyzed campaign commercial actually does not serve its purpose of presenting the work of the political leader Tusk and his government as concrete successes (Kolczyński 2012, 45).

As one of the TV campaign ads within the first promotional cycle "Poland under construction", it should put forward a positive image of the Prime Minister standing for re-election by means of the achievements of the previous office term. Instead, it presents Tusk as having not finished his project. There is no sense of dominance, sovereignty, or stability as was the case with Merkel in the CDU campaign commercial.

Due to such a fundamentally different image of the candidates in the two campaign commercials, the question arises if the PO campaign commercial has indeed missed its aim and if so, if this is a result of a lower degree of professionalism of Polish opposed to German TV campaign ads that, e.g., Musiałowska (2008) claims. From the dynamic perspective that is taken in this book, such a conclusion is unlikely. Instead, it is suggested that the entirely different images of Angela Merkel and Donald Tusk come along with different forms of audiovisual figurative meaning-making.

The CDU campaign commercial displays a cinematic staging and film-like composition and is thus subtler with regard to its central message that is primarily fed by the metonymical principle of contiguity and the affective experience evoked by the two emus. The PO campaign commercial, in turn, argues more explicitly and tries harder to convince. The successive activation and elaboration of the construction scenario from the beginning serves explanatory purposes: it starts from the foundation, proceeds to the continuation of building, takes a prospective look at the completion, and returns to the here and now and the explanation for its incompleteness. The fact of its incompleteness is at the end frankly admitted, but through the target-oriented successive elaboration the focus is on the reconstruction and how the result occurred. This emerges predominantly through verbal and, later on, multimodal activations and elaborations (through audiovisual images) of the experiential realm. At the peak of activation through the explicit verbal labeling in the utterance that "four difficult years are too little for realizing the plan of building a strong and rich Poland", the overall figurative theme is clearly presented. On this basis, the subsequent final sentence gets to the heart of the logical consequence and central message of the campaign commercial: "Some years of quiet are still necessary".

The audiovisual staging of the PO campaign commercial subordinates to this argumentative and more obvious promoting style that reminds of classical product- and campaign advertising. It supports and underpins the argument, the justification, and the apology why four years were not sufficient and some years of peace are still necessary. It does so by prominently staging and emphatically foregrounding the sensations of breathless hurry and tense pressure through the articulatory modalities of audiovisual staging, especially camera, montage, and sound design. Such a language-induced and highly condensed form (or rhetorical design) of audiovisual figurative meaning-making displays a higher degree of directness and explicitness than is the case in the CDU campaign commercial.

In regard to this, figurative meaning-making in campaign commercials unfolds temporally, attentionally, and above all experientially in a different way in each case despite the potential recourse to similar motives or the comparable use and arrangement of single articulatory modalities of audiovisual staging. Thus, neither the existence of a resembling visual motif, the use of a comparable technique of audiovisual staging, nor a similar figurative verbal expression in itself can provide sufficient insight into what kind of light is shed on the reference object (the candidate) and what kind of image is created of him or her. On the contrary, the particular concretization and perspectivation of the figurative imagery is profoundly linked to its specific context and rhetorical style of the campaign commercial and therefore cannot be generalized. Hence, instead of solely translating fixed imagery of linguistic or conceptual figurativity, campaign commercials constantly enable and create new and vital ideas, images, and scenarios on the basis of the situated interplay between the two dimensions of audiovisual figurative meaning-making.

As a consequence, new perspectives are opening up for social sciences research on campaign commercials. Being hitherto primarily quantitatively informed, it is with its fixed categories of aspects not able to account for their concrete form and configuration in the campaign commercials. Trent and Friedenberg's (1991) differentiation of incumbent and challenger strategies in campaign advertising, for instance, names for the first category among others the emphasis of achievements, the naming of political offices, or the presentation among politicians of other countries (cf. Holtz-Bacha and Kaid 1993, 62). These three aspects are certainly contained verbally and audiovisually in the CDU and the PO campaign commercial. However, how they emerge, are expressed and embedded, as well as what kind of role they play in the course of the campaign commercial, is not evident from the fact of their existence. The situated media context, i.e., the specific interplay of language and audiovisual staging is therefore a basic component of a detailed analysis of single campaign commercials as well as of comparative analyses. It is through the consideration of the self-same interplay that a profound qualitative differentiation of the PO and the CDU campaign commercial is even possible. As such, Trent and Friedenberg's above-mentioned aspects could be included in the analysis and considered in their particular form, configuration, and integration. This way, similarities and differences concerning the question how they relate to the emerging image of the candidates in campaign commercials could be demonstrated instead of schematically stating their mere existence.

8 Jarosław Kaczyński and Frank-Walter Steinmeier: A Door Opener and a Sober Problem Solution

Although this book does not pursue a social sciences informed take on mean-ing-making in campaign commercials, Trent and Friedenberg's (1991) differentia-tion of incumbent and challenger strategies provides a suitable starting point for the following two analyses. The campaign commercials in question are from the two major political opponents of the parties of Donald Tusk and Angela Merkel: the Polish Law and Justice party [*Prawa i Sprawiedliwość*] (PiS) and the Social Democratic Party of Germany [*Sozialdemokratische Partei Deutschlands*] (SPD), who were promoting their respective candidates Jarosław Kaczyński and Frank-Walter Steinmeier in the 2011 and 2009 parliamentary elections. This provides insight into what kind of political counter offer is provided by the candidates chal-lenging the incumbents Tusk and Merkel. Subscribing to Holtz-Bacha's account of campaign commercials as part of "interpretational culture" [*Deutungskultur*] (see Rohe 1987) that provide subjective, cognitive, affective, and evaluative orien-tation towards political phenomena for the members of a political system (Holtz-Bacha 2000, 16), the contrasting juxtaposition of incumbent and challenger TV campaign ads allows for comparing different foci, meanings, and images among the candidates in the context of the respective elections. The comparison of the challenger campaign commercials also sheds light on potential recurring motives or topics in their particular audiovisual composition within a situated media context. As such, it aims to contribute to a more detailed and nuanced view of the category of challenger strategies (see Trent and Friedenberg 1991).

As opposed to the two analyses of the CDU and the PO campaign commercial, this chapter is from the beginning comparatively oriented. It will start by pro-viding introductory information on the respective election campaign of the two parties PiS and SPD in the context of the elections of 2011 and 2009. As will be shown, on that basis alone remarkable differences become apparent. In the next step the two campaign commercials will also be reflected in their content-related and thematic outline. In this respect, some aspects that, according to Trent and Friedenberg, are characteristic for challenger strategies will be addressed in order to take them up and illustrate them in their specific and divergent form and integration into the respective audiovisual composition.

The focus and main objective of the analyses of the PiS and the SPD cam-paign commercial (both of which will be presented within a separate section) is on the particular interplay of the two dimensions of audiovisual figurativity

https://doi.org/10.1515/9783110578782-008

and what kind of image of the candidates it brings forward. For that reason, the structure of the analyses does not necessarily follow the one taken in the analyses of the CDU and the PO TV campaign ad. Rather, the main purpose is to take the particular interplay of the two dimensions optimally into account and thus to start from the dimension that makes significant contributions to the emergence and orchestration of figurative meaning in the respective campaign commercial. This is concomitant with the dynamic approach to audiovisual figurative meaning-making to stay as close to the material as possible in order to consider its specificity and respective dynamics also methodologically instead of working through all objects of investigation in a standard order (cf. also Müller and Kappelhoff 2018). After their analysis within separate sections, the PiS and the SPD campaign commercial are brought together and discussed with regard to their emergent figurative meaning and the respective interplay of the two dimensions. In this respect, they will additionally be juxtaposed with the CDU and the PO campaign commercial in order to arrive at a comprehensive picture of all emergent figurative meanings and candidate images.

8.1 Two Challengers, Different Foci: Self-Promotion as Opposition and as Governing Party

Both the Polish PiS party and the German SPD had very different initial conditions for the elections in question. The PiS party was in the opposition during the preceding legislative term and thus promoted itself as a counter proposition and alternative to the ruling Civic Platform (PO). The SPD, on the other hand, was in the difficult position of having been part of the grand coalition together with its opponent, the Christian Democratic Union (CDU). For that reason, an explicit attack on and negative campaigning against its coalition partner was problematic insofar as in so doing, the SPD would have compromised itself and furthermore risked the chance of continuing the coalition in case of missing the outright majority. These aspects are reflected in the style and contents of both parties' election campaigns and in the contrasting presentation of their candidates, also in the campaign commercials to be analyzed. It is, therefore, worthwhile to start from those contextual factors before coming to the question of audiovisual figurative meaning-making in the particular case of the two selected TV campaign ads.

The PiS party's candidate Jarosław Kaczyński was Donald Tusk's predecessor as prime minister from 2005 to 2007. However, its majority government together with the Self Defence of the Republic of Poland party [*Samoobrona Rzeczpospolitej Polski*] and the League of Polish Families party [*Liga Polskich Rodzin*] collapsed prematurely. Therefore, snap elections became necessary in 2007 from which the

PO came out as winner. As Szczerbiak (2013) argues, many voters of the PO at the elections in 2007 and 2011 were primarily motivated by fear of the PiS party's return to power. In order to improve its chances and image with the voters, the PiS party was "running a 'softer and gentler' campaign aimed at de-mobilising those Civic Platform voters who were motivated primarily by fear of Mr Kaczyński" (Szczerbiak 2013, 487). As candidate and party leader, Kaczyński had primarily attracted attention through his confrontational style and rather aggressive rhetoric (Kolczyński 2012, Szczerbiak 2013, Szułdrzyński 2011), wherefore the PiS party "attempted to construct a broader appeal" by focusing on social and economic topics with regard to Poland's future (Szczerbiak 2013, 487).

Its election campaign was highly praised in the national media: in the *Newsweek*'s interview with Anna Materska-Sosnowska from the Institute of Political Science at the University of Warsaw, she stressed the coherence of the party's campaign in general and the image of Kaczyński as a trustworthy head of the party in particular (Józefowicz 2011). The journalist Michał Szułdrzyński (2011) came to a similar conclusion: according to him, the PiS party was eager about evoking positive emotions on the part of the voters by focusing on aspirations and ambitions of the people instead of scaring them with negative campaigning. As opposed to previous election campaigns, the PiS omitted offensive attacks on its political competitor PO and made the future of Poland its central topic ("Poland deserves more" [*Polska zasługuje na więcej*]).

> Mr Kaczyński's party seized on the fact that many Poles felt that, even taking the economic crisis into account, Mr Tusk's government had not delivered the increase in opportunities that it had promised in 2007, a message exemplified by its main campaign slogan 'Poland Deserves More'. [...] Interestingly, Law and Justice also made a particularly strong pitch to younger voters, who were crucial in getting Civic Platform elected in 2007. Law and Justice correctly identified a 'glass ceiling' that many young Poles, especially those from smaller towns and rural areas, felt that they encountered and the fact that, in spite of economic growth, Poland still had high levels of youth unemployment and even many of those who managed to get a job struggled to obtain (much less pay) mortgages and support their families. (Szczerbiak 2013, 488)

A similar attempt to improve the image of the PiS party and an appeal to centrist voters was already made during the presidential elections in 2010 (Kolczyński 2012, 42) with the result that two rounds of voting were necessary, the second of which Kaczyński lost but with 47% of the votes (Szczerbiak 2013, 485). Building off this impact, the PiS complemented its focus on social and economic topics relevant for the average and young voters with a modern, progressive, and reliable image of its leader, Jarosław Kaczyński. In this respect, especially two moves are noteworthy: the publication of Kaczyński's book *The Poland of Our Dreams* [*Polska naszych marzeń*] (2011) and the premiere of the film LEADER (LIDER, 2011).

In the book, Kaczyński explained his opinion about the contemporary Poland and criticized the government for missing action with regard to current urgent problems (Jakubowski 2013, 35). The film, called the longest campaign commercial of the entire election campaign, was presented in a cinema and declared to have nothing to do with the PiS party's election campaign (Ostaszewski 2011). It lasted 24 minutes and staged the political story of Kaczyński in a pathetic style (Leszczuk-Fiedziukiewicz 2013, 94); however, there is doubt about its claimed informative nature (see Kolczyński 2012, Ostaszewski 2011).

The campaign commercial CHCEMY POLSKI RÓWNYCH SZANS ("We want a Poland of equal chances", advertising ageny Panplan) to be analzed is a similar case. It was released by the PiS more than one month before the elections took place (July 18, 2011) and was said to serve informational instead of canvassing purposes ("Tylko Kaczyński może otworzyć," 2011). With regard to its content, the chief of the election staff, Tomasz Poręba, explained that the 30-second-long video clip served as a starting point for the second part of the party's election campaign which aimed at the presentation of visions of a Poland of equal chances ("Tylko Kaczyński może otworzyć," 2011). According to Kolczyński (2012, 49), it is the best of the entire election campaign due to a dynamic presentation of and dealing with the topic of removing social barriers that have hindered Poles' chances and aspirations ("Tylko Kaczyński może otworzyć," 2011).

The campaign commercial starts by showing a group of various people heading for a modern glass building. When they get there, they stop in front of what is now shown to be closed doors. Inside the building, their backs to the front doors, a group of men formally dressed in suits sit together and talk, obviously ignoring the excluded. Two similarly dressed men arrive outside behind the group of the excluded and enter the building unnoticed through the back door, passing by the people outside as if they were not there. The scenario is interrupted by a faded-in slogan in red and blue letters, reading: "We want a Poland of equal chances" [*Chcemy Polski równych szans*].[1] Suddenly, Jarosław Kaczyński appears outside in front of the doors, energetically slides it open, and enters the building together with those previously excluded. The campaign commercial ends with the PiS party's logo and slogan "Time for courageous decisions" [*Czas na odważne decyzje*]. According to Poręba, it aims to deal with the educational and legal discrimination of the Poles by the current government and to point out that the PiS is the only party that wants to open these symbolic glass doors hindering their energy, enthusiasm, and potential ("Tylko Kaczyński może otworzyć," 2011).

---

1 The first two words are written in red, the last two words in blue, the colors of the PiS logo.

As opposed to such an obvious and explicit message with regard to the political opponent, the 2009 German federal election campaign has been declared the "most silent promotional event since the invention of letterpress" (Brauck and Müller 2009). According to Brauck and Müller, the election campaign was characterized by a fundamental lack of content and controversies; a fact that is especially reflected in the strong concentration on the candidates of the two major competing parties CDU and SPD. Both were grand coalition partners in the government for the legislative period from 2005 to 2009, in whose course the CDU was said to have adopted many topics of the SPD that had in turn lost its political profile (see, e.g., Casdorff 2009). Moreover, the collaborative government work was neither suitable as a target for criticism, nor for self-promotion. The prevailing lack of criticism during the federal election campaign is nevertheless remarkable because during the European election campaign some months earlier, the SPD had tried to attack the CDU and other opposing parties (Brauck and Müller 2009).[2]

In contrast, the SPD campaign commercial for the German parliamentary elections makes no mention of other parties or competitors and exclusively focuses on the chancellor candidate, Frank-Walter Steinmeier, and his programmatic issues. This concerns first of all his so-called Germany plan [*Deutschlandplan*], a long-term employment scheme, by which he presented his policy for the next decade. One of his aims was to achieve full employment by 2020 through the creation of four million jobs. However, the presentation of the plan on September 3, 2009 was a failure as the online magazine *Spiegel Online* disclosed details and major contents two days before the official presentation (Werner 2011, 43). The opposition thus had the opportunity to criticize the plan before it was completely and officially introduced; a setback that, as Werner (2011, 44) argues, the subsequent favorable coverage[3] could not change.

For the parliamentary election campaign, the SPD was supported by the advertising agency Butter from Düsseldorf (Rottbeck 2012, 177), which was already responsible for the party's 2005 parliamentary election campaign and the preceding 2009 European election campaign. Under the slogan "Our country is capable of more" [*Unser Land kann mehr*] the agency produced a campaign commercial

---

2 For instance, the Free Democratic Party [*Freie Demokratische Partei*] (FDP) was criticized for showing an upper torso with shirt and tie and a head of a shark complemented by the slogan "Financial sharks would vote for FDP" [*Finanzhaie würden FDP wählen*], or the CDU by means of the same upper torso and the head of a 50-cent piece next to the slogan "Dumping wages would vote for CDU" [*Dumpinglöhne würden CDU wählen*].

3 However, it plays a prominent role in the campaign commercial in order to demonstrate and underline the plan's sound reasoning and adequacy.

that makes the Germany plan its central and explicit topic and the (metonymical) flagship of the candidate Steinmeier who nearly disappears behind it.

The strong focus on and prominent promotion of the plan and Steinmeier makes the campaign commercial appear very much like an advertising spot presenting a product or a brand. A major reason for this impression is their recurrent explicit mention through a female voice-over that frames the campaign commercial, taking it from an initial introduction of the Germany plan and its potential to the explicit final request of voting for the SPD. Furthermore, the candidate's continuous direct appeal to the viewer (both verbally and visually by addressing the camera) evokes the impression of a traditional promotional event that straightforwardly and explicitly praises its product and tries to persuade the spectator to buy it.[4] Compared with the other campaign commercials, the SPD TV campaign ad thus addresses the viewer in the most proactive and explicit manner; thereby displaying the most noticeable direct effort to make its message clear and understood. However, Steinmeier only marginally promotes himself, instead promoting his Germany plan and the SPD's program.[5] The campaign commercial thus argues over its entire course with a clear will to convince, which remained subtle(r) in the other campaign commercials.

The 90-second-long TV campaign ad starts with three existential questions: "How do we want to live and work?" [*Wie wollen wir leben und arbeiten?*], "How do we close the gap] between rich and poor?" [*Wie schließen wir die Schere zwischen Arm und Reich?*], and "How do we create and ensure work?" [*Wie schaffen und sichern wir Arbeit?*]. These questions appear and dissapear as written text that comes continuously nearer and are additionally expressed verbally by the female voice-over. Immediately afterwards, this voice gives the answer to these initial questions: "Frank-Walter Steinmeier's Germany plan opens up a new perspective for our country" [*Frank-Walter Steinmeiers Deutschlandplan eröffnet unserem Land eine neue Perspektive*]. Simultaneously, different shots of Steinmeier are shown, mostly surrounded by or speaking in front of people.[6] Subsequently, various newspaper quotations, all of them positive reactions to

---

4 The direct addressing of the viewer was rare in the other campaign commercials, except for a final statement of the candidate at the end in the case of CDU and PiS.

5 According to Holtz-Bacha (2010, 182), this rejection of self-presentation leads to the problem that no image of Steinmeier's person emerges in the campaign commercial.

6 According to the executive director of the agency Butter, Frank Stauss, the aspect of being close to the people and having contact with them is Merkel's deficiency: "She does not have the common touch" (Brauck and Müller 2010). Therefore, Butter decided to show Steinmeier shaking hands and talking with workers, children, and retired people.

the plan, are faded in.[7] This way, Steinmeier's plan is explicitly proclaimed and approved as the adequate answer to the initial questions. In the following, the candidate himself faces the camera and addresses the spectator directly, explicitly arguing the case for his plan and the feasibility of its goals that are metonymically depicted through audiovisual illustrations. Steinmeier ends his argument by assuring that he believes in Germany's capability to achieve these goals and that he is willing to work hard for them. Together with a final image of Steinmeier and his wife waving their hands to their supporters, the female voice-over ends the campaign commercial by saying: "On September 27: SPD. Our country is capable of more" [*Am 27. September: SPD. Unser Land kann mehr*].

The campaign and political position of the two parties in the context of the 2011 and 2009 parliamentary elections display fundamental differences that are reflected in the content and thematic focus of the PiS and SPD campaign commercial. While the PiS concentrates on social and political aspects of ordinary citizens, such as the equality of opportunities and participation, and tries to establish the image of a qualified party leader, the SPD aims at an accentuated factual presentation of its program in order to convince by means of its content. In so doing, however, it is not able to create a vital image of its candidate. The following analysis illustrates in more detail how these contrasting conceptualizations in the two campaign commercials come about: they are due to fundamental differences in the respective interplay of the two dimensions of audiovisual figurative meaning-making. The Polish PiS party's campaign commercial gets along nearly without language, but predominantly brings about figurative meaning through audiovisual images in terms of "represented (i.e. depicted, in German 'dargestellt') visible or audible elements" (Schmitt 2015, 314) and cinematic expressive movement. It is only at a certain point that it is additionally made explicit through faded-in written language. Compared with this, the German SPD's campaign commercial is clearly led by language and complemented by single audiovisual illustrations. These, however, do not compose to a distinctive cinematic expressive movement corresponding to or complementing the verbally expressed figurative meaning, wherefore no consistent image of the candidate Steinmeier emerges.

---

7 "The plan has substance and a good foundation" [*Der Plan hat Substanz und ein gutes Fundament*], "More concrete than anything what hitherto could be found in the election programs of competitors" [*Konkreter als alles, was sich bislang in den Wahlprogrammen der Konkurrenz finden lässt*], "Economy and science praise the long-term objectivity" [*Wirtschaft und Wissenschaft loben die langfristige Zielsetzung*], "the focusing on the mid tier is welcome, too" [*Auch die Fokussierung auf den Mittelstand ist begrüßenswert*], "The SPD chancellor candidate obtains approval from the economy and from the unions" [*Zustimmung erhält der SPD Kanzlerkandidat aus der Wirtschaft und von den Gewerkschaften*].

8.2 Jarosław Kaczyński: Opening Doors and Conquering Hindrances

The PiS campaign commercial unfolds an emergent metaphorical meaning that is very similar to the CDU campaign commercial. It is the prominently staged separation of an outside and an inside between which a transparent pane of glass marks the border. Whereas it serves in the latter case to stress both the border and the difference in status as well as the omnipresence of the powerful sovereign Merkel, the glass facade in the PiS campaign commercial predominantly highlights separation, insuperability, and ignorance of the people who are inside and excluding others. Hence, although both campaign commercials use more or less the same experiential realm, the concrete emergent figurative meanings differ fundamentally: they display contrasting perspectives on the issue and thus give rise to dissimilar conceptualizations in their respective situated context. This again confirms the necessity of analyzing (audiovisual) figurative meaning in-depth in its particular context of use by staying as close to the material as possible in order to take account of such shades of meaning.

In the PiS party's campaign commercial, the glass facade strengthens the prominently staged opposition between the presented two groups of people and plays a central role for the overall figurative theme. These two groups are evidently the one that strides up to the modern glass building and is involuntarily stopped by its closed doors and the one that is sitting inside the building with their back to the people outside, entering stealthily through the back door and then walking past the row of excluded while pretending not to see them. With recourse to the remarks of the chief of the PiS party's election staff, Tomasz Poręba, that the campaign commercial aims to depict the discrimination of the Poles by the current government, the people who are shown evidently embody these actors.

Although their recognition and classification as such on the basis of Poręba's remarks appears to be self-evident, it is nevertheless also due to their particular audiovisual staging which moreover contributes significantly to their contrastive conceptualization. The perceived sharp contrast between the ordinary citizens outside and the business-like politicians inside is an outcome of metonymical profiling through audiovisual representation. For instance, the group outside distinguishes itself from the group inside by an observable difference and heterogeneity in age, clothing, and gender: younger and older people, casually and formally dressed, men and women. In contrast, the people inside are similarly dressed in a business style, are middle-aged, and exclusively men. The campaign commercial stages these two outwardly dissimilar groups audiovisually with specific experiences: the first group with quick and straightforward movement and being outside and excluded, the second group with immobility or little movement and being inside, excluding the outside.

This is primarily evoked by camera movement and visual composition that provide a clear-cut structure and division of the audiovisual image into a foreground and background as well as contrasting arrangements of visual elements and lines of gaze. For instance, the straightforward line of gaze of the excluded (to the camera) intersects with the sideward gaze of the people inside (i.e., the men sitting in armchairs and those walking past the glass facade). The arrangement of the two men in the armchairs who form a circle that is closed to the row of people outside concretizes this division of inside and outside, inclusion and exclusion. Moreover, the foreground that mainly amounts to the inside perspective is in sharp focus (e.g., the men in the armchairs), while the background that mainly amounts to the outside perspective is blurred (i.e., the excluded people standing in a row behind the glass facade). This clear-cut division is also highlighted through focus shifts from a sharp foreground to a sharp background (e.g., from the excluded in the foreground to insiders arriving unnoticed behind them), between which the glass facade functions as a kind of horizontal split and transition from the foreground to the background. The camera movement contrasts and highlights the respective movement qualities of the two groups and thus contributes to their contrasting perception: from tracking the quick and straightforward movement of the outsiders that is being stopped through the glass facade to a montage of medium-close shots and close-ups of puzzled faces in shallow focus. This fragmentation of the group to individuals who appear as a variation of the flat group formation unable to move along in front of the building gives rise to a feeling of being stopped and excluded. In contrast, the rather static quality of the circular formations of the men in suits inside is intensified through a static camera, and the dynamic parallel camera movement accompanying the walk of the two men past the row of the excluded increases the contrast between (moving) inside and (static) outside.

The outlined tension between inside and outside is furthermore strengthened through the underlying music that unfolds a powerful dynamic rhythm that presses forward. Its intensity and dynamics is withheld (primarily by omitting the drums) at the moment when the group outside is stopped in its straightforward movement, however, the rhythm that presses forward persists (through the electric guitar) in a kind of loop that waits for its final release. This way, a feeling of tension and suspense is evoked that corresponds to and complements the contrasting dynamics between inside and outside through camera movement and visual composition. The scenario is interrupted by the faded-in slogan in red and blue letters against a white background: "We want a Poland of equal chances" [*Chcemy Polski równych szans*]. With the following shot, the tension and contrasting dynamics dissolve. The PiS party's candidate Kaczyński is shown among the excluded people, energetically drawing back the glass doors of the building and granting the group its previously refused access. The people are shown streaming into the interior, the lobby, and offices where they are walking around and talking with each other (Kaczyński among them).

Apart from the cognitive processing and understanding that the drawing back of the glass doors provides access to the beforehand excluded, it is also the experience of a release of the previously unfolded tension and contrastive dynamics that contributes to this understanding. This becomes most tangible in the music. It comes in more intensely than before with high-pitched tones and a faster rhythm (with the drums coming in again) that is steadily pressing forward. Likewise, the dynamic and straightforward movement of the people starts again and is shown as slightly more energetic than before through a smoothly tracking camera and an opening of spatial depth. The latter equally resolves the previously prevailing tension of contrasting visual axes and elements by staging a well-balanced and harmonious half-round. Thereby, the audiovisual staging evokes an experience of balance, cohesion, and powerful dynamics. At the very end, Kaczyński is shown in a close-up, next to him the words "Premier Jarosław Kaczyński" and below the slogan "Time for courageous decisions" [*Czas na odważne decyzje*] that is expressed verbally as well.

In summary, visual composition, camera movement, and sound design merge into a movement pattern that brings about an experience of progress, balance, and cohesion (even intensified through the unfolded tension in the first half). This movement pattern amounts to one cinematic expressive movement unit (emu) that encompasses the whole TV campaign ad (Figure 13).

Admittedly, the question of whether the PiS campaign commercial consists of one or two emus is difficult to answer in this particular case. On the one hand, it prominently bears analogy to the CDU campaign commercial with its two emus between which a closure of its qualitative duration is perceptible (the transition from Merkel's recollection to the action image). The PiS campaign commercial also displays a kind of dichotomy between its first and second part that is discernable in terms of different sensations: initially tension and unevenness and then release, balance, and cohesion. In a way, the music also enters into a loop and pauses before it comes in again more intensely than before. The faded-in slogan "We want a Poland of equal chances" moreover seems to mark an explicit and prominently staged closure of the first and transition to the second part. However, these aspects are not as straightforward as it may seem. Rather than explicitly closing the first part and marking the beginning of the second one, the faded-in slogan seems to function as a hinge that connects the two. Moreover, the music only pauses for a while and does not remarkably change its basic quality. Finally, the expressive qualities of the first part are so closely linked to those of

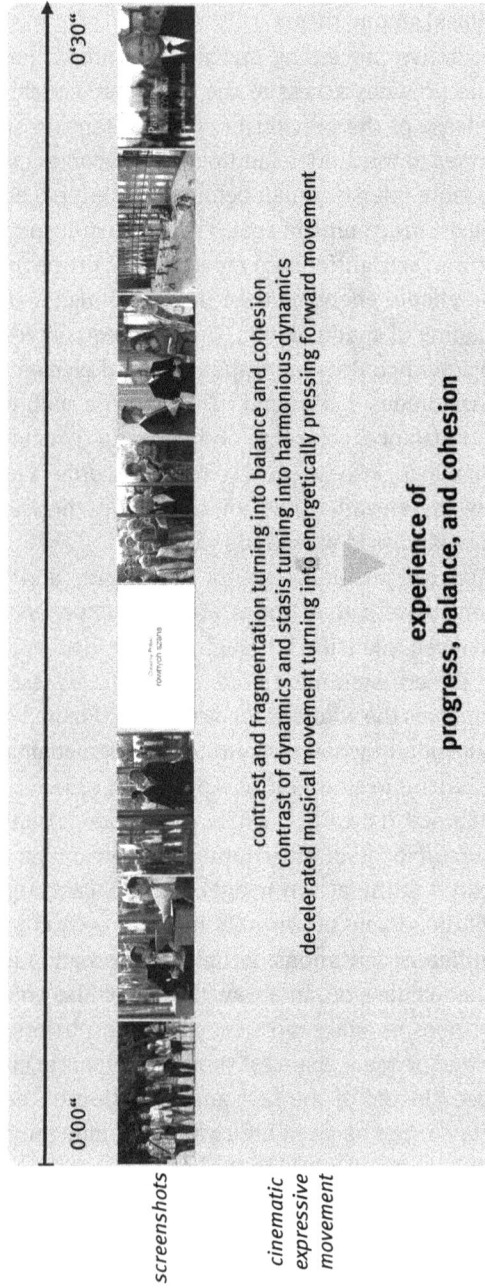

Figure 13: Tension turning into balance and cohesion (CHCEMY POLSKI RÓWNYCH SZANS)

the second part that they can be considered counterparts (tension vs. release; unevenness vs. balance; restraint vs. progress) and thereby provide a kind of negative space that anticipates its opposite ex negativo.

As such, the campaign commercial seems first and foremost moving towards the sensation of release, balance, and cohesion. For that reason, it is more likely that it consists of only one emu that in a highly condensed and intense manner addresses the viewer over the short course of 30 seconds. Through the interplay between expressive movement figuration and audiovisual representation the experience of release, balance, and cohesion is attributed to Jarosław Kaczyński who is shown opening the glass door. As a result, *Kaczyński is experienced and understood as eliminating tension and imbalance between an inside and outside through a state of balance.* What is more, the metonymical profiling of the depicted groups through audiovisual representation further specifies this emergent figurative meaning: *Kaczyński is experienced and understood as providing access to the so far segregated and excluded.*

It is noteworthy that this emergent figurative meaning – still without consideration of the verbal level – is close to the intended message of the campaign commercial as outlined by the chief of the election staff, Tomasz Poręba, namely, as presenting visions of a Poland of equal chances ("Tylko Kaczyński może otworzyć," 2011). In other words, the audiovisual staging unfolds a highly concrete image of what a Poland of equal chances means and what it would look and feel like. The explicit link between the experiential realm of bringing balance and having access, and the topic of equality and political participation is provided at two moments through faded-in written and additionally spoken language. Through the slogan "We want a Poland of equal chances" at the end of the campaign commercial's first half, an activation of metaphoricity occurs, connecting equal chances with having access (to a building). Remarkably enough, the audiovisual depiction of a door that separates people into groups inside and outside is at first glance contrary to what is expressed on the level of language, i.e., equal chances. What the viewer perceives due to the audiovisual staging is the opposite: unequal chances (Figure 14 below).

This contradiction between verbal and audiovisual imagery evokes a tension experienced by the viewer. At the same time, the audiovisual depiction corresponds to the verbal expression by providing ex negativo a highly concrete conceptualization of how chances are conceived of: *equal chances are seen as having admittance and access (to a building).* The experienced tension is pushing for a resolution,[8] which takes place in the second half of the campaign commercial.

---

8 This fact that is also reflected by the modal verb form 'we want'.

Now, words and audiovisual images match without any contradiction. What the viewer sees and experiences are actual equal chances: admittance and access to the building and the experience of free and unhindered movement (Figure 14 below). Thereby, the intermediately presented slogan calling for equal chances that was activated negatively by the audiovisual imagery of the first half is now activated multimodally a second time in a positively corresponding manner. As a result, the emergent metaphorical meaning (*equal chances as having admittance and access*) has a high degree of activation, especially with regard to its experiential realm whose sensory-motor experiences are spelled out comprehensively in terms of being excluded vs. being admitted.

The highly activated metaphorical meaning that makes civic participation in politics graspable and understandable in terms of a juxtaposition of being excluded and having access is finally elaborated as a key policy decision: by showing Kaczyński at the end in a close-up shot, next to him the words "Premier Jarosław Kaczyński" and below the slogan "Time for courageous decisions",[9] the idea and action of providing access (to civic participation) is linked to risk-taking and resoluteness. As it is Kaczyński who opens the door and makes civic participation possible, its metaphorical elaboration as a brave and resolute action is metonymically extended to him, its initiator, and provides the justification to vote for him as Prime Minister (Figure 14).

Through the interplay of the two dimensions of audiovisual figurative meaning-making, the sensation of release, balance, and cohesion (orchestrated through cinematic expressive movement) that is attributed to Jarosław Kaczyński combines with the multimodal activation of metaphoricity, i.e., being excluded as an unequal chance and having access as an equal chance. The interface of the two experiences and images, i.e., the moment of change or transition between them, is unambiguously provided on the level of audiovisual representation: Jarosław Kaczyński. As a result, an overall figurative theme emerges that can be formulated as follows: *JAROSŁAW KACZYNSKI IS EXPERIENCED AND UNDERSTOOD AS A DOOR OPENER FOR THE SO FAR SEGREGATED AND EXCLUDED CITIZENS, THEREBY MAKING FOR PARTICIPATORY EQUALITY.*

Audiovisual staging plays a predominant role for the emergence of figurative meaning in the PiS campaign commercial. In the CDU and the PO campaign commercial, multimodally activated figurativity has played an equally predominant role against audiovisual staging. In contrast, the PiS party's TV campaign ad

---

9 The very last shot is an equivalent to the intermediate one that reads "We want a Poland of equal chances". It refers in two lines, the upper in red, the lower in blue, to the party's Internet presence: "Our program: www.pis.org.pl" [*Nasz program: www.pis.org.pl*].

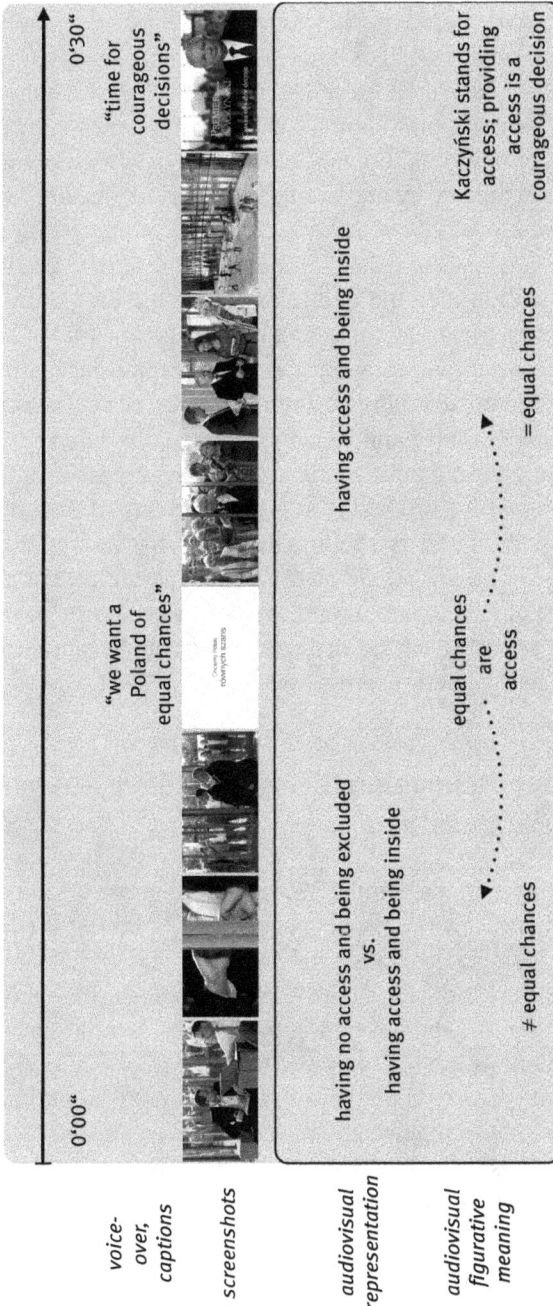

Figure 14: Contrasting unequal with equal chances (CHCEMY POLSKI RÓWNYCH SZANS)

unfolds the experiential realm of the overall figurative theme in a highly concrete manner while the audiovisual representation prepares the topic. In the end, language simply concretizes the latter – that is already present – by naming it explicitly ("Poland of equal chances"). For that reason, the PiS campaign commercial unfolds and expresses its overall figurative theme in a subtler manner (in contrast to the explicit form that prevails in the PO campaign commercial). Instead of making its political message highly explicit by spoken or written words, it evokes a vital feeling of its candidate by presenting him as a door opener, who releases tension and unevenness in favor of balance, cohesion, and progress.

The candidate Jarosław Kaczyński is inherently linked to the change in politics that is articulated in the form of a collective wish ("We want a Poland of equal chances"). More precisely, the called-for change to equal chances takes shape and form through the viewer's experience of a strong tension that releases immediately: as conceptualization of opening a barrier or door that previously separated people into excluded and included. As such, the emergent metaphorical meaning (despite the subordinate role of language) presents a highly concrete embodied perspective of looking at and conceiving of Kaczyński within the current (and potentially future) politics of Poland. In contrast, the SPD campaign commercial from the 2009 German parliamentary elections unfolds no such specific image of its protagonist and candidate, neither through language and multimodally activated figurativity nor through audiovisual staging and sensations evoked by cinematic expressive movement.

8.3 Frank-Walter Steinmeier: Giving a Realistic Answer to Existential Questions

Unlike the Polish PiS party, the German SPD had the dilemma of not having been in opposition but in office with its opponent, the CDU, during the terminating legislative period. With regard to the presentation of its program and the creation of an image of its candidate, Frank-Walter Steinmeier, the party therefore could not draw on the collaborative government work as a target for criticism nor for self-promotion. As the CDU was said to have furthermore adopted many of its topics, the SPD also could not rely on a distinct political profile (see, e.g., Casdorff 2009, Geise 2010). In this light, the campaign commercial "Our country is capable of more" [*Unser Land kann mehr*], produced by the advertising agency Butter (Rottbeck 2012, 177), displays a strong and explicit aiming at content-related profiling (especially in the field of labor and social affairs) and personal profiling of the candidate Steinmeier (Geise 2010, 162). It does so by bringing both key aspects together through a metonymical link: the Germany plan (a long-term employment scheme that Steinmeier introduced on September 3, 2009). This plan stands for Steinmeier, his creator, and as such it is the chief subject and protagonist of the campaign commercial, i.e., the promoted product that convinces the spectator. In this respect, the SPD TV campaign ad fundamentally differs from the other three campaign commercials that have been analyzed in this book. By explicitly mentioning Steinmeier and the plan by an additional speaker apart from the candidate himself and the prominent promotion of the latter's quality and public appreciation, it strongly reminds of a traditional advertising spot promoting a product or a brand by highlighting its advantages and additional values.

Such a classic line of argument structures the entire campaign commercial: it starts from a problematic issue, presents a solution, and provides evidence for it. The problematic issue is audiovisually staged by three existential questions at the beginning that are faded in as written language coming continuously nearer and are additionally expressed verbally by a female voice-over: "How do we want to live and work?", "How do we close the gap between rich and poor?", and "How do we create and ensure work?". After this straightforward start, the voice-over immediately gives the answer to these initial questions: "Frank-Walter Steinmeier's Germany plan opens up a new perspective for our country". By showing simultaneously different shots of Steinmeier – mostly surrounded by and talking with or to people – the creator is (through contiguity) metonymically linked with his product: the Germany plan stands for its creator Steinmeier. Accordingly, the explicitly expressed solution to the initial problematic issues is metonymically concretized: with Steinmeier representing the answer or solution to the existential social questions. Therefore, the various subsequently faded-in newspaper quotations that serve as evidence for the proposed solution – all of them positive reactions to and evaluations of the plan – not only confirm the plan itself, but basically also Steinmeier. In this regard, the first 38 seconds of the campaign commercial primarily bring about the central message by means of a classical argumentative structure of question, answer, and evidence in a straightforward manner (Figure 15).

What is remarkable is that in light of a strong presence of spoken and written language, there is little activated figurativity during this initial sequence of 38 seconds apart from the metonymical link between the Germany plan and its creator Steinmeier. Although various verbal metaphorical expressions are articulated by the female voice-over (e.g., "close the gap between rich and poor", "the plan has substance and a good foundation"), they are neither semantically connected to each other nor multimodally activated or elaborated. Hence, their imageries do not seem to be experientially present, wherefore the isolated verbal metaphorical expressions are sleeping instead of waking (cf. Müller 2008a, Müller and Tag 2010). Nevertheless, they are made salient through their simultaneous,

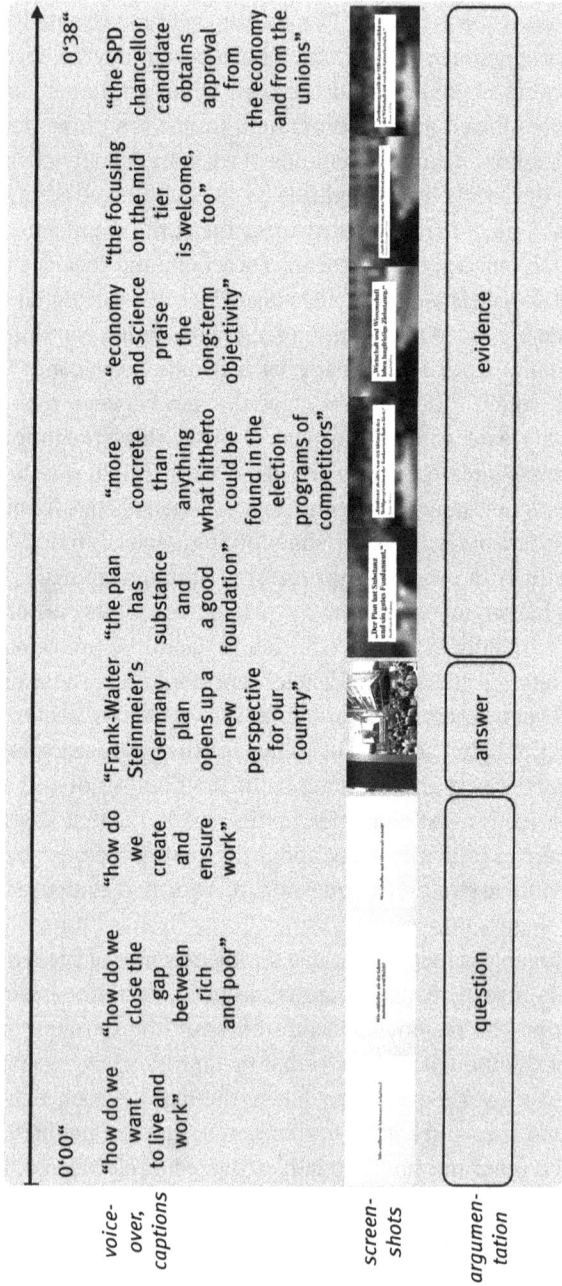

Figure 15: The Germany plan as reliable answer to a problematic issue (FRANK-WALTER STEINMEIER)

crossmodal[10] articulation in spoken (by the female voice-over) and written (by the faded-in newspaper quotations) language. According to the Iconicity Principle, such a double presence produces more meaning (Müller and Tag 2010, 94–95) even though the written language does not concretize the verbal figurative meaning experientially, but merely highlights the respective crossmodal moments attentionally within the course of the campaign commercial. Thereby, little peaks of attention are created for one thing. What is more, the newspaper reactions to the Germany plan are related to the existential questions from the beginning through their similar staging (i.e., by being expressed both verbally and in written form). Through this link between the problematic issues and the evidence, the in-between provided solution is (in addition to the explicit verbal line of argument) implicitly approved as an appropriate answer to the existential questions. In sum, the SPD campaign commercial is during its first 38 seconds primarily characterized by single attentional peaks that are foregrounded in the flow of time and both aesthetically and substantially related to each other. However, they do not give rise to a temporally, attentionally, and experientially unfolding figurative idea or scenario of the Germany plan or of Steinmeier.

This pattern of single condensed attentional peaks subsequently continues, whereby figurative meaning unfolds simultaneously in patches, but scarcely over a longer span of time. This becomes primarily evident when Steinmeier, who assumes the role of the speaker[11] after the faded-in newspaper headlines, speaks about his goals concerning Germany's future social and economic development ("With the right policy, we can make the breakthrough in the fight against unemployment in the next decade" [*Mit der richtigen Politik können wir im nächsten Jahrzehnt den Durchbruch schaffen im Kampf gegen die Arbeitslosigkeit*]). The corresponding measures that he verbally expresses are complemented by single audiovisual depictions. Thus, the phrase "with new products that save energy and protect the climate" [*mit neuen Produkten, die Energie sparen und das Klima schützen*] is audiovisually accompanied by glaring sunlight on a solar roof and by a flower meadow. As is the case with the Germany plan and Steinmeier, the verbally expressed aims for the future are metonymically depicted by contiguous aspects corresponding to them: the solar energy standing for new, energy-saving

---

10 The notion of crossmodality here serves as a distinction of such forms of double articulation from multimodal activations of figurativity where different modalities complement one another with regard to figurative meaning-making.

11 By talking directly to the camera, Steinmeier contrasts with the candidates in the other campaign commercials who do not address the viewer visually and verbally in such a direct manner. The only exception is Angela Merkel at the end of the CDU campaign commercial when she speaks her final statements to the camera.

products and the flower meadow standing for the climate. The phrase continues "with new jobs in health and care services and in culture and the media" [*mit neuen Arbeitsplätzen in Gesundheit und Pflege und in Kultur und Medien*], being audiovisually complemented by images of blood pressure measurement and a CT screen as well as a young man leading an older woman by the arm and people sitting behind computer screens. Here again, the audiovisual depictions activate metonymicity by presenting what is verbally expressed through one contiguous aspect.

All these audiovisual metonymies[12] are instances of short-time activations of figurative meaning that are, however, not semantically linked to each other, nor refer to something beyond themselves, as was the case in the CDU campaign commercial. In contrast, the single audiovisual depictions are heterogeneous in their staging; no connecting principle between them emerges and they remain rather isolated temporary peaks of activated figurative meaning. Such temporal dynamics of audiovisual figurativity that are characterized by single figurative moments also affect the attentional dynamics: they are condensed moments of activated metonymicity that recur in the temporal course but do so without any significant elaboration and therefore remain rather short-termed. The same holds for the experiential dynamics: the audiovisual concretizations create single moments of experiential concretization that appear less integrated but rather stand out compared to the rest of the composition. Basically, the audiovisual metonymies create little peaks of attention in the flow of the SPD campaign commercial that highlight meaning in patches, but do not intertwine and create a new level of meaning together (Figure 16). As a result, no consistent or overarching vital figurative conceptualization of the Germany plan or of the candidate Steinmeier arises.

Due to the prevailing of twofold (crossmodal) expressions that amount to overstatements of meaning, as well as isolated audiovisual illustrations and concretizations, a foregrounding of content occurs: the respective moments or sequences stand out in the flow of attention and are briefly experientially specified. In terms of content, this concerns exclusively programmatic issues of the Germany plan or of the party ('new products', 'new jobs'), not Steinmeier as the candidate. Hence, the target of figurative meaning in the campaign commercial is not Steinmeier himself, but what he stands for politically and programmatically.

---

12 Apart from the mentioned two examples of audiovisual metonymies, there is a third one shortly afterwards: while Steinmeier declares "We can offer a fair chance of good education to all children" [*Wir können allen Kindern eine faire Chance auf gute Bildung bieten*], what is shown are a girl and a boy holding the hands of adults, people studying in a library, and students in a lecture hall. These audiovisual images concretize and activate the verbally expressed 'children' and 'education' metonymically.

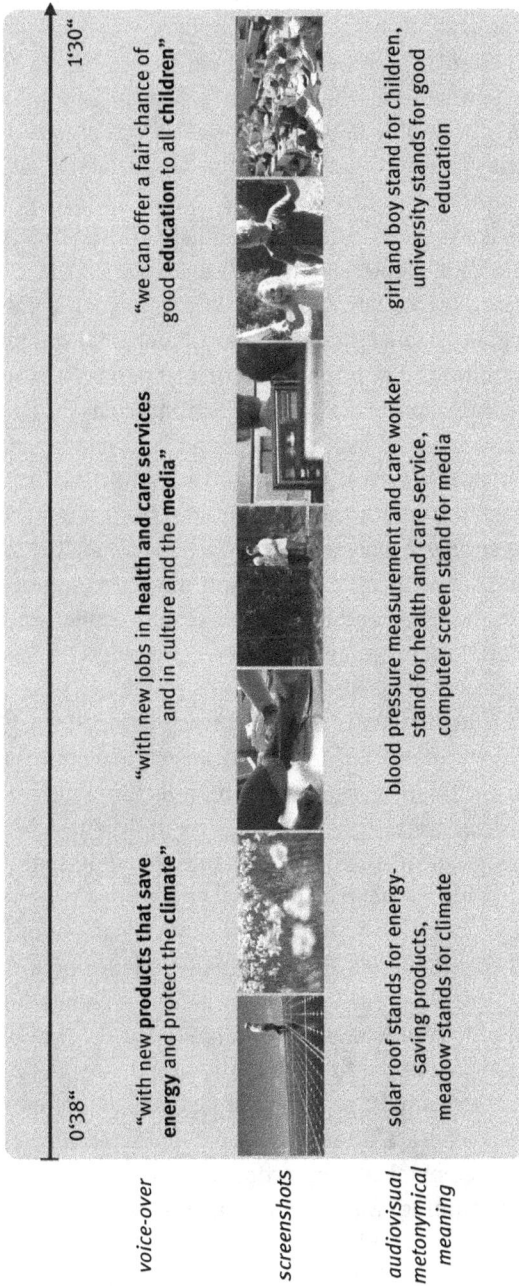

Figure 16: Short-time moments of metonymical meaning (FRANK-WALTER STEINMEIER)

This meaning-making process amounts to a selective illustration in patches instead of evoking an overall image. As such, it does not go beyond its mere illustrative function of making the goals of the Germany plan concrete and tangible.

This, in turn, corresponds to the overall emphatic emphasis that Steinmeier's Germany plan is authentic and realistic: primarily through verbal expressions such as "[the plan's] long-term objectivity", "[the plan is] more concrete than anything that could hitherto be found in the election programs of competitors", "these are ambitious goals, but they are feasible" [*das sind ehrgeizige Ziele, aber sie sind machbar*], and "our country is capable of more". What becomes apparent in these utterances is the focus on the authenticity and feasibility of the plan's goals, and the audiovisual depictions serve as evidence for this claim. That is to say, through the selective concretization and illustration of the plan's goals, they not only stand out in the flow of attention against moments and phases when no audiovisual illustration occurs, but also become experientially real for a given time. In this sense, the experiential dynamics of audiovisual figurativity come up with the figurative imagery as a concrete and vital image, i.e., as "a highly specific sensory-motor experience" (Müller and Schmitt 2015, 321). For example, the audiovisual concretization of "new products that save energy and protect the climate" by glaring sunlight, a solar roof, and a flower meadow provides a clear idea and sensation of how these products and unspoiled nature look and feel like. In this manner, the experiential dynamics of multimodally activated figurativity serve a predominantly argumentative goal. Concomitantly, the experiential exemplification expresses a specific view on the respective reference: a domain highlighting within a domain matrix in Croft's terms (2002 [1993], 178–179). When Steinmeier speaks, for instance, of "a fair chance to good education for all children", and a library with studying people and a lecture hall are shown, 'good education' is concretized and thus narrowed as university education. Such a predominantly argumentative and illustrative role of audiovisual images demonstrates that the campaign commercial does not create any image or tell a story; it makes a statement and seeks to do that convincingly by means of reason.

The temporal, attentional, and experiential dynamics of audiovisual figurativity thus serve primarily the rhetoric and visual argumentation of the claim to reality and feasibility of Steinmeier's Germany plan. In this way, the plan is displayed as the realistic answer to the initially raised questions. The argumentation is as follows: Germany is, as matter of fact, capable of more. This 'more' is the Germany plan whose authenticity is proven by audiovisual concretizations. Through the metonymical connection between the plan and its creator established at the beginning, the reasoning is likewise extended to the candidate Steinmeier, wherefore *Frank-Walter Steinmeier as well as his Germany plan is experienced and understood as the realistic answer to existential questions.*

However, the focus is on the Germany plan over the entire course of the campaign commercial (among others, through the audiovisual illustrations of the plan's verbally expressed goals). Only at the end, an explicit shift of focus from the plan to its creator takes place when Steinmeier says "I'm sure, our country is capable of more. And I promise you that I will work hard for it" [*Ich bin sicher: Unser Land kann mehr. Und ich verspreche Ihnen, dass ich hart dafür arbeite*]. The result of this imbalance is that the Germany plan is in the foreground and serves as the metonymical evidence for Steinmeier's political qualification. Viewing the campaign commercial, the spectator thus basically does not get a vital idea of him but rather of his Germany plan, which leads to conclusions about him.

In contrast to the campaign commercials of the CDU, the PO, and the PiS party, audiovisual staging is strongly subordinated and gives advantage to the content of the central message. For example, the underlying music's slightly pulsating start evokes a euphoric atmosphere. Although the beat intensifies when drums come in, the volume is restrained in turn, and the melody does not advance but remains in a loop. As a result, the rhythm does not unfold noticeable accelerations or decelerations; it remains moderate and does not push to the fore. The movement of the montage parallels this quality. It constantly changes from calm (e.g., the faded-in questions at the beginning or Steinmeier talking to the camera) to highly dynamic phases that are composed of various heterogeneous shots following one another in quick succession. The little camera movement strengthens this sensation of constant alternation between smooth and accelerating dynamics that encompasses the whole campaign commercial with no noticeable modification or development.[13] For that reason, the SPD campaign commercial consists of one cinematic expressive movement unit encompassing its entire length that is characterized by a steady and regular succession of (or alternation between) dynamic and calm movement. Unlike the emus in the other campaign commercials, it does not unfold its expressive quality in such a prominent manner.

This might be due to the fact that the SPD campaign commercial presents itself in an accentuated factual, sober, and realistic manner whereby language plays a predominant role and audiovisual staging mainly serves an illustrative and argumentative function. As such, also the experience that is evoked by the movement composition of music, montage, and camera movement reinforces the emergent figurative meaning that is induced through language. The steady and balanced rhythm unfolding from the alternation between powerful dynamics that are in the next moment restrained evokes a sensation of moderation and

---

13 This pattern is paralleled by the looping character of the underlying music persisting over the course of the campaign commercial.

regularity with Steinmeier and his Germany plan. In other words, *Steinmeier as his Germany plan is experienced and understood as a modest and balanced political actor.*

The fact that the experiential qualities of the movement composition do not play out in such a prominent manner, as was the case with the other campaign commercials, is also due to the fact that on the verbal level no consistent image or scenario of Steinmeier and his Germany plan emerges. Instead, the few isolated multimodal activations primarily foreground Steinmeier's and his program's authenticity and verisimilitude. In this respect, the sensations evoked by cinematic expressive movement underline the multimodally activated figurative meaning by unfolding an overall figurative theme that can be formulated as follows: *FRANK-WALTER STEINMEIER AS HIS GERMANY PLAN IS EXPERIENCED AND UNDERSTOOD AS THE SOBER AND REALISTIC ANSWER TO EXISTENTIAL QUESTIONS.*

This overall figurative theme as such emerges during the first 38 seconds of the campaign commercial; the rest of the time is filled with its verification and confirmation. This sober and argumentative style is paralleled by the voice quality. Steinmeier's voice and the female voice-over are synchronized in regard to their calm and certain tone. Corresponding to this tonal quality, a content-related orientation comes up: "*How do we want to* work and live?" – "*We have to* act resolutely!" – "*We can* achieve this and that aim!" Due to the repetition of the modal verbs (and their respective syntactic connection with the personal pronoun 'we' [*wir*]) in the particular sequences, they are made salient. Moreover, the recurrence of the prosodic features (sentence accent on the modal verbs) over the course of the campaign commercial unfolds a structure that relates the single sequences to each other and thus establishes a context that has as its subject the capabilities of 'we'. This 'we can' is (in a slightly modified form) reflected in the final sentence of the campaign commercial, "Our country is capable of more",[14] and thus strengthens the central message of Steinmeier regarding his program as being the realistic and sober answer to existential questions.

The predominance of language in the SPD campaign commercial has been demonstrated to bring about a particular form of audiovisual figurative meaning-making, namely one that emerges rather condensed and in patches in all three aspects of dynamics: speech initiates its concretization at particular moments in time in which figurative meaning is made salient and activated as

---

14 Here, the country together with a possessive pronoun substitutes for the first-person plural personal pronoun to express collective reference.

a short-term vital experience but does not bring about a profound and tangible image of the candidate, as was the case in the PiS campaign commercial. The latter unfolded a highly concrete experience and idea of Jarosław Kaczyński as a door opener for previously excluded citizens, releasing the citizens' power and energy and thereby leading to progress. Compared with this, the moderate and regular sensations that are evoked by the cinematic expressive movement in the SPD campaign commercial do not seem to be geared to Steinmeier in particular. Rather, the audiovisual staging appears to run parallel to language and to be hardly compositionally interrelated with it. This and further questions concerning the link between the different forms of audiovisual figurativity and the emergent candidate images are addressed from a comparative perspective in the subsequent section: first, by looking at the two challenger campaign commercials and then by considering the two incumbent campaign commercials.

8.4 Similarities and Differences Among Challenger and Incumbent Images

Social sciences research on campaign commercials has repeatedly underlined their similarity with product advertising concerning the emotional addressing of the viewers in order to achieve their positive identification with the promoted product: the candidate and his or her party. In this respect, they create – in the literal and equally in the figurative sense – an image of the candidate: on the surface, the audiovisual images of campaign commercials show him or her, e.g., Angela Merkel in the chancellery, Donald Tusk on his campaign trail with the citizens and at work with other politicians, Jarosław Kaczyński together with the excluded people, and Frank-Walter Steinmeier speaking in front of people and to the camera. Concomitantly, these images do not come up in a vacuum but are situated in a media context of audiovisual movement-images that the viewers make available to themselves in an embodied manner: "We are not making our world of objects, but we are instead *taking up* these objects in experience. In other words, objects are not so much *givens* as they are *takings*." (Johnson 2007, 75) As such, campaign commercials make political candidates present, concrete, vital, and tangible; they create an experientially and cognitively vital image of them on the part of the viewers.

Metaphor and metonymy play a crucial role in this process of image formation by enabling the viewer to make sense of the candidate on the basis of multimodally activated figurativity and sensations evoked by cinematic expressive movement. In the analyses of the selected four German and Polish campaign commercials, figurativity has turned out to be always context-bound and therefore highly specific. On this account, Kenneth L. Hacker's definition of political candidate images as "*re*presentations of political subjects" (Hacker 1995, xiv; emphasis mine), which suggests their ex ante givenness, should basically be reformulated as 'creations' or 'concretizations' of political subjects. Along with it, further factors such as voters' attitudes and emotions as well as evaluations of the candidate, also on the basis of conceptualizations from other presentational and communicative contexts, play a role for a voter's overall preference or rejection of a particular candidate. The emergent figurative images from campaign commercials are thus one component among others in the process of image formation.[15]

The analyses of the campaign commercials of the Polish PiS party and the German SPD have revealed clear differences in regard to the figurative meaning of their two protagonists Jarosław Kaczyński and Frank-Walter Steinmeier. These differences stand out despite clear parallels with regard to their political position during the respective elections and content-related analogies (e.g., call for change or emphasis on optimism for the future; cf. Holtz-Bacha and Kaid 1993, 62 drawing on Trent and Friedenberg's challenger strategies). While the PiS campaign commercial brings about an image of Kaczyński as somebody who will open doors for previously excluded citizens, releasing their power and energy and thereby leading to progress, the SPD campaign commercial in turn does not give rise to a concrete and tangible image of Steinmeier but rather of his Germany plan as the sober and realistic answer to existential questions. This remarkable contrast between the two campaign commercials, both of the figurative images themselves and of their emergence, is traceable to their distinct interrelatedness of language and audiovisual staging. In the case of the PiS campaign commercial, spoken and written language have been demonstrated not to play such a predominant role as in the SPD campaign commercial; they primarily convey in an explicit manner the target of the experiential grounds of figurative meaning provided by audiovisual staging (i.e., Poland). In the case of the SPD campaign commercial, in contrast, audiovisual staging subordinates to language by primarily conveying single illustrations of verbally expressed contents, whereas spoken language unfolds an argumentative structure (i.e., the Germany plan is the answer to existential questions) but no consistent – and activated – figurative meaning.

Thus, although both TV campaign ads thematically display the same challenger strategies, namely a call for change (PiS: admitting the excluded; SPD:

---

15 As such, they are obviously far from insignificant, as they are repeatedly referred to as relevant information sources and reference points for voters during election time (cf., e.g., Schicha and Dörner 2008, 14).

the Germany plan) and an optimistic perspective on the future (PiS: equalize and revitalize Poland; SPD: make the breakthrough against unemployment), the respective interplay of the two dimensions of audiovisual figurativity evokes completely different images of the two candidates, whereby the named strategies are affected in their significance and meaningfulness. That is to say, in the case of the PiS campaign commercial, the change and the optimism bring about a completely different effect and relevance in the context of a resolute door opener Kaczyński, who initiates dynamics and energy. This stands out in comparison to the case of the SPD campaign commercial and in the context of a candidate Steinmeier of whom no vital and tangible image emerges. This clearly suggests that Trent and Friedenberg's content-related categories need to be considered with regard to their respective emergence through audiovisual figurativity in order to arrive at a comprehensive understanding of their situated role and impact, and of the situated image of the candidate.

A similar contrast as the one discussed between the two challenger campaign commercials can be noticed in the two incumbent campaign commercials of the German CDU and the Polish PO party. Their respective protagonists, Angela Merkel and Donald Tusk, evoke similarly contrasting figurative meanings and thus also candidate images. In the first case, Merkel is experienced and understood as a powerful sovereign with civil roots who is nevertheless close to the people. Tusk, on the other hand, does not present such a sovereign image; he is experienced and understood as a pressured leading builder of the uncompleted construction project of Poland, who is asking for an extension of the deadline for completion. The two emergent meanings and images of the candidates are even more remarkable in direct juxtaposition when Trent and Friedenberg's incumbent strategies are also taken into consideration. Both campaign commercials display a content-related mention of the candidate's political office and an emphasis of what has been achieved so far (cf. Holtz-Bacha and Kaid 1993, 62 drawing on Trent and Friedenberg's incumbent strategies). However, the mere thematic presence of these two aspects does not allow for conclusions with regard to the respective image of the promoted candidate. In the CDU campaign commercial, their staging predominantly establishes the civil origin of Angela Merkel and her metonymical link with the people. In the PO campaign commercial, their staging in turn evokes the sensation of tension and pressure with Donald Tusk.

This distinct role and meaningfulness of the same incumbent strategies is again due to the respective audiovisual figurative meaning that emerges throughout the campaign commercials. In the case of the CDU TV campaign ad, it is the balanced interplay between an extended pattern of high-grade activated metonymicity and the viewers' vivid sensation of power and stability that in a well-composed and well-matched manner evokes the image of an absolutist sovereign who is above it all. In the case of the PO campaign commercial, figurative meaning emerges and develops predominantly through monomodal and multimodal activated figurativity and is as such complemented and underpinned by the affective experience of pressure and tension unfolded by its highly dynamic, heterogeneous, and seemingly unstructured audiovisual composition.

Such a different interplay and relation between the two dimensions of audiovisual figurativity has been mistakenly considered as a lack of professionalism: in her cross-national comparative study of political communication in Germany and Poland, Musiałowska (2008, 134) makes the following point with regard to Polish campaign commercials: "In many cases commercials were dominated by talking-head formats which weakened the overall spot's dynamics. As a consequence Polish ads achieved high professional standards not as often as German ads." Due to this evaluation as less professional, she tries to draw conclusions concerning their impact on the viewer: "The study did not provide empirical evidence referring to this issue. Still, it can be assumed that voters would find static talking-head formats more boring since they were accustomed to modern media formats showed in television programmes" (Musiałowska 2008, 207).

The film-analytical approach to cinematic expressive movement (Kappelhoff 2004, Kappelhoff and Bakels 2011, Scherer, Greifenstein, and Kappelhoff 2014) has shifted such a perspective on the viewer's experience of audiovisual media away from single and individually considered formal aspects and represented content, towards the audiovisual composition in its multimodal and temporal unfolding as expressive movement. Accordingly, it is not the use of, for example, certain special effects or the number of changes of camera perspectives that guarantees a particular impression or impact on the part of the viewer as Musiałowska suggests. Because of its dissimilarity to the well-composed TV campaign ad of the CDU, the PO campaign commercial is a suitable example to illustrate this point. Due to the obviously random content of its shots, their quick succession, and the apparent lack of an overall structure, it might appear less professional and barely reasonable, let alone appealing, to the viewer at a first glance. Nevertheless, the conducted transdisciplinary (film-analytical and cognitive-linguistic) analysis (see Chapter 7) has revealed how audiovisual figurativity creates indeed a productive "way of *understanding through experience*" (Müller and Schmidt 2015, 319) over its course; however, one that comes about in a more language-induced manner than in the case of the CDU campaign commercial.

The country-specific comparison of the four campaign commercials with regard to incumbent and challenger shows that the political situation and circumstances as well as the programmatic orientation of the respective party are reflected in the campaign commercials. The CDU campaign commercial in the context of the German parliamentary elections in 2009 focuses entirely on Merkel's character and political personality and makes it its political program and message. The SPD campaign commercial, on the other hand, seeks to focus in an accentuated manner on programmatic content and an objective line of argument instead of promoting Steinmeier's personality, whereby he, however, does not become concrete and tangible but remains rather vague. This indicates that the lack of an experiential basis affects figurative meaning-making and candidates' image formation in that it makes them less profound and comprehensible. The PO campaign commercial in the context of the Polish parliamentary elections in 2011 focuses on creating a vivid image of the justification of Tusk's re-election in terms of external circumstances. Thus, unlike the CDU campaign commercial, it does not argue the case for the electoral vote by means of Tusk's personality but lays the focus on the significance of an overall goal (i.e., a future Poland that is strong and rich). This different focus and political self-conception of Tusk is also reflected in the emergent figurative meaning, for it is the (image of a) huge and complex construction site that makes him the leading builder under pressure, not his personality or his competence. In contrast, the PiS campaign commercial reflects the integrative approach to address a wide range of voters by focusing on Kaczyński's political personality whose affective experience, similar to Merkel, becomes the political program and message.

Thus, the two Polish campaign commercials display the reverse pattern of concentration on personality and programmatic content than is the case with the German TV campaign ads: the incumbent Tusk focuses on the programmatic goal of a strong and rich future Poland, while the challenger Kaczyński draws on the experiential qualities of his personality. What this all amounts to is that an in-depth analysis of audiovisual figurativity makes an important contribution to the examination of challenger and incumbent strategies: it sheds light on the question of how these strategies, which are actually thematic aspects, come about, i.e., how they are audiovisually composed and unfolded within the campaign commercial.

In summary, the analyses of the four campaign commercials have therefore demonstrated

1) how diverse and multifaceted the figurate meanings emerging with the candidates can be;
2) how fundamentally these meanings shape the situated image of the candidate;
3) that the political position of incumbent or challenger does not necessarily come along with standardized candidate images of a sovereign and offensive opponent; and

4) that these three insights are significantly shaped by the respective interplay of language and audiovisual staging or, more precisely, the two dimensions of audiovisual figurativity in each and every campaign commercial.

In the concluding section, this issue will be discussed in greater detail.

8.5 Conclusion: The Intertwining of Language and Audiovisual Staging as Qualitative Criterion

Campaign commercials are supposed to make parties, as well as their programs and candidates, understandable and graspable, to literally give them a face, to create them an image. These faces or images are, however, not given a priori in terms of audiovisual representations but only emerge in the process of viewing the TV campaign ads. As Kappelhoff and Greifenstein (2016, 184) put it:

> [S]pectators themselves let moving images become visual representations in the modes of metaphor-making of "seeing one thing in terms of another" [...] and these representations indicate an artistically created, manufactured, fictional world in their every trait. [...] This is the sense in which we understand the reception of film images as poiesis, as an act of artistic production, which is to be found in media consumption itself [...].

In this respect, the campaign commercials of the PiS party and the SPD display clear differences in regard to the emergent figurative meaning of their two protagonists Jarosław Kaczyński and Frank-Walter Steinmeier as resulting from their distinct interplay between language and audiovisual staging. In the case of the PiS campaign commercial, the overall figurative theme is predominantly grounded in the modulation of affective experience through audiovisual staging and audiovisual representation. This way, figurative meaning unfolds temporally, attentionally, and experientially in an extensive pattern over the course of time. Through the audiovisually staged movement experience of withdrawn flowing powerful movement and its release by Kaczyński as the one who opens doors, figurative meaning emerges in a rather *subtle* manner. In the case of the TV campaign ad of the SPD, on the other hand, spoken and written language are prominently in the fore and create – by means of audiovisual illustrations and concretizations – a condensed pattern that is composed of single temporal, attentional, and experiential peaks. As a result, the respective contents are marked as salient and important in the course of the campaign commercial and audiovisual figurative meaning emerges in a far more *explicit and representational* manner.

Remarkably enough, the explicit form of figurative meaning-making in the SPD campaign commercial does not lead to a more concrete and tangible image of the candidate Steinmeier as compared to the PiS campaign commercial. Rather, its interrelatedness of speech and audiovisual staging in terms of twofold expressed meaning and single concretizations that differs fundamentally from the PiS campaign commercial leads to the "effect that the visuals [...] are perceived as mere illustrations, as doublings of the spoken word" (Scherer, Greifenstein, and Kappelhoff 2014, 2089). As such, the isolated moments of activated figurativity in the SPD campaign commercial amount to single overstatements of (figurative) meaning instead of activating an unfolding process of emergent interactions between two present realms and thus evoking a tangible image of the candidate Steinmeier.[16]

It is hence not sufficient to consider figurativity in audiovisual formats as if it emerged predominantly from language and single (static) pictures. Instead, only a comprehensive consideration of the dynamic link and composition of language and audiovisual staging makes it possible to qualitatively describe and differentiate the campaign commercials in respect to their emergent figurative meaning: the non-objective and rather subtle form of figurative meaning-making in the PiS campaign commercial creates a far more tangible image of the candidate Kaczyński than the explicit form does with Steinmeier in the SPD campaign commercial. The transdisciplinary perspective thus allows for detecting and explaining the qualitative differences between the two campaign commercials in a substantiated manner by reference to different forms of audiovisual figurativity. In the subsequent concluding chapter, these forms that have been introduced in Chapter 5 as different dominance phenomena among language and audiovisual staging (i.e., language over audiovisual staging, audiovisual staging over language, or a balanced interplay between the two) are related to the four campaign commercials and comparatively discussed with regard to their impact on figurative meaning-making and candidate image formation. On this basis, conclusions are drawn for future cognitive-linguistic research on (audiovisual) figurativity in political contexts of use in general as well as for future political, social, and media science research on campaign commercials.

---

16 In the case of the PiS campaign commercial such a dynamic process of what Scherer, Greifenstein, and Kappelhoff (2014, 2104–2105) have called "mapping in time" takes place over its entire course and apart from language.

9 Conclusion and Prospects

In the introduction to their edited volume *Political Language and Metaphor. Interpreting and Changing the World* (2008a), Terrell Carver and Jernej Pikalo distance themselves from a conception of metaphor in terms of a given meaningful entity. According to them, such an understanding has led to a neglect of its pragmatic aspects and inherent dynamic meaning-making. For that reason,

> the analysis of political metaphors should not just be about the interpretation of political metaphors, but also and above else about the creative-productive function that they have in politics and in political science itself. In other words, politics and political science are themselves linguistic phenomena and are thus *created and constructed through actions and activities as forms of life and knowledge* (Carver and Pikalo 2008b: 3; emphasis mine).

This active, dynamic, and productive nature that incidentally not only applies to metaphor but also to metonymy, has been a fundamental starting point for the theoretical and methodological framework developed in this book. Already on the basis of four campaign commercials, general variations in figurative meaning-making have become apparent, clearly suggesting that it is far from a standardized operation with changing content. A descriptive qualitative analysis of figurative meaning-making processes in a situated media context, therefore, is a research demand in order to close the gap Carver and Pikalo are mentioning. Audiovisual figurativity is not considered a translation of verbal figurative expressions into audiovisual images as Meyer-Lucht (2009) has called it and as numerous cognitive-linguistic studies have handled it to date.

The dynamic approach advocated and analysis undertaken in this book instead show that language is not the standard case of audiovisual figurativity but only one aspect among others. In this light, the role of audiovisual images as mere content duplications of verbal figurative expressions is hardly tenable from a dynamic perspective of audiovisual figurativity. Based on the elaborated temporal, attentional, and experiential dynamics, audiovisual images become graspable as high-grade specific concretizations and activations of verbally expressed figurative imagery. With its focus on the media specificity of audiovisual images as movement-images in Deleuze's (2008) sense, the film-analytical concept of cinematic expressive movement (Kappelhoff 2004; Kappelhoff and Bakels 2011) retrieves them from their subordinated role to language and allows for a transdisciplinary, more dynamic take on meaning-making in audiovisual contexts. In this respect, the audiovisual movement-image can be considered analogous to gestures (Müller and Kappelhoff 2018), which have their own specific forms and structures of meaning constitution and complement verbally expressed meaning in this manner instead of merely doubling it.

https://doi.org/10.1515/9783110578782-009

In the subsequent concluding sections, the findings of this work are brought together in a systematic manner. On that basis, implications for cognitive-linguistic research on audiovisual figurativity, as well as for political, social, and media science research on campaign commercials, is worked out. The main emphasis is initially placed on the synopsis and concluding comparative consideration of the results of analysis of the four campaign commercials. As such, it is particularly the relation between different forms of audiovisual figurative (and, thus, of explicit, subtle, or balanced) meaning-making and the respective conceptual and content-related orientation of the campaign commercials that will be elaborated upon. On this basis, conclusions can be drawn for cognitive-linguistic research and analysis of figurativity in political contexts of use. In the following section, the frame of reference for these insights will be extended by political, social, and media science research on campaign commercials. Here, figurative meaning-making has so far decidedly not been at the heart of investigation. As a prime example of embodied meaning-making or "understanding through experience" (Müller and Schmitt 2015), audiovisual figurativity as considered here bears the potential to open up a new perspective and thereby provide fresh insights for the political, social, and media studies examination of campaign commercials. The chapter concludes with reflections on implications of such an embodied understanding of audiovisual figurative meaning-making with regard to the notion of persuasion, which is a core topic both for figurativity in political communication in particular as well as for political and election campaign communication in general.

9.1 Variations of Audiovisual Figurative Meaning-Making

The comparative perspective taken in this chapter for the concluding discussion of the gained findings does not aim at presenting the developed emergent figurative meaning as an expression of entrenched cultural patterns of thinking in the respective language, i.e., in Polish or German. This study cannot put forward such an assumption as its data basis is too small and because such an equation of the level of use and the systems level of language amount to a generalization that the analysis does not target. Due to its film-analytical focus in respect to a specific presentational form, historical facts as well as peculiarities of the respective political and election system in the two countries are of minor relevance for this study and therefore only slightly taken into consideration. In comparing the commercials, they play a role to the extent that the analyzed campaign commercials occurred in the context of parliamentary elections in both countries that resulted in the formation of a new cabinet and the designation of a new head of government. Both the Chancellor of Germany and the Prime Minister of Poland are the heads of government in both countries. In this light, one campaign commercial of the incumbent and one of a challenger each were subjects of analysis. With the SPD and the CDU in Germany, and the PO and the PiS in Poland, the analysis refers to the (currently) two strongest parties in both countries. The objective of the comparison is, however, neither to extract party-specific positions or patterns of thinking from the figurative meaning found in the campaign commercials, nor to ascribe them to a culture-specific political or historical background.

In summary, the comparison of the campaign commercials' conception and content-related orientation aims to look at the role of the candidates in the election campaigns (i.e., incumbent and challenger). In this manner, the drawn conclusions remain close to the data. Significant differences between the two political systems render a simple equation impossible. They are, however, neither the aim of this study and therefore only briefly mentioned in the following: in Germany, the Chancellor is elected by the members of the Bundestag, while in Poland, the Prime Minister is appointed by the President of Poland. The two Polish parties PiS and PO are significantly younger than the German parties SPD and CDU. Apart from this, Poland's party system compared to Germany's is characterized by a strong discontinuity, e.g., with regard to the array of political parties, the balance of power among them, the formation of fractions and electoral alliances. Having clarified that, observations and insights that result from a concluding synopsis of all four analyses carried out in this study are presented and discussed below, not least with regard to their implications for cognitive-linguistic research and analysis of figurativity in political contexts of use.

The detailed analysis of the interplay between language and audiovisual staging in each of the four campaign commercials has led to accounting for the temporal, attentional, and experiential configurations of figurative meaning, i.e., where in the campaign commercial figurative meaning emerges and becomes activated, if this happens in particular moments only or continuously and consistently, what kind of sensory-motor and affective experiences are evoked and how they are modulated over the course of time. As such, figurativity in campaign commercials has been demonstrated to not unfold in the same manner as audiovisual illustrations of verbal metaphorical expressions, as often taken for granted. Instead, the analyses clearly show in what diverse ways figurative meaning emerges: through verbal figurative expressions that are activated through audiovisual images, through audiovisual representation, and through affective experiences that are orchestrated by audiovisual movement-images (i.e., cinematic expressive movements). These different ways have turned out not to occur in pure form but rather to intertwine over the course of time and thereby to develop figurative meaning dynamically to an overall figurative theme. A closer look at that interplay and its particular temporal, attentional, and experiential profile, allows for qualifying the overall process of audiovisual figurativity's dynamic unfolding in more detail on the level of the whole campaign commercial. In their case study of the dynamics of metaphorical meaning in two examples taken from conversational interaction, Müller and Tag attempt to develop an argument along these lines:

> Both examples also differ with regard to their respective foregrounding patterns. The first case is characterized by a condensed and mainly simultaneous foregrounding pattern, with a steady and fast increase of foregrounding of metaphoricity realized in a short amount of time. Meanwhile, the second example shows a highly complex simultaneous and linear foregrounding pattern that extends over a longer time span. (Müller and Tag 2010, 110)

However, they do not follow up on this observation in terms of drawing potential conclusions with regard to the implications of these different patterns for the situated context of use. This study takes this step by addressing the question of the emergent image of the promoted political candidates and the level to which they are made tangible and comprehensible. This is precisely what has turned out to be the main aspect of figurativity in campaign commercials: it literally creates an image of the candidates by making them available for being experienced and understood in a particular manner. In concrete terms, Angela Merkel is experienced and understood in terms of a powerful sovereign with civil roots who is close to the people; Donald Tusk as a leading builder under pressure asking for an extension of the deadline in order to finish his uncompleted project; Jarosław Kaczyński as a door opener for the so far segregated and excluded citizens, thereby making for participatory equality; and Frank-Walter Steinmeier as his Germany plan as a sober and realistic answer to existential questions. The reconstruction of these emergent figurative meanings that give rise to situated images of the four candidates from a dynamic view and transdisciplinary perspective, provides a basis for qualitatively comparing and differentiating the campaign commercials on a well-founded basis from the viewer's perspective. Admittedly, these emergent figurative meanings are not suggested to reflect actual psychological and physiological processes. Instead, they are grounded in a philosophical and phenomenological account of embodied meaning-making (cf., Müller and Kappelhoff 2018, Müller and Schmitt 2015; see also Johnson 2007).

The first considerable difference that shows up from the overall picture of all analyses is the one between the campaign commercials of the CDU, the PO, and the PiS compared with the SPD TV campaign ad. While the first three exhibit a clear intertwining of the two main modalities, language and audiovisual staging, and their respective dimensions of figurative meaning-making, the latter basically makes use of only one way, i.e., the multimodal (illustrative) activation of verbal figurative expressions through audiovisual images. In this respect, the former ones display a higher degree of composition of language and audiovisual staging as compared to the latter. The SPD campaign commercial actually gives the impression that language and audiovisual staging instead run parallel and barely intertwine with each other: this shows up in the clear predominance of language over audiovisual staging and the lack of consistent and sufficiently activated figurative meaning. As a result, a tangible image of the respective candidate emerges in the case of the first three campaign commercials, whereas in the case of the SPD campaign commercial, the candidate Frank-Walter Steinmeier remains vague and inconsistent. This clearly indicates that language and audiovisual staging cannot be separated from one another and that a static and simplistic conception of audiovisual figurativity as mere depiction of verbally expressed imagery is far from reality. Instead, there is need for a dynamic perspective that accounts for the temporal, attentional, and experiential dynamics of audiovisual figurative meaning in a situated media context.

Even among the three campaign commercials that give rise to a tangible image of the respective candidate, remarkable differences become apparent. Juxtaposing the PO with the CDU and the PiS campaign commercial demonstrates that the former's overall figurative theme emerges and unfolds primarily in language. The scenario of an uncompleted construction site and Donald Tusk as its leading builder is mainly unfolded monomodally through language. On this basis, it is further concretized through audiovisual images and affectively qualified through audiovisual staging. In contrast, the CDU and the PiS campaign commercial display no such predominance of language and instead an equal or stronger role of audiovisual staging that – without explicit verbal figurative expressions – makes present realms of experience that are related to others: in the case of Angela Merkel, it is the sensation of absolutist sovereign power and stability through visual composition, sound, and camera movement; in the case of Jarosław Kaczyński, it is the image of inclusion and exclusion and door opening as well as the sensation of releasing tension and providing balance.

A closer look at the particular temporal, attentional, and experiential profile of audiovisual figurative meaning-making of all four campaign commercials reveals further noteworthy variances. The PO TV campaign ad exhibits a condensed and pointed stepwise progression of audiovisual figurative meaning that increases noticeably in the second half through multimodal activations of the construction scenario and the explicit verbal mentioning of emergent figurative meaning ("four difficult years are too little in order to realize the plan of building a strong and rich Poland"). The PiS campaign commercial, on the other hand, features a prolonged and constantly high-grade activated profile to establish (through audiovisual representation) and elaborate its overall figurative theme throughout its entire course. Only at two points (in the middle and at the end) is it also verbally explicated through the faded-in slogans whereby the emergent figurative meaning is elaborated and foregrounded. The CDU campaign commercial displays a similar prolonged, but more complex profile as both dimensions of audiovisual figurative meaning-making (i.e., multimodal activation of figurativity and the affective experience of cinematic expressive movement) unfold continuously in an interrelated manner over its course. What is remarkable is that the audiovisual metonymies play a double role: on the one hand, they unfold figurative meaning simultaneously (e.g., Merkel's verbal expression 'empower families' corresponding with the image of a baby) and, taken together, they linearly foreground the principle of contiguity and the central metonymical link between Merkel and the German people over the course of the commercial. Quite different is the profile of audiovisual figurative meaning in the SPD campaign commercial where it unfolds in an extremely condensed and rather simultaneous pattern of single foregrounded but isolated moments of activated metonymicity that, however, do not compose a coherent image.

Generally speaking, the SPD and the PO campaign commercial, and the CDU and the PiS campaign commercial appear similar to each other and stand in opposition to the other pair. The predominance of language in the former two takes shape in condensed forms on the micro level and thereby develops a higher degree of explicitness of the emergent figurative meaning. This is due to the direct relation between language and audiovisual staging in the SPD TV campaign ad and the monomodal elaboration of metaphorical meaning in the PO campaign commercial. In the first case, the audiovisual images relate closely to the verbal expressions with which they create an audiovisual metonymy. Thereby, these metonymies have a clear, explicit, and as such rather illustrating character that leaves little room for interpretation which is indeed not intended because the SPD campaign commercial wants to argue and create unambiguous precedents. In the case of the PO campaign commercial, the room for interpretation is a bit more open due to the less direct audiovisual depiction of the imagery: the viewer is never shown a building site as a whole but always single images that activate the construction scenario. Nevertheless, due to the predominant elaboration through language and the subdominant role of audiovisual staging, the emergent metaphorical meaning first and foremost plays out in an explicit manner.

The predominance of audiovisual staging and almost complete absence of language in the CDU and the PiS campaign commercial, on the other hand, takes shape in prolonged and highly activated forms on the micro level and thereby develops a higher degree of subtlety of the emergent figurative meaning. In the latter of the two, language plays a subdominant role: it merely serves to explain the audiovisually evoked metaphorical scenario of inclusion and exclusion. Because the faded-in language does, however, not relate directly to the audiovisual representation, as in the case of the SPD campaign commercial, the emergent figurative meaning of the PiS campaign commercial develops in a rather subtle manner. In contrast, the CDU campaign commercial exhibits a balance between language and audiovisual staging that takes shape in interconnected simultaneous and extended forms on the micro level and thereby develops a balanced interplay between explicitness and subtlety of the emergent figurative meaning. Language unfolds both simultaneous explicit metonymical meanings, but concomitantly points beyond it and foregrounds the non-explicit principle of contiguity. Furthermore, language makes figurative meaning explicit in patches (e.g., "I was not born a chancellor" which exhibits an alternation between 'I' and 'we' in the first contemplative part, or the final slogan "We have the power"). However, it primarily relates less directly to the audiovisual images, wherefore a balanced interplay between language and audiovisual staging, between explicitness and subtlety shapes the emergent figurative meaning.

From an overall view on all forms of the interplay between language and audiovisual staging on the micro level there arises a tendency on the macro level either towards language or towards audiovisual staging or equally to both of them. These three different dominance phenomena in the two dimensions of audiovisual figurative meaning-making (i.e., predominance of language over audiovisual staging; balance between language and audiovisual staging; predominance of audiovisual staging over language) that have been introduced in Chapter 5 can now be attributed to the campaign commercials under discussion. In Figure 17, their allocation to the respective TV campaign ad is illustrated.

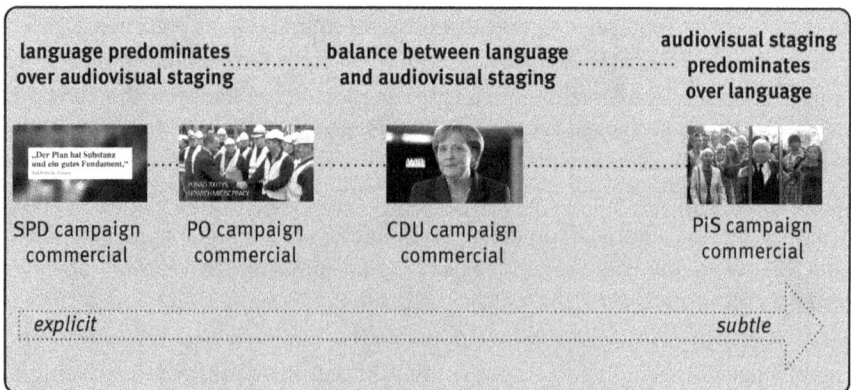

Figure 17: Campaign commercials as variant forms of audiovisual figurativity

The three forms of audiovisual figurativity are not understood in terms of distinct, mutual exclusive categories but as a continuum with smooth transitions between the single forms. This becomes particularly evident in the case of the PO campaign commercial that displays a predominance of language over audiovisual staging as does the SPD campaign commercial to be sure, but its language and audiovisual staging are more strongly interrelated than the latter's. That is to say, while the PO campaign commercial is language-induced, the SPD campaign commercial is language-driven. Therefore, the PO campaign commercial is not completely assigned to the form of predominant language, like the SPD campaign commercial, but instead between it and the balanced interplay of language and audiovisual staging.

Hence, from the SPD, across the PO and the CDU and, finally, to the PiS campaign commercial, an increasing degree of subtlety and of the temporal, attentional, and experiential extent of audiovisual figurative meaning-making can be stated. On this basis, and due to the detailed transdisciplinary analysis, it is now possible to examine the four campaign commercials qualitatively on a well-founded basis from the viewer's perspective. In contrast to previous studies that proposed that Polish campaign commercials were unprofessional compared to German ones (e.g., Musiałowska 2008), they have turned out to equally give rise to elaborate figurative meaning and thereby make the promoted candidate tangible and comprehensible like their German equivalents. Remarkably, the campaign commercial of the Polish PiS makes for an even more tangible image of its candidate Jarosław Kaczyński than the campaign commercial of the German SPD. Although the former unfolds figurative meaning primarily through audiovisual representation and affective experience orchestrated by audiovisual movement patterns, the few instances of language are well-composed with them and thereby give rise to a consistent and vital image of Kaczyński. In the SPD campaign commercial, on the other hand, language is barely related to audiovisual staging: apart from single, isolated moments of activated figurativity, no consistent idea and image of the candidate emerges. The dynamic approach to audiovisual figurative meaning-making thus offers deeper insights into the meaning-making process of campaign commercials than surface analyses of the represented or linguistic content and used audiovisual techniques. The findings of the campaign commercials of the two major German and Polish parties could be further complemented by analyses of campaign commercials of the minor parties in Germany and Poland in order to test Holtz-Bacha and Kaid's (1993) hypothesis that they were unprofessional and boring due to conventional patterns and production technique as well as long text passages. Such a comparative analysis, however, goes beyond the scope of this book and is subject to further investigation.

Another, more basic factor that has an impact on the process and thus also on the form and quality of audiovisual figurative meaning in campaign commercials is their limited duration, which gives rise to rather short-termed patterns in general. Nevertheless, slight differences and variations among the four campaign commercials stand out: those with a shorter duration (i.e., PiS and PO with 30 respectively 45 seconds) exhibit a more pointed meaning-making process, whereas those with a longer duration (i.e., CDU with 90 seconds) tend to display a wider extension and unfolding of figurative meaning.[1] This also becomes apparent in the complexity of cinematic expressive movement patterns: the PiS and the PO campaign commercial consist of only one expressive movement unit (emu), whereas the CDU TV campaign ad features two emus and thus a small dramaturgy. By contrast, the SPD campaign commercial consists of only one emu, but this one addresses the viewer in a rather restrained manner because it is overshadowed by language and displays a low degree of composition. Hence, the mere number of emus does not reveal anything about the way and intensity of affectively addressing the viewer.

Apart from this, the respective movement qualities are an influential factor as well as the interplay of dominant and subdominant articulatory modalities of audiovisual staging that compose it. In this respect, the CDU, the PO, and the PiS campaign commercial all address the viewer in an intense manner, but vary in view of their respective degree of explicitness or subtleness: while the movement qualities in the PO and the PiS campaign commercial are strongly foregrounded in the underlying music and visual composition, they are in the CDU campaign commercial rather subtly staged in the visual composition, underlying music, and camera movement which has to do with the rather calm and moderate quality itself. As the SPD campaign commercial unfolds a mainly heterogeneous audiovisual movement pattern that could at best be described by an alternation of dynamics (through the quick succession of shots illustrating the goals of the Germany plan) and rest (through showing Steinmeier speaking to the camera), it is primarily the dynamic sequences[2] that address the viewer more intensely than the calm ones. However, this kind of addressing amounts primarily to a short-term attentional and sensory-motor experiential appeal.

---

[1] In spite of its 90 seconds of duration, the SPD campaign commercial does not follow this pattern as it displays a rather scattered figurative meaning-making process that mainly plays out on the verbal level.

[2] With regard to the attentional dynamics, the dynamic sequences are also those of activated figurativity when the audiovisual images illustrate what is verbally expressed by Steinmeier's voice over and thus create audiovisual metonymies.

The overall comparison of all campaign commercials discloses further observations that are relevant to cognitive linguistics: metonymy plays a role in each of
them to a varying extent. In the CDU TV campaign ad, it unfolds as a pattern that
foregrounds the principle of contiguity and the central link of the candidate Merkel
and the German people. In the case of the PO campaign commercial, it virtually
forms an anti-pattern that highlights heterogeneity and makes Tusk's workload
and pressure tangible. In the PiS campaign commercial, metonymy complements
and classifies the affective and representational contrast between excluded and
included by qualifying the two shown groups as citizens and politicians. In the
case of the SPD campaign commercial, metonymy serves for illustrating single
goals of the Germany plan and concomitantly putting forward an individual perspective on them, i.e., what 'good education' or 'families' means and looks like
(for Steinmeier). This clearly illustrates that metaphor is not the only figurative
mode that plays a role in audiovisual figurative meaning-making and in making
candidates tangible in campaign commercials. A more comprehensive view of figurativity that considers its various forms and configurations as well as the particular interplay of metaphor and metonymy is thus fruitful and desirable.

The imagery of a house or a building in general is a recurrent motive in all
four campaign commercials, however, with a different role and with varying
configurations. In the CDU TV campaign ad, it plays a prominent role in terms
of Merkel's office and as a remarkable boundary between inside and outside,
past and present and future. As such, it supports her double role, i.e., the emergent figurative meaning of being both sovereign and having civil roots. The PO
campaign commercial creates an entirely different image of a house or building,
namely as an experiential scenario of a hitherto unfinished but to be realized
vision of a future Poland. As such, it serves as an excuse and absolution for Tusk's
terminating office term and simultaneously as a justification for his re-election.
In the PiS party's campaign commercial, the building plays the most prominent
role as compared with the other three campaign commercials: it provides the
realm for experiencing and understanding politics, both in a negative (drawing
a remarkable boundary between inside and outside) and in a positive way (open
and big enough for everybody, transparent). The SPD campaign commercial, in
turn, is the only one in which it is only marginally and shortly present, namely
on the verbal level: as a metaphorical conceptualization of the Germany plan that
is, however, barely activated ("The plan has substance and a good foundation").
This metaphorical expression is reminiscent of a stable and solid building or
house, but it is not further elaborated and thus remains one among other heterogeneous verbal figurative expressions that form no consistent whole.

It would be going too far to speak of audiovisual and verbal instances of a
conceptual POLITICS IS A HOUSE metaphor for this is not the line of thought

that this study is following, i.e., to prioritize the conceptual system level against the level of use. Instead, it focuses on embodied meaning-making in a situated media context and not as an instantiation of a pre-existing mapping between conceptual domains. As such, it explicitly does not aim to make claims about the psychological reality, in terms of (un-)consciousness or deliberateness, of the analyzed emergent figurative meaning in the campaign commercials. With such a clear focus on the situated emergence and unfolding of figurative meaning, the analyses at best suggest the assumption of the house or building as a systematic metaphor in Lynne Cameron's sense[3] (2007, Cameron, Low, and Maslen 2010). However, the extremely small corpus of four campaign commercials that, more-over, originate from different elections in different countries in different years makes this hypothesis rather improbable.

9.2 Campaign Commercials as Political Symbolizations

What kinds of insights can this study with its cognitive-linguistic research topic of audiovisual figurativity in four selected campaign commercials provide for political communication research? To begin with, the most obvious and certainly straightforward link between the two disciplines lies in the fact that

> [...] politics is heavily depended upon communication between and among political actors, citizens, and the media, and even can be regarded a form of communication in itself, polit-ical communication research is highly relevant to modern societies [...] Political communi-cation research by its very nature is interdisciplinary and comprises scholars from a wide range of theoretical approaches, methodological backgrounds, and academic disciplines of which media and communication studies and political science are the most important, but by far not the only ones. (Reinemann 2014, 1)

However clear and self-evident this may appear – there is a long-lasting dissoci-ation between the two disciplines. Although linguistics, verbal communication, and rhetorical analysis were highly relevant for the emergence of the field, they were replaced by social psychology, political science, and mass communication in the post-war phase due to a strong focus on the effects of media influence on society (Reinemann 2014, 9). Within political communication research this led to the dissociation between the humanities and the social sciences in favor of the latter, which had theoretical and methodological consequences:

---

3 According to Cameron, systematic metaphors are "aggregated samples of actual use of lan-guage from a specific discourse event" and "dynamic mappings that reflect a temporary stabili-sation in online language use" (Cameron 2006).

> This tradition [...] established a long-lasting, dominant research paradigm marked by key concepts like opinion and attitude, the notion of political communication as a process, a strong focus on media effects as well as a preference for quantitative empirical research. (Reinemann 2014, 10)

In other words, those disciplines that deal with the basic conditions and principles of communication were (and still are) underrepresented in the research field. As a result, individual subdisciplines and approaches (e.g., politolinguistics, critical discourse analysis) have emerged on the part of the humanities that examine the field of political communication separately. Given its interdisciplinary nature as pointed out by Reinemann (2014), this isolation is regrettable as the research expertise of the social sciences and the humanities could complement each other in a fruitful way.

While political communication in the context of election campaigns has only become a research topic within linguistics in recent years (e.g., Cienki and Giansante 2014, Forchtner, Krzyżanowski, and Wodak 2013), "[t]he desire to understand campaign effects became a major driving force in the development of political communication research. Even today, a considerable amount of political communication research is done in the context of election campaigns" (Reinemann 2014, 4). In this, political communication is always established as the "strategic use of communication to reach voters directly through different forms of controlled communication or indirectly through the news media, or as different modes of communication and campaigning" (Strömbäck and Kiousis 2014, 110). It stands to reason that this presupposition is why most research carried out in this field takes meaning in the examined forms of communication for granted and therefore focuses on identifying and analyzing strategic and effective aspects on the level of content.

Political communication research on campaign commercials predominantly aims at the analysis of their contents and their effects on the spectators, respectively the voters (see Chapter 1). In this respect, the "hegemony of quantitative social science" (Delia 1987, 71) is most obviously manifest in quantitative content analysis (e.g., Holtz-Bacha 2000, Jakubowski 1998), illustrating the distribution of coded categories (e.g., parts of verbal language, elements on the level of representation, or single articulatory modalities of audiovisual staging) in the campaign commercials (mostly in the form of tables and diagrams). The concomitant abstraction and decontextualization of single formal and audiovisually represented elements and their comparative juxtaposition with other instantiations neglects their situatedness, emergence, and particular quality in a situated media context. Furthermore, the focus on the represented content does not take into account the media-specific mode of perception of audiovisual images (cf. Müller and Kappelhoff 2018) and the concomitant emergence of meaning through cinematic expressivity.

This work contributes to previous, quantitatively informed political communication research by involving the aspect of meaning-making in campaign commercials in consideration of the media specificity of audiovisual images. In doing so, it takes one important step back in examining and analyzing the TV campaign ads and asks for the conditions of how the so far exclusively examined, and taken-for-granted, visual representation and processes of fictionalization come into being (cf. Kappelhoff and Greifenstein 2016). From the transdisciplinary perspective taken in this book, it is through the figurative principle of experiencing and understanding one thing in terms of another that these two come into being in the first place:

> This fictionalization can be reconstructed as *processes of metaphorization*. Indeed, one can view the formation of metaphor itself as a fundamental driving force of any fictionalization. Metaphor can be described as a process of changing, correlating, and projecting two different complexes of experience, sensory units, perceptual schemata, or sources of the image. If metaphor links two different realms of experience, then the processes of forming metaphors should open up a way to access the processes of fictionalization as arrangements of film experiences, which spectators concretely traverse in the process of seeing and hearing. (Kappelhoff and Greifenstein 2016, 184)

This link between the establishing of figurativity and the process of constructing a fictional cinematic world puts forward a constitutive and overarching meaning-making principle of audiovisual images: it is not realized through the audiovisual representation of reality but is only created in and through the viewer. Transferring and applying this idea to the analysis of campaign commercials and considering the spectator as meaning-maker in the process of viewing opens up an alternative complementary approach to the question of their experience. In this manner, campaign commercials are not ex ante regarded as abstract strategic tools aiming at persuasion but are first and foremost considered with regard to their mediality: namely, as a part and expression of political discourse. In other words, they are conceived of as audiovisual images that orchestrate the perception of viewers, thereby bringing forth a communicative situation and entering into discourse. Such an orientation to the process of seeing and hearing positions the TV campaign ads as an interactive form of meaning-making instead of focusing exclusively on the production side and its intentions.

This is also compatible with the notion of political "interpretational culture" [*Deutungskultur*] that Holtz-Bacha (2000) has adopted from Karl Rohe (1990). Holtz-Bacha uses the term in order to mark and classify campaign commercials as part of political culture through which competing proposals of sense and interpretation among the different parties within a political system become graspable, either resulting in the confirmation or the transformation of socioculture

(Holtz-Bacha 2000, 16–21). Therefore, she refers to the campaign commercials as symbolic politics by which political parties attempt to define and construct political reality. Holtz-Bacha particularly emphasizes this aspect in order to justify her content-analytical access and the neglect of the effectiveness of the campaign commercials. The complete focus on the production side and its interpretative proposal, however, implies a separation or gap between the TV campaign ads and the viewers whereby the latter seems to be subjected to them from the start, merely relevant as a target audience and therefore only playing a passive role.

In contrast, the analysis of the emergence of audiovisual figurative meaning proceeds from a close link between the campaign commercials and the viewers that consists of their affective and cognitive addressing in a situated media context. As a result, the viewers are considered as being actively involved in the process of symbolization that occurs within the political interpretational culture (cf. Beichelt 2004, 155). It is them who bring into being and figure the candidates and parties, the points of view and aims in their own body when viewing the TV campaign ads. This reflexive perceptual experience of audiovisual images that is characterized by the bodily experience of a foreign subjective perception (Sobchack 1992) corresponds to the relation between the socioculture and the culture of interpretation. Socioculture refers to the taken-for-granted level of political culture that is not repeatedly brought into question, constituted by passed-on interpretative patterns as represented by everyday political life (Holtz-Bacha 2000, 18). These patterns are reflected and negotiated in a subjective perspective on the interpretational culture and can, in so doing, find their way into socioculture. Equally, the campaign commercials give rise to a fictional perceptual world that refers to the reality of everyday experience in the form of an as-if experience: "[W]e perceive a foreign way of sensing the world as if it were our own sense of perception, our feeling for the world." (Greifenstein and Kappelhoff 2016, 188) That is to say, the construction of the world in the TV campaign ads as fiction relates to a shared experience of the reality, but it does so in a subjective, evaluative, and situated manner, and thereby reflects and transforms its reference object.

In this light, the respective point of view, expressed in the campaign commercials and materializing as a bodily experience on the part of the viewer, can be understood as an exchange relationship between socioculture and interpretational culture and as a social practice of constructing political reality. In this sense, this study puts forward a cultural-science informed perspective on the exploration of the political (cf. Schwelling 2004, 12): it examines the TV campaign ads as communicative encounters and exchange between political parties and voters in their entirety and situatedness. This qualitative focus naturally goes along with a limited scope concerning the quantifiability and generalizability of the gained results. Nevertheless, it proposes a closer examination of supposed overall tendencies or recurrent patterns in the aesthetic arrangement of the campaign commercials that are mostly deduced from isolated abstracted elements (e.g., Holtz-Bacha 2000) by taking a closer look at their respective configuration and staging. In doing so, they remain embedded in their immediate situated context, i.e., the respective candidates, parties, election period, and political context to which they refer directly.

In this sense, the TV campaign ads are considered as audiovisual access to the political. By now, social sciences have treated images in political communication first and foremost with skepticism and have adopted a rather negative attitude in dealing with them (Hofmann 2004, 309). Symbolic politics – in contrast to 'real' politics – has mostly been conceived of and neglected as mere visual and make-believe presentation of political results (Hofmann 2004, 309), whereby their communicative reality-constituting function has not been taken into consideration. Marion Müller, however, explicitly points out that there is a nexus between political symbolizations and cultural self-understanding:

> A society's image production is a direct expression of its cultural self-understanding. From a cultural-sciences perspective images can be conceived of as sources for political structures and processes, opening up a qualitative access to the understanding of political-cultural patterns of reproduction and communication. (Müller 2004, 335; translation mine)

With regard to fiction films, Siegfried Kracauer has similarly argued the case for a critical media analysis in order to reveal inventories of social mentality. According to him, films do not reflect explicit beliefs but rather psychological dispositions, which he considers as deep layers of a collective mentality, located below the level of consciousness (Kracauer [1947] 1984, 12).

Campaign commercials take up these cultural collective dispositions and relate them to a subjective experiential reality. In these audiovisual descriptions and new descriptions of a shared world, the political community is questioned and related to the situated experiential reality of film-viewing. TV campaign ads thereby produce a thinking that measures the space of commonality (see Kappelhoff 2018). In this respect, the discourse taking place in the process of viewing the campaign commercials and the subject of this book is also relevant for comparative political communication research. Such a comparative perspective, however, neither refers to country-specific contextual conditions[4] of political

---

4 In connection with the "seemingly outdated country category" Pfetsch and Esser (2014, 87, 94) point out that "many studies comparing election communication were unable to demonstrate stark differences in campaign style [...], marketing orientation [...], the use of advertising [...] or web campaigning [...], and consequently did not succeed at attributing differences to the impact of country-specific contextual conditions".

communication nor to supposed entrenched culture-specific concepts or ideas of politics. Instead, it refers to the respective description and new description of a shared world through subjective experience which only gives rise to the audio-visual representations and images of candidates and political parties as (figurative) meaning. Against this backdrop, the previous understanding of figurativity in political communication as a strategic persuasive tool or even as ideological tool of persuasion (cf. Androshchuk 2014) is questioned and reconsidered in the final section.

9.3 Reframing Persuasion towards Meaning-Making and Understanding

The research discussions of campaign commercials (in the social sciences) and of figurativity in political communication (in linguistics) display one common feature: both are led somewhat one-dimensionally, videlicet foremost with respect to their strategic use for the purpose of persuading the addressee. Charteris-Black, for instance, declares right at the beginning of his book *Corpus Approaches to Political Metaphor*:

> Metaphor is a figure of speech that is typically used in persuasion; this is because it represents a novel way of viewing the world that offers some fresh insight. Because metaphor is persuasive it is frequently employed discursively in rhetorical and argumentative language such as political speeches. (Charteris-Black 2004, 7)

Androshchuk similarly presupposes the occurrence of metaphors in political discourse as an intended influencing of the addressee by a speaker. According to him, the use of metaphor is never objective and rather expresses an individual worldview (Androshchuk 2014, 97). Based on that assumption, he formulates the main objective of the use of political metaphor as gaining influence on the consciousness of the audience and manipulating it by controlling thoughts, emotions, and behavior (Androshchuk 2014, 274). A similar epistemological interest guides Holtz-Bacha in her study of campaign commercials in Germany. Considering them as interpretational proposals of political parties for the voters, she focuses on strategies of images and arguments by which the parties try to give voters an understanding of their way of looking at things, their political programs, and their staff during election campaigns (Holtz-Bacha 2000, 230–231). A similar reasoning can be found with Dörner and Schicha (2008, 9) who state that the TV campaign ads are all about presenting the candidates and parties in the proper (positive) light in order to force the voting decision in a strategic manner.

These examples show that scholars in both fields of research repeatedly make recourse to an encroaching assertion and implementation of a subjective way of thinking and to the shrewd arousal of emotions in order to explain the persuasion of addressees. What is notable is that the discussion is thus from the first led in a critical and pejorative manner. Charteris-Black's and Androshchuk's works on metaphor in political language exemplify such a rhetorical political approach and moreover illustrate that the notion of persuasion is frequently used in an inconsistent manner and mostly vaguely defined. Referring to Garth Jowett's and Victoria O'Donnell's work *Propaganda and Persuasion* (1992), Charteris-Black puts forward a definition of persuasion that conceives of it as an "interactive communicative process in which a message sender aims to influence the beliefs, attitudes and behaviour of the message receiver" (Charteris-Black 2005, 9). Although he uses the term 'interactive', the further explanation clearly reveals that he subscribes to a unidirectional model of communication (i.e., a sender-receiver model; see Shannon and Weaver 1945) that is oriented towards one-sided communication instead of having both parts involved in mutual participation: "the *active* role of the sender is characterised by deliberate intentions" while "the receivers' role is *passive*" (Charteris-Black 2005, 9; emphasis mine). With that said, the use of metaphors is exclusively linked to the sender and his purposes, and their persuasive effectiveness consists in the one-to-one eventuation of the intended impact on the part of the receiver.[5]

Petra Gehring has criticized such a one-sided conception from a philosophical perspective as falling short by making metaphors buttons that a rhetor, charismatic leader, or agitator can press in order to mobilize a multitude of people. In this respect, the power of metaphor is characterized as bearing too much impact wherefore it appears as an improper instrument for emotionalization and persuasion (Gehring 2015, 45). It is these aspects of insidiousness and inevitability that Charteris-Black uses for his argument as well:

> Metaphor draws on the unconscious emotional associations of words, the values of which are rooted in cultural knowledge. For this reason it potentially has a highly persuasive force because of its activation of both conscious and unconscious resources to influence our intellectual and emotional response, both directly – through describing and analysing political issues – and indirectly by influencing how we feel about things. (Charteris-Black 2005, 30)

---

[5] In this respect, Charteris-Black's notion of persuasion is tantamount to the purposefulness of all communication as assumed by speech act theory (see Austin 1962, Searle 1969), in particular to the successful accomplishment of the perlocutionary act.

According to him, metaphor evokes an intellectual response by drawing on shared culturally rooted belief systems that are brought together with addressed political topics and thereby open up new ideas and fresh insights (Charteris-Black 2005, 20). Equally, it provokes emotional responses as the "associative power of language" always associated particular words or expressions with positive or negative experiences within a given culture (Charteris-Black 2005, 20). One example that Charteris-Black is drawing on is Margret Thatcher's speech to the Conservative Party Conference in 1987, in which she contrasted the policy of the British Labor party and the Conservative Party by linking them to death and life forces:

> An evaluative framework is created by the contrast that is set up between two interaction chains of metaphor. The first is associated with the negative feelings aroused by death images and includes: *cut the heart, snuff out, dying, sapping, decay*; the other is associated with the positive feelings aroused by life images: *spark, give back heart, growing, recovery, take root, sprang.* [...] Inevitably, these associations are likely to arouse powerful feelings. (Charteris-Black 2005, 18–19)

From such a perspective, metaphors are considered to execute a psychological constraint and determinism upon the addressees by drawing on a "pre-rational universe of not yet articulated worlds of feelings" (Gehring 2015, 45–46, 51; translation mine). The argument of culturally rooted underlying values and experiential patterns is used in a similar manner to Lakoff and Turner: ex negativo, it serves the purpose of suggesting that what is most subconscious or unconscious is most entrenched and therefore most activated and influential on human thinking (Lakoff and Turner 1989, 129). Such presumed collectively shared concepts on a systems level are nevertheless hardly vindicable and traceable. Furthermore, they do not necessarily have to hold for the individual level of language use. In this sense, the idea of linguistic determinism (i.e., the direct impact of language on the human mind) suggests paradoxically the failure of language as truthful argument and similarly its exploitation in bad faith (Gehring 2015, 51).

While the persuasive aspect of metaphor for Charteris-Black consists in subtly evoking particular associations and emotions regarding political issues and topics, Androshchuk goes one step further by arguing that such an evocation of conscious or unconscious emotions stimulates a specific line of thought that leads to a certain reaction or behavior on the part of the addressee (Androshchuk 2014, 10). In the first case, the persuasive influence refers predominantly to the understanding and perception of things; in the second case, it moreover leads to certain actions. What is hereby addressed – and partially confounded – on the basis of the same line of argument are entirely different levels of effectiveness (conceptual, psychological, behavioral). Notwithstanding the above, a conception of persuasive power as Charteris-Black and Androshchuk propose suggests that things were different without metaphor (cf. Gehring 2015, 48). As a result, the power that is attributed to metaphor is characterized as being a falsification that exerts manipulative influence on the addressee by forcing a specific view and opinion on a mass of recipients, in particular in the case of limited background knowledge about the addressed topic. Such manipulative circumstances, however, are rather tantamount to 'dominance' (Gehring 2015, 48), especially due to the unequal distribution of power among speaker and addressees: the unidirectional communication, the one-sided impact, activity versus passivity, producer versus recipient.

In his book *Topos und Metapher* (2007), Jörg Jost – from a pragmatic and rhetorical point of view – criticizes such a power gap in the conceptions of persuasion by adducing the dilemma of the perlocutionary act:

> The speaker can intend persuading, but he cannot induce the perlocutionary effect (of having persuaded). The self-same cannot be achieved in a rule-governed way and by no means be constrained. This can be reasoned by the missing link of the perlocutionary act to conventionality and expectable (conventional) answers/reactions; in the case of illocutions, the speaker can anticipate them already in the stage of production. (Jost 2007, 160; translation mine)

Both social sciences research on campaign commercials and cognitive-linguistic research on metaphor (and metonymy) in political discourse, has generally focused one-sidedly towards the persuasive impact and not been taking that dilemma into account. As a way out of the self-same and with recourse to Aristotle, Jost proposes to consider the illocutionary act in regard to the achievement of the perlocutionary goal (i.e., persuasion).

> According to Aristotle's rhetorical conception, rhetorical speech acts cannot be reduced to the formula [...] 'As a result of having said x, I have persuaded him'. That would mean to take the second step before the first, which is expressed in the illocutionary formula 'Having said x, I have done y' respectively 'Having said x, I have reasoned. (Jost 2007, 162; translation mine)

As a result, the way to persuasion leads through reasoning or, in other words: "Persuasion is only possible through making oneself understood, respectively having understood leads the way into persuasion." (Jost 2007, 161, 165; translation mine) Gehring equally argues in favor of such an orientation towards the preceding process of meaning-making and understanding with regard to the examination of metaphor in political discourse. In this light, she points to the close connection between politics and language: "Political action is at least implicitly conceived of as being constantly accompanied by linguistic action. Whoever conducts empirical research, has to consider politics in relation to horizons of meaning, not solely to behavioristic schemata." (Gehring 2015, 49–50; translation mine) This book is a contribution to meet this claim and the proposal of a reorientation both within social sciences research on campaign commercials and linguistic research on figurativity in political discourse.

The dynamic approach to audiovisual figurativity does not focus on an intentionally acting producer and figurativity as a fixed meaningful product that is implemented purposefully and influences the (passive) recipient persuasively. As Gehring (2015, 54) has illustrated, such a conception ascribes certain helplessness to the political audience whereby the political space of reception appears to be a childlike one that requires care and does not harmonize with figurativity. Instead, the dynamic approach proceeds from an analysis of the material, i.e., from film analysis, which naturally does not rule out the skillful composition of audiovisual images by professionals but does not make it its starting point.[6] It does not take figurative meaning for granted (i.e., as given) but focuses on the process of its 'taking' (cf. Johnson 2007, 75), i.e., its emergence in a situated media context to which it is inherently linked. In doing so, the dynamic approach takes one basic step back as compared to other studies. This step, however, gives direction to a modified understanding of the effectiveness and power of figurative meaning in political discourse.

Instead of thinking it from the first implicitly in contradistinction to an actual "suchness" [*Sosein*] (i.e., 'reality' or 'truth') by what it appears as a falsification of an alleged objectivity, the dynamic approach to audiovisual figurative meaning-making sets its reality-constituting potential as the benchmark. This way, particular situational-related configurations of possibilities come to the fore (cf. Gehring 2015, 48). In practical terms, that means that, for instance, the experiencing and understanding of Angela Merkel as a powerful sovereign with civil roots who is close to the people, leads to an image or idea of the German Chancellor as a "non-arbitrary possibility of reality" (Gehring 2015, 48; translation mine) that emerges in the process of viewing the campaign commercial. It is neither the reproductive reflection of an alleged objective reality, nor completely abstract or arbitrary; it has a reflexive character in its specific relatedness: by experiencing and understanding something in terms of something else, by experiencing a foreign sensation of the world as if it were one's own (cf. Sobchack 1992). In this respect figurativity is a "machine of possibilities par excellence" (Gehring 2015, 49; translation mine). Through the temporal, attentional, and

---

6 Metaphors and metonymies are not particularly persuasive just because they are metaphors and metonymies (cf. Gehring 2015, 52–53).

experiential dynamics the interplay of activated figurativity and the affective experience of cinematic expressive movement gives rise to

> two emerging experiential realms that interact [...] in film and audio-visuals. Both of these fields or realms are supposed to be imaginarily and perceptively present while spectators experience audio-visual media (films, TV shows, etc.). Notably, the mapping of those realms does not primarily build upon assumed similarities, but grounds in relations evoked by the concrete audio-visual context (Schmitt, Greifenstein, and Kappelhoff 2014, 2105).

It is in that sense that figurativity opens up possibilities for viewing spectators: the two emergent experiential realms provide them with the grounds for making sense of the candidates and their political program. In other words: viewers are *enabled* to construct audiovisual figurative meaning in a dynamic and embodied process "from the experiential qualities staged in each and every scene" (Müller and Schmitt 2015, 322). Such an enablement of vividness and insight through audiovisual figurativity entails in the first instance the construction of meaning and the ensuring of understanding before there can be talk of persuasion or attitude change. As Jost underlines, this holds equally true for communicative situations with primarily strategic and success-oriented action, such as campaign commercials: "The listener has to understand what the speaker is telling him; otherwise the strategic action cannot succeed either" (Jost 2007, 44–45; translation mine).

Conceiving of metaphor and metonymy in political communication (just as campaign commercials in general) as strategic, reality-simplifying, and falsifying attack on people's minds (e.g., Androshchuk 2014, Charteris-Black 2005, Goatly 2007) by which a producer deceitfully forces his view and opinion on a mass of recipients, underestimates their productive reality-constituting possibility potential. Taking the self-same as a starting point for the question of what makes figurativity powerful, one arrives at a different conception of power: "From a modal perspective it is about forms of a relative ruling out of possibilities right up to enabling former impossibilities" in a situated context (Gehring 2015, 48; translation mine). What makes figurativity powerful then, cannot least be its specificity and relative adequacy (Gehring 2015, 54) in making politics palpable, vivid, and comprehensible.

Bibliography

Abbott, Michael, and Charles Forceville. 2011. "Visual Representation of Emotion in Manga: 'Loss of Control' is 'Loss of Hands' in Azumanga Daioh Volume 4." *Language and Literature* 20 (2): 91–112.

Ahrens, Kathleen. 2011. "Examining Conceptual Metaphor Models Through Lexical Frequency Patterns: A Case Study of U.S. Presidential Speeches." In *Windows to the Mind. Metaphor, Metonymy and Conceptual Blending*, edited by Sandra Handl and Hans-Jörg Schmid, 167–184. Berlin/New York: De Gruyter Mouton.

Albers, Hagen. 2010. "Politik im 'Social Web'. Der Onlinewahlkampf 2009." In *Die Bundestagswahl 2009. Analysen der Wahl-, Parteien-, Kommunikations- und Regierungsforschung*, edited by Karl-Rudolf Korte, 227–238. Wiesbaden: Verlag für Sozialwissenschaften.

Androshchuk, Bohdan. 2014. *Die Metapher als ideologisches Instrument der Persuasion im deutschsprachigen politischen Diskurs. Eine Untersuchung anhand der Familienpolitik der 16. Legislaturperiode des Deutschen Bundestages*. Hamburg: Dr. Kovač.

Arnheim, Rudolf. 1932. *Film als Kunst*. Berlin: Rowohlt.

Arnheim, Rudolf. 1978. *Kunst und Sehen*. Berlin: De Gruyter.

Atkin, Charles, and Gary Heald. 1976. "Effects of Political Advertising." *Public Opinion Quarterly* 40: 216–228.

Austin, John Langshaw. 1962. *How to Do Things with Words*. Oxford: Oxford University Press.

Bakels, Jan-Hendrik. 2014. "Embodying Audio-Visual Media. Concepts and Transdisciplinary Perspectives." In *Body – Language – Communication. An International Handbook on Multimodality in Human Interaction. (Handbooks of Linguistics and Communication Science 38.2.)*, edited by Cornelia Müller, Alan Cienki, Ellen Fricke, Silva H. Ladewig, David McNeill, and Jana Bressem, 2048–2061. Berlin/Boston: De Gruyter Mouton.

Balázs, Béla. 2010. "Visible Man or the Culture of Film." In *Béla Balázs: Early Film Theory*, edited by Erica Carter, 1–90. Oxford: Berghahn Books. Original edition 1924.

Barcelona, Antonio. 2000. "The Cognitive Theory of Metaphor and Metonymy." In *Metaphor and Metonymy at the Crossroads. A Cognitive Perspective*, edited by Antonio Barcelona, 1–28. Berlin/New York: Mouton de Gruyter.

Barcelona, Antonio. 2009. "Motivation of Construction Meaning and Form. The Roles of Metonymy and Inference." In *Metonymy and Metaphor in Grammar*, edited by Klaus-Uwe Panther, Linda Thornburg, and Antonio Barcelona, 363–401. Amsterdam: John Benjamins.

Barker, Jennifer M. 2009. *The Tactile Eye. Touch and the Cinematic Experience*. Berkeley, CA: University of California Press.

Barsalou, Lawrence W. 1999. "Perceptual Symbol Systems." *Behavioral and Brain Sciences* 22 (4): 577–660.

Barsalou, Lawrence W. 2008. "Grounded Cognition." *Annual Review of Psychology* 59: 617–645.

Barth, Hermann. 1990. *Psychagogische Strategien des filmischen Diskurses in G. W. Pabsts Kameradschaft (Deutschland 1931)*. München: Schaudig Bauer Ledig.

Bartsch, Anne, and Susanne Hübner. 2004. "Emotionale Kommunikation. Ein integratives Modell." PhD, Martin-Luther University Halle, accessed 25 November 2016 http://sundoc.bibliothek.uni-halle.de/diss-online/04/07H050/prom.pdf

Bateman, John A., and Karl-Heinrich Schmidt. 2012. *Multimodal Film Analysis. How Films Mean*. New York/London: Routledge.

https://doi.org/10.1515/9783110578782-010

Beichelt, Timm. 2004. "Herrschaftskultur. Symbolisierung von Politik am Beispiel der bundesdeutschen Außenpolitik." In *Politikwissenschaft als Kulturwissenschadt. Theorien, Methoden, Problemstellungen*, edited by Birgit Schwelling, 151–169. Wiesbaden: Verlag für Sozialwissenschaften.

Bialek, Catrin. 2007. "Frau Merkels Sinn für gute Kreation." *Handelsblatt* 01 November 2007 accessed 25 November 2016 http://www.handelsblatt.com/unternehmen/management/politik-werbung-frau-merkels-sinn-fuer-gute-kreation-seite-2/2880868-2.html

Bieber, Christoph. 2009. "Das 'Kanzlerduell' als Multimedia-Debatte. Politische Kommunikation und Bürgerbeteiligung zwischen TV und Internet." In *Die Bundestagswahl 2009. Analysen der Wahl-, Parteien-, Kommunikations und Regierungsforschung*, edited by Karl-Rudolf Korte, 239–261. Wiesbaden: Verlag für Sozialwissenschaften.

Black, Max. 1962. *Models and Metaphors. Studies in Language and Philosophy*. Ithaca, NY: Cornell University Press.

Black, Max. 1993. "More about Metaphor." In *Metaphor and Thought*, edited by Andrew Ortony, 19–41. Cambridge: Cambridge University Press. Original edition 1977.

Bordwell, David. 2008. *Poetics of Cinema*. New York, NY: Routledge.

Bounegru, Liliana, and Charles Forceville. 2011. "Metaphors in Editorial Cartoons Representing the Global Financial Crisis." *Visual Communication* 10 (2): 209–229.

Bowen, Lawrence. 1994. "Time of Voting Decision and Use of Political Advertising: The Slade Gorton-Brock Adams Senatorial Campaign." *Journalism & Mass Communication Quarterly* 71 (3): 665–675.

Bratman, Michael. 1987. *Intention, Plans, and Practical Reason*. Cambridge, MA: Harvard University Press.

Brauck, Markus, and Martin U. Müller. 2009. "Kampagnenanalyse: Das Elend des Kuschel-Wahlkampfs." *Spiegel online* 28 September 2009, accessed 25 November 2016 http://www.spiegel.de/kultur/gesellschaft/kampagnenanalyse-das-elend-des-kuschel-wahlkampfs-a-651770.html

Brosda, Carsten, and Johannes Schwarz. 2001. "'Amerikanisierung' der Politikvermittlung? Gesellschaftswandel – Medienwandel – Politikwandel." *vorgänge – Zeitschrift für Bürgerrechte und Gesellschaftspolitik* 154: 70–76.

Bucher, Hans-Jürgen. 2012. "Multimodalität – ein universelles Merkmal der Medienkommunikation: Zum Verhältnis von Medienangebot und Medienrezeption." In *Interaktionale Rezeptionsforschung. Theorie und Methode der Blickaufzeichnung in der Medienforschung*, edited by Hans-Jürgen Bucher and Peter Schumacher, 51–82. Wiesbaden: Springer Fachmedien.

Bühler, Karl. 1933. *Ausdruckstheorie: Das System an der Geschichte aufgezeigt*. Jena: Fischer.

Bühler, Karl. 1990. *Theory of Language. The Representational Function of Language*. Amsterdam: John Benjamins Publishing. Original edition 1934.

Burkhardt, Armin. 1988. "Sprache in der Politik. Linguistische Grundbegriffe und Methoden." *English Amerikanische Studien* 10: 333–358.

Cameron, Lynne. 1999a. "Identifying and Describing Metaphors in Spoken Discourse Data." In *Researching and Applying Metaphor*, edited by Lynne Cameron and Graham Low, 105–132. Cambridge: Cambridge University Press.

Cameron, Lynne. 1999b. "Operationalising 'Metaphor' for Applied Linguistic Research." In *Researching and Applying Metaphor*, edited by Lynne Cameron and Graham Low, 3–28. Cambridge: Cambridge University Press.

Cameron, Lynne. 2006. "Metaphor Analysis Project. Procedure for Metaphor Analysis. Building Metaphor Groupings." The Open University, accessed 25 April 2018 (via the internet archive). https://web.archive.org/web/20111001231254/ http://creet.open.ac.uk/projects/metaphor-analysis/building.cfm

Cameron, Lynne. 2007. "Patterns of Metaphor Use in Reconciliation Talk." *Discourse & Society* 18 (2): 197–222.

Cameron, Lynne. 2008a. "Metaphor and Talk." In *The Cambridge Handbook of Metaphor and Thought*, edited by Raymond W. Jr. Gibbs, 197–211. Cambridge University Press: Cambridge.

Cameron, Lynne. 2008b. "Metaphor Shifting in the Dynamics of Talk." *Pragmatics and Beyond New Series* 173.

Cameron, Lynne. 2010. "The Discourse Dynamics Framework for Metaphor." In *Metaphor Analysis. Research Practice in Applied Linguistics, Social Sciences and the Humanities*, edited by Lynne Cameron and Robert Maslen, 77–96. London: Equinox.

Cameron, Lynne. 2011. *Metaphor and Reconciliation. The Discourse Dynamics of Empathy in Post-Conflict Conversations*. New York, NY: Routledge.

Cameron, Lynne. 2018. "From Metaphor to Metaphorizing: How Cinematic Metaphor Opens up Metaphor Studies." In *Cinematic Metaphor in Perspective. Reflections on a Transdisciplinary Framework*, edited by Sarah Greifenstein, Dorothea Horst, Thomas Scherer, Christina Schmitt, Hermann Kappelhoff, and Cornelia Müller, 17–35. Berlin/Boston: Walter de Gruyter.

Cameron, Lynne, Graham Low, and Robert Maslen. 2010. "Finding Systematicity in Metaphor Use." In *Metaphor Analysis. Research Practice in Applied Linguistics, Social Sciences and the Humanities*, edited by Lynne Cameron and Robert Maslen, 117–146. London: Equinox.

Cameron, Lynne, and Robert Maslen, eds. 2010. *Metaphor Analysis: Research Practice in Applied Linguistics, Social Sciences and the Humanities*. London: Equinox.

Cameron, Lynne, Robert Maslen, Zazie Todd, John Maule, Peter Stratton, and Neil Stanley. 2009. "The Discourse Dynamics Approach to Metaphor and Metaphor-Led Discourse Analysis." *Metaphor and Symbol* 24 (2): 63–89.

Carroll, Noël. 1996. *Theorizing the Moving Image*. Cambridge: Cambridge University Press.

Carroll, Noël. 2001. *Beyond Aesthetics. Philosophical Essays*. Cambridge: Cambridge University Press. Original edition 1994.

Carver, Terrell, and Jernej Pikalo. 2008a. *Political Language and Metaphor. Interpreting and Changing the World*. London: Routledge.

Carver, Terrell, and Jernej Pikalo. 2008b. "Editors' Introduction." In *Political Language and Metaphor. Interpreting and Changing the World*, edited by Terrell Carver and Jernej Pikalo, 1–11. London: Routledge.

Casdorff, Stephan-Andreas. 2009. "Was die CDU der SPD voraus hat." *ZEIT Online* 04 September 2009, accessed 25 November 2016 http://www.zeit.de/online/2009/36/cdu-spd-regierung

Catalano, Theresa, and Linda Waugh. 2013. "The Language of Money. How Verbal and Visual Metonymy Shapes Public Opinion About Financial Events." *International Journal of Language Studies* 7(2): 31–60.

Chafe, Wallace. 1994. *Discourse, Consciousness, and Time. The Flow and Displacement of Conscious Experience in Speaking and Writing*. Chicago/London: University of Chicago Press.

Chafe, Wallace. 1996. "How Consciousness Shapes Language." *Pragmatics and Cognition* 4 (1): 55–64.

Charteris-Black, Jonathan. 2004. *Corpus Approaches to Critical Metaphor Analysis.* Basingstoke: Palgrave Macmillan.

Charteris-Black, Jonathan. 2005. *Politicians and Rhetoric. The Persuasive Power of Metaphor.* Basingstoke: Palgrave Macmillan.

Charteris-Black, Jonathan. 2013. *Analysing Political Speeches: Rhetoric, Discourse and Metaphor.* Basingstoke: Palgrave Macmillan.

Chodakowski, Tomasz. 2012. "Tuskobus II wyjeżdża z zajezdni. Czyli gdzie i kiedy wypatrywać premiera?" *Wyborcza.pl* 15 October 2012, accessed 25 November 2016 http://wyborcza. pl/1,76842,12674316,Tuskobus_II_wyjezdza_z_zajezdni__Czyli_gdzie_i_kiedy.html

Christiansen, Paul. 2018. *Orchestrating Public Opinion. How Music Persuades in Television Political Ads for US Presidential Campaigns, 1952–2016.* Amsterdam: Amsterdam University Press.

Cienki, Alan. 1998. "Metaphoric Gestures and Some of Their Relations to Verbal Metaphoric Expressions." In *Discourse and Cognition: Bridging the Gap*, edited by Jean-Pierre Koenig, 189–204. Stanford, CA: Center for the Study of Language and Information.

Cienki, Alan. 2004. "Bush's and Gore's Language and Gestures in the 2000 US Presidential Debates." *Journal of Language and Politics* 3 (3): 409–440.

Cienki, Alan. 2005. "Researching Conceptual Metaphors That (May) Underlie Political Discourse." Paper at ECPR Workshop on Metaphor in Political Science, Grenada, Spain, accessed 26 September 2016 https://ecpr.eu/Filestore/PaperProposal/60476c8f-960f-40d2-9194-c342a40cf7c6.pdf

Cienki, Alan. 2013. "Cognitive Linguistics: Spoken Language and Gesture as Expressions of Conceptualization." In *Body – Language – Communication: An International Handbook on Multimodality in Human Interaction. (Handbooks of Linguistics and Communication Science 38.1.)*, edited by Cornelia Müller, Alan Cienki, Ellen Fricke, Silva H. Ladewig, David McNeill, and Sedinha Teßendorf, 182–201. Berlin/Boston: De Gruyter Mouton.

Cienki, Alan, and Gianluca Giansante. 2014. "Conversational Framing in Televised Political Discourse: A Comparison from the 2008 Elections in the United States and Italy." *Journal of Language and Politics* 13 (2): 255–288.

Cienki, Alan, and Cornelia Müller, eds. 2008a. *Metaphor and Gesture.* Amsterdam: John Benjamins Publishing Company.

Cienki, Alan, and Cornelia Müller. 2008b. "Metaphor, Gesture, and Thought." In *The Cambridge Handbook of Metaphor and Thought*, edited by Raymond W. Jr. Gibbs, 483–501. Cambridge: Cambridge University Press.

Cienki, Alan, and Cornelia Müller. 2014. "Ways of Viewing Metaphor in Gesture." In *Body – Language – Communication: An International Handbook on Multimodality in Human Interaction. (Handbooks of Linguistics and Communication Science 38.2.)*, edited by Cornelia Müller, Alan Cienki, Ellen Fricke, Silva H. Ladewig, David McNeill, and Jana Bressem, 1766–1781. Berlin/Boston: De Gruyter Mouton.

Clifton, N. Roy. 1983. *The Figure in Film.* Mississauga: Associated University Presses.

Coëgnarts, Maarten, and Peter Kravanja. 2012. "Towards an Embodied Poetics of Cinema. The Metaphoric Construction of Abstract Meaning in Film." *Alphaville* (Issue 4, Winter 2012): 1–18.

Coëgnarts, Maarten, and Peter Kravanja. 2014. "Metaphor, Bodily Meaning, and Cinema." *Image [&] Narrative* 15 (1).

Coëgnarts, Maarten, and Peter Kravanja, eds. 2015. *Embodied Cognition and Cinema*. Leuven: Leuven University Press.

Croft, William. 1993. "The Role of Domains in the Interpretation of Metaphor and Metonymy." *Cognitive Linguistics* 4 (4): 335–370.

Croft, William, and Alan D. Cruse. 2004. *Cognitive Linguistics*. Cambridge: Cambridge University Press.

Cwalina, Wojciech. 2000. *Telewizyjna Reklama Polityczna. Emocje i Poznanie w Kształtowaniu Preferencji Wyborczych*. Lublin: Towarzystwo Naukowe KUL.

Cwalina, Wojciech, Andrzej Falkowski, and Lynda Lee Kaid. 2000. "Role of Advertising in Forming the Image of Politicians: Comparative Analysis of Poland, France, and Germany." *Media Psychology* 2 (2): 146–199.

Cwalina, Wojciech, Andrzej Falkowski, and Bohdan Roznowski. 1999. "Television Spots in Polish Presidential Elections." In *Television and Politics in Evolving European Democracies*, edited by Lynda Lee Kaid, 45–60. New York NY: Nova Science Publishers.

De Jaegher, Hanne, and Ezequiel Di Paolo. 2007. "Participatory Sense-Making." *Phenomenology and the Cognitive Sciences* 6 (4): 485–507.

Debatin, Bernhard. 1994. "Cinematic Metaphors." *The Semiotic Review of Books* 5 (2): 6–8.

Deignan, Alice. 2010. "The Cognitive View of Metaphor: Conceptual Metaphor Theory." In *Metaphor Analysis. Research Practice in Applied Linguistics, Social Sciences and the Humanities*, edited by Lynne Cameron and Robert Maslen, 44–56. London: Equinox.

Deleuze, Gilles. 2008. *Cinema 2. The Time Image*. London: Continuum. Original edition 1985.

Delia, Jesse G. 1987. "Communication Research: A History." In *Handbook of Communication Science*, edited by Charles R. Berger and Steven H. Chaffee, 20–99. Beverly Hills, CA: Sage.

Dewey, John. 1980. *Art as Experience*. New York, NY: Putnam.

Dirven, René. 2002. "Metonymy and Metaphor: Different Mental Strategies of Conceptualisation." In *Metaphor and Metonymy in Comparison and Contrast*, edited by René Dirven and Ralf Pörings, 75–111. Berlin/New York: Mouton de Gruyter.

Dörner, Andreas. 1998. "Das politisch Imaginäre. Vom Nutzen der Filmanalyse für die Politische Kulturforschung." In *Visuelle Politik. Filmpolitik und die visuelle Konstruktion des Politischen*, edited by Wilhelm Hofmann, 199–219. Baden-Baden: Nomos.

Dörner, Andreas. 2001. *Politainment. Politik in der medialen Erlebnisgesellschaft*. Frankfurt: Fischer

Dörner, Andreas. 2006. "Politik als Fiktion." *Aus Politik und Zeitgeschichte* 7: 3–11.

Dörner, Andreas, and Ludgera Vogt. 2008. "Politik, Ästhetik und Wahlwerbespots." In *Politik im Spot-Format. Zur Semantik, Pragmatik und Ästhetik politischer Werbung in Deutschland*, edited by Andreas Dörner and Christian Schicha, 37–59. Wiesbaden: Verlag für Sozialwissenschaften.

Dröge, Franz, Winfried Lerg, and Rainer Weißenborn. 1969. "Zur Technik politischer Propaganda in der Demokratie. Analyse der Fernseh-Wahlsendungen der Parteien im Wahlkampf 1969." In *Fernsehen in Deutschland. Die Bundestagswahl 1969 als journalistische Aufgabe*, edited by Christian Longolius, 107–144. Mainz: v. Hase u. Koehler.

Dziok, Marek. 2011. "Kampania wyborcza – nowe zasady." 03 February 2011, accessed 25 November 2016 http://www.wyborydosejmu.pl/2011/02/wybory-2011-reklama-tv-i-radiowa-zakazana

Edelman, Murray. 1971. *Politics as Symbolic Action: Mass Arousal and Quiescence*. New York, NY: Academic Press.

Eggertsson, Gunnar T., and Charles Forceville. 2009. "Multimodal Expressions of the HUMAN VICTIM IS ANIMAL Metaphor in Horror Films." In *Multimodal Metaphor,* edited by Charles Forceville and Eduardo Urios-Aparisi, 429–449. Berlin/New York: Mouton de Gruyter.

Eisenstein, Sergej M. 1951a. "A Dialectic Approach to Film Form." In *Film Form. Essays in Film Theory*, edited and translated by Jay Leyda, 45–63. London: Dennis Dobson Ltd. Original edition 1929.

Eisenstein, Sergej M. 1951b. "Dickens, Griffith, and the Film Today." In *Film Form. Essays in Film Theory*, edited and translated by Jay Leyda, 195–255. London: Dennis Dobson Ltd. Original edition 1944.

Eisenstein, Sergej M. 1982. "The Montage of Attractions." In *Eisenstein at Work*, edited by Jay Leyda and Zina Voynow, 17–20. New York, NY: Pantheon Books. Original edition 1924.

Elder, Charles D., and Roger W. Cobb. 1983. *The Political Uses of Symbols*. New York, NY: Longman.

Empirische Medienästhetik (internet portal): eMAEX – a standardized method of analyzing qualities of filmic expression, accessed 25 November 2016 http://www.empirische-medie-naesthetik.fu-berlin.de/en/emaex-system/emaex_kurzversion/index.html

Engelkamp, Johannes. 1998. "Gedächtnis für Bilder." In *Bild – Bildwahrnehmung – Bildverarbeitung*, edited by Klaus Sachs-Hombach and Klaus Rehkämper, 227–242. Wiesbaden: Deutscher Universitätsverlag.

Engelke, Henning. 2013. "Susanne K. Langer und Parker Tyler über Film als 'multimodales Medium'." In *Multimodale Bilder. Zur synkretistischen Struktur des Filmischen*, edited by Lars C. Grabbe, Patrick Rupert-Kruse, and Norbert M. Schmitz, 171–187. Darmstadt: Büchner.

Esser, Frank, Christina Holtz-Bacha, and Eva-Maria Lessinger. 2005. "Sparsam in jeder Hinsicht. Die Fernsehwerbung der Parteien im Europawahlkampf 2004." In *Europawahl 2004. Die Massenmedien im Europawahlkampf*, edited by Christina Holtz-Bacha, 65–89. Wiesbaden: Verlag für Sozialwissenschaften.

Esser, Frank, and Barbara Pfetsch. 2004. *Comparing Political Communication. Theories, Cases, and Challenges*. New York, NY: Cambridge University Press.

Fahlenbrach, Kathrin. 2005. "Aesthetics and Audiovisual Metaphors in Media Perception." *CLCWeb. Comparative Literature and Culture* 7 (4): 1–9.

Fahlenbrach, Kathrin. 2007. "Audiovisuelle Metaphern und Emotionen im Sounddesign." In *Audiovisuelle Emotionen. Emotionsdarstellung und Emotionsvermittlung durch audiovisuelle Medienangebote*, edited by Anne Bartsch, Jens Eder, and Kathrin Fahlenbrach, 330–349. Köln: Herbert von Halem.

Fahlenbrach, Kathrin 2008. "Emotions in Sound. Audiovisual Metaphors in the Sound Design of Narrative Films." *Projections: The Journal for Movies and Mind*. 2 (2): 85–103.

Fahlenbrach, Kathrin. 2010. *Audiovisuelle Metaphern. Zur Körper- und Affektästhetik in Film und Fernsehen*. Marburg: Schüren.

Fahlenbrach, Kathrin. 2016. "Audiovisual Metaphors as Embodied Narratives in Moving Images." In *Embodied Metaphors in Film, Television and Video Games. Cognitive Approaches*, edited by Kathrin Fahlenbrach, 33–50. New York, NY: Routledge, Taylor & Francis Group.

Fillmore, Charles J. 1982. "Frame Semantics." In *Linguistics in the Morning Calm*, edited by Linguistic Society of Korea, 111–137. Seoul: Hanshin.

Forceville, Charles. 1996. *Pictorial Metaphor in Advertising*. London/New York: Routledge.

Forceville, Charles. 2002. "The Identification of Target and Source in Pictorial Metaphors." *Journal of Pragmatics* 34 (1): 1–14.

Forceville, Charles. 2007a. "Cybercourse in Pictorial and Multimodal Metaphor", accessed 29 September 2016 http://www.chass.utoronto.ca/epc/srb/cyber/cforcevilleout.pdf

Forceville, Charles. 2007b. "Multimodal Metaphor in Ten Dutch TV Commercials." *The Public Journal of Semiotics* 1 (1): 15–34.

Forceville, Charles. 2008a. "Metaphor in Pictures and Multimodal Representations." In *The Cambridge Handbook of Metaphor and Thought*, edited by Raymond W. Jr. Gibbs, 462–482. Cambridge: Cambridge University Press.

Forceville, Charles. 2008b. "Pictorial and Multimodal Metaphor in Commercials." In *Go Figure! New Directions in Advertising Rhetoric*, edited by Edward F. McQuarrie and Barbara J. Phillips, 272–310. Armonk, NY: ME Sharpe.

Forceville, Charles. 2009a. "Non-Verbal and Multimodal Metaphor in a Cognitivist Framework. Agendas for Research." In *Multimodal Metaphor*, edited by Charles Forceville and Eduardo Urios-Aparisi 19–42. Berlin/Boston: Mouton de Gruyter.

Forceville, Charles. 2009b. "The Role of Non-Verbal Sound and Music in Multimodal Metaphor." In *Multimodal Metaphor*, edited by Charles Forceville and Eduardo Urios-Aparisi, 383–400. Berlin/New York: Mouton de Gruyter.

Forceville, Charles. 2011. "Pictorial Runes in 'Tintin and the Picaros'." *Journal of Pragmatics* 43 (3): 875–890.

Forceville, Charles. 2017. "From Image Schema to Metaphor in Discourse. The FORCE Schemas in Animation Films." In *Metaphor. Embodied Cognition and Discourse*, edited by Beate Hampe, 239–256. Cambridge: Cambridge University Press.

Forceville, Charles, and Marloes Jeulink. 2011. "The Flesh and Blood of Embodied Understanding: The Source-Path-Goal Schema in Animation Film." *Pragmatics & Cognition* 19 (1): 37–59.

Forceville, Charles, and Eduardo Urios-Aparisi, eds. 2009. *Multimodal Metaphor, Applications of Cognitive Linguistics*. Berlin: Mouton de Gruyter.

Forchtner, Bernhard, Michał Krzyzanowski, and Ruth Wodak. 2013. "Mediatization, Right-Wing Populism, and Political Campaigning: The Case of the Austrian Freedom Party." In *Media Talk and Political Elections in Europe and America*, edited by Mats Ekström and Andrew Tolson, 205–228. Basingstoke: Palgrave Macmillan.

Fricke, Ellen. 2008. "Grundlagen einer multimodalen Grammatik des Deutschen. Syntaktische Strukturen und Funktionen." Habilitation, European University Viadrina, Frankfurt Oder. Manuscript.

Fuchs, Thomas, and Hanne De Jaegher. 2009. "Enactive Intersubjectivity. Participatory Sense-Making and Mutual Incorporation." *Phenomenology and the Cognitive Sciences* 8 (4): 465–486.

Gehring, Petra. 2015. "Was macht Metaphern mächtig?" In *Politik der Metapher*, edited by Andreas Hölzl, Matthias, Klumm, Mara Matičević, Thomas Scharinger, Johannes Ungelenk, and Nora Zapf, 41–56. Würzburg: Königshausen & Neumann.

Geise, Stephanie. 2010. "'Unser Land kann mehr…' Visuelle Wahlkampfstrategien in der Plakatkommunikation zur Bundestagswahl 2009." *Zeitschrift für Politikberatung* 3 (2): 151–175.

Gellner, Winand, and Gerd Strohmeier. 2004. "The 'Double' Public. Germany After Reunification." In *The Berlin Republic: German Unification and a Decade of Changes*, edited by Winand Gellner and John D. Robertson, 58–81. London/Portland: Routledge.

Gerstenkorn, Jacques. 1995. *La Métaphore au Cinéma. Les Figures d'Analogie dans les Films de Fiction*. Paris: Klincksieck.

Gibbs, Raymond W. Jr. 1993. "Process and Products in Making Sense of Tropes." In *Metaphor and Thought*, edited by Andrew Ortony, 252–276. Cambridge: Cambridge University Press.

Gibbs, Raymond W. Jr. 1998. "The Fight Over Metaphor in Thought and Language." In *Figurative Language and Thought*, edited by Albert N. Katz, Cristina Cacciari, Raymond W. Gibbs, and Mark Turner, 88–118. New York, NY: Oxford University Press.

Gibbs, Raymond W. Jr. 1999a. "Speaking and Thinking With Metonymy." In *Metonymy in Language and Thought*, edited by Klaus-Uwe Panther and Günter Radden, 61–76. Amsterdam: John Benjamins.

Gibbs, Raymond W. Jr. 1999b. "Taking Metaphor Out of Our Heads and Putting It into the Cultural World." In *Metaphor in Cognitive Linguistics*, edited by Raymond W. Jr. Gibbs and Gerard Steen, 145–166. Amsterdam: John Benjamins.

Gibbs, Raymond W. Jr., ed. 2008. *The Cambridge Handbook of Metaphor and Thought*. Cambridge University Press: Cambridge.

Gibbs, Raymond W. Jr. 2011. "Are 'Deliberate' Metaphors Really Deliberate? A Question of Human Consciousness and Action." *Metaphor and the Social World* 1 (1): 26–52.

Gibbs, Raymond W. Jr. 2018. "Our Metaphorical Experiences of Film." In *Cinematic Metaphor in Perspective. Reflections on a Transdisciplinary Framework*, edited by Sarah Greifenstein, Dorothea Horst, Thomas Scherer, Christina Schmitt, Hermann Kappelhoff, and Cornelia Müller, 120–138. Berlin/Boston: Walter de Gruyter.

Gibbs, Raymond W. Jr., and Lynne Cameron. 2008. "The Social-cognitive Dynamics of Metaphor Performance." *Cognitive Systems Research* 9 (1–2): 64–75.

Gibbs, Raymond W. Jr., and Herbert L. Colston. 1995. "The Cognitive Psychological Reality of Image Schemas and their Transformations." *Cognitive Linguistics* 6 (4): 347–378.

Gibbs, Raymond W. Jr., and Gerard Steen, eds. 1993. *Metaphor in Cognitive Linguistics*. Amsterdam/Philadelphia: John Benjamins.

Girnth, Heiko. 2015. *Sprache und Sprachverwendung in der Politik: Eine Einführung in die linguistische Analyse öffentlich-politischer Kommunikation*. Berlin/Boston: Walter de Gruyter.

Goatly, Andrew. 2007. *Washing the Brain – Metaphor and Hidden Ideology*. Amsterdam/Philadelphia: John Benjamins.

Goossens, Louis. 1990. "Metaphtonymy. The Interaction of Metaphor and Metonymy in Expressions for Linguistic Action." *Cognitive Linguistics* 1 (3): 323–340.

Grady, Joseph E. 1997. "Foundations of Meaning: Primary Metaphors and Primary Scenes." PhD, University of California, Berkeley.

Greifenstein, Sarah, and Hermann Kappelhoff. 2014. "The Discovery of the Acting Body." In *Body – Language – Communication. An International Handbook on Multimodality in Human Interaction. (Handbooks of Linguistics and Communication Science 38.2.)*, edited by Cornelia Müller, Alan Cienki, Ellen Fricke, Silva H. Ladewig, David McNeill, and Jana Bressem, 2070–2080. Berlin/Boston: De Gruyter Mouton.

Hacker, Kenneth L., ed. 1995. *Candidate Images in Presidential Elections*. Westport, CT: Praeger.

Hampe, Beate, ed. 2017. *Metaphor: Embodied Cognition and Discourse*. Cambridge: Cambridge University Press.

Hofmann, Wilhelm. 2004. "Die politische Kultur des Auges. Der pictorial turn als Aspekt des cultural turn in der Politikwissenschaft." In *Politikwissenschaft als Kulturwissenschaft*.

Theorien, Methoden, Problemstellungen, edited by Birgit Schwelling, 309–334. Wiesbaden: Verlag für Sozialwissenschaften.

Holly, Werner. 1991. "Wir sind Europa. Die Fernsehwerbespots der SPD zur Europawahl 1989." In *Begriffe besetzen. Strategien des Sprachgebrauchs in der Politik*, edited by Frank Liedtke, Martin Wengeler, and Karin Böke, 258–275. Opladen: Westdeutscher Verlag.

Holm, Kerstin. 2005. "Verwandte Seele: Eine Zarin für die Kanzlerin." *FAZ.net* 24 October 2005, accessed 29 September 2016 http://www.faz.net/aktuell/feuilleton/katharina-die-grosse-verwandte-seele-eine-zarin-fuer-die-kanzlerin-1279955.html

Holtz-Bacha, Christina. 1994. "Entfremdung von der Politik durch 'Fernseh-Politik'? Zur Videomalaise-These." In *Politische Kommunikation in Hörfunk und Fernsehen*, edited by Otfried Jarren, 123–133. Opladen: Leske + Budrich.

Holtz-Bacha, Christina. 2000. *Wahlwerbung als politische Kultur. Parteienspots im Fernsehen 1957–1998*. Wiesbaden: Westdeutscher Verlag.

Holtz-Bacha, Christina. 2006. "Personalisiert und emotional. Strategien des modernen Wahlkampfes." *Aus Politik und Zeitgeschichte* 7: 11–19.

Holtz-Bacha, Christina. 2010. "Politik häppchenweise. Die Fernsehwahlwerbung der Parteien zu Europa- und Bundestagswahl." In *Die Massenmedien im Wahlkampf: das Wahljahr 2009*, edited by Christina Holtz-Bacha, 166–188. Wiesbaden: Verlag für Sozialwissenschaften.

Holtz-Bacha, Christina, and Lynda Lee Kaid. 1993. "Wahlspots im Fernsehen. Eine Analyse der Parteienwerbung zur Bundestagswahl 1990." In *Die Massenmedien im Wahlkampf. Untersuchungen aus dem Wahljahr 1990*, edited by Christina Holtz-Bacha und Lynda Lee Kaid, 46–71. Opladen: Westdeutscher Verlag.

Holtz-Bacha, Christina, and Lynda Lee Kaid. 1996. "'Simply the best'. Parteienspots im Bundestagwahlkampf 1994 – Inhalt und Rezeption." In *Wahlen und Wahlkampf in den Medien. Untersuchungen aus dem Wahljahr 1994*, edited by Christina Holtz-Bacha, 177–207. Opladen: Westdeutscher Verlag.

Jakobson, Roman. 1987. "Quest for the Essence of Language." In *Language in Literature*, edited by Krystyna Pomorska and Stephen Rudy, 413–427. Cambridge, MA: Belknap Press of Harvard University Press. Original edition 1965.

Jakobson, Roman. 1990. "Two Aspects of Language and Two Types of Aphasic Disturbances." In *On Language*, edited by Linda R. Waugh and Monique Monville-Burston, 115–133. Cambridge, MA: Belknap Press of Harvard University Press. Original edition 1956.

Jakobson, Roman, and Krystyna Pomorska. 1983. *Dialogues*. Cambridge, MA: Massachusetts Institute of Technology Press.

Jakubowski, Alex. 1998. *Parteienkommunikation in Wahlwerbespots. Eine systemtheoretische und inhaltsanalytische Untersuchung von Wahlwerbespots zur Bundestagswahl 1994*. Opladen: Westdeutscher Verlag.

Jakubowski, Paweł. 2013. "Marketing wyborczy partii politycznych w kampanii parlamentarnej 2011. Analiza strategii i technik wyborczych." In *Współczesne Kampanie Wyborcze w Polsce i na Świecie*, edited by Paweł Jakubowski and Ewelina Kancik, 31–53. Lublin: Wydawnictwo UMCS.

Jensen, Thomas Wiben. 2017. "Doing Metaphor: An Ecological Perspective on Metaphoricity in Discourse." In *Metaphor: Embodied Cognition and Discourse*, edited by Beate Hampe, 257–276. Cambridge: Cambridge University Press.

Jensen, Thomas Wiben, and Elena Cuffari. 2014. "Doubleness in Experience: Towards a Distributed Enactive Approach to Metaphoricity." *Metaphor and Symbol* 29 (4): 278–297.

Johnson, Mark. 1987. *The Body in the Mind. The Bodily Basis of Meaning, Imagination, and Reason*. Chicago, IL: University of Chicago Press.

Johnson, Mark. 2007. *The Meaning of the Body. Aesthetics of Human Understanding*. Chicago, IL: Chicago University Press

Joost, Gesche. 2008. *Bild-Sprache. Die audio-visuelle Rhetorik des Films*. Bielefeld: transcript.

Joslyn, Richard A. 1980. "The Content of Political Spot Ads." *Journalism Quarterly* 57: 92–98.

Jost, Jörg. 2007. *Topos und Metapher. Zur Pragmatik und Rhetorik des Verständlichmachens*. Heidelberg: Winter.

Jowett, Garth, and Victoria O'Donnell. 1992. *Propaganda and Persuasion*. London/Newbury Park: Sage.

Józefowicz, Maciej. 2011. "'Najbardziej spójną kampanię miało PiS'. Materska-Sosnowska dla 'Newsweeka'." *Newsweek* 07 October 2011, accessed 29 September 2016 http://polska. newsweek.pl/-najbardziej-spojna-kampanie-mialo-pis—materska-sosnowska-dla-newsweeka-,83062,1,1.html

Kaid, Lynda Lee. 1982. "Paid Television Advertising and Candidate Name Identification." *Campaigns & Elections* 3: 34–36.

Kaid, Lynda Lee, and Anne Johnston. 2001. *Videostyle in Presidential Campaigns: Style and Content of Televised Political Advertising*. Westport, CT: Praeger Publishers.

Kanzog, Klaus. 2001. *Grundkurs Filmsemiotik*. Munich: Diskurs-Film-Verlag Schaudig & Ledig.

Kappelhoff, Hermann. 2004. *Matrix der Gefühle. Das Kino, das Melodrama und das Theater der Empfindsamkeit*. Berlin: Vorwerk 8.

Kappelhoff, Hermann. 2010–2014. Database. Mobilization of Emotions in War Films. Berlin: CeDiS – Freie Universität Berlin.

Kappelhoff, Hermann. 2018. *Frontlines of Community. Hollywood Between War and Democracy*. Translated by Daniel Hendricks. Berlin/Boston: Walter de Gruyter.

Kappelhoff, Hermann, and Jan-Hendrik Bakels. 2011. "Das Zuschauergefühl. Möglichkeiten qualitativer Medienanalyse." *Zeitschrift für Medienwissenschaft* 5 (2): 78–95.

Kappelhoff, Hermann, Jan-Hendrik Bakels, Hye-Jeung Chung, David Gaertner, Sarah Greifenstein, Matthias Grotkopp, Michael Lück, Christian Pischel, Cilli Pogodda, Franziska Seewald, Christina Schmitt, and Anna Steininger. "eMAEX – Ansätze und Potentiale einer systematisierten Methode zur Untersuchung filmischer Ausdrucksqualitäten." Internet portal *Empirische Medienästhetik*, accessed 24 November 2016 http:// www.empirische-medienaesthetik.fu-berlin.de/media/emaex_methode_deutsch/ eMAEX-_-Ansaetze-und-Potentiale-einer-systematisierten-Methode-zur-Untersuchung-filmischer-Ausdrucksqualitaeten.pdf?1401464494

Kappelhoff, Hermann, Jan-Hendrik Bakels, and Sarah Greifenstein. forthcoming/2019. *Die Poiesis des Filme-Sehens. Methoden der Analyse audiovisueller Bilder*. Berlin/Boston: Walter de Gruyter.

Kappelhoff, Hermann, David Gaertner, and Cilli Pogodda. 2013. *Mobilisierung der Sinne. Der Hollywood-Kriegsfilm zwischen Genrekino und Historie*. Berlin: Vorwerk 8.

Kappelhoff, Hermann, and Sarah Greifenstein. 2016. "Audiovisual Metaphors. Embodied Meaning and Processes of Fictionalization." In *Embodied Metaphors in Film, Television, and Video Games*, edited by Kathrin Fahlenbrach, 183–201. New York, NY: Routledge.

Kappelhoff, Hermann, and Cornelia Müller. 2011. "Embodied Meaning Construction. Multimodal Metaphor and Expressive Movement in Speech, Gesture, and Feature Film." *Metaphor and the Social World* 1 (2): 121–153.

Klein, Josef. 1993. "Wort-Alchemie. Die Operationen der Begriffe-Besetzer." In *Sprachliche Aufmerksamkeit. Glossen und Marginalien zur Sprache der Gegenwart*, edited by Wolf Peter Klein and Walther Dieckmann, 102–110. Heidelberg: Winter.

Klein, Tobias. 1992. "Zum Wandel des Kommunikationsstils in Wahlwerbespots von 1972 bis 1990." PhD, University Erlangen-Nürnberg.

Kolczyński, Mariusz. 2012. "W pułapce politycznej rutiny – Reklama polityczna w kampanii parlamentarnej 2011." *Roczniki Nauk Społecznych* 4, 40 (3): 33–53.

Kolle Rebbe. 2007. "Kolle Rebbe wird Lead-Agentur der CDU Deutschlands." Press release, accessed 24 November 2016 URL: http://www.kolle-rebbe.de/news/von-kolle-rebbe/kolle-rebbe-wird-lead-agentur-der-cdu-deutschlands

Kolter, Astrid, Silva H. Ladewig, Michela Summa, Cornelia Müller, Sabine C. Koch, and Thomas Fuchs. 2012. "Body Memory and the Emergence of Metaphor in Movement and Speech. An Interdisciplinary Case Study." In *Body, Memory, Metaphor, and Movement*, edited by Sabine C. Koch, Thomas Fuchs, and Cornelia Müller, 201–226. Amsterdam: John Benjamins.

Kövecses, Zoltán. 2000. *Metaphor and Emotion: Language, Culture and Body in Human Feeling*. Cambridge: Cambridge University Press.

Kowalczyk, Krzysztof. 2012. "Wybory bez alternatywy? Kampania Platformy Obywatelskiej w wyborach parlamentarnych w 2011 roku." In *Wybory Parlamentarne 2011*, edited by Agnieszka Turska-Kawa and Waldemar Wojtasik, 255–274. Katowice: Uniwersytet Śląski w Katowicach.

Kracauer, Siegfried. 1984. *Von Caligari zu Hitler. Eine psychologische Geschichte des deutschen Films*. Frankfurt/Main: Suhrkamp. Original edition 1947.

Kress, Gunther, and Theo van Leeuwen. 1998. "Front Pages: (The Critical) Analysis of Newspaper Layout." In *Approaches to Media Discourse*, edited by Allan Bell and Peter Garrett, 186–219. Oxford: Blackwell Publishers.

Kroeber-Riel, Werner. 1993. *Bildkommunikation. Imagerystrategien für die Werbung*. Munich: Vahlen.

Lacan, Jacques. 1995. "The Instance of the Letter in the Unconscious, or Reason Since Freud." In *Écrits. A Selection*, 493–441. London: Routledge. Original edition 1957.

Lacan, Jacques. 1977. *Écrits. A Selection*. Translated by Alan Sheridan. London: Tavistock/Routledge. Original edition 1966.

Lakoff, George. 1987. *Women, Fire, and Dangerous Things. What Categories Reveal About the Mind*. Chicago, IL: University of Chicago Press.

Lakoff, George. 1993. "The Contemporary Theory of Metaphor." In *Metaphor and Thought*, edited by Andrew Ortony, 202–251. Cambridge: Cambridge University Press.

Lakoff, George. 1996. *Moral Politics: What Conservatives Know that Liberals Don't*. Second edition (2002) published as *Moral Politics: How Liberals and Conservatives Think*. Chicago, IL: University of Chicago Press.

Lakoff, George. 2008. *The Political Mind. A Cognitive Scientist's Guide to Your Brain and Its Politics*. London: Penguin.

Lakoff, George, and Mark Johnson. 1980. *Metaphors We Live By*. Chicago, IL: University of Chicago Press.

Lakoff, George, and Mark Johnson. 1999. *Philosophy in the Flesh*. New York, NY: Basic Books.

Lakoff, George, and Mark Turner. 1989. *More Than Cool Reason. A Field Guide to Poetic Metaphors*. Chicago: Chicago University Press.

Lakoff, George, and Elisabeth Wehling. 2008. *Auf leisen Sohlen ins Gehirn. Politische Sprache und ihre heimliche Macht*. Heidelberg: Carl-Auer Verlag.

Landesmedienanstalten 2013. "Rechtliche Hinweise der Landesmedienanstalten zu den Wahlsendezeiten für politische Parteien im bundesweit verbreiteten privaten Rundfunk vom 19. März 2013", accessed 24 November 2016 http://www.die-medienanstalten.de/fileadmin/Download/Positionen/Gemeinsame_Positionen/Rechtliche_Hinweise_zu_den_Wahlsendezeiten_2013_01.pdf

Langacker, Ronald W. 2001. "Dynamicity in Grammar." *Axiomathes* 12: 7–33.

Leszczuk-Fiedziukiewicz, Anna. 2013. "Strategie celebrytyzacji polityki na przykładzie medialnego obrazu kampanii parlamentarnej w 2011 r.." *Nowe Media* 4, accessed 25 November 2016 http://dx.doi.org/10.12775/NM.2013.004

Littlemore, Jeannette. 2015. *Metonymy. Hidden Shortcuts in Language, Thought and Communication*. Cambridge: Cambridge University Press.

Marks, Laura U. 2000. *The Skin of the Film. Intercultural Cinema, Embodiment, and the Senses*. Durham: Duke University Press.

Martinelli, Kathleen A., and Steven H. Chaffee. 1995. "Measuring New-Voter Learning Via Three Channels of Political Information." *Journalism and Mass Communication Quarterly* 72 (1): 18–32.

Mazur, Marek. 2005. "Negatywna telewizyjna reklama polityczna. Doswiadczenia amerykanskie i polskie." In *Kampania Wyborcza: Marketingowe Aspekty Komunikowania Politycznego*, edited by Bogusława Dobek-Ostrowska, 91–93. Wrocław: Wydawnictwo Uniwersytetu Wrocławskiego.

McLuhan, Marshall. 1964. *Understanding Media. The Extensions of Man*. New York, NY: New American Library.

Merleau-Ponty, Maurice. 1962. *Phenomenology of Perception*. Translated by Colin Smith. London/New York: Routledge & Kegan Paul. Original edition 1945.

Metz, Christian. 1982. *The Imaginary Signifier. Psychoanalysis and The Cinema*. Translated by Celia Britton, Annwyl Williams, Ben Brewster, and Alfred Guzzetti. Bloomington, IN: Indiana University Press. Original edition 1975.

Meyer-Lucht, Robin. 2009. "CDU-Spot: Angela Merkel hat auch von Ronald Reagan gelernt." *Carta* 06 September 2009, accessed 25 November 2016 http://www.carta.info/14345/cdu-werbespot-angela-merkel-ronald-reagan-wahlkampf/

Mio, Jeffery Scott. 1997. "Metaphor and Politics." *Metaphor and Symbol* 12 (2): 113–133.

Mitry, Jean. 2000. *Semiotics and the Analysis of Film*. Bloomington, IN: Indiana University Press. Original edition 1987.

Mittelberg, Irene. 2006. "Metaphor and Metonymy in Language and Gesture. Discourse Evidence for Multimodal Models of Grammar." Phd, Cornell University.

Mittelberg, Irene. 2008. "Peircean Semiotics Meets Conceptual Metaphor. Iconic Modes in Gestural Representations of Grammar." In *Metaphor and Gesture*, edited by Alan Cienki and Cornelia Müller, 115–154. Amsterdam: John Benjamins.

Mittelberg, Irene. 2010. "Interne und externe Metonymie. Jakobsonsche Kontiguitätsbeziehungen in redebegleitenden Gesten." *Sprache und Literatur* 41 (1): 112–143.

Mittelberg, Irene. 2013. "The Exbodied Mind. Cognitive-Semiotic Principles as Motivating Forces in Gesture." In *Body – Language – Communication. An International Handbook on Multimodality in Human Interaction. (Handbooks of Linguistics and Communication Science 38.1.)*, edited by Cornelia Müller, Alan Cienki, Ellen Fricke, Silva H. Ladewig, David McNeill, and Sedinha Tessendorf, 750–779. Berlin/Boston: De Gruyter Mouton.

Mittelberg, Irene, and Linda R. Waugh. 2009. "Metonymy First, Metaphor Second. A Cognitive-Semiotic Approach to Multimodal Figures of Thought in Co-Speech Gesture." In *Multimodal Metaphor*, edited by Charles Forceville and Eduardo Urios-Aparisi, 329–356. Berlin/New York: Mouton de Gruyter.

Mittelberg, Irene, and Linda R. Waugh. 2014. "Gestures and Metonymy." In *Body – Language – Communication. An International Handbook on Multimodality in Human Interaction. (Handbooks of Linguistics and Communication Science 38.2.)*, edited by Cornelia Müller, Alan Cienki, Ellen Fricke, Silva Ladewig, David McNeill, and Jana Bressem, 1747–1766. Berlin/Boston: De Gruyter Mouton.

Müller, Cornelia. 1998. *Redebegleitende Gesten. Kulturgeschichte, Theorie, Sprachvergleich*. Berlin: Arno Spitz.

Müller, Cornelia. 2008a. *Metaphors Dead and Alive, Sleeping and Waking. A Dynamic View*. Chicago, IL: University of Chicago Press.

Müller, Cornelia. 2008b. "What Gestures Reveal About the Nature of Metaphor." In *Metaphor and Gesture*, edited by Alan Cienki and Cornelia Müller, 219–245. Amsterdam: John Benjamins.

Müller, Cornelia. 2011. "Are 'Deliberate' Metaphors Really Special? Deliberateness in the Light of Metaphor Activation." *Metaphor and the Social World* 1 (1): 61–66.

Müller, Cornelia. 2013. "Gestures as a Medium of Expression. The Linguistic Potential of Gestures." In *Body – Language – Communication. An International Handbook on Multimodality in Human Interaction. (Handbooks of Linguistics and Communication Science 38.1.)*, edited by Cornelia Müller, Alan Cienki, Ellen Fricke, Silva H. Ladewig, David McNeill, and Sedinha Tessendorf, 202–217. Berlin/Boston: De Gruyter Mouton.

Müller, Cornelia. 2014. "Gestural Modes of Representation as Techniques of Depiction." In *Body – Language – Communication: An International Handbook on Multimodality in Human Interaction. (Handbooks of Linguistics and Communication Science 38.2.)*, edited by Cornelia Müller, Alan Cienki, Ellen Fricke, Silva H. Ladewig, David McNeill, and Jana Bressem, 1687–1702. Berlin/Boston: De Gruyter Mouton.

Müller, Cornelia, and Alan Cienki. 2009. "Words, Gestures, and Beyond. Forms of Multimodal Metaphor in the Use of Spoken Language." In *Multimodal Metaphor*, edited by Charles Forceville and Eduardo Urios-Aparisi, 297–328. Berlin/New York: Mouton de Gruyter.

Müller, Cornelia, and Hermann Kappelhoff. 2018. *Cinematic Metaphor. Experience – Affectivity – Temporality*. In collaboration with Sarah Greifenstein, Dorothea Horst, Thomas Scherer, and Christina Schmitt. Berlin/Boston: Walter de Gruyter.

Müller, Cornelia, and Silva H. Ladewig. 2013. "Metaphors for Sensorimotor Experiences. Gestures as Embodied and Dynamic Conceptualizations of Balance in Dance Lessons." In *Language and the Creative Mind*, edited by Michael Borkent, Barbara Dancygier, and Jennifer Hinnell, 295–324. Stanford, CA: CSLI Publications.

Müller, Cornelia, and Christina Schmitt. 2015. "Audio-Visual Metaphors of the Financial Crisis. Meaning Making and the Flow of Experience." *Revista Brasileira de Linguística Aplicada* 15 (2): 311–342.

Müller, Cornelia, and Susanne Tag. 2010. "The Dynamics of Metaphor. Foregrounding and Activation of Metaphoricity in Conversational Interaction." *Cognitive Semiotics* 10 (6): 85–120.

Müller, Marion G. 2004. "Politologie und Ikonologie. Visuelle Interpretation als politologisches Verfahren." In *Politikwissenschaft als Kulturwissenschaft. Theorien, Methoden, Problemstellungen*, edited by Birgit Schwelling, 335–349. Wiesbaden: Verlag für Sozialwissenschaften.

Münsterberg, Hugo. 2002. The Photoplay – A Psychological Study. In *Hugo Münsterberg on Film. The Photoplay – A Psychological Study and Other Writings*, edited by Allan Langdale. New York, NY: Routledge. Original edition 1916.

Musiałowska, Ewa Anna. 2008. "Political Communication in Germany and Poland." PhD, Technische Universität, Dresden, accessed 16 June 2018 http://www.qucosa.de/fileadmin/data/qucosa/documents/165/1216216577378-7378.pdf

Musolff, Andreas. 2000. *Mirror Images of Europe. Metaphors in the Public Debate About Europe in Britain and Germany*. Munich: Iudicium.

Musolff, Andreas. 2004. *Metaphor and Political Discourse. Analogical Reasoning in Debates About Europe*. Basingstoke: Palgrave Macmillan.

Musolff, Andreas. 2012. "The Study of Metaphor as Part of Critical Discourse Analysis." *Critical Discourse Studies* 9 (3): 301–310.

Musolff, Andreas. 2016. *Political Metaphor Analysis. Discourse and Scenarios*. London/New York: Bloomsbury.

Musolff, Andreas, and Jörg Zinken, eds. 2009. *Metaphor and Discourse*. Basingstoke/New York: Palgrave Macmillan.

Oakley, Todd. 2009. *From Attention to Meaning. Explorations in Semiotics, Linguistics, and Rhetoric*. Bern: Peter Lang

Ortiz, María J. 2015. "Films and Embodied Metaphors of Emotions." In *Embodied Cognition and Cinema*, edited by Peter Kravanja and Maarten Coëgnarts, 203–220. Leuven: Leuven University Press.

Ortony, Andrew, ed. 1979. *Metaphor and Thought*. Cambridge: Cambridge University Press.

Ostaszewski, Maciej. 2011. "'Lider' – najdłuższy spot wyborczy tej kampanii." *Gazeta Wyborcza* 26 September 2011, accessed 25 November 2016 http://wyborcza.pl/1,76842,10360490,_Lider____najdluzszy_spot_wyborczy_tej_kampanii.html

Pagel, Gerda. 1989. *Lacan zur Einführung*. Hamburg: Junius.

Payne, J. Gregory, John Marlier, and Robert A. Baukus. 1989. "Polispots in the 1988 Presidential Primaries. Separating the Nominees From the Rest of the Guys." *American Behavioral Scientist* 32 (4): 365–381.

Peirce, Charles S. 1960. *Collected Papers of Charles Sanders Peirce (1931–1958). Vol. I. Principles of Philosophy, Vol. II. Elements of Logic*. Edited by C. Hartsthorne and P. Weiss. Cambridge, MA: The Belknap Press of Harvard University Press.

Peszyński, Wojciech. 2012. "Telewizyjny obraz kampanii parlamentarnej w 2011 roku." In *Wybory Parlamentarne 2011*, edited by Agnieszka Turska-Kawa and Waldemar Wojtasik, 185–202. Katowice: Uniwersytet Śląski w Katowicach.

Petrica, Monica. 2011. "'Overt' vs. 'Covert' Cultural Variance in Metaphor Usage: 'Europe' vs. Malta and the EU-Membership Debate." In *Windows to the Mind. Metaphor, Metonymy and Conceptual Blending*, edited by Sandra Handl and Hans-Jörg Schmid, 143–166. Berlin/New York: De Gruyter Mouton.

Pfetsch, Barbara, and Frank Esser. 2014. "Political Communication in Comparative Perspective: Key Concepts and New Insights." In *Political Communication*, edited by Carsten Reinemann, 87–105. Berlin/Boston: De Gruyter Mouton.

Pfetsch, Barbara, and Rüdiger Schmitt-Beck. 1994. "Amerikanisierung von Wahlkämpfen? Kommunikationsstrategien und Massenmedien im politischen Mobilisierungsprozeß." In *Politik und Medien. Analysen zur Entwicklung der politischen Kommunikation*, edited by Michael Jäckel and Peter Winterhoff-Spurk, 231–252. Berlin: Vistas.

Pfister, René. 2013. "Die Entfremdung." *Der Spiegel* 37/2013: 22–28.

Plessner, Helmuth. 1970. *Laughing and Crying: A Study of the Limits of Human Behavior.* Evanston, IL: Northwestern University Press. Original edition 1941.

Podschuweit, Nicole. 2007. *Wirkungen von Wahlwerbung. Aufmerksamkeitsstärke, Verarbeitung, Erinnerungsleistung und Entscheidungsrelevanz.* München: Fischer.

Pragglejaz Group. 2007. "MIP: A Method for Identifying Metaphorically Used Words in Discourse." *Metaphor and Symbol* 22 (1): 1–39

Prümm, Karl. 2008. "Großes Kino im Sekundenformat. Kinematographische Codes in den Wahlwerbespots der Parteien." In *Politik im Spot-Format. Zur Semantik, Pragmatik und Ästhetik politischer Werbung in Deutschland*, edited by Andreas Dörner and Christian Schicha, 181–188. Wiesbaden: Verlag für Sozialwissenschaften.

Pulvermüller, Friedemann. 1999. "Words in the Brain's Language." *Behavioral and Brain Sciences* 22 (2): 253–336.

Radden, Günter. 2000. "How Metonymic Are Metaphors?" In *Metaphor and Metonymy at the Crossroads. A Cognitive Perspective*, edited by Antonio Barcelona, 93–108. Berlin/New York: Mouton de Gruyter.

Radden, Günter, and Zoltán Kövecses. 1999. "Towards a Theory of Metonymy." In *Metonymy in Language and Thought*, edited by Klaus-Uwe Panther and Günter Radden, 17–59. Amsterdam: John Benjamins.

Reinemann, Carsten, ed. 2014. *Political Communication.* Berlin/Boston: De Gruyter Mouton.

Richards, Ivor A. 1936. *The Philosophy of Rhetoric.* New York/London: Oxford University Press.

Ricœur, Paul. 1986. *Die lebendige Metapher.* Munich: Wilhelm Fink.

Riedel, Peter. 2008. "Bausteine einer historischen Poetik des Wahlwerbespots." In *Politik im Spot-Format. Zur Semantik, Pragmatik und Ästhetik politischer Werbung in Deutschland*, edited by Andreas Dörner and Christian Schicha, 18–204. Wiesbaden: Verlag für Sozialwissenschaften.

Ritchie, David. 2010. "Between Mind and Language: A Journey Worth Taking." In *Metaphor Analysis. Research Practice in Applied Linguistics, Social Sciences and the Humanities*, edited by Lynne Cameron and Robert Maslen, 57–76. London: Equinox.

Rohe, Karl. 1987. "Politische Kultur und der kulturelle Aspekt von politischer Wirklichkeit – Konzeptionelle und typologische Überlegungen zu Gegenstand und Fragestellung Politischer Kultur-Forschung." In *Politische Kultur in Deutschland: Bilanz und Perspektiven der Forschung*, edited by Dirk Berg-Schlosser and Jakob Schissler, 39–48. Westdeutscher Verlag: Opladen.

Rohe, Karl. 1990. "Politische Kultur und ihre Analyse. Probleme und Perspektiven in der Politischen Kulturforschung." *Historische Zeitschrift* 250: 321–346.

Römmele, Andrea, and Jürgen Falter. 2002. "Professionalisierung bundesdeutscher Wahlkämpfe, oder: Wie amerikanisch kann es werden?" In *Moderner Wahlkampf. Blick hinter die Kulissen*, edited by Thomas Berg, 49–64. Opladen: Leske + Budrich.

Rothschild, Michael L., and Michael L. Ray. 1974. "Involvement and Political Advertising Effect: An Exploratory Experiment." *Communication Research* 1 (3): 264–285.

Rottbeck, Britta. 2012. *Der Online-Wahlkampf der Volksparteien 2009: Eine empirische Analyse.* Dordrecht: Springer.

Ruiz de Mendoza, Francisco J. 1997. "Cognitive and Pragmatic Aspects of Metonymy." *Cuadernos de Filología Inglesa* 6 (2): 161–178.

Rundfunkstaatsvertrag ("Interstate Broadcasting Agreement") 2016. accessed 25 November
    2016 https://www.ard.de/download/538848/Staatsvertrag_fuer_Rundfunk_und_
    Telemedien_in_der_Fassung_des_20__Aenderungsstaatsvertrags__vom_8__bis_16__
    12—2016.pdf
Sarcinelli, Ulrich. 2009. *Politische Kommunikation in Deutschland. Zur Politikvermittlung im
    demokratischen System*. Wiesbaden: Verlag für Sozialwissenschaften.
Scherer, Thomas, Sarah Greifenstein, and Hermann Kappelhoff. 2014. "Expressive Movements
    in Audiovisual Media. Modulating Affective Experience." In *Body – Language –
    Communication. An International Handbook on Multimodality in Human Interaction.
    (Handbooks of Linguistics and Communication Science 38.2.)*, edited by Cornelia Müller,
    Alan Cienki, Ellen Fricke, Silva H. Ladewig, David McNeill, and Jana Bressem, 2081–2092.
    Berlin/Boston: De Gruyter Mouton.
Scheuermann, Arne. 2009. *Zur Theorie des Filmemachens. Flugzeugabstürze, Affekttechniken.
    Film als rhetorisches Design*. Munich: Ed.Text + Kritik.
Schicha, Christian, and Andreas Dörner, eds. 2008. *Politik im Spot-Format. Zur Semantik,
    Pragmatik und Ästhetik politischer Werbung in Deutschland*. Wiesbaden: Verlag für
    Sozialwissenschaften.
Schmitt, Christina. forthcoming/2019. *Wahrnehmen, fühlen, verstehen. Metaphorisieren und
    audiovisuelle Bilder*. Berlin/Boston: Walter de Gruyter.
Schmitt, Christina. 2015. "Embodied Meaning in Audio-Visuals: First Steps Towards a Notion
    of Mode." In *Building Bridges for Multimodal Research. International Perspectives on
    Theories and Practices of Multimodal Analysis*, edited by Janina Wildfeuer, 309–325. Bern/
    New York: Peter Lang.
Schmitt, Christina, Sarah Greifenstein, and Hermann Kappelhoff. 2014. "Expressive Movement
    and Metaphoric Meaning-Making in Audio-Visual Media." In *Body – Language –
    Communication. An International Handbook on Multimodality in Human Interaction.
    (Handbooks of Linguistics and Communication Science 38.2.)*, edited by Cornelia Müller,
    Alan Cienki, Ellen Fricke, Silva H. Ladewig, David McNeill, and Jana Bressem, 2092–2112.
    Berlin/Boston: De Gruyter Mouton.
Schwelling, Birgit. 2004. "Der kulturelle Blick auf politische Phänomene. Theorien, Methoden,
    Problemstellungen." In *Politikwissenschaft als Kulturwissenschaft. Theorien, Methoden,
    Problemstellungen* edited by Birgit Schwelling, 11–29. Wiesbaden: Verlag für Sozialwis-
    senschaften.
Searle, John. 1969. *Speech Acts. An Essay in the Philosophy of Language*. Cambridge:
    Cambridge University Press.
Searle, John. 1993. "Metaphor." In *Metaphor and Thought*, edited by Andrew Ortony, 83–111.
    Cambridge: Cambridge University Press. Original edition 1979.
Semetko, Holli A., and Klaus Schoenbach. 1994. *Germany's "Unity Election". Voters and the
    Media*. Hampton, NJ: Cresskill.
Semino, Elena. 2008. *Metaphor in Discourse*. Cambridge/New York: Cambridge University
    Press.
Semino, Elena, and Zsófia Demjén, eds. 2017. *The Routledge Handbook of Metaphor and
    Language*. Abingdon: Routledge.
Shannon, Claude Elwood, and Warren Weaver 1945. *The Mathematical Theory of
    Communication*. Urbana, IL: University of Illinois.
Sheets-Johnstone, Maxine. 2011. *The Primacy of Movement*. Amsterdam: John Benjamins.
    Original edition 1999.

Siebel, Frank. 2007. "Der Mythos von der Amerikanisierung. Über die Leistungen und die zwiespältige Rolle von Qualitätsmedien in mediatisierten Wahlkämpfen." PhD, University Dortmund, accessed 25 November 2016 https://eldorado.tu-dortmund.de/bitstream/2003/26376/1/Band_1_Der_Mythos_von_der_Amerikanisierung.pdf

Simmel, Georg. 1995. "Aesthetik des Porträts." In *Aufsätze und Abhandlungen, 1901–1908*, edited by Rüdiger Kramme and Alessandro Cavalli, 321–332. Frankfurt/M.: Suhrkamp. Original edition 1905.

Sinclair, Jon R. 1995. "Reforming Television's Role in American Political Campaigns: Rationale for the Elimination of Paid Political Advertisements." *Communications and the Law* 17: 65–97.

Slobin, Dan. I. 1996. "From 'Thought and Language' to 'Thinking for Speaking'." In *Rethinking Linguistic Relativity*, edited by John Joseph Gumperz und Stephen C. Levinson, 70–96. Cambridge: Cambridge University Press.

Sobchack, Vivian. 1990. "The Active Eye: A Phenomenology of Cinematic Vision." *Quarterly Review of Film & Video* 12 (3): 21–36.

Sobchack, Vivian. 1992. *The Address of the Eye. A Phenomenology of Film Experience.* Princeton, NJ: Princeton University.

Sobchack, Vivian. 2004. *Carnal Thoughts. Embodiment and Moving Image Culture.* Berkeley, CA: Universitiy of California Press.

Steen, Gerard. 2006. "The Paradox of Metaphor: Why We Need a Three-Dimensional Model of Metaphor." *Metaphor and Symbol* 23 (4): 213–241.

Steen, Gerard. 2011. "What Does 'Really Deliberate' Really Mean? More Thoughts on Metaphor and Consciousness." *Metaphor and the Social World* 1 (1): 53–56.

Steen, Gerard, Aletta G. Dorst, J. Berenike Herrmann, Anna Kaal, Tina Krennmayr, and Trijntje Pasma. 2010. *A Method for Linguistic Metaphor Identification. From MIP to MIPVU.* Amsterdam/Philadelphia: John Benjamins.

Stenvoll, Dag 2008. "Slippery Slopes in Political Discourse." In *Political Language and Metaphor. Interpreting and Changing the World*, edited by Terrell Carver and Jernej Pikalo, 28–40. London: Routledge.

Strömbäck, Jesper, and Spiro Kiousis. 2014. "Strategic Political Communication in Election Campaigns." In *Political Communication*, edited by Carsten Reinemann, 109–128. Berlin: Mouton de Gruyter.

Szczerbiak, Aleks. 2013. "Poland (Mainly) Chooses Stability and Continuity: The October 2011 Polish Parliamentary Election." *Perspectives on European Politics and Society* 14 (4): 480–504.

Szułdrzyński, Michał. 2011. "Spójny przekaz, miły lider." *Rzeczpospolita* 10 October 2011, accessed 25 November 2016 http://www.rp.pl/artykul/730354.html

Talmy, Leonard. 2000. *Toward a Cognitive Semantics – Vol. 1: Concept Structuring Systems.* Cambridge, MA: MIT Press.

Talmy, Leonard. 2007. "Attention Phenomena." In *The Oxford Handbook of Cognitive Linguistics*, edited by Dirk Geeraerts and Hubert Cuyckens, 264–293. Oxford: Oxford University Press.

TK: "Dwudniowe wybory i zakaz używania billboardów niezgodne z konstytucją." *Gazeta.pl* 20 July 2011, accessed 08 January 2015 http://wiadomosci.gazeta.pl/wiadomosci/1,114873,9976424,TK__Dwudniowe_wybory_i_zakaz_uzywania_billboardow.html

Trent, Judith, and Robert V. Friedenberg. 1991. *Political Campaign Communication. Principles and Practices.* New York, NY: Praeger.

Turska-Kawa, Agnieszka, and Waldemar Wojtasik, eds. 2012. *Wybory Parlamentarne 2011*. Katowice: Uniwersytet Śląski w Katowicach.

"Tylko Kaczyński może otworzyć szklane drzwi. PiS ma nowy spot." *Newsweek* 18 July 2011, accessed 25 November 2016 http://polska.newsweek.pl/tylko-kaczynski-moze-ot-worzyc-szklane-drzwi–pis-ma-nowy-spot,79641,1,1.html

Urios-Aparisi, Eduardo. 2009. "Interaction of Multimodal Metaphor and Metonymy in TV Commercials: Four Case Studies." In *Multimodal Metaphor*, edited by Charles Forceville and Eduardo Urios-Aparisi, 95–117. Berlin/New York: Mouton de Gruyter.

Urios-Aparisi, Eduardo. 2014. "Figures of Film. Metaphor, Metonymy, and Repetition." *Image [&] Narrative* 15(1): 102–113.

Van Dijk, Teun. 1998. *Ideology: A Multidisciplinary Approach*. London: Sage

Varela, Francisco J., Evan Thompson, and Eleanor Rosch. 1991. *The Embodied Mind: Cognitive Science and Human Experience*. Cambridge, MA: MIT Press.

Ventola, Eija, Cassily Charles, and Martin Kaltenbacher, eds. 2004. *Perspectives on Multimodality*. Amsterdam/Philadelphia: John Benjamins Publishing.

Voss, Christiane. 2011. "Film Experience and the Formation of Illusion. The Spectator as 'Surrogate Body' for the Cinema." *Cinema Journal* 50 (4): 136–150.

Vygotsky, Lev S. 1978. *Mind in Society. The Development of Higher Psychological Processes*. Cambridge, MA: Harvard University Press

Vygotsky, Lev S. 1986. *Thought and Language*. Translated by Alex Kozulin. Cambridge, MA: MIT Press. Original edition 1934.

Wachtel, Martin. 1988. *Die Darstellung von Vertrauenswürdigkeit in Wahlwerbespots. Eine argumentationsanalytische und semiotische Untersuchung zum Bundestagswahlkampf 1987*. Tübingen: M. Niemeyer.

Wagner, Jochen W. 2005. *Deutsche Wahlwerbekampagnen made in USA? Amerikanisierung oder Modernisierung bundesrepublikanischer Wahlkampagnen*. Wiesbaden: Verlag für Sozialwissenschaften.

Wehling, Elisabeth. 2016. *Politisches Framing. Wie eine Nation sich ihr Denken einredet – und daraus Politik macht*. Cologne: Halem.

Wengeler, Martin, and Alexander Ziem. 2015. "Sprache in Politik und Gesellschaft." In *Handbuch Sprache und Wissen Vol. 1*, edited by Ekkehard Felder und Andreas Gardt, 493–518. Berlin/Boston: De Gruyter Mouton.

Werner, Tilo. 2011. *Kandidat Steinmeier und Kanzlerin Merkel: Image-Konstruktion im Fernsehen*. Norderstedt: Books on Demand.

Whittock, Trevor. 1990. *Metaphor and Film*. Cambridge: Cambridge University Press.

Wilson, Nicole L., and Raymond W. Gibbs Jr. 2007. "Real and Imagined Body Movement Primes Metaphor Comprehension." *Cognitive Science* 31: 721–731.

Winsbro, Jack. 1987. "Misrepresentation in Political Advertising: The Role of Legal Sanctions." *Emory Law Journal* 36: 853–916.

Wodak, Ruth, and Paul Chilton, eds. 2005. A *New Agenda in (Critical) Discourse Analysis: Theory, Methodology and Interdisciplinarity*. Amsterdam: John Benjamins.

Wodak, Ruth, and Michael Meyer, eds. 2009. *Methods of Critical Discourse Analysis: Introducing Qualitative Methods*. London: Sage.

Yu, Ning. 2009. "Nonverbal and Multimodal Manifestations of Metaphors and Metonymies. A Case Study." In *Multimodal Metaphor*, edited by Charles Forceville and Eduardo Urios-Aparisi, 119–146. Berlin/New York: Mouton de Gruyter.

Audiovisual Sources

ANGELA MERKEL, Agentur Kolle Rebbe, GER 2009
FRANK-WALTER STEINMEIER, Agentur Butter, GER 2009
PREMIER DONALD TUSK, Agencja Mindshare, PL 2011
CHCEMY POLSKI RÓWNYCH SZANS, Agencja Panplan, PL 2011

https://doi.org/10.1515/9783110578782-011

List of Figures

If not indicated otherwise, all figures were created by the author.
All screenshots were captured by the author.

https://doi.org/10.1515/9783110578782-012

Name Index

https://doi.org/10.1515/9783110578782-013

Subject Index

www.ingramcontent.com/pod-product-compliance
Lightning Source LLC
Chambersburg PA
CBHW050348270326
41926CB00016B/3645

* 9 7 8 3 1 1 0 7 0 9 0 6 3 *